THE AUBURN AVENUE CHRONICLES

VOLUME ONE

THE AUBURN AVENUE CHRONICLES

The Complete Collection of *Blog & Mablog* Posts on the Federal Vision

VOLUME ONE

2004–JULY 2007

DOUGLAS WILSON

BLOG & MABLOG
PRESS AND TIRE CENTER
MOSCOW, IDAHO

Blog & Mablog Press and Tire Center
Moscow, Idaho
www.dougwils.com

Cover design and interior layout: Valerie Anne Bost
Cover image: "En Barnedaab (A Baptism)," Michael Ancher, 1888.

Printing Version: 20200803

For Steve and Wendy Wilkins

CONTENTS

INTRODUCTION

The controversy over what came to be called the Federal Vision was big enough, and extended enough, that by this time some young bucks who were just ten years old when the controversy broke are now in seminary and are thinking of doing a research paper on the controversy. I thought it might be a good idea to put my particular contributions to that controversy into a form that is easily accessible.

That form comes in the shape of this e-book, originally available as a PDF, or Mobi, or EPUB and now in print through the magic of Amazon's Kindle Direct in case a seminary library wants to have a hard copy of it. This puppy weighs in at over 300,000 words. If it is a puppy, it is kind of a Tibetan mastiff, and printing limitations forced us to Solomonically divide it into two volumes. Volume One includes this Introduction and posts from April 2004 to July 2007. Volume Two picks up in August 2007 and carries on through March 2017. It also includes an appendix with 2003–4 correspondence from a private email list. The page numbering is continuous between the two volumes.

If anyone wants to read the sum of the matter, I would recommend you just read the entry entitled "Federal Vision No Mas" (January 17, 2017). I will only say here what I said a number of times in the controversy. From the beginning of the controversy to the end of it, and down to the present, I have been a Westminsterian Puritan. The only place where I diverge from the standard Reformed take on these issues is in my agreement with child communion—which I believe can be harmonized with that larger system, while remain robustly Calvinistic and evangelical. If anyone believes that I have shifted my views during the course of this controversy, I would simply invite them to read through this straightforward chronological record of what I wrote.

There are some housekeeping issues that I ought to address as well. This is a collection of the blog posts that I wrote in the course of that controversy, and they are submitted in simple chronological order. They have been lightly edited, with that editing being limited to the cleaning up of obvious typos and various grammatical infelicities.

Published as blog posts, there were numerous links to other posts, and these links may no longer be good. There were some places where we were able to correct the link. If the link is good, then if someone wants to use this in a footnote, then it would probably be best to consider the date of my post as the access date. In some cases, we were able to find current URLs for the same content, in which case there is a footnote supplied. For the print edition, we rechecked all hyperlinks, footnoted all viable (as of April 2020) URLs, and also noted when a particular resource was no longer available. Of course even more may be obsolete by the time you read this, but perhaps you may be clever enough to find them via the Wayback Machine.*

It is also the case that there is a north/south problem because of the original blog format. On a blog, the earlier posts are located below the newer ones. In a book, it goes the other way. The reason I bring this up, is that I will occasionally refer to an earlier installment, and the "below" language is retained. If that happens, don't be fooled—look *above*.

As *Blog & Mablog* has switched platforms a time or two over the years, some things were unfortunately lost along the way. We've done our best to catch any quotes that may originally have been block quotations without quotation marks, but a few may have slipped past. We trust the context will be clear enough to indicate who said what. Photos were all stripped out at some juncture, though we did manage to dig up and replace one. And if you were hoping to go read the posts *in situ* and delve into the comments sections, you will be disappointed, as comments before a certain date were not raptured along with the main content.

* archive.org/web

The *form* of my citations has been closer to the jeans-and-T-shirt end of the formatting spectrum, and not so much the white-tie-and-tails end, but that comes from the nature of the medium. It must be confessed that this thing is kind of a slab of theological controversial writing, and so I do confess it. But at the same time, I believe there is a lot of edifying theology here—distinctions that the Reformed used to make still need to be made, as long as the people of God need to be pastored. I trust that the experience of reading this will be edifying over all, even if it includes working through some of the blunders I later repudiate and repent of.

Don't try to get through it in one sitting.

DOUGLAS WILSON
Christ Church
Reformation Day 2018
Revised April 2020 for the print edition

APRIL–JUNE 2004

NICODEMUS AND JUDAS

APRIL 24, 2004

The current controversy over the objectivity of the covenant is caused, in part, by the penchant certain theologians have for ignoring the importance of plot lines in story. These plot lines obviously show up in the stories of Scripture, and consequently, a lot of confusion results from theologians treating plot problems as though they were math problems. But Nicodemus was a card-carrying member of the Sanhedrin, the body which condemned Jesus. And Judas was a card-carrying member of the Twelve. Plot involves plot twists, of the kind one ought not to get while doing a math problem. "And then the 7 betrayed his fellow odd numbers and became a 6!"

JOHN ROBBINS IS A HOOT

APRIL 27, 2004

The most recent *Trinity Review* put out by John Robbins is dedicated to extinguishing the heresies of my good friend Peter Leithart. Congratulations to Peter are in order. It has been a long time coming, and he was beginning to worry. Of course for a Robbins to try to deal with a Leithart in this fashion is like trying to put out a bonfire by pelting it with wadded up Kleenex soaked in kerosene.

As Robbins is one who prides himself on his strict adherence to *logic* ("all rise!"), I was particularly pleased with this one from the article in question: "There never was a time when the proposition 'April 19, 2004, was a sunny day in Unicoi, Tennessee' was not true." Of course to say this, he has to maintain that this proposition was true on April 18, 2004. But the proposition, on April 18, is clearly claiming that April 19, 2004 is a *past* event. After all, it says, 'April 19, 2004, *was* a sunny day . . .' What fresh irrationalism is this? Take it away. I am not amused and would be alone.

For those who do not go to the link provided, here is a sample quote, which shows that putting John Robbins in charge of fighting heresy is like making Typhoid Mary the director of the Center for Disease Control. Robbins saith, "Truth, not historical events, has primacy. Christianity is not events, nor is it based on events." Maybe he doesn't think the resurrection counts as an event. And if Christ be not raised . . .

For those who would like to see the entire article (and if you do, you are probably the kind of motorist who slows down to gawk at automobile accidents), here it be.*

AS CLEAR AS I CAN
APRIL 29, 2004

Many bystanders have been trying to figure out what the whole "Auburn Avenue" controversy is all about. As one of the players in this, I feel it is my duty to try to make this as clear as I can.

Some Lutherans are concerned about us because they have heard that somebody might be questioning justification by faith alone. At the same time, southern Presbyterian TRs are concerned about us because we seem awfully Lutheran to them, and everyone knows how weak the Lutherans are on justification by faith alone. Some good folks at Westminster West think that one of our central problems is our denial of the covenant of works. But David Engelsma of the Protestant Reformed Church has come out swinging against us because we are developing the natural and logical consequences of the doctrine of the covenant held by the OPC, PCA, and URC, and which happens to be the doctrine of the covenant held by all of our critics.

I am glad to have been of assistance.

* Updated link: trinityfoundation.org/PDF/The%20Trinity%20Review%2000195%20AgainstChristianity.pdf.

THE IRENIC BOMBSHELL
MAY 4, 2004

The Auburn Avenue Hubbub (AAH) of course has a number of texts going. But those who are theologically astute have no doubt noticed some subtexts also. One of those subtexts is the question about the covenant of works and the covenant of grace, and the grounding of those covenants. Fundamentally, what is the relationship of any covenant that God makes with man to His own eternal and triune nature? Ralph Smith carefully addresses this question in his small book *Eternal Covenant: How the Trinity Reshapes Covenant Theology* (it can be found at http://www.canonpress.org/pages/bibstudies.asp† and I urge you all to find it there). This book makes sense out of a good deal of what sometimes appears to be an irrational controversy.

This book is an irenic bombshell. It shows (in my view, *decisively*) how the contemporary dichotomy between a covenant of works and a covenant of grace is fundamentally a man-centered approach to salvation. Faithful to the Reformed tradition, Ralph Smith nevertheless blows up (irenically) a few current Reformed shibboleths. For all who would understand the current fracas, this book is a must.

WAS JESUS FAITHLESS?
MAY 11, 2004

What I would like to do in brief compass is explain how a particular understanding of a pre-Fall covenant of works requires us to say that Jesus was faithless. In short, I want to explain the problem some have with our rejection of their covenant of works, and then explain the problem with that problem.

The view we reject is that the covenant with Adam *must* be considered a covenant of works, based on Adam's merit or demerit. But those who defend this position say that it is necessary because the first Adam sets the pattern for the second Adam. And if Adam did not merit (or demerit) anything in the Garden, then we cannot be saved by Christ's merit. And if we cannot be saved by Christ's merit, then we must be saved by our own merit. And that is works-salvation, and that is why people are talking as though the gospel of grace were at stake.

† This title has since gone out of print..

Here is the problem with that problem. If Adam had not fallen, would he have been under any obligation to say "thank you" to God? And when Jesus was obeying His Father, even to the point of the cross, was He doing so *in faith*? If He was doing so in faith, then that means the problem with the first Adam was his *unbelief*, and not an action that brought about raw demerit.

The problem is the use of the word *merit*, which does not imply a covenant relationship. Rather than saying we are saved by Christ's merit (Bible verse?), we should rather say that we are saved by Christ's *obedience*. This is because obedience implies and requires a relationship—with the someone He was obeying, the same one in whom He was trusting. A man cannot merit anything by grace through faith. But a man can obey by grace through faith. Adam disobeyed through His unbelief. And Jesus Christ is our faithful High Priest.

But if Christ must win our salvation for us through raw merit, and not through obedience, this means that Christ must be considered faithless. Our opponents must face up to this conundrum. If Jesus merited our salvation through His faith in His Father, then it isn't really what they mean by merit. But if Jesus obeyed God in faith, and that obedience is our only possible salvation, then what is the fuss about?

AUBURN AVENUE HUBBUB (AAH) COOL QUOTE 1
MAY 11, 2004

> More and more it has occurred to me that the big issues between the Anabaptists and the Reformers of classical Protestantism are still among the biggest unresolved agonies of modern American Protestantism.
> —Hughes Oliphant Old, *The Shaping of the Reformed Baptismal Rite* (Grand Rapids, MI: Eerdmans, 1992), p. x.

AUBURN AVENUE HUBBUB (AAH) COOL QUOTE 2
MAY 11, 2004

> All who are baptized into the name of the Father, and of the Son, and of the Holy Ghost, recognizing the Trinity of Persons in the Godhead, the incarnation of the Son and his priestly sacrifice, whether they be

> Greeks, or Arminians, or Romanists, or Lutherans, or Calvinists, or the simple souls who do not know what to call themselves, are our brethren. Baptism is our common countersign. It is the common rallying standard at the head of our several columns.
>
> —A.A. Hodge, *Evangelical Theology* (Carlisle, PA: Banner of Truth, 1976), p. 338

AUBURN AVENUE HUBBUB (AAH) COOL QUOTE 3
MAY 12, 2004

> But to protect the importance of faith we do not have to deny His presence, which is what many people, in opposition to formalism, want to do. They say, 'No, we don't want to find Christ in the water, we want to find him just by faith.' But Luther and Calvin's point is that the water bears Christ to us . . . Does baptism relate to regeneration? Sure it does. When we look, in faith, to our baptism, we are sure we are regenerate.
>
> —Robert Godfrey, at the Blue Ridge Bible Conference (6/16/97)

MONOCOVENANTALISM, A GREAT WORD, OR WHAT?
MAY 14, 2004

One of the charges leveled against me for my Auburn Avenuing is that of monocovenantalism. But what is that, exactly?

If the critics mean that I hold that there has only been one covenant throughout the history of mankind, then the charge is false. God made one covenant with mankind in Adam, and He made a distinct and separate restorative covenant with mankind in Christ. So that would be two covenants, not one. The covenants are also distinct in that it was possible for Adam to fall, and it was not possible for Christ to fall. Further, the first covenant did not have to deal with the forgiveness of sin, and the second covenant was remedial, dealing with sin after the fact.

So why am I accused of being a "monocovenantalist"? The reason appears to be that I assert that both covenants were to be kept by the grace of God through faith. God spoke His Word, and both Adam and Christ had a covenanted obligation to believe Him, and to act accordingly. Adam did not, and Christ did. But the assigned way for both covenants to be kept was through simple trust in God.

Further, several prominent men on the other side of this flap have acknowledged to me privately that, had Adam stood, it would have been by the grace of God, appropriated by the faith of Adam. So if I am a monocovenantalist, so are they. But I am not, and neither are they.

But that is no reason to stop fighting, now is it?

AUBURN AVENUE HUBBUB (AAH) COOL QUOTE 4
MAY 16, 2004

> Before baptism, the minister is to use some words of instruction, touching the institution, nature, use, and ends of this sacrament, shewing . . . that they [children] are *Christians*, and federally holy *before* baptism, and therefore are they baptized.
>
> —*Westminster Directory for the Publick Worship of God*, emphasis mine

I GOT A QUESTION
MAY 17, 2004

So here it is.

Q. What should the Reformed establishment do with a teaching or doctrine that emphasizes our need to believe *all* the promises of God, especially those promises that concern our children? Keep in mind that this is a doctrine that underscores the necessity of faith from first to last. The purveyors of said doctrine (as in, like, me) believe that we are justified by faith, through faith, unto faith, on faith, under faith, and everything else a squirrel can do to a tree. All faith, all the time, all the way down.

A. Well, of course, the only appropriate response would be to question the commitment of said fellows to *sola fide*. And have conferences.

And this is why I prefer my theology Auburn. Rather than Blonde.

FAITH UNPLUGGED
MAY 18, 2004

I guess I should be pleased that I caught up with Peter Leithart. The April edition of *The Trinity Review* is a chapter from a book called *Not Reformed At*

All, which presents itself as a response to my *"Reformed" is Not Enough**. I am tempted to write another book entitled *And Both Are Too Much.*

One striking thing about this piece is the repeated use of the phrase "justification by belief" (instead of "justification by faith") This highlights, as I suppose, the, um, heterodox Clarkian approach that wants us to be justified by assent to propositions.

So then, we are living in a time when *assensus* can be severed from *fiducia*, and the *fiducia* thrown away like it was a wrapper, and this can be done in the name of a defense of Reformed orthodoxy! Maybe LaHaye and Jenkins are right and it is the last days.

THANKS FOR NOTHING
MAY 18, 2004

In my post on monocovenantalism (5/14/04), I said that some prominent folks on the other side of the AAH had agreed with me that had Adam stood, it would have been by the grace of God appropriated by faith. One of those gentlemen has since contacted me, saying that this misrepresents his views. He believes that Adam would have stood by faith, but not by grace. He said, "had Adam fulfilled the covenant of works he would have presented his own works." So then, in once sense I am happy to clarify his views (even though I did not name him). But I am sorry that the view as amended is a lot more unbiblical than it was before.

What does the Bible say about works? It is tied, necessarily, to the principle of *boasting* (Rom. 3:27). In other words, had Adam stood by His own works, he had no obligation to say "thank you" to God, for "thank you" presupposes a *gift*, and a gift is *grace*. The Bible contrasts works with election (Rom. 9:11). The Bible treats works as a paycheck in principle (Rom. 6:23; 11:6). If grace is excluded from the Garden, *then so is gratitude.*

And Eve said, "Adam, let us give thanks to God for our great deliverance!"

"No need for that, honey. I withstood the serpent all by myself. It was my own intrinsic righteousness at work here."

* Douglas Wilson, *"Reformed" Is Not Enough: Recovering the Objectivity of the Covenant* (Moscow, ID: Canon, 2002).

"But still, Adam, shouldn't we acknowledge that our obedience was a gift from God?"

"Woman, you clearly don't understand the deeper issues of theology. No wonder that serpent had you going for a bit."

"Yes, but only for a bit. God gave me insight to the nature of his lies. I am so grateful, and I think we should thank Him together."

"But, dear, you are being grateful to the wrong person. We must of course thank God for the Garden, and for the fruit, and for one another. But who should be thanked for this particular act of obedience? Me. *Me.*"

"Well, I do thank you. But can't we thank God too? Doesn't He ordain all things? Shouldn't we see this obedience of ours as His grace to us?"

"Trust me, Eve. I do know there are subtleties involved. But the only way to preserve a true God-centeredness for all our children in the ages to come is for us to acknowledge that God did not do this. I did it. Me."

"But I feel so empty not thanking God for this grace."

"I understand that feeling, at least in part. Maybe we can compromise. When the Lord comes walking in the cool of the day this evening, we can make a point of thanking Him."

"Adam, that's wonderful! What shall we thank Him for?"

"Thanks for nothing. But we needn't put it that way of course."

THE COUNCIL OF TRENT FINALLY REPENTS!
MAY 19, 2004

In response to my *Thanks for Nothing* post (5/18/04), one correspondent argued that this was essentially the same position that Trent affirmed. It was a bit hard to follow, but I will do my best to replicate it here. If the creature's works are the ground of his justification (which I was *denying*, actually), but the creature can only do such works by grace through faith, then it follows that the creature is saved by grace through faith, but the grace and faith are no longer alone. Somehow.

But the problem is that I was asserting the sovereign, inexhaustible, exhaustive, glorious, high-octane grace, jet fuel grace, grace all-the-way-down kind of grace prior to the Fall. The creature always and for everything must give thanks to God, for every blessed thing comes from His hand, and to Him goes all the glory. As in, *soli Deo gloria*! To be contrasted with this *new* version of reformational thunder, which appears to be *soli Deo gloria nisi ante lapsum*. All glory to God, except before the Fall, when Adam gets a cut.

Had Adam withstood temptation in the Garden, the Lord would have said, "Well done, good and faithful servant," and Adam in return would have (*rightly*) given all the glory to God. "I was a good and faithful servant because it was a gift from Your hand, and Your hand alone." All grace, all the time, in every direction, run it out over the horizon and don't stop then.

All grace as the ground of any possible justification. No works as the ground of any possible justification. Works are bad as ground of any possible justification.

(Background muttering, building to a crescendo) "Word games! More word games! What is he trying to say? Wilson insists that sovereign and exhaustive grace is the sole ground of any creature's obedience, anywhere, any time (and he think no works can be the ground of justification anywhere, works, bah!). Since when Wilson defends *tota gratia* he must be sneaking in works, we will fool them all. We will deny works by affirming them."

If this doesn't make sense to you, don't worry about it. Not your problem.

COMMON GRACE. UH OH.
MAY 20, 2004

I just can't stay off this monocovenantal thing. This whole fracas is a real head scratcher, and the word *grace* appears to be the thing that causes the great game of paradigm bumper cars to begin. But this is highly selective. The fact that I want to use the word *grace* to describe the unearned favor of God that was bestowed on unfallen Adam is highly offensive to our critics. And yet (most of them, I think) would not object to the word *grace* being applied to unregenerate reprobates after the Fall, as in the phrase *common grace*. Unfallen Adam, no grace at all. Local abortionist, common grace is the order of the day.

Why are the critics struggling with something that is so simple?

1. God's favor was shown to the unfallen Adam, the grace of creation. All glory goes to God.
2. God's favor would have been shown to Adam had he not fallen, the grace of sovereign preservation. All glory would have gone to God.
3. God's favor was shown to the unfallen Christ, the grace of sovereign preservation. All glory to God.
4. God's favor is shown to the reprobate, the common grace of earthly goods and postponed judgment. All glory to God.
5. God's favor is shown to us, His believers, the grace of salvation from sin. All glory to God.

"Too much grace around here! Too much emphasis on the fundamental *graciousness* of God. *You* must not be Reformed!"

JUSTIFICATION BY SAYING THE RIGHT THING ABOUT JUSTIFICATION

MAY 24, 2004

If I taste too many more delicious ironies, I think I will become a theological diabetic. The latest one is the way in which John Robbins has taken to denying justification by faith alone. Justification by faith alone is *not* accomplished by asserting justification by faith alone. Justification by faith alone occurs when a sinner trusts in Jesus.

There will be men who affirm justification by faith alone who will be in Hell, and there will be men who do *not* affirm justification by faith alone who will be in Heaven. This is because this particular tenet of the faith is *true*. But however true it is, and it is true, it is not our Savior. It, like every other faithful servant, points to the Savior. It can only point this way because justification by faith alone is true.

Requiring people to affirm justification by faith alone in order to get saved is like requiring a two-year-old to get a degree in electrical engineering before he is allowed to turn on the lights. Allowing men to be ordained who cannot explain justification by faith alone from the Scriptures, men like John Robbins, is like letting your two-year-old install your electrical system.

But some still do not get this basic distinction. When you point to a stick on the ground, a dog might mistake this signal, and look at your finger and not the stick. But the finger is pointing at something *else*.

Affirming justification by faith alone is a work. It is different than the sheer gift of God that is simply trusting Jesus. Affirming *sola fide* is a work that is most necessary for ordination, not for salvation. For some reason, John Robbins has turned this around.

ANABAPTISTS IN PURITAN FACE PAINT
MAY 29, 2004

When was the first appearance of the strict regulative principle? And what does this tell us about certain deep affinities between certain streams of the Reformed faith and the streams of other communions?

I have before charged that some of the pietists in the Reformed world are completely at odds with their own heritage. And when they encounter living, breathing examples of men in line with their Reformed fathers, they bring them up on charges, saying that they have departed from orthodoxy. But *they* are the ones who departed. Thus they build the tombs of the prophets, and name their seminaries and churches after men they do not care to understand.

In short, I am saying that many of our staunch Reformed brethren are actually anabaptists in Puritan face paint.

This is why the first appearance of the strict regulative principle ("that which is not commanded is forbidden") as opposed to the Reformed regulative principle ("worship must be according to Scripture") is quite instructive.

The anabaptist Conrad Grebel was writing to the radical Thomas Muntzer in September of 1524. He praised a number of things that Muntzer was saying, but he had this criticism, that Muntzer allowed singing in worship. And here comes the origin of a whole lot of trouble in the sectarian world of our reformational backwaters. "Whatever we are not taught by clear passage or examples must be regarded as forbidden, just as if it were written: 'This do not; sing not.'"

The Auburn Avenue Hubbub (AAH) is happening because we have not yet resolved the boundary lines between the magisterial reformation and the radical reformation. And some folks who live near the border don't know what country they are in. Think of it as kind of an ecclesiastical Alsace Lorraine.

AUBURN AVENUE HUBBUB (AAH) COOL QUOTE 5
MAY 29, 2004

> Now in particular I ask you to pray with me that as I baptize this child with water and receive him into the number of Christians, that God himself inwardly baptize him with his Spirit and hold him in the number of his elect.
>
> —John Oecolampadius, *Basel Service Book of 1526*

AUBURN AVENUE HUBBUB (AAH) COOL QUOTE 6
JUNE 7, 2004

> Almighty God, Heavenly Father, we give you eternal praise and thanks, that you have granted and bestowed upon this child your fellowship, that you have born him again to yourself through your holy baptism, that he has been incorporated into Your beloved Son, our only Savior, and is now your child and heir.
>
> *—Strasbourg Psalter of 1537*

JOHN ROBBINS AND THE COUNCIL OF TRENT
JUNE 8, 2004

The controversy over justification by faith shows no signs of letting up. Every day I hear from some new quarter that the hubbub continues. One of the larger ironies in all this is that men who have abandoned the historic, Protestant understanding of faith have accused other men (who have not abandoned it) of doing precisely that. Thus we have closet Tridentine writer like John Robbins accusing faithful Protestants of adopting the errors of Rome on the question of justification by faith.

Naming is central in all this. Because the initial controversy was caused by a surprise attack, those making the charges had the luxury of naming as they pleased. Thus, the Auburn group was falsely accused of drifting Romeward. And initially the controversy was shaped by this. False accusations were made, and then accurately denied. "You deny *sola fide*." "Actually, we don't."

But if there must be a controversy, the next stage in it is most necessary. We need to show how the charge needs to be turned around. Many of those who are attacking us have adopted the same basic definition of faith as was held by the Council of Trent—that is, that faith is assent to raw propositions, and is primarily an intellectual transaction. Trent held that faith was primarily an act of the intellect, and that is what John Robbins holds. The difference between them is that Trent went on to say that this raw assent was not enough, and had to be supplemented by works somehow. Robbins thinks that this lonely faith is the instrument of justification. In contrast to both Trent and Robbins, the historic Reformers held that saving faith did not need to be supplemented from the outside in any way because one component of this faith was *fiducia*, or loving trust. For the Reformers, faith was a gift from God, and when God gives faith, He does not give anything other than a living, obedient faith. Being the kind of God He is, this living faith is the only kind of faith He can give.

So the debate is not whether we are justified by faith alone. The debate is over what kind of faith God actually gives. And many of our hostile brothers need abandon their heterodox opinions, *and return to the historic Reformed faith.*

STRANGE ALLIANCES
JUNE 9, 2004

A specter is haunting the Reformed world—the specter of biblically grounded teaching on marriage, family, and elder qualifications. The threat is causing new ecumenical alliances to form, all calculated to meet the rising and imminent danger. TR Frank Smith is teaming up with openness theology, rabid anti-theonomist John Robbins is shoulder to shoulder with the theonomist Joe Morecraft, crypto-Lutherans in the west are cheek by jowl with anti-Lutherans in the east, and the lion lies down with the lamb.

Of course, it won't do to try to distract attention away from the general familial disarray in the current Reformed establishment by saying that one disagrees with the teaching that husbands should love their wives as Christ loved the church. That wouldn't fly. So one must say, regretfully, that the family books are all very well, but it is "unfortunate that the author is heterodox on justification," or that "he owns half of Las Vegas and is a gambling impresario." *That's* the ticket!

What saith *sola Scriptura*? "Remember them which have the rule over you, who have spoken unto you the word of God: whose faith follow, *considering the end of their conversation*" (Heb. 13:7). "Ye shall know them *by their fruits*. Do men gather grapes of thorns, or figs of thistles?" (Matt. 7:16). But enough with the embarrassingly scriptural *ad hominem*. Some men want to defend ministerial credentials through shibbolethian propositions, making the truth walk around on stilts. Others, more biblically, want to do it through sons and daughters, children who love God and His Christ, and who embody and live the glories of propositional truth in an imitative and incarnate fashion.

By the way, another book on the family is at the printers now, and is due out within the next few weeks. It is entitled *My Life for Yours*. Let us, as the apostle Paul might say, keep on keeping on.

WHEN STUCK, TRY THEOLOGICAL INNOVATION
JUNE 12, 2004

How is it that we are assailed for having a high (and very Reformed) view of the sacraments, when others, like the Lutherans and the Westminster West cadre, are given a pass by the anabaptist reformed? The answer that is given to this question is that there is a basic compatibility between the covenant of works and the covenant of grace (as it is currently understood in the American Reformed world), and law and gospel (as it is understood by the Lutherans). It is claimed that these concepts function in largely the same way, and hence, since we deny that the unfallen Adam was assigned the task of earning merit badges (and want to say that the covenant of life made with him was fundamentally *gracious*), our motives and our persons are therefore suspect.

But of course the covenant of works and the law (in the history of Reformed theology) do *not* function in the same way, and those who are trying to get out of a dicey debate situation by equating them (or even *kinda* equating them) are frankly beginning to flail. Those who doubt this assertion need to answer just a few basic questions at presbytery.

1. Is the Reformed believer today to use the covenant of works as a rule of life?
2. Would you please expound on the third use of the covenant of works?
3. In the life of the believer today is my entire duty to my neighbor summed up in the covenant of works? For he who loves his neighbor keeps the covenant of works.
4. Can the believer be under the covenant of works and the covenant of grace at the same time? Please explain, and feel free to use the blackboard

AUBURN AVENUE HUBBUB (AAH) COOL QUOTE 7
JUNE 14, 2004

> Surely the Sacraments can remind us of grace, help us to appreciate grace, and exhort us to walk in grace, but do they actually give us the grace promised in the Gospel? The Reformed and Presbyterian confessions answer "yes" without hesitation. A Sacrament not only consists of the signs (water, bread and wine), but of the things signified (new birth, forgiveness, life everlasting). And yet, the experience of Reformed and Presbyterians churches in the odd world of American revivalism has challenged the confessional perspective.
>
> —Michael Horton

CROSSFIRE
JUNE 14, 2004

As Stevie Ray Vaughn might have put it, "I'm caught in the crossfire." The East Coast Reformed Police say that it is all right to believe in a kind of baptismal regeneration so long as you also believe in a prelapsarian meritorious covenant of works. And the West Coast Reformed Police are saying that so long as you believe in a prelapsarian meritorious covenant of works, it is all right to be a evangelical anabaptist who practices wet dedications. The only ones who are decidedly *not* okay are those who say that God was covenantally gracious to Adam before the Fall. For some reason. That has not yet been explained.

AUBURN AVENUE KERFUFFLE (AAK) AND TRANSITIVE VERBS

JUNE 17, 2004

Always trying to be helpful, I would like to suggest something else that might help good Reformed folks out of the impasse we have gotten ourselves into. In the current debate over faith alone, obedient faith, faith and obedience, and so on, we have a tendency to reify things like faith and obedience, and then talk about them like they were two billiard balls. Then, when one of the Auburn guys talks about obedient faith, it seems to others like we are trying to get two billiard balls to occupy the same space at the same time. Everyone knows that obedience in sanctification is *this* billiard ball, and that faith is *that* billiard ball. And they do not mush together well.

But the problem is that faith is an abstract noun that describes the action of a multitude of verbs—numerous actions of believing. Obedience does the same thing—and refers to numerous actions of obeying, generally considered.

But an abstract noun should never forget that in its abstract form it never does what it is talking about. "Love," as found in the dictionary, does not have a beloved. But love, in order to exist in the world, requires a beloved. This is another way of saying that *love* is a transitive verb. So is *obey*. So is *believe*.

Now in order for someone to check out someone else's Protestant *bona fides* (such as mine, for instance), it is necessary to ask what I understand the direct object of any given sentence to be.

When I say obedient faith, the question should be "faith that obeys *what*?" or "obedience that believes *what*?"

The response should *not* be "Faith obeys? That sounds like obedience. Obedience sounds like works. Works? Akkk!"

Saving faith obeys the gospel, and only the gospel. Saving obedience believes in Jesus Christ, and saving obedience does nothing *but* believe in Jesus Christ. What is the direct object? God in Christ, Christ on the cross, Christ ascended.

YELLING AT MY WINDSHIELD
JUNE 19, 2004

I have begun listening to the audio recordings of the recent conference at Westminster West on The Foolishness of the Gospel and will make a few comments here from time to time as circumstances warrant. Initially, just a few remarks.

While it is quite true that Scripture speaks of the foolishness of the gospel, it is equally true that Scripture speaks of the foolishness of foolishness. Beware of affirming the consequent.

Second, it simply will not do to *assume* that the historic doctrine of justification under attack, and then to defend it against all imaginary comers. There are two issues here. One is exegetical theology—what did Paul actually say? But there is also historical theology—what was the *actual* position of the Reformers? By "position" I mean those things which they taught, wrote, said, and put in their catechisms. To treat the "Federal Vision" as a self-conscious *challenge* to the historic Protestant doctrine of justification when a number of us claim to be *recovering* the historic Protestant doctrine of justification is a bit thick.

And third, to mush E.P. Sanders, N.T. Wright, Norman Shepherd, Steve Wilkins, *et al.*, all together, "the better to generalize with," and then defend this hopeless process because E.P. Sanders did it to the first century Jews is enough to make me call for the smelling salts.

"I object to how your leader E.P. Sanders blurs the distinctions between disparate groups among first century Jews."

"E.P. Sanders is not my leader."

"And therefore I will do the same to you. For he is your leader."

"Um . . . being from a podunk town in northern Idaho, I'm not used to this level of scholarly discourse. What can I say to this? Is *not*."

"This process your leader has employed is fatally flawed. And that is why I employ it on his minions like you—to show that it is fatally flawed. A *reductio ad absurdum*, as it were."

"I agree that this is screwy process, and it is part of the reason why I don't listen to E.P. Sanders. It is also part of the reason why I don't listen to Westminster West."

But alas, I *am* listening to Westminster West. And I have a significant number of these CDs to go. I am listening to them in my pick-up truck, so if anyone in the Moscow area sees me driving around yelling at my windshield, this datum is likely to have something to do with it.

YELLING AT MY WINDSHIELD, PART TWO
JUNE 21, 2004

Maybe this doesn't count as yelling at my windshield, because I would like to respond to something from the Westminster conference that was reported in *Christian Renewal.* That means my windshield wasn't anywhere near when I read this.

Dr. Hywel Jones was reported as saying this: "Justification is the realization that one is pardoned of all sin, accepted by God without works of any kind, and this motivates and supports one in doing the will of God as nothing else does."

This is not the only difference between us and our, um, discussion partners, but it is a significant one. Notice what Dr. Jones is saying here—"Justification *is the realization* that one is pardoned . . . ." Emphasis is mine.

In contrast, we believe that justification is the grace of God on our behalf through the obedience of Jesus Christ alone. That obedience is ours through our union with Christ, and consequently all that Jesus ever believed and did is reckoned to our account.

Our discussion partners apparently think that justification is a process within us that includes believing the right things about justification. Notice again. "Justification is the realization . . . ."

Now is this an imputed realization or an infused realization?

If I may, allow me to edit Dr. Jones's statement back into orthodoxy. "Justification is the pardon of all sin, in which we are accepted by God without works *or realizations* of any kind, and this motivates and supports one in doing the will of God as nothing else does."

AUBURN AVENUE HUBBUB (AAH) COOL QUOTE 8
JUNE 28, 2004

> Through the outpouring of water is meant that the one on whom the water is sprinkled belongs to the Church and the people of God, that just as water washes away the smudges and stains of our bodies, so also the one upon whom there is this outpouring, being received by grace, is washed with the blood of Jesus and pledged to a new life.
> —Heinrich Bullinger

YELLING AT MY WINDSHIELD, PART 3
JUNE 28, 2004

In his talk on "Justification Under Fire," Dr. Baugh works through three positions. First he takes on the New Perspective. Then he moves on to Norman Shepherd. And third he addresses the Federal Vision, which he regards as having adopted and advanced the positions of Shepherd.

When he gets to (as the Victorians would have put it) the present writer, this is how his argument proceeds:

1. After a few brief comments, read quote from Wilson;
2. Allow time for laughter from audience;
3. Move on.

This is not to say that Dr. Baugh is not advancing his position by this means. Far from it. In his brief comments, he does not argue exegetically or theologically, but he does an admirable job in how he contextualizes what he reads. But unfortunately, that context is entirely of his own manufacturing.

For example, he read one quote from the special issue of *Credenda* entitled A Pauline Take on the New Perspective [click here to see for yourself*], which said that amillennial crypto-Lutherans and revivalistic Reformed fundamentalists

* credenda.org/issues/index.php?issue=15-5. No longer available.

had drifted from their confessional roots, and this is why they were opposed to the New Perspective. Ho, ho, ho from the audience, and contemporary scholarship then advanced to the next point.

The problem with this is that Dr. Baugh neglected to mention that this issue of *Credenda* was my *critique* of the New Perspective, that according to *his* definition of the NP I am not among them, and that the basic arguments he advanced against the NP I fully share and argued for in that issue (which he *appears* to have read). But no one listening to this tape as an introduction to the controversy could possibly have gathered any of this.

What are we to make of it? This is a classic example of misrepresenting an opponent by means of nothing but true statements. If one of my students were to write home, "Dear Mom, Had a great day in class today. Mr. Wilson came in sober," the fact that everything written was true will not prevent Mom from coming to false conclusions.

So one conclusion of ours should be that Westminster West is not to be trusted for an accurate assessment of the various positions in this controversy. Someone down there apparently bought a spray can of Careful-Distinctions-B-Gone.

YELLING AT MY WINDSHIELD, PART 4
JUNE 28, 2004

At the conclusion of his talk, Dr. Baugh offered some salient comments on the first verses of Galatians 5, over against various forms of covenant nomism. And shoot, I AGREED WITH HIM (the "all caps" are so that theological scholars might pick up on this particular nuance) in his critique of the idea that we get into the covenant by grace and stay in by our obedience. Never heard anything so crazy in my life. Anyhow, because at that point I AGREED SO FUNDAMENTALLY WITH DR. BAUGH, I was interested to hear what he did next. But alas, he did not keep up the pace.

He came next to that "faith working by love" part (Gal. 5:6). He said (a little briskly, I might add) that our faith is alive, and does works of love, because it has been justified. Huh, I thought, looking out my windshield.

I thought faith was the instrument of justification in the *ordo salutis*, and therefore preceeded it. In other words, faith is what it is before justification gets to it, because justification doesn't happen without the instrumentality of faith, which has to be what it is in order for justification to happen at all. If you follow me. If you don't, it is all right. Has happened before, most recently in Escondido.

So let me put this another way. When God gives the gift of faith, the instrument that will be used (any nano-second now) to appropriate the imputed gift of justification, is that faith changed when the justification happens? Is *dead* faith the instrument of justification, and then under the influence of imputed righteousness it changes into living faith in order to do all that sanctification stuff? Or is it living faith from the get go? If the latter, then what did Dr. Baugh mean by saying it was living because of justification? It seems that faith working by love appropriates the gift of righteousness. That's what I think, but I am the heretic, and so I don't trust myself anymore.

By the way, did I mention that I AGREED COMPLETELY with Dr. Baugh's critique of covenant nomism?

YELLING AT MY WINDSHIELD, PART 5
JUNE 29, 2004

Just finished listening to Michael Horton's contribution to the Westminster conference. He made lots of fine points, and is clearly well-read in all the literature that surrounds this particular embarrassment to Christian discourse.

Nevertheless, some fundamental misapplications are still there, and the stumbling block is that pesky word *merit*. I am reminded of that section in *Pirates of Penzance*: "When you say, *offen*, do you mean *offen*, a person who has lost his parents, or *offen*, frequently?"

Horton believes that we have gone back to the medieval category of *congruent merit*, and this frankly baffles me. Whenever I see *congruent merit* on the street, I never fail to heap opprobrium on his pointy little head. Congruent merit is nothing if not synergistic, and when you are high octane predestinarians, as all the Federal Vision men are, congruent merit is simply a theological impossibility. Horton may not like what we are articulating, and we would be happy to discuss it. But it is not congruent merit, or any kind of merit at all.

Near the end of his talk, he rejects the idea that we "get in" by grace, and "stay in" by works. As do I, with enthusiasm. We get in by grace, we remain in by grace, we walk by grace, we talk by grace, we persevere by grace, we eat dinner by grace, we go to church by grace. We get in by grace. We stay in by grace. We finish by grace. *Sola gratia. Tota gratia. Tota et sola gratia.* Grace, grace, grace.

But you know me. Mr. Ambiguous.

YELLING AT MY WINDSHIELD, PART 6
JUNE 30, 2004

I am mostly through Dr. Clark's talk on the active obedience of Christ. In one part of his lecture, he gives a great long list of theologians who affirm and believe in the active obedience of Christ. Missing from this section of his lecture was a sentence like the following: "Douglas Wilson, well known advocate of the Federal Vision, also affirms the active obedience of Christ, and declares with Machen there is no hope without it." Had the sentence been included it would have been accurate and everything, but it frankly would have ruined the symmetry of the occasion. And some of the faithful would have left scratching their heads.

YELLING AT MY WINDSHIELD, PART 7
JUNE 30, 2004

Dr. Clark makes the statement that we bad guys are teaching somewhere that Christ lived, not a life of perfect condign merit, but rather a life of okay congruent merit. Where we affirmed this, I am sure I don't know. Maybe one of us is writing for WTJ under a pen name. And maybe he is on drugs while he is doing this. And maybe the editor was distracted and published it anyway. And maybe Dr. Clark forgot to footnote this outrageous claim that we somehow teach that Jesus did not live a life of perfect obedience. But we are claiming this somewhere, for those who only have eyes to see.

JULY–SEPTEMBER 2004

YELLING AT MY WINDSHIELD, PART EIGHT
JULY 1, 2004

I finished listening to Dr. Clark's lecture on the active obedience of Christ. Jeepers. I never knew I believed and taught such things as alleged, and we here at Christ Church have launched a full-scale investigation to determine why it was that I was never informed.

YELLING AT MY WINDSHIELD, PART NINE
JULY 2, 2004

I am a good chunk of the way through Robert Godfrey's talk on *sola fide*, and even drove around a little extra at lunch to hear more of it. Really fine talk, actually, and I am not saying this satirically at all, although there is *some* irony involved. If anyone wants to know what DW's position on *sola fide* is, just check out what Robert Godfrey has to say. Me and Godfrey, just like this (holding up two intertwined fingers). Good exposition of Calvin's exposition of Paul, and they all stated accurately what I believe on this subject (Paul, Calvin, and Godfrey). Let me add my own voice to this lovefest. "Me, too!"

The irony is that on this subject Godfrey and I are in complete harmony. Just like ham and eggs. But this means that *something* is seriously out of joint somewhere. Either he *ought* to be in serious trouble with the rest of his amigos down there, or I ought *not* to be. I wonder which it is.

Just for the record (again): *We are justified by grace through faith, and we are justified by this grace from first to last, through the instrumentality of faith from first to last.*

So where does the problem lie? Here is the report card:

Exegesis of Paul: A

Exegesis of Calvin: A

Exegesis of Luther: A

Exegesis of Federal Vision: D minus

AUBURN AVENUE HUBBUB (AAH) COOL QUOTE 9
JULY 2, 2004

> His covenant with Adam was gracious in character, sovereignly imposed, mutually binding, called for trust and submission on Adam's part, and carried sanctions (blessings or curse). When Adam fell into sin, God mercifully re-established a covenantal relationship with him, one in which the gracious and promissory character of the covenant was accentuated even further—in the promise of a coming Savior, a promise which is progressively unfolded and elaborated upon throughout the Old Testament. —Greg L. Bahnsen, "Cross-Examination: Practical Implications of Covenant Theology," *The Counsel of Chalcedon*, December, 1992.

YELLING AT MY WINDSHIELD, PART TEN
JULY 2, 2004

Robert Godfrey raises a great question concerning objections to Pauline theology. If what we teach is not generating the same objections that Paul's teaching did, then the chances are good that we are not *preaching* the same thing he did. If our preaching of grace does not provoke the charge of antinomianism from the legalists, then we are not having the same effect on the legalists that Paul did. I accept the argument, which I think is a *very* good one, and I also accept the challenge.

Dr. Godfrey says that he cannot see the Federal Vision writings having that effect on anyone. But that is probably because he is not a legalist (and cannot think like one), coupled with the fact that he ought to get out a little more. But as far as quite a few *others* are concerned, I have gotten the antinomian wind in my sails and do not give two cents for the law of God. And for his opposition to Regulative Principle Dour Party (RPDP) lots of people think that Schlissel is the original antinomian orangutan. But the closest Dr. Godfrey has gotten to the precipice of antinomianism is that he was once tempted to sing a hymn instead of a psalm.

For good measure, doubling the effectiveness of this particular argument, for *their* part the antinomians think I'm a legalist. And to retrofit an argument of Chesterton's, this is probably not because I am wicked enough to encompass multiple contradictory sins, but rather that any stick is good enough to beat me with.

Over the course of the last few years, I have been accumulating so many slanderous accusations of evil doing that the local landfill had to start charging the Wilson family extra. If *this* is to be the test of orthodoxy (and in part, it ought to be), I will glad to be welcomed back into the ranks of the faithful by an official emissary of Westminster West, and will sit by the phone waiting for their call. At last, a test I can pass with ease.

Why, (and you will *scarcely* believe this), just the other day I was listening in my pick-up to a tape by a gentleman named Dr. Scott Clark, and *he* said that we Federal Vision types did not believe that Jesus lived a life of perfect, sinless obedience! I was so flummoxed by this that I pulled my truck over to the side of the road, and had to lay myself down on the highway with my feet on the bumper just to get the blood back into my head. Then when the state patrolman asked me what I thought I was doing, I explained it to *him*, and he couldn't believe it either. Actually, I made this last little bit up—just a little fib—but that's okay. We're all under grace.

I well remember when I first learned this argument that Dr. Godfrey presented—I was standing in front of a local LDS study center handing out literature, and one of the fellows who came out to talk to me said something like this, "If what you are saying is true, then what is to prevent us all from living a life of sin?" That's when I *first* heard the echo of Romans 6.

Just curious. When was the last time Westminster West had to fight off charges of rampant antinomianism? Anybody heard recently that the seminarians down there are party commandoes? That they frequent casinos? That the administration winks at such sin?

YELLING AT MY WINDSHIELD, PART ELEVEN
JULY 3, 2004

Finishing up Dr. Godfrey's tape, I realized that it was not until the last couple minutes that I encountered any doctrinal or theological disagreement. Of course, he was wrong about the Federal Vision throughout, but his treatment of Paul and Calvin was admirable. Would that he handled what we have written with the same care.

But there was disagreement on substance right at the end. Dr. Godfrey cited Romans 5, "Therefore we have peace with God . . ." and went on to say that Paul does not say, "We have peace with God, but beware! You might lose it." The problem with this is that it is simply wrong. That is precisely what Paul spends the 11th chapter of Romans doing. The Jews fell from their position on the olive tree—you Romans, beware! What Dr. Godfrey says here is simply a glaring exegetical error.

And keep in mind that I agreed with everything he said about *sola fide*. But exegetically, this *has* to be harmonized with the doctrine of *covenantal apostasy*, which Paul addresses in Romans 11. This harmonization is right at the center of the Federal Vision project and does not depend on any of the medieval scarecrows that were being produced at this Westminster conference. Congruent merit, *bah!* Arminianism, *ptooey!* Semi-Pelagianianism, *ha!* I spit in their general direction.

Romans 11 must not be treated as the invisible chapter in Reformed systematics. It must be incorporated. It is fully consistent with what Dr. Godfrey said about *sola fide*. But if you speak as though Romans 4–5 and Romans 11 *are part of the same apostolic argument*, be prepared to be attacked as one who is attacking the gospel.

YELLING AT MY WINDSHIELD, PART TWELVE
JULY 3, 2004

Dr. Hywel Jones begins his lecture by noting that in the weeks and months to come, some of us on the other side will "cry foul." And that is precisely what I have been doing in these posts—crying foul. Dr. Jones goes on to say that when someone is struck under the fifth rib, this is precisely the response we should expect from them.

But the problem is not that we have been struck, it is that we have been struck by people who manifestly have not done their homework. There are times when a blow under the fifth rib *should* arouse a concern about a foul blow. Joab and Abner come to mind.

I don't think our discussion partners at the Ft. Lauderdale colloquium understood us. But I will say this—they *labored* to understand us. The results of that labor can be found here.* But this is simply not the case with our critics at Westminster West—and it shows. The tragedy is that I believe that both Dr. Horton and Dr. Godfrey have the wherewithal to understand us. Had that labor been invested the way it ought to have been, this conference would not have been the standing embarrassment to the seminary that it is.

GONE FOR A WHILE, BACK IN A BIT
JULY 4, 2004

Heading out of town for a week or thereabouts, and I don't know if I will have Internet access there. If I do, I will post as I can, but I am afraid that my pick-up and CD player are staying right here in Idaho. Therefore, I will not be yelling at my windshield for the time being. This is a shame really, because I think my windshield was actually starting to get it.

YELLING AT MY WINDSHIELD, PART THIRTEEN
JULY 14, 2004

I have resumed my duties of listening to the Westminster West conference tapes, and have made it all the way to the Q&A. Imagine my surprise when these worthy gentlemen (in effect) all denied the imputation of the active obedience of Christ. A question was asked which quoted my statement from *Credenda*, to the effect that I believed that the faith and faithfulness of Jesus Christ was imputed to us. "What do you make of that?"

* cmfnow.com

The answers all showed that they did not understand the plain statement being made, and the plain statement being made was an affirmation of the imputation of Christ's active obedience. They began discussing a bunch of things that I was *not* talking about, and missed the whole point. One of them even said that Christ's faith was utterly different from ours, because He was trusting in God, and not in a mediator.

Of course he was trusting in God! Of course He was not trusting in a mediator! He *is* the mediator! I wrote (in English, just for the record), that the faith and faithfulness of Christ were *imputed* to us. His faith was *imputed* to us. His faithfulness was *imputed* to us. One of these gentlemen said (I did not recognize the voice) that I was thereby equating Christ's faith with our faith. The problem with this analysis is that it is (sorry, windshield) THE OPPOSITE of what I was saying.

When I read a cultbuster book, like Walter Martin's *Kingdom of the Cults*, I come away knowing what the cult thinks, why they think it, where they say it, and how they defend it. Listening to these tapes all I hear is hopeless muddle and confusion. This muddle is the result of a fundamental conviction that Norman Shepherd, N.T. Wright, the NPP, and the Federal Vision are all engaging in the same basic set of monkeyshines. This fundamental conviction is Not To Be Questioned, despite plain statements to the contrary.

It is like the old joke about the guy who was convinced he was dead, and so he went to a shrink. The shrink decided not to take the direct approach, and showed the gentleman over a series of weeks the incontrovertible proof that dead men don't bleed. He showed him encyclopedia articles, medical journals, took him to the morgue, and what not. After an arduous number of weeks, the man was finally convinced. "Dead men don't bleed." Whereupon the shrink took out a pin and pricked the man's thumb and a drop of blood appeared. The man's face turned ashen white. "Dead men bleed after all!"

How is their confusion on this point a denial of imputation of Christ's active obedience? In order for Christ's obedience to be truly imputed to us, it has to include the motive force, and not just the motions of his body. But the motive force was faith in His Father. (That is, faith in His *Father*. Who ever said anything about some other mediator? Not me.) So the imputation of Christ's active obedience must include His faith——His reasons for obeying. And the imputation of His faithfulness is simply the imputation of the visible aspects of His obedience.

That's what I said. And that's what they all disagreed with.

YELLING AT MY WINDSHIELD, FINIS
JULY 14, 2004

I am thinking of getting a tattoo. I know, I have argued against it elsewhere, but here's my thinking. I could have the Shorter Catechism tattooed on my back, and then the guys at Westminster West would have to believe me, right? And maybe I'd get really sick with ink poisoning with a tattoo that big, and they would visit me in the hospital, and we would have us a Reformed reconciliation. What I mean by Reformed reconciliation is, "Don't hold your breath." I am starting to feel as lonely as one of Ken Sande's Peacemaker counselors at a Scottish revival.

Seriously, just a few last comments about this particular conference and on to greener pastures with me.

First, my experience with Norman Shepherd is pretty limited. I have read *Call of Grace* once, and it is a short book. But there is all this yelling and hollering about him, so a fellow like me doesn't have much to go on. However, the one thing I *do* have the privilege of going on is my first-hand knowledge of how *my* words have been handled. And if they have misunderstood just half of his positions as I know they have misunderstood mine, then Shepherd must be one orthodox dude.

Second, the Federal Vision is not a heresy. But if it *were*, this caliber of critique would not be keeping us heretics up nights. As a case in point, for the record *again*, here are my positions. I believe in and openly teach:

1. Predestination
2. Total inability

3. Sovereign election.
4. Particular redemption
5. Resurrecting grace
6. Perseverance of the elect saints
7. *Tota et sola fide*
8. *Tota et sola gratia*
9. *Tota et sola Scriptura*
10. *Totus et solus Christus*
11. *Toti et soli Deo gloria*
12. The objectivity of the covenant.
13. And that baptism and the Lord's Supper are effectual means of salvation for worthy receivers, which is to say, to those who trust in Christ alone by grace alone through faith alone according to the gospel found in the Scriptures alone, with all the glory going to God alone.

And what does this position get labeled as in the Westminster Q & A session? *Pelagianism.* I must say, it is the strangest form of Pelagianism as ever *I* encountered. This whole controversy is starting to resemble the Jabberwocky on stilts.

Third, various references were made to a book they are working on. I will let you know if they represent my views accurately in that book. They did not in this conference.

Time to soothe my windshield with a little Norah Jones.

YELLING AT MY WINDSHIELD, POST SCRIPT
JULY 15, 2004–

Okay. Just one more thing on these audio recordings. Robert Godfrey was asked about the full-throated support that Cornelius Van Til gave to Norman Shepherd during the Westminster East controversy. In his response, Godfrey basically said that during this period Van Til was not as sharp as he used to be, that despite this, he was a thorough-going confessionalist, and that he was out of the loop anyway, getting his information from Richard Gaffin. Godfrey then went on to say that, all these things notwithstanding, even if Van Til knew his own mind fully in his support of Shepherd, nothing requires us all to accept everything Van Til held as though it came down from an oracle on the mount. A number of others reinforced this point, and there was a good deal of oracular joking around.

But this misses the point completely. The question is not whether Van Til *must* be an oracle, or whether current Reformed theologians must agree with him. The question is why I and my friends are assailed for being heretics because we *might* agree with Shepherd in some things, and Van Til, when he enthusiastically supported Shepherd, is simply "not an oracle." Why not say what your position seems to entail, and condemn Van Til as a heretic? And John Murray while you are at it? If I agreed to be considered a non-oracle by the men at Westminster (which shouldn't be too hard), can we drop all this "assault on the gospel" foolishness?

Related to this, why the attack on me and my friends instead of on Richard Gaffin, who was apparently feeding all the bum dope to Van Til? Not that I want anybody to attack Richard Gaffin, but this Esconditic zeal for the gospel looks like it is choosing political targets of opportunity instead of standing for principle. Why the attack on a church of another denomination in *Idaho* when The Contagion is obviously present in one's very own Sister Seminary? It is as though Paul, deciding that withstanding Peter to his face at Antioch for hypocrisy would be too dicey politically, started an argument over *sola fide* with the church janitor in the parking lot.

AND ANOTHER THING
JULY 15, 2004

Along the same lines as the previous post, the latest *Modern Reformation* has a short article on "American Tragedy: Jonathan Edwards on Justification." The article maintains that Edwards was, in significant respects, closer to the Thomists than to the Reformers on the question of justification. I waited for the other shoe to drop—e.g., Edwards was a heretic, covenant and justification under attack, etc.—but nothing. Nothing but an eerie silence.

One reason why they don't finish their syllogisms should be obvious. If you write off Van Til, John Murray, and Jonathan Edwards as not Reformed, and heretical to boot, you start to look like those Turbulent Waters Revival Books johnnies, who are the only Christians left in the world.

YELLING AT MY COPY OF MODERN REFORMATION
JULY 15, 2004

Actually I am not yelling at all. This is merely a poetic conceit, kind of like George Herbert yelling at his pulley.

I want to raise a question I have asked before, only in different terms. According to our discussion partners, within the Covenant of Grace does the Covenant of Works have any members? Are the elect simultaneously members of both covenants? If members of both, please explain. No man can have two masters. If of one only, then why do the residual terms of the covenant we are *not* member of have any force or authority at all, even as directions for living?

AS REFORMED AS I WANNA BE
JULY 18, 2004

In their recent book, *Not Reformed At All,* John Robbins and Sean Gerety ask the following, somewhat rhetorically. "Is Wilson suggesting that because parents are Christians, their baptized children also are Christians?"

No, not at all. Baptism is not necessary. The *unbaptized* children of Christians are Christians. That's why we baptize them. But I do wonder why John Robbins thinks we should baptize them. I also wonder why he thinks I am out of conformity with the Westminster position, and he is not, for which, see below.

> Before baptism, the minister is to use some words of instruction, touching the institution, nature, use, and ends of this sacrament, shewing . . . that they [children] are *Christians,* and federally holy *before* baptism, and therefore are they baptized. (*Westminster Directory for the Publick Worship of God,* emphasis mine)

SLOW MOTION HELICOPTER CRASHES
JULY 18, 2004

Okay, then. My previous post gave away the fact that I have been reading *Not Reformed At All*[*] by Robbins and Gerety. Just three comments. First, I have read up through page 63 with that curious sense of fascination that one has while watching slow motion videotape of helicopter crashes. Second, why is it that rationalists and propositionalists and logicians are the most unreasonable people in the world? Why is it that they cannot follow an argument to save their soul? Fortunately, the salvation of their souls does not depend on following arguments (*sola fide*!), but still, the fact is troublesome. Third, the graphic design of the cover is superb, and is the best argument the book contains, at least in the first 63 pages. But alas, a great cover on a book like this is like that woman in Proverbs without discretion. If someone is looking for a well-reasoned, thoughtful critique of the Auburn position, it ain't here. But try getting a look at the cover sometime.

UNCORKING THE WHOLE JUG
JULY 20, 2004

Every faithful servant of God has to learn how to respond to the lies that are told about him. One reaction is to do precisely that, *react*, and respond in the flesh. If someone slaps you in the face, that initial reaction is probably what the flesh wants you to do. The reason for responding has less to do with the honor of God than it has to do with the fundamental desire to "get even." But Paul teaches us not to take vengeance, not because vengeance is wrong, but because vengeance is Mine, saith the Lord. Vindication is the Lord's.

But it is important to emphasize that the desire to get even is a fleshly response because of the motives; the problem is *not* that it is an actual response in the physical world. Another carnal reaction is what we might call the pacifist option. Taking the truth that God is the one who vindicates, it is assumed that this must mean no action or words or defense on the part of the

* John W. Robbins and Sean Gerety, *Not Reformed at All: Medievalism in "Reformed" Churches* (Dallas: Trinity Foundation, 2004).

slandered is ever appropriate. If someone says something in his own defense, it is simply assumed that he is angling for his own vindication, not the Lord's. But we don't apply this foolishness to other aspects of our lives, nor should we. I thank God for the food, but I also buy the food with the paycheck that I earned. The biblical position on all such matters is *trust*, not quietism. If someone defends himself vigorously against slander (as the apostle Paul frequently did), this is not evidence that he was not trusting God.

From time to time, I have contemplated writing a narrative story of the events of the last couple years—on all the controversies, and how all of them have come together into one grand donnybrook. And what a story it would be! But I have put this off for various reasons. One, I want to be sure that I am not reacting in the flesh. Thomas Watson put it well, "Better to be wronged than to do wrong," and waiting a bit while making such a decision seems to be prudent. Second, the elders of Christ Church have told me not to worry about defending myself, and they have done a very capable job of saying and doing everything that *needs* to be said and done. One of the things a telling of this story would do is reveal what a group of stalwarts they have been. Third, a complete story would reflect badly on people who should have known better, people I don't want to hurt in the telling. And there is no real way to tell this story without uncorking the whole jug.

But for the present, I will say one thing. The Psalms are *amazingly* relevant. Not only do they describe what is going on, they also are very descriptive about how the story ends. Diggers of pits fall into them, and vindication is the Lord's.

REFORMED JUST A SKOSH
JULY 21, 2004

From time to time, I want to make a few comments on passages of the Robbins/Gerety *Not Reformed At All* book. The passages generally have this in common—they are marked with exclamation marks in the margins, sometimes more than one, in my personal copy of this book. I will not be yelling at these margins for, as everyone knows, it does no good to yell at inanimate objects.

In their discussion of authority and tradition, these gentlemen reveal that they have not mastered a basic distinction in this argument. They take me to task for saying the traditions of the Church are not infallible, and yet claiming at the same time they are authoritative.

"This is the same position on church tradition—it is both authoritative and fallible—that many so-called scholars take about the Scriptures. One must ask of Wilson, as we ask of them, what epistemic authority does error have? Why are we obliged to believe something that might be false?" (p. 27).

I have been asked a question, and I answer the call!

First, if we are not obliged to believe error, as Robbins claims, then I wonder what he is doing publishing a book full of them. What did he *want* us to do with them?

Second, to answer the question seriously, error has no *epistemic* authority at all. If a father commands his young daughter to make meat loaf with five times more salt than the recipe demands, she can know that he is being silly even while she graciously makes the meatloaf. His folly has no epistemic authority over her at all. She is not required to believe it is going to be edible. But is there no authority here? This question they ask me is the fruit of hyper-propositionalism. If everything in the universe is a proposition with a little T or F beside it, then of course, everything reduces to epistemic issues. But the universe is not like that (what is the propositional value of the music in Handel's *Messiah*?), and everything does not so reduce.

Third, what possible relevance does it have to bring up scholars who deny the infallibility of the Scriptures in a debate with someone who affirms *sola Scriptura*? Scripture alone provides an ultimate and infallible word. Other spiritual authorities exist—parents and pastors, to cite two—but they are not ultimate (appeal can always be made past them to the Scriptures) and they are not infallible (they can and do err, like me and John Robbins).

And last, I am thinking of inventing a new school of theology, since that is all the rage these days, and Robbins has already shown us the way. But instead of hyper-propositionalism, I think we need to pay some attention to the neglected prepositions of Scriptures. I call this school of thought hyper-prepositionalism, and want to reduce everything to words like, *above, to, on, under*, and so on. I think this is the key to answering the rampant unbelief of our day.

Hyper-propositionalists, please note: the paragraph above is a trap. Beware of it.

THE WHOLE TRUTH AND NOTHING BUT THE TRUTH JULY 22, 2004

In *Not Reformed At All*, at the bottom on page 29, Robbins/Gerety breathlessly announce that I have denied the very concept of truth. They put it this way. "In 1999 Wilson published an essay titled 'The Great Logic Fraud' in his book *The Paideia of God*. It expresses his revolt against excellence, precision, and logic. That essay belies any claim Wilson might make to be believe the system of truth in the *Westminster Confession*. In the essay, Wilson even denies that 2 + 2 = 4 is true. His exact words are, for those who might find my accusation incredible, 'Because of our realist assumptions in mathematics, we have come to believe that 15 + 20 = 35 is true. But it is evidently not true.'"

Ah, but there is more. In that essay, I went on to say (in the very *next* sentence) that "15 unicorns plus 20 unicorns will not get 35 unicorns, try as you may. Of course, on the other hand, 15 turnips plus 20 turnips will result in 35 turnips, *and it will do so every time*. The structure of the addition table is sound, and the 'argument' is valid. And if unicorns existed, we would wind up with 35 of them. But this means the argument is valid, not true" [emphasis added]. I was talking about truth and validity (an elementary distinction in logic, one we teach to our eighth graders), not truth and falsity, or truth and relativism.

From this distance, it is impossible to say if the Robbins/Gerety problem is one of paradigm-induced incompetence, paradigm-induced dishonesty, ordinary incompetence, ordinary dishonesty, or some mixture of the four. And so I do not presume to say. But I *can* say that Robbins/Gerety are not to be trusted in representing to their reading public anything about what I have to say. Somebody is struggling with the concept of truth, all right.

THEOLOGICAL SPAM
JULY 23, 2004

My spam filter catches hundreds of invitations a day—invitations to check out these mortgage rates, these crazy chicks, these unbelievable cell phone offers, and more. One nagging question concerns why these companies go to all this effort. Does anybody *actually* get their mortgage this way? And the answer has to be *yes*. Otherwise, there would not be all this traffic. The percentages may be extremely low, but apparently (judging from the volume of invitations) there is enough of a response to keep these fellows in business.

And this is why I am taking the time to answer John Robbins. However much he has discredited himself in the responsible Reformed world (consigning C.S. Lewis to Hell, attacking the Apostles' Creed, and much, much more), he still has a hearing in certain quarters. And some of the people who listen to him are dear Christian people.

On page 33 of *Not Reformed At All*, Robbins/Gerety say: "Wilson lets us know that by redefining this word, he is simultaneously re-structuring all other doctrines. Please keep that in mind as we examine what he says." The word under discussion here is *Christian*.

The thing to emphasize at this point is that Robbins/Gerety are incapable of understanding what their opponents are saying. They say, "It is not Wilson's point that 'the word *Christian* can be used in two senses.' That is trivial, and he is being disingenuous." But of course, that is precisely my point. The word *Christian* has more than one legitimate biblical usage, and I want to use them both.

Jesus said to make disciples by baptizing them as such. Such disciples were first called Christians at Antioch. This is the category I understand as *Christian by covenant*.

But there is another category—those who are born again to God, those who worship in Spirit and truth, those who are regenerate, and any other phrase you might take from traditional soteriology. This is the kind of Christian who goes to Heaven when he dies.

Why can't Robbins/Gerety understand this? They don't *want* to.

LOGIC 101
JULY 29, 2004

Throughout their book, Robbins and Gerety show a genuine inability or unwillingness to engage with the arguments I present for the objectivity of the covenant. For example, one of my common illustrations for what I am talking about is the covenant of marriage. A husband is covenantally a husband, and whether or not he is a faithful husband is a separate question. All husbands are married, but not all husbands are faithful to their marriage vows. In the same way, all the baptized are covenantally bound to Christ, but not all such Christians are faithful to their baptismal vows. (And faithfulness to these vows consists of *faith alone*, incidentally, and not by works as some slanderously report me as saying.)

But look at how Robbins/Gerety misconstrue this illustration and argument. "Wilson's denial of the class 'nominal husband,' implies that all fornicators are husbands, just as his denial of 'nominal Christian' implies that all hypocrites are Christians" (p. 115).

The apostle Paul had to deal with a similar problem——teachers of the law who knew nothing about the law (1 Tim. 1:7). Robbins and Gerety make a great fuss over the inviolability of logic (which I agree with, by the way, since the character of God is the basis for all rational thought), but after they have claimed great things for logic, they go on to show that they don't understand how it works. In this instance, they are guilty of affirming the consequent. They do this in an oblique way, by misrepresenting my argument as though I were affirming the consequent.

This particular fallacy is committed when someone says, "If p, then q. Q. Therefore p." "If he studies hard, he will get a good grade. He got a good grade, therefore he must have studied hard." Well, no. He might have bribed the teacher, got lucky on a multiple-choice test, etc. Reasoning this way is called affirming the consequent.

I argued that every husband bound by covenant is obligated to keep that covenant, whether he does so or not. All husbands are *obligated* to refrain from adultery, whether they do or not. If they do not, this does not make them nonhusbands, it makes them adulterers. Robbins and Gerety respond to this by saying that a "fornicator remains a fornicator—he does not become a husband—by participating in some of the activities of a husband" (p. 116).

Let me make this concrete, in order to illustrate fully the intellectual dishonesty of how they are arguing. I said that all horses are horses, even those that are black. Robbins and Gerety respond that Wilson thinks—ho,ho,ho!—that being black makes you a horse!

I say that all husbands are husbands, even those who have sex with women to whom they are not married. Robbins and Gerety respond that this entails saying all who have sex with a woman they are not married to are therefore husbands. Really? I would like to see them try to sketch this on the blackboard.

Those who are tempted to listen to what John Robbins puts out need to understand that he is either unwilling or incapable of following the arguments he has assumed the role of refuting. This has been shown repeatedly. For those on the other side of this fracas, you need to find another champion. He is not really helping you out. I say this because if too much more of this goes on, we will be accused of secretly paying The Trinity Foundation to maintain their position as our real-life straw man.

A HANDY GUIDE FOR NAVIGATING THEOLOGICAL CONTROVERSIES

AUGUST 3, 2004

For all those interested second-year seminary students who are watching the varied logomachies being undertaken on their behalf by their elders in the gates of Zion, it seems that someone ought to have prepared a handy guide like this long before now. But they haven't, and you know how it goes. But you can't tell the players without a scorecard.

In some disputes, the answer to these questions runs along the lines of "neither," but in those cases it is best to abandon all interest in *that* dispute anyway and give yourself to a perusal of Monday Night Football.

That said, here are some basic questions to help keep things sorted out:

1. Which side is capable of stating the position of their opposition in terms that the opposition would own and recognize?

2. Which side is threatened and behaves as though it is threatened?
3. Which side has a donor base that would dry up if they did not point to a "threat to the gospel" to keep the money coming in? Which side has a donor base that would dry up if they successfully preserved the unity of the Spirit in the bond of peace?
4. Which side takes offense when extreme members of their party are answered?
5. Which side behaves as though it is competing for a market share?
6. Which side is characterized by grimness, and which by gladness?
7. Which side resorts to theological dishonesty in representing the arguments and positions of their adversaries? And refuses to be held accountable for it?
8. Which side looks as though they are trying to position themselves to be the next Ligonier when R.C. Sproul retires?
9. Which side resorts to Bulverisms in accounting for the motives of the opposition?

Answer key:

1. *Good*
2. *Bad*
3. *Bad, bad*
4. *Bad*
5. *Bad*
6. *Bad and good, respectively*
7. *Bad, bad*
8. *Really bad*
9. *Bad, except when insightfully done, as here*

THE POTENCY OF SOLA FIDE
AUGUST 7, 2004

One of the reasons why John Robbins and Sean Gerety are not to be trusted is because of their deliberate misrepresentations, as has been shown in previous posts. But there is another problem that runs throughout the book, which would be better classified as an inability to grasp the argument. For example, consider this:

> In opposition to this counterfeit covenant, Paul teaches a Covenant of Grace in which "*the promise might be sure to all the seed.*" There is no sure promise of salvation in Wilson's counterfeit covenant. His appeal to ritual baptism for assurance is asinine, for he admits that some baptized people go to Hell. (Robbins and Gerety, p. 90)

Now the problem here, ironically, is an inability to understand *sola fide*. God makes promises in His Word and in His sacraments. But a man can have a Bible and go to Hell. He can read his Bible and go to Hell. He can hear the Bible preached and go to Hell. He can nod his head *yeah, uh huh* at what the Bible says and go to Hell. But nevertheless, the Bible still contains the promises. What secures the promises for an individual? What is the instrument that causes an individual to close with Christ? *Faith* and *faith alone*.

The same is true of the sacraments. When the Reformers taught Christians to "look to their baptism," they were not teaching them to look there *faithlessly*. A faithful statement of "look to the Bible, look to your baptism, look to the Supper" is actually saying look to Christ, and look where He has promised to meet with you. And do this in faith. Faith alone is that which enables a man to see the promise of God (the promise who is Christ Himself) in what would otherwise be paper and ink, water, bread and wine. Let me use the words of Martin Luther's wonderful baptismal hymn to make the point I am making, and which Robbins and Gerety are missing.

> The eye of sense alone is dim, and nothing sees but water;
> Faith sees Christ Jesus and in Him the Lamb ordained for slaughter;
> It sees the cleansing fountain, red with the dear blood of Jesus,
> Which from the sins, inherited from fallen Adam, frees us
> And from our own misdoings.

When I tell someone to look to Scripture, I am not telling them to trust in leather bindings, ink and high-quality paper—though some people do trust in their Nehushtan Bibles in just this way. And there are people who superstitiously come to offend Jesus through their use of unbelieving ritual, water and bread and wine. Their condemnation is just.

But Robbins and Gerety cannot imagine how a man might look to his baptism and see, with Martin Luther, Christ Jesus and the Lamb ordained for slaughter. In short, they cannot grasp the potency of faith alone.

UPCOMING DEBATE
AUG 10, 2004

I am looking forward to my debate with James White this fall. I am currently halfway through his book *The Roman Catholic Controversy*, which is actually quite good. I agree with bunches and bunches of it. The debate, for those not up to speed, has to do with whether Roman Catholics are members of the New Covenant. I am taking the affirmative, and Dr. White the negative. The debate does *not* have to do with whether or not I approve of the errors of Rome. Well, actually, it might have to do with that in John Robbins's mind, but ol' John is marching to a different drummer. Those who are interested in more information on the debate can click here*.

ANSWERING ALL THE QUESTIONS
AUG 11, 2004

When trust breaks down, it is hard to say anything without the suspicious seizing upon whatever it is and twisting it to suit themselves. This is just another way of saying that when trust breaks down, one of the first things that people forget is that affirmation of innocence until guilt is established and proven is a biblical requirement. And within confessional churches, *orthodoxy is a given* unless the contrary is proven in accordance with how the Bible says things are to be proven. This is the context in which I am debating. This means that in this debate, Steve Schlissel, Michael Horton, Cal Beisner, Rick Phillips, Steve Wilkins, Robert Godfrey, are all orthodox Christians, and should be treated as such. If there is a case to be made for changing our

* aomin.org

conviction of this truth, then the case should be made in an appropriate way, and in the appropriate place.

But not everyone is treating *my* words in this way, and so it is necessary to make adjustments, as best you can, before you say anything publicly. That said, let me risk something . . . again. Theological models are designed to represent important biblical truths. Pointing to the inadequacy of a particular model in some of its details is not the same thing as rejecting the important biblical truths illustrated by the model.

The *ordo salutis* is one such model. Many of those who are nervous about what we are saying about the traditional Reformed *ordo salutis* are nervous because they think we are challenging the central truth that the model is pointing to—which is false.

The purpose of a model is to explain and illustrate, and not to provide a photograph. For example, the model of an atom in a high school science class looks an awful lot like a tiny little solar system. And this helps explain a number of basic concepts. But if someone assumes, in their subsequent study of sub-atomic physics, that the tiny solar system model is correct in every detail, they will soon encounter things that they simply cannot explain. This is what has happened with many who are holding to the traditional *ordo salutis* in a wooden way—to mix the metaphor, they are treating it as though it were a paper-mache "solar system" atom, hanging from the ceiling of a high school science classroom. There are important truths hanging there, but the model simply does not answer all the questions.

Lest anyone take this general statement as further justification for increasing nervousness about what I am saying, let me reiterate what important truth the traditional Reformed *ordo salutis* protects, a truth which I heartily affirm. Here is it. "Salvation is monergistic. Salvation is all of grace. A man does not bring about his own regeneration. He does not prepare himself for regeneration. Justification is also a matter of free grace, wherein the righteousness of Jesus Christ is imputed to the sinner. This righteousness is imputed to him, not infused within him. The order of regeneration, repentance, faith, justification, and sanctification protects and illustrates this, and rightly so."

But here are some questions that the model does not answer. This is not said so that we would jettison the model, but rather so that we would refine it. This is not said as a challenge to the central truth of the model. Those who agree with me that these questions do not threaten the distinctively Reformed understanding of salvation need to work together with us to explore these questions. But those who insist upon seeing these questions as a threat need to do more than just fulminate. If the paper-mache *ordo* is the only way to go, they need to show *how* their approach fully answers these questions. Note, in either case, the questions need to be answered. I reiterate again that this entire battle is for the hearts and minds of second-year seminarians. In the presence of those who are following the argument, and who understand it, these issues really need to be engaged. Those debating us really need to answer the following questions in some manner.

1. Justification is fourth, and sanctification is fifth in this *ordo*. Justification is imputed, and sanctification is infused. But regeneration is first on the list. Now regeneration is a gift (from God alone) of a righteous heart in the place of an unrighteous heart. So in some manner, it involves a transfer of righteousness. Now, is regeneration an imputed transfer of righteousness, or an infused transfer of righteousness? Or a third way?
2. If imputed, then does this make regeneration a part of justification? And if it is that, then how can faith be the sole instrument of justification because faith is the fruit of regeneration?
3. If infused, then does this make regeneration a part of sanctification? If so, then how can sanctification precede justification? And is the regenerate heart justified before it exercises faith? Or is it an unjustified regenerate heart?
4. If a third way, please explain.

These questions fade into the background when we think of them in terms of union with Christ, and stop trying to measure them with a stopwatch. But when we think of this union with Christ in a non-chronological way (and rather a covenantal way), this generates new questions. And the way we address these new questions must preserve what we knew and affirmed in our embrace of the old model as traditionally affirmed. And I do. Salvation is of the Lord, and let him who boasts, boast in the Lord.

JESUS OR ARISTOTLE?

AUG 12, 2004

I have to begin by saying that it should be self-evident that logical fallacies exist, and that they should be avoided. Having the mind of Christ includes avoiding the kinds of confusions and mistakes in reasoning that are so characteristic of our time. I think it was John Stott who said that fuzzy-mindedness is one of the sins of the age.

That said, it needs to be reaffirmed yet again that for Christians *the standard is Scripture*. But the problem is that good little Christians tend to make a standard for themselves out of bits and pieces of good advice, lessons, and lectures that they picked up over the years from their teachers and other intimidating authorities.

When I tell people what I believe is going on in various controversies (including the Auburn flap) a common response is that I should limit myself to the argument, stick to the issue, and not go bringing in the character of my opponents. This is because the *ad hominem* is a logical fallacy, they say. Well, actually it is a fallacy of distraction, not a fallacy of logical structure, and this is a good thing. Sometimes the character of an opponent *is* the issue, and it is not a distraction to bring it up, still less a *fallacy* of distraction. Think of a lying witness on the stand—a good attorney will go after his credibility precisely because his credibility *is* the issue. When Jesus attacked the hypocrisy of Pharisees, He was not indulging in fallacious reasoning. Rather, He was teaching us how to reason in any comparable situation.

If I am losing an argument on the merits and I tell my adversary that his mother is a lizard, I am doing this to distract attention away from the fact that he has the better part of the argument. If I start a fight because I am losing the argument, then I really am guilty of trying to distract attention away from my lost cause. And this really is an intellectual sin.

But this was not Eve's problem. She had the opposite problem in that she did not consider the character of the one who brought the argument. She considered the argument apart from considering the source of the argument. The serpent was up to no good, as she ought to have known. And Adam knew the character of the God who had given him the requirement to stay away from the tree in the middle of the garden. Adam also ought to have known the serpent was up to no good.

Jesus specifically instructed us to weigh the competing claims of theologians, writers, authors, preachers, teachers, and pastors *on the basis of fruit.* Some want to devour the sheep; they are wolves in sheep's clothing. Pretend for a moment that it was not Jesus who came up with that metaphor. I can imagine many people telling the hapless one who said it that he really ought to content himself with addressing the *arguments* of that strange-looking sheep over there, and to stop trying to pull the fleece off to reveal the wolf beneath. "That sort of *ad lupum* argument (or is it *ad ovem?* Can't be sure.) hardly does credit to your position."

When we are told in Hebrews to remember our rulers and instructors in the Scriptures, we are required to *follow their faith* (not just the argument they laid out on the blackboard), and we are to do so *while considering the outcome of their conduct.* We are to consider the fruit of their lives. "Remember those who rule over you, who have spoken the word of God to you, whose faith follow, considering the outcome of their conduct" (Heb. 13:7, NKJV). An elder must be "one who rules his own house well, having his children in submission with all reverence (for if a man does not know how to rule his own house, how will he take care of the church of God?)" (1 Tim. 3:4–5, NKJV)

The Auburn Avenue controversy is a controversy about our theology of children. What does it mean to be a covenant child? What is the covenantal position of those who are born into Christian families? Does God promise us generational succession within the covenant? How are such promises to be apprehended? What does the Bible command us to do as we consider such controversies? This is not the only thing we are commanded to do, but it is right at the center of what we are commanded to do—we are to look at the children. Whether this is "disobedience to Aristotle" is debatable, but it is certainly obedience to the Lord Jesus.

MY SANE BAPTIST FRIEND
AUGUST 13, 2004

I recently had an email exchange with someone I shall call my "sane Baptist friend," or SBF for short. He had some questions about the Auburn Avenue deal, and I thought our exchange might prove helpful to others. There are a couple back-and-forths here. For ease of following, my original words are underlined, his words are in bold and mine are in *italics*.

Dear SBF,

My answers are interspersed below. And if you give permission, I would like to post a portion of this exchange on my blog (with your name removed so that people wouldn't jump to conclusions about you. I would just call you a "sane Baptist friend"). I have been trying to answer a lot of these same questions for a lot of people, and I think this might help.

At 06:20 AM 8/13/2004, you wrote:

Dear Doug,

Thanks for your message, and please forgive me for this delayed reply. It's been a hectic week on several fronts. You wrote:

I heard from _________ that you might be concerned that I had gone wobbly. Just a couple quick comments, along with an invitation to ask me anything your heart desires, at any time.

Thanks for that. I hope you know that I have great respect for you. Of course, as a Baptist, I can't help regarding Presbyterian sacramentalism as somewhat wobbly. Still, I wouldn't normally criticize a Presbyterian just for being Presbyterian. But *"Reformed" Is Not Enough* seems to advocate a view of church, sacraments, and soteriology that wobbles to the point of teetering dangerously.

Right. And my problem is not with Baptists who think Prebyterian sacramentalism is wobbly. It is with Presbyterians who think it is. Perhaps we can agree on this—that many of our critics in the Reformed world need to become more consistent with their critiques of us by becoming Reformed Baptists?

1. I affirm the imputation of the active and passive obedience of Christ to every regenerate believer, apart from which no one has any hope of salvation. No hope without it, as Machen put it. Everything that Christ is and did is credited to the elect believer at the moment of justification, and faith (itself a gift from God, lest any boast) is the sole instrument for appropriating God's grace to us in Christ.

2. Lesbian Eskimo bishops must be excommunicated without one moment's delay, and God is very angry with those who tolerate such abominations in the Church. May I never be in that number, or look to any of the faithful as though I might be.

Thanks for those clarifications. I do still have a few questions:

1. Would you also say the imputed righteousness of Christ is the sole and sufficient ground of our justification? Saying it's essential is not quite the same thing as saying it's sufficient.

Yes. I would say it is the sufficient ground of our individual justification. Without it, there is no individual justification. With it, there must be individual justification.

2. Why wouldn't your ecclesiology constrain you to conclude that any body that would deliberately ordain practicing lesbians as bishops is no true church?

There are several aspects to this reply. First, for example, I am fully supportive of what the Third World Anglicans appear to be doing in their discipline of the renegade Americans, Englishmen, and Canadians. I believe that this sort of disciplinary action ought to occur, and I support it wherever it does occur. In short, I support disciplinary against individual clerics who are practicing homosexuals, and support as well disciplinary action against those ecclesiastical bodies that deliberately ordain such people. I think that ought to happen.

But the second thing is this. What I believe ought to be done does not make me believe that it is automatically done. Suppose a wife has a husband who is rampantly and unrepentantly promiscuous. I think she ought to divorce him. But until she does divorce him, he is still her husband. In a similar way, the American Episcopal Church ought to be disciplined by Christendom, but she hasn't been yet.

And one other thing. We should remember that things have been worse than this in the history of the faith, and God (who raises the dead) has brought about Reformations. On the verge of murdering the Messiah, Caiphas, being high priest that year, prophesied.

3. You do still seem to be suggesting that we daren't put the lesbian bishop in the Jude 4–13; 17–19 category until and unless she has been formally excommunicated. Have I misunderstood what you're saying?

Yes, there is a misunderstanding here. Paul denounces as false brethren men who had not been formally excommunicated, and I believe we can do the same. Go back to my earlier illustration. I think false husbands should be both denounced and divorced. And if there is a faithful Christian in the diocese that now has a homosexual bishop, a man who ought to be deposed and excommunicated, that faithful Christian can and should denounce the infidelity whether or not any excommunication has happened or will happen. But until it happens, that person is objectively in some sense a Christian, just as the husband pre-divorce is objectively in some sense a husband.

4. If your view of church and sacraments obliges you to regard a lesbian Eskimo bishop as "a New Testament Christian"—i.e., if her baptism (and ordination) are "efficacious" irrespective of her lack of faith or moral fitness—how does your view differ from the notion that the sacraments automatically confer grace ex opere operato? I'm having a hard time seeing any meaningful distinction.

An essential part of understanding this is the notion of blessings and curses in the covenant. I do not hold to an ex opere operato result from baptism if we are talking about baptismal grace or blessing. I hold to an ex opere operato covenant connection, which increases the judgment if the person is faithless. This is because the blessings of the covenant are appropriated sola fide, by evangelical faith alone. All others who despise the covenant through their unbelief, while receiving the mark that obligates them to have faith, receive a much stricter judgment.

I appreciate your taking time to write. I can only imagine how busy you must be these days. Since we last corresponded about the Auburn controversy (probably a year and a half ago) I've tried to keep up with how you have answered your critics. (I try to read your blog regularly but can't do it daily.) No doubt my Baptist presuppositions are a definite handicap as I try to make sense of what you're saying, but I have to say that your position seems more ambiguous to me now than before you began trying to clarify it.

Sorry about that. Hope this helps.

AUBURN AVENUE HUBBUB (AAH) COOL QUOTE 10
AUG 17, 2004

> This is why God has to stoop down to us, which he does by means of the sacraments. This, then, is how we put on the Lord Jesus Christ at baptism . . . . Thus, you see that our baptism becomes precious to us when we use it as a shield to deflect all assailing doubts.
> —John Calvin, *Sermons on Galatians*, (Carlisle, PA: Banner of Truth, 1997), 346.

HERESY STEW
AUG 23, 2004

Having become a heretic in the broader Reformed world, I am sometimes asked how I did it. What is the recipe? How might a young man who wants to cook up something similar go about the business?

Here is the good news. You probably have the ingredients in your library . . . kitchen . . . having trouble sustaining the metaphor. Anyway you can cook up your own batch of heresy stew, and you don't even have to use suspect items purchased at the Grocery Store of Rome, or the Mini-Mart of Pop Evangelicalism.

Everything can be assembled if you simply read and pay attention to the following: *Given for You*, by Keith Mathison, *Resurrection and Redemption* by Richard Gaffin, "The Church: Its Definition in Terms of 'Visible' and 'Invisible' Invalid" by John Murray, and assorted other stuff published by impeccable publishing houses located in places like Carlisle and Phillipsburg.

The best I can figure, these publishers don't mind you cooking up this kind of stew, for, after all, the ingredients are all still available from them (for a modest price). But they do want you to throw the stew out after you have cooked it. No serving it to anybody. Reformed people eating stuff instead of thinking stuff appears to be what has gotten everybody riled.

REFORMATION AND OUR CHILDREN
AUG 24, 2004

> Behold, I will send you Elijah the prophet before the coming of the great and dreadful day of the Lord: And he shall turn the heart of the fathers to the children, and the heart of the children to their fathers, lest I come and smite the earth with a curse. (Mal. 4:5–6)

One of the great marks of a true, God-given reformation is the characteristic described here by the prophet Malachi. The hearts of fathers are turned to their children. The hearts of children are turned to their fathers. This characteristic is not at odds with correct theology, rather it depends upon it. And any vaunted "correct theology" that does not issue forth in this result is either false theology, or what might be called true-on-paper theology. Jesus was noted as a teacher because he taught with authority, and not like the scribes. This did not make everything the scribes said false. They sat in Moses' seat, the Lord said. What they *said* was true enough. But how is it to be lived? How does it translate into everyday application?

I have said on different occasions that the Auburn Avenue controversy is all about our children. How is that? Not only so, but some of the other controversies that have arisen are directly related to this as well. And how is that?

A brief glance at the books and tape sets off to the right should quickly show that our ministry has a particular driving emphasis—on marriage, family, children, discipline, and education. This is not because this is an area where theology is irrelevant, but rather because this is where theology is undeniably enfleshed. I am fond of saying that your theology comes out your fingertips, and whatever it is that is coming out your fingertips *is* your theology. Therefore, orthodox Reformed theology *means* loving your wife as Christ loved the church. Orthodox Reformed theology *means* bring up your children in the nurture and admonition of the Lord.

For many years, we have emphasized that parents should believe God for the salvation of their children, should love and nurture their children accordingly, that elders and pastors have a profound obligation before the Lord to lead the way in this, that the elder qualifications in 1 Timothy 3 about managing households well are widely and routinely disobeyed in the Church, and that reformation will not occur unless all this is addressed in a lived-out, loved-out fashion. If I have memorized all of the Westminster Larger Catechism, but speak harshly to my wife, then, as the apostle Paul noted, my theology is just so much balloon juice.

All of this converges. The covenant is not an abstraction. The covenant exists in history, and extends over generations. Generations involve children. And covenantal reformation therefore means . . . turning the fathers back to their children. Reformation does not mean turning the fathers back to big, fat books of theology—except to the extent, and *only* to the extent, that God uses such theology to turn fathers back to their children. Further, when this happens, the hearts of the children are turned back to their fathers. Is a man genuinely Reformed? I don't know. Do his children love him, and faithfully serve his God? If a man's children do not love him, and do not faithfully love, worship and serve his God, and then that man presumes to engage in theological polemics, we should not be surprised when we are suddenly surrounded with sounding brass and tinkling cymbals.

We are engaged in pursuing theological and liturgical reformation, but we are pursuing familial reformation as one of the most important indicators of how we are doing. As God blesses, we will continue to do this. Some of the attacks on our ministry have been calculated to make people think we have abandoned our standards (on elder qualifications, for example), which we have not. Some of them are calculated to drag the debate back into the realm of abstractions, rather than within the realm of the covenant itself. But if we think biblically, we are not to debate the covenant in the classroom, as though the ins and outs of this were merely to be followed like a proof from Euclid. Paul asks the Thessalonians, what is his joy? What is his crown? Is it not *you*? Authentication of ministry is to be found in people, and when a minister is a family man, that authentication is to be found both in *little* people and in grown people who grew up in his household. Biblical ministry, and biblical qualifications for ministry, are always written on human hearts.

By the grace of God, every Saturday night, our household begins our extended family's observance of the Lord's Day. Not counting guests and boarders, with just our family, there are fourteen of us. In a few months, there will be seventeen. All of us love and serve the Lord Jesus Christ. "Knox, what day is it?" "It's the Lord's Day." "Jemma, why is this the Lord's Day?" "Because Jesus rose from the dead." "Bel, what kind of day is it?" "A sweet day." "Rory, what did God make in the beginning?" "Light." And as I look at this exuberant gathering of saints—a shadowy type of what "here am I, and the children you have given me" actually means—I rejoice that the lines have indeed fallen for me in pleasant places. This is *all* the grace of God, and this is what we declare.

This will seem to some as though it is just more "covenant confusion." But following the glazed rolls around the table, following the love in the conversation, following the theological argument, and following the gospel of sheer unmerited grace, *are all the same thing*. And what is that "thing?" It is faith, the gift of God, lest any boast.

SHOW ME A TOKEN
AUGUST 26, 2004

Nothing reveals a person's approach to epistemology more rapidly than trouble-shooting in conflict does. "What's the trouble here? How did the trouble start?" Almost always the way this kind of question is answered serves to extend and continue the trouble.

When Ahab decided to start worshiping Baal, the end result of this was a drought that turned Israel brown. Jezebel persuaded him to start worshipping the idols of green, and the first thing that happened was lots of brown everywhere. But the interesting thing was that when Ahab and Elijah encountered one another after three years of this drought, they *still* had differing interpretations. Ahab thought Elijah was the trouble, and Elijah thought that Ahab and his idols were the trouble (1 Kings 18:17–18). Scripture tells us clearly that Achan was a troubler of Israel (1 Chron. 2:7). Is that how *he* thought of it? Is that what Achan's mom thought? Let's get her on CNN to tell *her* side.

Whenever we get to this point in the polemical proceedings, continued conversation (as mere talk) is fruitless. Those who are stubborn remain stubborn. Those who are faithful remain faithful. Those who are ignorant remain ignorant. Over the last several years, in our various controversies, I have seen a remarkable amount of treachery, dishonesty, and invincible ignorance. But if this is the case, then how are these things ever to be resolved?

But as we answer this question, we have to take care. Giving up on endless discussion, dispute, debate, etc. is not the same thing as giving up generally. When we tend to think that to give up on talking is the same as giving up period, this indicates that perhaps our faith was in our words, and not in Christ.

Theological impasses are resolved in two ways——the first is obviously the ultimate way in which God will sort out everything in the final judgment. We will not enter eternity still trying to tie up all the loose ends. God will bring everything together, and the entire story will make wonderful and perfect sense.

But what about in the meantime? The second way a sovereign God resolves many of these issues is through how He governs the course of history. The names of many honored saints today have that position precisely because of the abuse they were willing to endure at the time. Athanasius is not against the entire Christian world now (*contra mundum*) precisely because he was willing to be in that position then.

When controversy erupts in the Christian world, there are the two sides of the dispute, and then there is a large, getting-up-to-speed group in the middle that spends its time trying to figure out who started it. And regardless of who started it, some members of this middle group usually take St. Paul, or Athanasius, or some other faithful Tishbite aside, and urge them to be more gentlemanly in how they fight the Lord's battles.

And more words won't sort it out. We must appeal to God, who sees it all. "Shew me a token for good; that they which hate me may see it, and be ashamed: because thou, LORD, hast holpen me, and comforted me" (Ps. 86:17).

WINESKINS AND OTHER METAPHORS
SEPTEMBER 2, 2004

A recent letter writer to *Touchstone* magazine (responding to a review of a couple of D.G. Hart's books) says this: "If one wishes to locate a separate Protestant 'confessional' tradition, where should one go? Conservative American Protestantism is root and branch a tradition that depends for its existence and vitality on revivalism and the historical forms we describe as Evangelical. A theologically orthodox Protestant *who would stay Protestant* must make peace with that fact—and all its related ironies and tensions."

As a confessional Protestant, I have no trouble with accepting this assessment, as far as it goes, but it doesn't go nearly far enough. Not only do confessional Protestants have to make their peace with revivalism, the kind of movement to which they generally object, they also have to make their peace with genuine movements of the Holy Spirit, which can be far more troublesome. In the revivalist stream, the institutional Church often suffers at the hands of nutjobs, and they come and punch holes in the wineskins with the icepick of fanaticism. This does create ironies and tensions. But the new wine of the Spirit is sometimes *just* as unkind to the wineskins. As we recall, there was a time when virtually every trained theologian in Jerusalem voted to kill the Messiah.

A high view of the institutional (and confessional) Church does not necessitate a view that we can now see where the wind comes from or where it is going. One of the things we confessional Protestants confess is that God converts how, when and where He pleases. When He does this, He is bringing His bride to a glorious consummation, and at that day, there will be no wrinkle or spot. The tensions will have been removed.

We don't have to choose. High Church Puritanism is possible and highly desirable. But if you *make* me choose, I prefer the Ringling Brothers tent of Evangelicalism to the marble mausoleum of Rome.

MORE ON ROBBINS
SEPTEMBER 16, 2004

In a recent *Trinity Review*, John Robbins tackles the work of Richard Gaffin, and spends quite a bit of energy fulminating about the departures of said theologian from the traditional Reformed *ordo salutis*. In the course of his discussion, Robbins says, "Believers do not die with Christ 'existentially' or 'experimentally,' but legally. They do not possess Christ's perfect righteousness 'in the inner man.' Christ's righteousness is imputed, not infused. His act and righteousness are legally, not experientially, theirs."

And if we are talking about the (isolated) justification of the individual believer, this is quite right. But such things can never be absolutely isolated. And it appears clear that Robbins does not even understand the nature of the problem that Gaffin is wrestling with.

Let me try to bring it home by asking Robbins a question. What is regeneration? That *is* an existential and experimental reality. God takes away a heart of stone and replaces it with a heart of flesh. Now, when does regeneration occur? According to the traditional *ordo*, which Robbins is defending, regeneration is first, then repentance, then faith, then justification. Imputation arrives with justification. What is the righteousness that this new heart has, both experientially and practically? It is an infused righteousness. Regeneration is not imputed, right? Regeneration is a change of heart, from an unrighteous heart that hates God to a righteous (but still imperfect) heart that loves Him, repents of sin, and believes in Him.

Now, according to the traditional *ordo* (that Robbins is defending), this means that if faith is the instrument of justification (not the ground), and if faith arises naturally from this new heart (which is there because it was "infused"), difficulties arise.

At the end of the day, this means that Robbins is defending infused righteousness as the instrument of imputed righteousness. Gaffin, and others, are aware of the threat this model (when taken woodenly) poses to monergistic grace. By defending *sola gratia* in one place, it threatens it in another.

So let me say it again. The traditional *ordo*, if taken as the only possible model for considering these things, gives us a problematic order.

1. Regeneration (infused righteousness);
2. Repentance and faith (fruit of infused righteousness;
3. Justification (imputed righteousness);
4. Etc.

So let's talk about union with Christ. And Richard Gaffin has done just that, in an admirable way.

WHERE IS THE PULPIT?
SEPTEMBER 24, 2004

One of the common mistakes in creating hypothetical scenarios to test where someone "comes down" in the Federal Vision controversy is the mistake of saying, "How do you preach to the baptized? Do you preach as though they are unconverted, needing constantly to question? Or that they are converted, in need of encouragement?"

The question is far too broad. Which baptized are we preaching to? Are we preaching in Thyatira? Ephesus? Laodicea? Corinth? Rome?

WHAT IS A CHRISTIAN?
SEPTEMBER 25, 2004

One of the stories circulating out there is that the Federal Vision folks have changed the definitions of words, words like *Christian* or *justification*. This is said because it is simply assumed (not demonstrated) that any expansion of a word's uses must necessarily include an abandonment of previous uses. I was brought up in an evangelical home, and was taught that a genuine Christian was the kind of Christian who goes to heaven when he dies. This is an important (and precious) use of the word. I agree with it as strongly as I ever did. But somehow, because of a slavish and superstitious reverence for that one definition as the only possible definition, my recognition that the word can be used in other senses has completely thrown some people.

Suppose there were two young boys, Sammy and Dougie. Both of them were pleased one day to start receiving an allowance from their fathers, and they received a *quarter* a week. They both enjoyed the allowance, and Dougie particularly liked the sound of the word *quarter*. He used it a lot. One day, years later, when Dougie was in third grade, he learned *another* definition of the same word. The class was learning fractions, and he learned that *quarter* could refer to things other than the coin. You could divide pies into quarters for example. Proud of his new knowledge, he came into his house one afternoon with his friend Sammy, and asked his mother, who was cutting up a pie, if he could have a *quarter*.

"You want a coin?" Sammy asked.

"No," Dougie said, "I would like a fourth of the pie. I am famished."

"That's not how you used to use that word," Sammy said. "You've changed."

"No, I've not changed. I still think *quarter* means a silver coin. I just don't think that is the only thing it means. But it still means that for sure. See, here is a *quarter* in my pocket."

"No," Sammy said. "I heard you. You just called a piece of pie a *quarter*."

"Well, yes. But that is not a change."

Sammy still looked dubious. "Well, I don't like it. But I'll go for it if you admit that the two words *quarter* have absolutely nothing to do with each other."

"Well, I can't do that. They do have something in common—a *quarter* is a fourth of a dollar and a *quarter* is a fourth of a pie."

"See! We can't be friends anymore. You are using the word differently than you used to, and, worst of all, you won't even admit that you have changed. *Quarter* means a silver coin. Now you say it means a piece of pie. Which is it? Yes or no. A coin or pie? No matter what you say, that's change."

"Now when you said *change*," Dougie said. "Do you mean going from one state to another? Or do you mean coins in your pocket? Because . . ."

But with that, Dougie's mother interrupted, told them both *to stop being silly*, and shooed them out into the back yard.

OCTOBER–DECEMBER 2004

FAITH ALONE
OCTOBER 1, 2004

Faith is the alone instrument that God uses to bring justification to the individual believer. This faith that He uses is the real thing, living faith, faith that looks to Christ alone (apart from any defective works that person might have). But a very common form of "defective works" would have to include defective theories of justification by faith alone. *Because justification by faith alone is true*, it is possible for someone who is screwed up on justification (in his theology) to be actually saved. And because justification by faith alone is true, it is possible for someone with an orthodox theology on the subject to be actually looking at His correct theory instead of to Christ alone, and so he is lost. Rome is wrong on justification, and so Rome is not qualified to teach the saints of God. But precisely *because* Rome is wrong on justification, it is possible for particular Roman Catholics within her pale to be saved.

PLUS NOTHING
OCTOBER 1, 2004

The points made in the previous post apply in another way to the problem posed for *sola fide* by theological Arminianism. To be faithful to Scripture we have to reject all notions of faith-plus-something-else salvation. Salvation must be all of God.

The ground of our salvation must be Christ and His work alone. Just as we are lost through our union with Adam, so we are saved through our union with Christ in His perfect life, death, burial, resurrection, and ascension.

When we speak of the *ground* of salvation, we are talking about the basis for it, the reason for it. Everyone who comes to salvation is saved because of the person and work of the Lord Jesus Christ, *plus nothing.* His work is the sole reason we are saved.

But does this mean that we do nothing? And if we do something, is that something "our part" which is the partner with God who does "His part"? Not at all. Of course, we do something (we repent and believe), but everything we do is built upon the foundation of Christ's work. We do not extend our work out from Christ's work; rather, we build our work upon Christ's work. We do not build out, we build up.

But in order to build upon God's work, instead of extending out from God's work, it is necessary for us to grasp the biblical truth that both repentance and faith are gifts of God. Repentance and faith don't get us grace; repentance and faith *are* grace.

But this distinction between the ground of our salvation and the instrument of our salvation is only possible if faith is *God's* instrument for saving us, not *our* instrument for getting the job done. If it were *our* instrument, then our wielding of that instrument would necessarily become part of the ground of our salvation—that upon which our salvation rests. "Even so then, at this present time there is a remnant according to the election of grace. And if by grace, then it is no longer of works; otherwise grace is no longer grace. But if it is of works, it is no longer grace; otherwise work is no longer work" (Rom. 11:5–6, NKJV).

But we don't have to depend on theological extrapolations. This is what the Bible says. Apart from repentance we cannot believe, and apart from faith we cannot be saved. And both repentance and faith are gifts from God.

First, we see that the Bible speaks of repentance being *granted* to us. "When they heard these things they became silent; and they glorified God, saying, 'Then *God has also granted* to the Gentiles *repentance* to life'" (Acts 11:28, NKJV).

The apostle Paul speaks the same way. "And a servant of the Lord must not quarrel but be gentle to all, able to teach, patient, in humility correcting those who are in opposition, *if God perhaps will grant them repentance*, so that they may know the truth, and that they may come to their senses and escape the snare of the devil, having been taken captive by him to do his will" (2 Tim. 2:24–26, NKJV).

The same thing is true of faith. "For to you *it has been granted* on behalf of Christ, *not only to believe* in Him, but also to suffer for His sake . . ." (Phil.1:29, NKJV).

Luke describes Christians as those who have believed *through* grace, not "believed *in* grace." "And when he desired to cross to Achaia, the brethren wrote, exhorting the disciples to receive him; and when he arrived, he greatly helped those *who had believed through grace*; for he vigorously refuted the Jews publicly, showing from the Scriptures that Jesus is the Christ" (Acts 18:27, NKJV).

The conclusion is plain. God gives the gifts of repentance and faith, so that no one can boast. "For by grace you have been saved through faith, and that not of yourselves; it [i.e., *faith*] is the gift of God, not of works, lest anyone should boast. For we are His workmanship, created in Christ Jesus for good works, which God prepared beforehand that we should walk in them" (Eph. 2:8–10, NKJV).

The first good work we were created for is conversion—turning away from sin in repentance, and turning to God in faith. This work we do because we are God's workmanship, and the work we do was prepared beforehand by God so that we could walk in that work.

And what is the work of God? "Jesus answered and said to them, 'This is the work of God, that you believe in Him whom He sent'" (John 6:29, NKJV). This is the work of *God*, that *you believe.*

Now if this is true, and it is, then what becomes of those who deny it? What becomes of those who believe, contrary to Scripture, that faith is *our* contribution? Are they lost? The biblical answer is—of course not. We are saved by faith in Christ, plus nothing. We not saved by faith in Christ, plus a passing grade on the theology exam.

This is where self-righteous Calvinists so often trip up. Imagine an exam that God made us all take. It has ten questions on it, each of them amounting to something like "Who saves you?" with the correct answer being "Jesus." Two men take the exam—an arch Calvinist and an Arminian. Further in our supposal, imagine the exams are being graded by John Owen, John

Murray, and the apostle Paul. The Calvinist got a 100% and the Arminian scored an 80%. The Arminian had put down a couple of things about "God voting for him, the devil voting against him, and so he broke the tie, voting for God." The Calvinist dances back to his desk, trusting in his 100%, and the Arminian bowed his head and asked God to be merciful to him, a B-minus Christian. Which one went home justified?

The Arminian was justified *because his answer was wrong.* The Calvinist went home unjustified because the glory of all those right answers dazzled his eyes.

So there it is—faith in Jesus, plus nothing else. *Nothing* else.

TALKING REASONABLY TO MY WINDSHIELD
OCTOBER 2, 2004

A friend recently gave me a couple of CDs of a recent broadcast of The White Horse Inn with Michael Horton. While I was listening to the program (I am not done yet) a couple of comments caught my attention. I think that if we worked though the issues surrounding these comments, we might have the possibility of coming to an understanding. That is why I am talking reasonably to my windshield, and not yelling at it.

The comment was made that to see the covenant of works made with Adam as a gracious covenant has the effect of making the covenant of grace into a legal covenant. On the surface this seems absurd—to turn a watermelon into a tomato is surely not the same thing as turning a tomato into a watermelon. But his reasons for saying this showed that it was not an absurdity at all. A previously hidden assumption came out a moment later when one of the participants revealed that he is hearing us say, when we say that the covenant of works was *gracious*, that God in the Garden of Eden somehow relaxed the standard for Adam. In other words, "grace" is being heard as "cutting of slack." Now if this *were* what we meant, then it does follow that grace and law are being blurred and confused. But we are not using grace as meaning the standards are lowered. We mean by grace the exhaustive sovereignty of divine favor.

In the covenant that God had with Adam in the Garden, there was no lowering of the standards at all. Adam was obligated, by the grace of God, to a perfect obedience. The only thing we mean about this covenant being gracious is that if Adam had obeyed perfectly (which he was obligated to do, in every sense of the word), he would then have had the additional obligation to thank *God* for that perfect obedience. In other words, the only thing we are saying here is that, had Adam obeyed, that obedience would not have been autonomous. But if Adam had obeyed, that obedience would have been perfect—otherwise it would not have been obedience at all.

Grace does not ever involve a lowering of divine standards of righteousness. The grace of God brought to us a way of salvation in which God would be both just *and* the one who justifies.

RAISING EYEBROWS AT MY WINDSHIELD
OCTOBER 4, 2004

I am continuing to listen to the White Horse Inn series on covenant confusion and was duly astonished by something Michael Horton said. By registering this astonishment, I am not saying that I differ with him on this necessarily, but just that I was surprised to hear him talking this way. He said that Jesus Christ, by His perfect sinless life, fulfilled all the requirements of the covenant of works. *Amen*. In saying *amen*, I am not abandoning my previous assertions that the covenant of works was fundamentally gracious, but the point here is a different one.

Here is the rub. In order to fulfill the requirements of the covenant of works, the Lord Jesus would have had to have been a *member* of that covenant. The terms of the covenant would have to be a requirement for Him to fulfill. The covenant would have to pertain to Him somehow. Now, how was He a member of it? Was Adam His federal head? No, that would mean that Adam's sin would have to be imputed to Him. But Christ could not have fulfilled that covenant unless he was a party to the covenant, and in what sense was it possible for Him to be a party to it?

Further, that obedience of the Lord Jesus Christ, both active and passive, is imputed to us, as believers in Jesus. Amen again. But this means that the particular obedience that is reckoned to our account is *obedience to the terms of the covenant of works.* And this means that my justified status is that of one who is obedient (through Christ) to the covenant of works. In other words, the covenant of grace is God's instrument for making us fulfill the terms of the covenant of works, and the covenant of works never goes away—because we are constantly in need of the imputed righteousness of Christ. And so this imputed righteousness of Christ is a righteousness *defined* by the covenant of works. Through the imputed righteous of Christ, I am now obedient (by grace through faith alone, lest anyone from the Trinity Foundation read this and think to write another book). So through Christ alone I am obedient now. Obedient to what? Now, there is a point here, I promise.

All this means that Michael Horton is a monocovenantalist of some stripe. What is imputed to me in the covenant of grace? Covenant-of-works-obedience-through-Christ, that's what. This means that the continuing validity of the covenant of works is a distinguishing feature of the covenant of grace and is an essential part of it. These covenants are joined at the hip, at least according to Horton.

Now I have denied in the past being a monocovenantalist because it seems clear to me that two federal heads necessitate two covenants. No man can serve two masters, and one static covenant cannot have two heads. But it is equally clear that throughout the course of history the headship of Adam is "swallowed up" by the headship of Christ. This is the sense that I believe Horton was pointing to. History matters in all this. At the eschaton, there will only be one covenant, the new covenant. And that new covenant will include within it all the terms of the broken covenant of works, now restored through the obedience of Christ. The point is a simple one—so long as I need the obedience of Christ reckoned to me (which is constantly and always), I will always have some relation to the covenant of works. Through Adam, I was a disobedient son of a broken covenant (of works). Through Christ alone, by the covenant of grace, I am an obedient son of a restored covenant (of works).

My thanks to Michael Horton for this suggestive and stimulating line of thought.

CAN WE PLAY TOO?
OCTOBER 6, 2004

I finished listening to the White Horse covenant confusion series. Covenant confusion is right. We have a lot of knots to untie.

The center of the problem concerns the use of the word *grace* in speaking of God's relationship to Adam before the Fall. Because the word *grace* is linked in their minds to the idea of overcoming demerit, it is assumed that we must either be asserting some sort of fallenness in the created order, even though God said it was all very good, or we are abusing a perfectly good theological word like *grace* when we could be using other words like goodness, kindness, etc.

And so I return to a question I have posed before, and have not even received an attempt at an answer. What about common grace?

We agree that a firm distinction must be maintained between the *creational grace* enjoyed by Adam in the Garden and the *redemptive grace* that God bestowed on His elect in Christ. The word *grace* signifies divine favor, and divine favor to an innocent creature and a fallen sinner will necessarily be manifested in different ways.

But in these broadcasts, it was insisted that grace can only be used to describe unmerited favor to sinners, favor that overcomes their sins and demerit. The word *charis* in the Scripture does mean this overwhelmingly—but not exclusively. Jesus grew in grace. The grace of God was upon Him (Luke 2:40).

God's goodness to Adam in the Garden was expressed through a multitude of *gifts*—a world, a body, a life, a wife, a Garden, and all the trees but one. None of this is redemptive, none of it implies any deficiency on Adam's part. This is *creational grace*.

After Adam broke the covenant of creation, God determined to restore what had been done through another covenant. This new covenant had a new federal head, the second Adam. This new covenant was *redemptive grace*. It *does* presuppose sin. When grace is extended to sinners, it is manifested differently.

Fine, our opponents might say. We agree that God was good to Adam before the Fall, but why do you insist on calling it grace? Well, not because we want a controversy, or because we are trying to be perverse. We call it this because this is what we think it is. God was gifting Adam.

And this is why I am astonished that those who are fighting our use of *creational grace* for unfallen Adam in this way are not rejecting the far more problematic concept of common grace for *fallen* Adam. If the gifts of God bestowed on an unfallen man cannot be called grace (without running the risk of being dubbed a heretic), then how can the gifts of God bestowed on fallen (and reprobate) men be called grace?

In other words, our opponents are saying (in effect) that Adam enjoyed no grace from God at all until he disobeyed, and then he started enjoying common grace. Moreover, Cain enjoyed common grace his entire life. But before the Fall, no grace at all.

But if grace must overcome demerit, then why is common grace for the reprobate called grace at all? It does not overcome demerit. The answer might be that we understand common grace to be a theological phrase with a stipulated meaning. Okay. Can we play too? Creational grace is *not* redemptive grace.

AUBURN AVENUE HUBBUB (AAH) COOL QUOTE 11
OCTOBER 7, 2004

> In the original creation of the world God made us perfect with the perfection of nature, which consists in our having everything due to our nature. But over and above what is due to our nature there were later added to the human race certain perfections that were solely owing to divine grace. Among these is faith, which is a 'gift of God,' as is clear from Ephesians 2.8.
>
> —Thomas Aquinas, *Exposition of Boethius' De Trinitate*, Question 3, article 1, reply to objection 2.

PRESBYTERY EXAM
NOVEMBER 3, 2004

A few weeks ago, I was examined at the presbytery meeting of the Confederation of Reformed Evangelical Churches (CREC). The exam consisted of a written portion, and a three hour oral exam, all of it on the doctrinal issues surrounding the Auburn Avenue business. If you are a glutton for punishment, or if you are up on charges for having read *Reforming Marriage* once, or if you are an insatiable theology wonk, you may find all that stuff by clicking here*.

JUST BACK FROM L.A.
NOVEMBER 6, 2004

I just arrived back in town from a debate jaunt down to L.A. The hosts of the debate, Alpha/Omega Ministries, were gracious in every respect, and I enjoyed meeting James White, and thoroughly enjoyed our debate. The event was videotaped and will be available sometime soon. When it is, I will post a link here.

In some respects, the debate was another round of what I have called "paradigm bumper cars," but I thought that some of the exchanges were particularly helpful and revealing for those who stand to profit from this debate the most. I have said before that this whole thing is a battle for the second-year seminarians, and I believe they will be able to gather a lot from this exchange.

My thanks again to James White and his colleagues for the gracious reception, and for the debate. My opening statement will be in the next post. I was under a full court press by the time limit, and so some portions of the opening statement were dropped and showed up later in the debate. But this is how it was originally written.

OPENING STATEMENT
NOVEMBER 6, 2004

"Are Roman Catholics Members of the New Covenant?" a Debate with James White

I would like to begin by offering my thanks to Alpha/Omega ministries for inviting me to this event, and to James White for engaging in this debate with me. I have been looking forward to it, and I am genuinely glad to be here. I would also like to thank the many in attendance here, some of whom

* Current link: cmfnow.com/douglaswilson2004crecpresbyteryexam.aspx

have come a great distance. It is a great pleasure to be able to address an issue of some importance in a way that I hope will be truly edifying to the larger Christian community.

Before proceeding to my argument, I would like to begin with an assertion so there will be no confusion about my position concerning the Church of Rome. I detest the errors of Rome, and I pray for the day of her repentance. Among those errors I would include the idolatry of the Mass, the use of images in worship, their profound confusion on the matter of faith and works, Purgatory, Mariolatry, merit, the saints, the papacy, and much more. In preparation for this debate, I read James White's book *The Roman Catholic Controversy*, which I thought was quite good. Judging from that book, I do not know of any *distinctive* Roman doctrine concerning which James White and I would disagree.

At the same time, I believe our Lord's teaching requires us to detest our own failings more than those of others, and, as a classical Protestant, I can only lament what the larger Protestant world has become. As someone who wants to be fully identified as a dedicated, convinced, and practicing Protestant-one who by the grace of God is going to die in the evangelical faith he was brought up in-honesty still compels me to state that I detest *our* sectarianism, in-fighting, gimcrack evangelism, hostility to covenant connections, and lack of historical awareness. These are our besetting sins, and I believe the best way to demand that Rome repent is *to show them how*. And no, repentance does not require returning to Rome. But it does require returning to the Scriptures, and it does require a new reformation. I fully believe that the issues we are discussing tonight are not at all peripheral to that reformation.

Before proceeding to my positive case, I would also like to make a brief preliminary argument (in order to set boundaries for what others might do with our discussion). I appreciate how James White has already framed his understanding of our debate, and so these remarks are not directed to him. But as one who has been condemned as a heretic by certain scribes in the Reformed Sanhedrin, some of whom could not locate their confessional hinder parts even if allowed to use both hands, I really cannot afford to participate in a debate like this without making certain things abundantly clear. I am sure you understand my dilemma-and *perhaps* your heart goes out to me.

At the center, this debate is really going to revolve around the question of whether or not Protestant churches should "receive" Roman Catholic baptism, thereby acknowledging it (at *some* level) to be a valid new covenant baptism. This means that part of this statement will necessarily be an exercise in historical theology, and not just an exegetical question.

I understand (fully) that just because certain Reformers held to a position does not automatically make that position scriptural or right. Synods and councils have erred and do err. But bringing this up might prevent modern adherents of these same positions (like me) from having to endure the absurd charge of having abandoned the Reformed faith.

From 1517, when the Reformation broke out, down to 1845, when J.H. Thornwell and Charles Hodge differed at the General Assembly of that year over this issue, the *overwhelming* position of the Reformed churches was that of receiving Roman Catholic baptism. This was not an issue that can be dismissed as an unexamined holdover from the medieval era. It was *thoroughly* examined, and *regularly* debated. This was one of the defining issues that distinguished the magisterial reformation from the radical reformation.

As I said, this in itself does not make one position or the other right. To determine that, we must turn ultimately to Scripture, as I will seek to do in a few moments. But it does mean that a man *should* be able to hold this same position today without fear of being labeled sympathetic to Rome. This is not the road to Rome; it is the road our fathers took *out* of Rome. The magisterial Reformation was not closet popery, and yet some of us today who hold to certain positions articulated and defended in the magisterial Reformation too often have to endure this kind of profound misunderstanding.

So, who held to the view that Roman Catholic baptism was a valid administration of new covenant baptism? Among others, I would like to name (as my cohorts in crime) John Calvin, John Knox, Theodore Beza, William Perkins, Samuel Rutherford, Richard Baxter, Francis Turretin, Charles Hodge, and A.A. Hodge. Providing implicit support for this view would be the position outlined by the Westminster Confession of Faith. I am not going to quote extensively from all these gentlemen because we do need to get to the scriptural arguments. But I want to make it perfectly clear that this debate we are having is a comparatively recent *intramural* Reformed debate (since 1845), and it does not represent a clash between light and darkness, good and evil, Klingons and Smurfs.

So here are just a few quotations, to give you some idea of where I got my unsavory opinions. Bad companions, as they say, corrupt good morals.

The French Confession of 1559

"Yet nevertheless, because there is yet some small trace of a Church in the papacy, and that baptism as it is in the substance, hath been still continued . . . we confess that they which are thus baptized do not need a second baptism."

John Calvin

"Such in the present day are our Catabaptists, who deny that we are duly baptized, because we were baptized in the Papacy by wicked men and idolaters; hence they furiously insist on anabaptism." —*Institutes*, IV.15.16–17

"So it is with Baptism; it is a sacred and immutable testimony of the grace of God, *though it were administered by the devil*, though all who may partake of it were ungodly and polluted as to their own persons." —Commentary on Amos 5:26

John Knox

"No more ought we to iterate baptism, by whomsoever it was ministered unto us in our infancy; but if God of his mercy [should] call us from blindness, he maketh our baptism, how corrupt that ever it was, available unto us, by the power of the Holy Spirit." —Letter, 1556

Samuel Rutherford

Samuel Rutherford provides us with an interesting case, because he not only argues for the legitimacy of Roman Catholic baptism, but does so while arguing for the legitimacy and necessity of Roman Catholic *orders.* Virtually all Protestants accepted baptism performed by Roman Catholic priests, while there was debate on, for example, baptism performed by Roman Catholic midwives. "[John] Robinson [the Separatist] and our brethren acknowledge that the Church of Rome hath true baptism, even as the vessels of the Lord's house profaned in Babylon may be carried back to the temple . . . But I answer, if baptism be valid in Rome [then] so are the ministers baptizers." —"The Validity of Roman Catholic Ministry" in *The Due Right of Presbyteries,* 1644 (Rutherford is not arguing a *reductio* here, but rather was arguing for the validity of Roman Catholic *ordination.*)

A.A. Hodge

"All who are baptized into the name of the Father, and of the Son, and of the Holy Ghost, recognizing the Trinity of Persons in the Godhead, the incarnation of the Son and his priestly sacrifice, whether they be Greeks, or Arminians, or Romanists, or Lutherans, or Calvinists, or the simple souls who do not know what to call themselves, *are our brethren.* Baptism is our common countersign. It is the common rallying standard at the head of our several columns." —*Evangelical Theology* (Carlisle, PA: Banner of Truth, 1976), p. 338.

Note that Hodge called Roman Catholics *his brethren.* Note only so, but he managed that particular stunt in a Banner of Truth book. Nevertheless, despite this cloud of witnesses, if I am in error on this, and shown to be in error from the Scriptures, I hope before God that I would receive the truth in humility, and confess my fault. But if I were prevailed upon to do this, I would be confessing a characteristic *Reformed* fault, held by virtually all of our Reformed fathers for 328 years. I would also hope that those same

Reformed fathers would be equally correctable on this issue, although Knox might present a little trouble. But in any case, for all of them, the arguments would need to be pretty good, and better than the arguments presented to them in their day.

Scriptural Argumentation

If the scriptural phrase *new covenant* is to be taken as synonymous with the *elect*, or the *invisible church*, then of course we cannot answer our question in the affirmative. With such an understanding, we could not say that Roman Catholics are members of the new covenant. But of course, because we would now be dealing with the secret decree and the invisible church, we also could not say that Southern Baptists were members of the new covenant, or Free Methodists, or Presbyterians. While I think that the doctrine of sovereign election is an important doctrinal truth, and one that I heartily affirm, I do not believe that this is strictly in view when the Bible uses the phrase *new covenant*. The number of the elect and the members of the new covenant are not an interchangeable set of names-until the last day. Put in familiar categories, the new covenant people in the New Testament are the visible church, not the invisible church.

And as we consider this question, it all comes down to whether or not the Bible teaches that the *new covenant* can be broken by any of the members of that covenant. Does the new covenant contain covenant-breakers? And because all of us in Adam are in some sense covenant breakers because of the first covenant made with man, the *covenant of life* made with Adam in the garden, I am pushing the question further. I am asking if the new covenant contains any covenant-breakers of the new covenant itself. Can the new covenant *itself* be broken?

I want to begin by setting a scriptural pattern, and I want to show how this pattern can be seen as culminating in a specific apostolic warning to the Church at Rome, which is the subject of our proposition being debated tonight.

Of how much sorer punishment, suppose ye, shall he be thought worthy, who hath trodden under foot the Son of God, and hath counted *the blood of the covenant, wherewith he was sanctified*, an unholy thing, and hath done despite unto the Spirit of grace? (Heb. 10: 29)

The book of Hebrews was written to *a new covenant people*, and it was written in order to head off a looming apostasy. That is what the entire book is about. In this verse, we learn that the sanctions of the new covenant are *more* severe than the sanctions under Moses—"sorer punishment." The new covenant does not contain "no sanctions," it contains "more severe sanctions." If we allow the New Testament to define what Jeremiah meant when he prophesied of the new covenant, we will spend most of our time with the entire book of Hebrews. This book is where we receive an extended and inspired commentary on this prophecy of Jeremiah, and that commentary makes it plain that apostasy is a very real threat for new covenant members. Members of the visible church can and do fall away from Christ.

Now is apostasy a possibility for those who are decretally elect? Of course not, but here in this passage we find new covenant members who will receive sorer punishment because they trampled the Son of God underfoot, and reckoned *the blood of the covenant*, the blood which sanctified them, as an unholy thing.

For various reasons, we have a tendency to draw *contrasts* between the old and new covenant people at precisely those places where the New Testament draws *parallels*.

> Wherefore (as the Holy Ghost saith, To day if ye will hear his voice, Harden not your hearts, as in the provocation, in the day of temptation in the wilderness: When *your fathers* tempted me, proved me, and saw my works forty years. Wherefore I was grieved with that generation, and said, They do alway err in their heart; and they have not known my ways. So I sware in my wrath, They shall not enter into my rest.) Take heed, *brethren*, lest there be *in any of you an evil heart of unbelief*, in departing from the living God. But exhort one another daily, while it is called To day; lest any of you be hardened through the deceitfulness of sin. For we are made partakers of Christ,

> if we hold the beginning of our confidence stedfast unto the end. (Hebrews 3: 7–14)

We are not told that in the new covenant it is impossible for new covenant members to depart from the living God. We are not told that in the new covenant there will be no bodies scattered over the wilderness. We are warned, solemnly, again and again, about the dangers of hardening our hearts *in just the way* that our fathers the Jews did. Now whatever this means, it cannot mean that in the new covenant such hardening of heart is an impossibility. Again, for clarity's sake, I want to assert that such apostasy, such hardening of heart, *is* an impossibility for the elect. And again, just for the record, I am so Calvinistic it makes my back teeth ache. And if the Synod of Dort had come up with six replies to the Remonstrants, then I would be a six-point Calvinist.

In another place, the Corinthian Gentiles were beginning to boast, and puff themselves up a little. *We* have baptism. *We* have the Lord's Table. *We* have spiritual food and spiritual drink. *We* have Christ. Not so fast, Paul said. So did the Jews in the wilderness, and their bodies were scattered across the wilderness to provide a solemn example for *you*.

> Moreover, brethren, I would not that ye should be ignorant, how that all our fathers were under the cloud, and all passed through the sea; And were all baptized unto Moses in the cloud and in the sea; And did all eat the same spiritual meat; And did all drink the same spiritual drink: for they drank of that spiritual Rock that followed them: and that Rock was Christ. But with many of them God was not well pleased: for they were overthrown in the wilderness. Now these things were our examples, to the intent we should not lust after evil things, as they also lusted. (1 Cor. 10: 1–6)

In short, *our* fathers are *our* examples, and with a number of them God was *not* well pleased. But what does all this have to do with the Roman Catholic Church? Rome has fallen into the errors it has because she has refused to heed the warning explicitly given by the apostle Paul to that specific church-a warning very much like the ones we have just been considering.

The apostle could already see the stirrings of hubris in that church, in that ancient capital city, and so he spoke to it bluntly. The apostle Paul saw (with remarkable prescience) that the Church at Rome *was going to be a problem*, and he addressed it forthrightly. And the only thing that is more remarkable than the Church of Rome ignoring these Pauline warnings aimed straight at *her* besetting sins is that fact that Protestants have also largely ignored the fact that these warning were directed at *Rome*.

> For if the firstfruit be holy, the lump is also holy: and if the root be holy, so are the branches. And if some of the branches be broken off, and thou, being a wild olive tree, wert grafted in among them, and with them partakest of the root and fatness of the olive tree; Boast not against the branches. But if thou boast, thou bearest not the root, but the root thee. Thou wilt say then, The branches were broken off, that I might be grafted in. Well; because of unbelief they were broken off, and thou standest by faith. Be not highminded, but fear: For if God spared not the natural branches, take heed lest he also spare not thee. Behold therefore the goodness and severity of God: on them which fell, severity; but toward thee, goodness, if thou continue in his goodness: otherwise thou also shalt be cut off. (Rom. 11:16–22)

"Rome, thou shalt be cut off." Why? Because of unbelief and covenant presumption. Luther said it well when he said that *sola fide* is the article of a standing or falling church, and here is the text. Unbelief caused the Jews to be broken off, and "thou *standest* by faith." Now this is not a statement that Rome *has* fallen into complete apostasy, but it certainly is a statement that Rome is *capable* of complete apostasy. She *can* fall away, she is not indefectible.

This being the case, then why could we not say that Rome has been broken off because of her formal and judicial denial of *sola fide* at the Council of Trent? Four comments:

First, the unbelief for which the Jews were cut off in AD 70 was a problem that had plagued them for centuries. God does not operate on a covenant hair trigger. All day long He holds out His hands to a disobedient people.

Second, if we drum out of the new covenant anyone who does not hold to a pure understanding of *sola fide*, then we have not only gotten rid of Rome, but also of most Protestants. Take, as one example of a Protestant Trent, this statement from the Free Will Baptist Articles of Faith. "The human will is free and self-controlled, having power to yield to the influence of the truth and the Spirit, or to resist them and perish." Would we accept *their* baptisms? Well, of course we would.

Third, if we require a pure understanding of *sola fide* in order to be included in the new covenant, then we have denied *sola fide*. It is not faith plus a passing grade on the ordination exam. It is not faith plus *anything*. It is God-given faith in Jesus, period.

Fourth, this is not an issue to be decided by this individual or that one. Either God will do it in a signal and unmistakable way, as He did with the Jews in AD 70, or He will do it working through an ecumenical council of the continuing and faithful church. And unfortunately, the Protestant church is too fragmented to make the kind of statement that one day soon might need to be made. We are too much in need of repentance on this point to be entrusted with any judgment of the lack of repentance on the part of others. But more on this in a moment.

It is important for me to acknowledge that this has not always been my position. In the past I have maintained (although I cannot find *where* I said this) that Rome was guilty of a final apostasy at Trent, where in solemn ecumenical council she anathematized any who faithfully held the biblical gospel. This is no longer my position, and if my worthy opponent has found a quotation of mine that says this, and returns to this point to press me with it, I will merely say, "I changed my mind, and it is a practice I commend to you." It is nevertheless still my position that what happened at Trent *deserved* removal from the olive tree, that is, from the catholic church. But I am now convinced that such a removal has not yet occurred. God does not always give us what we deserve.

Why is this no longer my position? First, I find no signal event of providence that could be interpreted this way. No blazing meteor has landed on the Vatican, while crying out, "Come out from among her, and be ye separate." Secondly, there has been no concerted ecumenical rejection of Rome as entirely and completely apostate. It might be countered that the Westminster Assembly should count, and they reckoned the papacy as the antichrist. Does that not matter? No, because that Assembly occurred 198 years *before* classical Protestants began rejecting Roman Catholic baptisms in 1845. The men of Westminster would have been on my side in this debate-again, consider men like Rutherford.

The apostle Paul gives us a textual basis for all this in Ephesians:

> I therefore, the prisoner of the Lord, beseech you that ye walk worthy of the vocation wherewith ye are called, With all lowliness and meekness, with longsuffering, forbearing one another in love; Endeavouring to keep the unity of the Spirit in the bond of peace. There is one body, and one Spirit, even as ye are called in one hope of your calling; One Lord, one faith, one baptism, One God and Father of all, who is above all, and through all, and in you all. (Eph. 4:1–6)

The unity of the Spirit in the bond of peace, which we are required to preserve, is foundationally Trinitarian. One God and Father. One Lord. One Spirit. Woven in with this Trinitarian reality is the phrase "one baptism." Baptism into the triune name means what *God* says it means, and not what the men performing it say or think about it. Let God be true, and every man a liar (Rom. 3:4).

In principle, could anything happen in the future that would make Roman Catholic baptism "unreceivable" by faithful Protestant churches-with or without a Protestant ecumenical council? Yes, and I honestly don't know if it is far off or not. The Roman church is shot through with theological liberalism, which Machen correctly identified as another religion entirely. And it is interesting to note in passing how Machen spoke of Rome in this regard:

> Yet how great is the common heritage which unites the Roman Catholic Church, with its maintenance of the authority of Holy Scripture and with its acceptance of the great early creeds, to devout Protestants today! . . . The Church of Rome may represent a perversion of the Christian religion; but naturalistic liberalism is not Christianity at all (*Christianity and Liberalism*, p. 52).

But Rome now has a bad dose of that same liberalism. Couple this with feminism, the appeal of Mariolatry to the natural man, and it is quite possible that Mary will eventually get her big promotion, and people will be baptized into the name of a Quaternity. When the creedal core has rotted out, the liturgy cannot remain indefinitely the same. We see this in the mainline denominations which abandoned the faith in substance, but kept the old triune form *for a time*, a form which we should receive. Let God be true. But the rot has to spread, and eventually people will be baptized in the name of God the Mother, or Allah, or Shiva. And of course, all such baptisms are no baptisms at all.

So then, Trinitarian baptism, baptism into the triune name, places an individual into an objective covenant relationship with Christ. This does not mean that he is automatically regenerate, or that he is necessarily among the elect. The baptism, however, constitutes a word from God, and it requires of that person that he repent and believe in the Lord Jesus Christ. If he does not, then he is a covenant breaker, and God will remove him from the covenant. If he repents and believes, then he is keeping covenant through the perfect righteousness of Jesus, the only perfect covenant keeper. If he repents sometime after his baptism, he does not need to be baptized again. This is the position of our Reformed forefathers, and it is a position that is fair and orderly.

The conclusion is that I believe that *faithless* Roman Catholics are in fact members of the new covenant. Otherwise, how could they be covenant breakers? To illustrate our difference, James White believes faithless Roman Catholics to be guilty of the sin of spiritual fornication. I believe them to be guilty of *the far more serious sin of spiritual adultery*. Part of my mission here tonight is to encourage my brother to be a little harder on Rome.

MYSTERY THEOLOGY THEATER
NOVEMBER 16, 2004

Color Commentary on
A Précis of the Federal Vision (FV)
Précis by the Mississippi Valley Presbytery (PCA)
Play by Play Commentary by Douglas Wilson in italics

'Proponents of the FV identify themselves as Reformed. *You betcher.* Most appeal to the writings of the sixteenth century Reformers in support of their views. *But this is only because they were obliging enough to provide us with all those neat quotations, and to teach us all these things in the first place.* Many regard the Reformed thought of the British Puritan and American Presbyterian traditions to have capitulated to the Enlightenment, what is termed Revivalism, and what is termed baptistic theology. *I don't think it is quite that bad, but statements like this one aren't helping.*

FV proponents define the covenant as an objective relationship that is independent of the covenant member's subjective considerations of the strength or nature of his membership. *Right. Marriage is marriage, whether the marriage is a good one or a bad one.*

FV proponents also define the covenant as essentially a vital relationship between God and the covenant member. *What? Huh?* Downplayed are the legal and forensic dimensions of the covenant. *Huh? What?* Membership within the covenant is conceived in an undifferentiated manner: the distinction between a non-communicant and a communicant member of the church is either downplayed or eliminated. *Non-communicant members of the church? I just gotta get me some new Bible software. I can't find this stuff anywhere.*

FV proponents argue that this doctrine of the covenant requires reformulation of the doctrine of the Trinity. *Learning and applying the doctrine of the Trinity is not the same thing as reformulating it.* The divine unity is framed in terms of covenantal relationship among the three persons.

FV proponents deny the traditional doctrine of the covenant of works. *I keep forgetting. Are we against tradition or for it?* One proponent has denied the imputation of Adam's sin to his posterity. *And another proponent affirms it while standing on his chair!*

FV proponents deny the imputation of Christ's active (and perhaps passive) obedience to the believer for justification. *When did I do that? I don't remember. It was dark. They were big.* The "righteousness" of the believer in justification is sometimes said to be the believer's covenantal faithfulness. Justification is defined in terms of a process not a definite act *nuh uh*; and good works are said to be necessary to justification, particularly to the believer's "final justification" at the Day of Judgment. One proponent has argued for not fewer than three instruments of justification: faith, covenantal faithfulness, and baptism. *As opposed to the four they argue for—preaching, hearing, faith, and convincing the session that something happened in your heart.*

Following Norman Shepherd, FV proponents argue that election must be understood in terms of the covenant, not *vice versa.* The result is formulations of election that render one's election a process and a function of one's covenantal obedience. *I give up. I don't care anymore.* Coupled with this is a denial of the traditional doctrine *[more tradition! but different from Rome's!]* of the visible and invisible church and a practical denial of the distinction between common and saving operations of the Spirit as distinguishing the sincere believer from the hypocrite. *So what do we think does distinguish them?* One proponent has even denied the doctrine of individual regeneration. *Oh? Does that mean the rest of us didn't?*

FV proponents point to objective grounds for one's assurance while practically denying subjective grounds for one's assurance. *Except for the entire chapter I wrote on subjective assurance in RINE**. For assurance, the believer is directed away from discerning the inward and spiritual graces unique to the regenerate person, *and we all know how much assurance that produces,* and is directed towards his water baptism.

FV explanations of apostasy suggest that a believer may genuinely possess Christ's redemptive benefits and yet lose them. *I would give up some more, but I already did that.*

* Here and throughout, RINE stands for *"Reformed" Is Not Enough.*

FV proponents understand the doctrine of the sacramental union to mean that the sign and the thing signified invariably accompany one another. *I agree with this assessment, provided I can understand it as meaning that the sign and thing signified frequently do not accompany one another.* Baptismal efficacy is affirmed, therefore, of every recipient of the sacrament. *I agree with this too, provided I am allowed to change it into what I actually do believe.* All the blessings and benefits of Christ's work are sometimes said to be conferred upon the recipient in baptism. Baptism is assigned a place in the doctrine of the Christian life that denigrates the place of preaching as the instrument of conversion. *Preaching is an instrument of conversion? Holy moly! What happened to sola fide?*

DISTINGUISHING AND CONSTRUING
NOVEMBER 16, 2004

> "There's an ill *fama* of you gone abroad, Mr Sempill, and it is my duty as your elder in the Lord's service to satisfy myself thereanent. It is reported that you pervert the doctrine of election into grace, maintaining that this blessed estate may be forfeit by a failure in good works, as if the filthy rags of man's righteousness were mair than the bite of a flea in face of the eternal purposes of God."
>
> "I say that a man who believes that his redemption through Christ gives him a license to sin is more doubly damned than if he had never had a glimpse of grace."
>
> "But ye maun distinguish. The point is far finer than that, sir. I will construe your words, for there is an interpretation of them which is rank heresy."
>
> The task of construing and distinguishing did not fare well, for every few minutes the teeth of Mr. Proudfoot were shaken in his head by his horse's vagaries. He had just reached a point of inordinate subtley, when the track of Bold branched off, and his animal, recognising at last the road home, darted down it at a rough gallop. The last seen of the minister of Bold was a massive figure swaying like a ship in a gale, and

still, if one might trust the echoes the wind brought back, distinguishing and construing.
—John Buchan, *Witch Wood*

AUBURN AVENUE HUBBUB (AAH) COOL QUOTE 12
NOVEMBER 18, 2004

From *Death of Death* by John Owen

> [Christ's] own exaltation, indeed, and power over all flesh, and his appointment to be Judge of the quick and the dead, was a consequent of his deep humiliation and suffering; but that it was the effect and product of it, procured *meritoriously* by it, that it was the end aimed at by him in his making satisfaction for sin, that we deny.

IF FEDERAL VISION WERE A BEER
NOVEMBER 26, 2004

My friend Cal Beisner sent me a copy of a new P&R book, which I just finished reading this morning. The book was entitled *Justification and the New Perspectives on Paul*, so guess what it was about. Overall I would rate it as a very fine book, one that I highly recommend, but one with a handful of unfortunate spots.

The author, Guy Waters, studied under E.P. Sanders, and so this book should be read for what it is—a careful, sane, and nuanced criticism of the various forms of the New Perspective from someone who is well qualified to offer that criticism.

The book begins with a background history of modern critical thinking on Paul (Bultmann and such) and treats various figures in the development of the New Perspective (and as the title indicates, there is more than one New Perspective). Waters works through Stendahl, Sanders, Raisanen (sorry, can't do those little Scandanavian dot thingies over the gentleman's a's), Dunn, and N.T. Wright.

In descending order, I agreed enthusiastically with Waters's criticism of Sanders and Raisanen, I agreed almost entirely with his criticism of Dunn, and largely with his criticism of N.T. Wright. I do think there were a few places where Waters does not do justice to Wright (e.g., pp. 133, 142), where he fills in what Wright "must be saying." But the section where Waters describes why N.T. Wright is so attractive (and genuinely helpful) to many among the Reformed was really insightful, and I thought, dead on.

The unfortunate spots in this book are small, but unfortunately, still *there*. The last eight pages of the book undertake to deal with Norman Shepherd and the summary doctrinal statement of the session of the Auburn Avenue Presbyterian Church. To attempt this in the scope of just a few pages, and as the conclusion of a book dedicated to the New Perspective, can be counted on to confuse and mislead. And if there is one controversy where we could use a little less of that, it has been this one.

More than once in this whole farce, it would have been a good idea for everyone to look down and double-check the color of their own uniform. Allow me to throw together a bunch of random facts that should show clearly that this should have been done in these 8 pages. Norman Shepherd's project has almost nothing to do with the New Perspective. Richard Gaffin wrote a cover blurb for *Call of Grace*, Shepherd's book, put out by P&R, the same folks who put out *Waters's* book. But Richard Gaffin is *commended* in the bibliography of Waters's book for writing a fine critique of the New Perspective. In fact, at this next Auburn Avenue conference, Richard Gaffin is going to be engaged in a critical but amicable discussion with N.T. Wright. Now, when we Federal Vision troublemakers are sitting there listening to the discussion between Gaffin and Wright, though Christian charity will radiate from us in every direction like heat from a stove, where shall our *doctrinal* sympathies be? Mine will be with Gaffin; his concerns are mine. This means, according to the bibliography, that since his concerns are the concerns of Waters, my concerns are those of Waters. But Gaffin is friendly to Shepherd, and I don't know who is on what team anymore.

Now it is quite possible that I am lined up with Gaffin because I am a Federal Vision Amber, and that some of the Federal Vision Lagers might sympathize more with Wright. Maybe, but I don't think so. And in any case, the whole thing is way too complicated to undertake a treatment in 8 pages. The only thing that those 8 pages will do is reinforce the *false* impression that the

Federal Vision is just another form of the New Perspective, but with minor adaptations to the American Reformed scene.

This is particularly problematic for me since it has been about *a year* since the special issue of *Credenda* came out, critiquing the New Perspective. The central concerns I laid out in *A Pauline Take on the New Perspective* line up very nicely with the central concerns of Waters's book. So why are *agreements* being ignored?

Still, one last positive comment. Even in this unfortunate conclusion to an otherwise fine book, Waters still writes like a gentleman and a Christian. It is evident that he is not in the business of hyperventilating, heaving dead cats, or getting spittle on his keyboard. He seeks to make distinctions worth making, even in this section, and I believe that doctrinal discussion with a man like this would be a discussion well worth having.

HORTON AND WILSON
NOVEMBER 30, 2004

Yesterday I had a very productive conversation with Michael Horton, arranged by the good folks at St. Anne's Pub, an audio journal. The proceedings were of course taped, and will be available from them in a week or so. While you are there, please check out the other things being done by that most valuable ministry. A CD version of our discussion will be available from Canon Press.*

Coincidentally, I just finished reading Alister McGrath's *The Intellectual Origins of the European Reformation*. That book accented one of the things that is tripping us up, centuries later, in this conversation. And that, it seems to me, is the tendency to blur uses and applications of something with the inherent nature of that something. The three *uses* of the law are very different from the inherent *nature* of the law. And when I look at a passage ("law or gospel?"), it is easy to miss the fact that this is a question of hermeneutical *use*, and not a statement about the inherent nature of the law (or the gospel), or the scriptural passage I am looking at for that matter.

* Currently available at wordmp3.com/details.aspx?id=1158..

What the text is saying, and what the text is doing to me, may be two different things entirely. At any rate, I hope the conversation shows that productive conversation on these issues is possible, and I hope that we can widen the discussion——if for no other reason to identify the places where we genuinely differ, getting rid of superficial or apparent disagreements. Anyhow, if you are at all interested in this issue, try to get this recording when it is available.

TRAILER COMMITTEE
NOVEMBER 30, 2004

A few days ago, I mentioned Guy Waters's book on the New Perspective on Paul, and did not heap scorn upon it. Rather, I commended it, all but the last eight pages, which really were unfortunate.

When I wrote that review, I did not know that Guy Waters was on the committee for Mississippi Valley Presbyery that recently (*pre*)released a committee report on all this Stuff. It seems funny to me to have a report like this circulating in public before the presbytery has a chance to approve it (or not). But I am a stranger to the ways of the Presbyterians' MVP (heh heh), and so what do I know? Maybe it is like the movie industry where they release trailers before releasing the movie, in order to stir up interest. Anyhow, the trailers had something on Shepherd, something on the New Perspective, something on Auburn Ave, etc. A few days ago, I provided a color commentary on the section devoted to the Federal Vision, which made a dog's breakfast out of what we are supposed to believe.

Nevertheless, I continue to appreciate Waters's book (may its pages never yellow!), but the last eight pages showed that he *does* confound things that ought not to be confounded. And the MVP committee trailers show that some of those same things are being confounded by this trailer committee. The vast majority of Waters's book shows that he is capable of critical analysis *that is fair to those he is criticizing*. So far, this does not appear to be true of the committee he is on.

My thanks to the reader who pointed out Waters's membership on this committee.

FAITH, DEAD OR ALIVE?
DECEMBER 6, 2004

In my recent conversation with Michael Horton, he raised a question that I did not get a chance to answer in the course of our discussion. He had a problem with the fact that I had said somewhere that "works is the animating principle of faith."

By saying this, I do not mean that faith is one thing, and that works are another, and that when you put the two of them together, you get an autonomous basis for commending yourself to God in the day of judgment. We are saved by grace through faith, period. But what is the nature of that faith? Is it alive, or dead? And if it is alive, then what is the qualitative nature of that life?

The answer to that question can be found in James 2:26, using James's theological vocabulary (and *not* Paul's!). "For as the body without the spirit is dead, so faith without works is dead also."

For James, the spirit is the animating principle of the body. Without the spirit, the body is unanimated, i.e., dead. This relationship is identical to the relationship of faith without works (James tells us). Faith without works is like a body without the spirit. In this analogy (which is in the Bible), faith is compared to the body, and the works are compared to the spirit. I was simply trying to be faithful to what James said.

I recognize that James and Paul have differing stipulated vocabularies. "Works" is a word that does not refer to the same thing for the two men. Paul is at war with dead works, and James is at war with dead faith. We are the heirs of both men, and ought to be at war with both dead works and dead faith. The enemy is death, not faith or works. Works for James is fruit for Paul. But within the clear usage that James gives us, it is indisputable that works is the animating principle of faith.

WHEN PROBLEMS GLARE
DEC 6, 2004

He may not be thrilled with this commendation, but in a recent journal article (*Mid-America Journal of Theology*), Alan Strange has an outstanding review of Gordon Clark's *What Is Saving Faith?*

He praises where praise is due and points out glaring problems where said problems glare. And as Strange notes several times in the article, the nature of saving faith is a "significant factor in the current debates about justification."

And the question that this review article raises is this: What on earth are *Clarkians* (like John Robbins) doing in the forefront of "defending" traditional Reformed orthodoxy on this subject when their position necessarily involves a rejection of traditional Reformed orthodoxy on this subject? Is saving faith really intellectual assent to propositions?

FEDERAL AUDIO STUFF AVAILABLE
DEC 13, 2004

A week or so ago I mentioned that the folks at St. Anne's Public House had interviewed me together with Michael Horton on issues related to the Federal Vision. Well, the glad day when that interview can be made available has arrived, and so here it is.* Of course, I was there when we recorded it, but I just had a chance to listen to it again and was very encouraged. We were doctrinally close in a number of areas, some of them predictable, and some of them not. If you are following this subject at all, you need to give it a listen. While you are there at the Canon website, you can also check out the recording of my doctrinal examination at the most recent CREC presbytery. And a hearty thank you to Christ Church in Spokane for setting up this forum, and for putting out the St. Anne's Pub.

YEAH, UH HUH FAITH
DECEMBER 13, 2004

John Robbins says the following, in an ostensible defense of Protestant orthodoxy. Gordon Clark apparently closed the back door "through which much of this Neolegalism has entered the churches: the notions that saving faith is different from belief, and more than belief, and that it is 'commitment' as well" (*The Current Justification Controversy*, p. 74).

* Currently available at wordmp3.com/details.aspx?id=1158..

The fact that someone who believes that saving faith is nothing more or less than mental assent to propositions has somehow come to be regarded as a defender of the Reformed faith is a remarkable phenomenon, and worthy of study.

AUBURN AVENUE HUBBUB (AAH) COOL QUOTE 13
DEC 17, 2004

> This covenant is variously styled, from one or other of these several elements. Thus, it is called the 'covenant of works,' because perfect obedience was its condition, and to distinguish it from the covenant of grace, which rests our salvation on a different basis altogether. It is also called the 'covenant of life.' because life was promised on condition of the obedience. It is also called a 'legal covenant,' because it demanded the literal fulfillment of the claims of the moral law as the condition of God's favour. *This covenant was also in its essence a covenant of grace*, in that it graciously promised life in the society of God as the freely-granted reward of an obedience already unconditionally due. Nevertheless it was a covenant of works and of law with respect to its demands and conditions.
> —A.A. Hodge, *The Confession of Faith* (Carlisle, PA: Banner of Truth, 1958), p. 122, although the emphasis is emphasis here is *mine*.

SOME RESPONSES TO DR. FESKO
DEC 18, 2004

Dr. Fesko is an Adjunct Professor of Theology at RTS, Atlanta, and is serving on a study commission of the OPC, a group tasked check out the Federal Vision. He recently released a paper toward that end, entitled "The Federal Vision and the Covenant of Works." To that paper, I offer a few comments.

The first comment belongs in the "talking past one another" department. Dr. Fesko says, "The traditional view posits Adam in a covenantal relationship that is conditioned by obedience in order to obtain eternal life. The Federal Vision, on the other hand, sees Adam in a covenantal relationship that is conditioned by a need for maturity . . ." Well, okay thus far. But how would that maturity be reached? By personal and perpetual *obedience*, that's how. The issue we have with the covenant of works is not on the need for *obedience*. It is whether or not that obedience is necessarily related to something *else* called *merit*.

For a second example, Dr. Fesko says, "We must ask, however, where in the Scriptures do we see a covenant defined only as a relationship. While relationships certainly take place within the context of a covenant, we must recognize that Scripture sees a covenant primarily as an agreement."

This is the kind of *unnecessary* disagreement that is just exasperating. We do have substantive disagreements, and we should be discussing them. But this is not one of them. To say that Scripture sees a covenant primarily as an agreement, setting it in opposition to seeing covenant as relationship, is simply missing what an agreement is. An agreement is an agreement between persons. *It is a relationship*. An agreement is an agreed upon relation.

A lease agreement form sitting on the shelf of a stationery store is just a form. It is not an agreement until persons make the agreement.

SMITH AND FESKO
DEC 18, 2004

Dr. Fesko also objected to seeing the covenant as part of the triune life and spent a good bit of time answering some of the points raised by Ralph Smith on that score. "The legal element in the covenant is not a problem unless one argues, as does the Federal Vision, that covenant is part of the *opera ad intra* of the Trinity."

But the covenants that are made with men are not exact reenactments of the covenantal nature of God. There are aspects of God's nature that are communicable, and aspects that are not. Nevertheless, there should be no problem in acknowledging that there are elements in our covenants, such as the legal aspect, that *answer to* something in the divine nature. What we are looking for is not a Platonic form of "legal element," but rather a transcendent and divine basis for all that we experience in covenant. I have begotten children, and the Father has begotten His Son eternally. These are not even remotely identical, but they do answer to one another, and the Bible encourages us to see it that way. So when I submit to a legal stipulation of a covenant, this is not even remotely identical to the Son obeying the will of the Father, taking the form of a servant, and dying for us. But they do answer to one another somehow.

JORDAN AND FESKO
DEC 18, 2004

Dr. Fesko also takes issue with Jim Jordan on the subject of death and maturity. Before defending Jordan's point, let me agree with Dr. Fesko's objection on his use of terms. To use the word *death* to describe the transformation/glorification/maturation of Adam, had he not sinned, is, in my judgment, prone to do nothing but mislead. This is so on two counts. First, one of the driving themes of the Federal Vision is that we must be allowed to speak as Scripture speaks, and we should strive to function within those categories. But, as Dr. Fesko points out, the Bible describes death as an enemy, something introduced to the world by Adam's *sin*. (Incidentally, I am looking forward to Dr. Fesko using this point, which is a very good one, to critique all the old-earthers out there who think that the fossil record of death somehow could *predate* Adam.) To use the term *death* to refer to an unfallen transformation to a higher degree of glory is, at the very least, a non-biblical way of speaking. And this leads to the misunderstandings that are likely to occur among the saint as a result, which is my second point. This is comparable to saying something like, "Had the serpent not sinned, and had Eve not been deceived, and had Adam not rebelled, they would have all walked in the garden in warm satanic fellowship, which, as we know, is the best kind of creaturely fellowship there is. Therefore, let us promote a *godly* satanic fellowship today." There are too many *ifs* here, and our theology starts to inch out on to the skinny branches. What is the use in saying that if we had some ham, we could make a ham and cheese sandwich, if we had some cheese?

That said, Jordan's *point*, to which Dr. Fesko also objects, should be considered incontrovertible. There should be no disagreement among the Reformed that Adam's condition was probationary. Had Adam not sinned, is there any doubt that he would have been glorified? Is there any doubt that this transformation would have resulted in Adam coming to full maturity? In fact, I think that Jim's point is so obviously *true* that the only thing that could have thrown Dr. Fesko off the point is the use of that word *death*.

WILSON AND FESKO
DEC 18, 2004

Dr. Fesko's critique interacts mostly with Jim Jordan, Rich Lusk, and Ralph Smith. In his critique, he frequently misses the point being made by these men, although I also believe he raises some legitimate questions. But when he comes to summarize his concerns, he does so in a way that expands his critique to include others, including me.

Dr. Fesko says this: "The evidence has demonstrated that the Federal Vision does not merely represent one variant of reformed theology but an entirely different system of doctrine. They deny the primary authority of Scripture in theology, the covenant of works, the adversarial nature of death, the ability of man to obey the command in the garden, the traditional distinction of the active and passive obedience of Christ, the imputation of the active obedience of Christ, the historic understanding of the work of Christ, and the traditional definition of faith. What is troubling is that proponents of the Federal Vision claim they are building upon the historic reformed faith. One writer, for example, states that 'we do understand ourselves to be in the *middle* of the mainstream of historic Reformed orthodoxy."

Note the reference to the "Federal Vision" as a whole in the first sentence, the words "they deny" that begin the second sentence, the catalog of doctrinal problems that follow, and then his quotation of my essay on union with Christ in *The Auburn Avenue Theology*. He is guilty at this point of what can only be described as extraordinary sloppiness. Let me run through his catalog of our deficiencies to show what I mean. In my responses I am speaking only for myself, although I believe many of the same responses would apply also to other Federal Vision types. Moreover, my responses on these points are very much part of the public record of this controversy.

Dr. Fesko says:

1. They deny the primary authority of Scripture in theology. *But I affirm it, stoutly.*
2. They deny the covenant of works. *If you mean a covenant of obedience, I affirm it. But if you mean a covenant of autonomous merit, I deny it. There is likely a true disagreement here.*
3. They deny the adversarial nature of death. *But I affirm that death is an enemy, an adversary, and that this is necessarily so.*
4. They deny the ability of man to obey the command in the garden. *I affirm the ability of man to have obeyed God in the garden. And had he obeyed, he would have thanked God for His gracious preservation.*
5. They deny the traditional distinction of the active and passive obedience of Christ. *I affirm the traditional distinction between the active and passive obedience of Christ.*
6. They deny the imputation of the active obedience of Christ. *Turns out that I affirm it. Like Machen said, no hope without it.*
7. They deny the historic understanding of the work of Christ. *I affirm it. Me and Leon Morris are fishing buddies.*
8. They deny the traditional definition of faith. *I affirm the traditional definition of faith, which rests upon Christ alone as He is offered in the gospel.*

This is an accuracy rate that is (at its *highest*, depending on how the covenant of works discussion goes) *around twelve percent.* And then Dr. Fesko quotes *me* as *defending* this collage of misrepresentations as being in the middle of the Reformed mainstream. This is more than embarrassing. If Dr. Fesko wants the OPC study commission to be received with anything other than a horse laugh, he needs to take far better care in gathering his facts. This is such a striking misrepresentation, that I would like to take this opportunity to call upon Dr. Fesko, who is a godly Christian gentleman, to retract that portion of his paper, and to apologize for it.

2005

AUBURN 2005

JAN 7, 2005

The Auburn Avenue Pastors' Conference 2005 just concluded this last Wednesday, and I just got back from Louisiana last night. I'd like to briefly review the conference in three posts. Here in the first one I would like to thank the conference organizers and the participants for a very helpful conference, both in terms of structure and theme.

The structure and theme were a set of parallel lectures on the theology of Paul by Richard Gaffin and N.T. Wright, each of them giving five lectures. In the question and answer sessions, each session would begin with the lecturers asking one another questions before we got to the questions from the audience.

The conference was not a debate, but it was very helpful in highlighting areas of agreement between a classical (historical/redemptive) expression of the Reformed faith represented by Gaffin, and a conservative expression of the New Perspective on Paul represented by Wright. In addition, the set up was well suited for showcasing where there is continuing and significant disagreement.

The last thing about this topic has to do with the helpfulness of this kind of irenic theological discussion. Nothing was more apparent than that there is a great deal to talk about and work through. Each speaker was very respectful of the other, and the way the conference was set up it is probable that a good many misunderstandings were cleared up, and no whacking great new ones were generated. This expression of gratitude is not so that we will never differ in some sort of false ecumenism, but rather that we might get to the *actual* differences. In many ways, it was a very satisfying conference.

RICHARD GAFFIN AT AUBURN 2005
JAN 7, 2004

Richard Gaffin is a gracious Christian gentleman, who really knows his subject. I learned a great deal from his talks and appreciated how careful he was being. Some of this was no doubt because of the setting, for, after all, he was speaking at the Auburn Avenue Pastors' Conference. This means that his words are going to be gone over in a painstaking way by examiners with unsympathetic eyes, not to mention a small contingent of people who don't know what "careful" means. Because they *will* not be careful, Dr. Gaffin needed to be. This meant that Gaffin's talks could not really be described as stemwinders, but they were thorough, solid, and very good. He did not jump into the fray *in media res*, but rather started with a prolegomenon, and laid his foundation stones carefully. Some listening to the lecture tapes might initially wonder at the method ("what's his point?", but he was simply being diligent in his approach. By the time he was done with his talks, the value of the early preparation work should have been evident.

The most helpful thing to me personally was his treatment of the sense in which we may speak of future justification. Without denying the declarative (and definitive "once-for-all-ness") nature of justification in the life of the believer, Gaffin did a *masterful* job of showing how the central "already/not yet" elements of Paul's theology have to be taken into account when we talk about the final vindication of God's people in the resurrection. No one could honestly think that Gaffin was saying that God will justify us on the basis of our own autonomous works, and yet he did full justice to the language of Paul on this, particularly when it came to the question of our adoption as sons. This adoption as sons is described by Paul as finalized in the redemption of our bodies. If adoption has a forensic component, as Dr. Gaffin showed, then this means that this declarative and forensic component has a future manifestation. This is just a thumbnail sketch of his argument, and so I refer you to the tapes.

I am very grateful to Dr. Gaffin for his agreement to speak at the conference, for the work he did in preparing for it, and for the help he was to me in his lectures. It was an honor to meet him, and to talk about some of the larger controversies we are all involved in. If more in the Reformed establishment responded to so-called "new stuff" in the sober and sane way that Gaffin has, all of us would be a lot better off. N.T. Wright said during the conference that if New Testament studies had been flowing in a Ridderbosian channel (my expression, not his), the reaction of Sanders to Lutheranism (and Lutheranism gone to seed in folks like Bultmann) would have been unnecessary. In my view, the same compliment should be accorded to Gaffin and his work. That in the New Perspective which is a healthy corrective to older errors actually antedates the advent of the New Perspective.

N.T. WRIGHT AT AUBURN 2005
JAN 7, 2004

The bulk of my review of N.T. Wright's presentations at Auburn 2005 will be occupied with concerned observations and/or criticisms, so I need to establish the context of all this in the first couple of paragraphs. In all my years of listening to Christian speakers, I have to say that I have never heard anyone so gifted, or so compelling. He is a very great gift of God to the Church at large, and to the Church of England particularly. He was witty, humble and self-deprecating, very effective as a speaker, and a *master* of the raw material under discussion. He spoke as though all the text of all Scripture were laid out flat before him on a table, and he could instantly point to any place in Scripture and show its relevance to the topic under discussion. I have never seen anyone who had so much Scripture instantly at his fingertips. This gift of God to the Church at large is currently the Bishop of Durham, and the Church of England is in the midst of a very great crisis indeed. This is the crisis provoked by the arrogant ordination of a practicing homosexual as a bishop by the bishops of the American Episcopal Church. I don't know if we can be optimistic about the outcome, but *if* something good comes from it, I think Wright will be involved in that good. When I went to the conference, I was already appreciative of much of Wright's work, and came away with a much deeper appreciation of him. His talks were extraordinarily edifying.

That said, just a few comments. Much of this comes from things he said in the course of his talks, some from things in the air, and some of it from questions I was able to ask him.

One of the great emphases in Wright is the impossibility of depoliticizing the gospel. His talk on eschatology (I think it was Tuesday night) was simply stupendous, and he notes, rightly, that the restoration of humanity in Christ cannot be tucked away in some private place. These things cannot be done in a corner. But when Wright comes to make the (necessary) applications of this, his socialistic environment manifests itself. In England, and in some of the circles he visits in America, he is considered something of a dangerous conservative, and this is *something* of an optical illusion. Wright needs to come to grips with the fact that *many* Americans who are attracted to what he is saying about the public nature of discipleship will not make the same political applications of this truth that he would. To him, one public application of the lordship of Christ means the forgiveness of Third World debts. The way believing Americans would apply it would be more likely to involve protecting gun ownership. All this serves to warn us—the Church needs to work through a lot of things before we take the show on the road. Americans would be prone to simply reproduce our radical individualism in the name of Jesus, which is not helped if the English evangelicals simply reproduce the quasi-socialism that they are used to—in the name of Jesus.

Related to this is Wright's acceptance of women's ordination. How someone who knows Paul the way Wright knows Paul can process this is simply beyond me. But because Wright generally is so masterful in things Pauline, I think something like this is a good reminder for us. We should be extremely grateful for Wright, but not so dazzled that we allow him to slip something in that is manifestly not true (and in this case, something that is at odds with Wright's larger project). The whole thing reminds me of the old joke told about Charles Spurgeon (by a Presbyterian): God gave so many gifts to Spurgeon that He knew we would be tempted to idolize him . . . so He made him a Baptist.

Then there is the question of whether Saul (before the Damascus road experience) was blameless according to the law. Paul *says* that he was in Philippians

3:6, a point made by Wright at the conference. But is Paul saying that he really was blameless, or that he *thought* he was (to the admiration of all his fellow Pharisees)? I asked Wright if he thought that Paul and Zacharias, who is also described as blameless in his observance of the law (Luke 1:6), would have gotten along. Wright said he thought Zacharias would have thought Paul a dangerous hothead, which I think is exactly right. But being a dangerous hothead is not blameless. Paul describes himself as having been an insolent man, which was *not* okay according to the law. Wright acknowledged that Paul did have something wrong with him, but this issue lies right at the heart of all the "boundary marker" questions. Zacharias was a covenant-keeping Jew, and Saul was a covenant-breaking Jew. I was happy that Wright acknowledged a difference of some sort between them but concerned that he doesn't appear to see the relevance of this to one of the big New Perspective issues.

The last point regards inerrancy. Wright is *clearly* committed to the functional authority of Scripture, but the way he answered the question looked like a dodge. I believe he has an important point to make about inerrancy (and the problems of precisionism), but the question itself is not a matter of American categories. Perhaps I can note more about this later.

THE B.T.K. KILLER AND THE OBJECTIVITY OF THE COVENANT

MARCH 4, 2005

The recent arrest of Dennis Rader for the infamous B.T.K. killings presents an interesting dilemma for those who want to maintain, as I do, the objectivity of the covenant. For the sake of this discussion, I want to assume that the reports are true that Rader has confessed to a number of the killings, and that Rader is in fact guilty. If that were not the case, then our discussion should revolve around rules of evidence, and what constitutes proof.

The thing that makes this a problem for the objectivity of the covenant is that Rader does not meet the standard profile of a serial killer. He is a family man, and the president of his congregation, Christ Lutheran Church. His pastor has visited him in prison and has said some things that provoke these musings now. After his visit, Rader's pastor said, "We are not going to cut him off. I could tell that he was relieved . . . He is still a part of the body of Christ—and that is something some people will have a hard time hearing."

Now some might say that this is the "objectivity of the covenant" coming back at us with a vengeance. Here is a man who has confessed to a number of horrendous murders over a span of decades and who remains a member of a Trinitarian church. He is baptized and has not been excommunicated. His pastor certainly seems to think (in some measure) in terms of Dennis Rader's objective standing within the covenant. But how are we to process this? Here are some preliminary thoughts.

1. No one has ever done anything so horrendous that God's forgiveness in Christ cannot reach him. Salvation is according to grace, not according to works. Of course Rader does not deserve to be saved. No one does.
2. Because Rader was a member of a Christian church, he had a standing obligation to repent of his grotesque sins, and believe in Christ.
3. His confessed behavior indicates that he was in defiance of this covenantal obligation over an extended period of time, over decades.
4. This does not mean that he cannot repent *now*, but the Bible must be the only rule for us in defining what actual repentance looks like. There is a sorrow that leads only to death, but a godly sorrow leads to repentance without regret.
5. In a situation like this one, again, assuming the confessions of guilt, what would repentance look like? In short, what sort of repentance should Christ Lutheran Church accept, so that Rader might remain a member, and not be "cut off," as his pastor put it?
6. A genuinely repentant man in such circumstances must confess everything, fully and completely, and this would include any crimes he has not been charged with. The chances are good that the authorities do not know everything he has done. He must plead guilty in court to any crimes he committed, publicly declare that he has sought God's forgiveness, and ask for forgiveness from the families of the victims. So that they might know that this is not just talk, Rader must strive to receive the death penalty. A

repentant man who had done these things would evidence his repentance in his whole-hearted desire to be executed. In this, he should echo the words of the apostle Paul. "For if I be an offender, or have committed any thing worthy of death, I refuse not to die" (Acts. 25:11).

7. If in substance he manifests repentance this way, that repentance should be *accepted* by his brothers and sisters in Christ, and he should willingly go to his death a communicant member of Christ Lutheran Church. If he does *not* do these things, if his declared repentance is only an emotional sorrow that does not bear the marks of true repentance, then he should be excommunicated from his church.

The situation is obviously filled with tangles, and I do not envy Rader's pastor at all. He was right that a godly response to the situation contains things that "some people will have a hard time hearing." But the difficulty should cut across the political spectrum. Those who think that the grace of God could never come to someone like Rader will have a hard time hearing about any kind of forgiveness for such a man. And those who think that forgiveness must mean a removal of all consequences will have a hard time hearing that a repentant man in such a case must ask to be executed and must be supported in this desire by his church. But there it is.

THREE STUMBLING BLOCKS
MARCH 15, 2005

When it appears that the Holy Spirit has begun to create new wine in the church, why do Christian leaders sometimes fail to drink it?

Let us begin by acknowledging that sometimes it is because they are courageous and insightful. Athanasius was against the world, and the new wine of Arianism was actually stump water with clever marketing. The same kind of thing could be said of all the slick hype over ministry in a postmodern matrix, whatever that is supposed to mean.

But let us assume for a moment that the Holy Spirit really has begun to work in a significant way, and that entrenched religious authorities oppose that work. What are some of the reasons given in Scripture for why they might want to do this? Three basic motivations come to mind:

Envy

Jesus was opposed because of envy, a reality that even Pilate could see (Matt. 27:18; Mark 15:10). When Paul preached in Antioch, things were going great until the local authorities saw the large multitude that showed up to hear Paul preach the next week. So they were filled with envy (Acts 13:45). The same thing happened in Thessalonica (Acts 17:5). This is a human problem—not only were Jewish leaders afflicted with it, so were *Christian* preachers (Phil. 1:15). When someone teaches or preaches with authority, and not like the scribes, there have been times when the scribes haven't taken it too well. Sometimes the new wine can't get into the old wineskin, not because of the old wine, but because the skin is stuffed full of learned scribes, writing treatises on what it was like back in the glory days, back before we drank all the old wine.

Fear

in John 12:42, we are told that many of the rulers (leaders, teachers, etc) believed in Jesus. But they did not admit this publicly because they were cowed by a powerful, conservative faction within the church. They loved the praise of men more than the praise of God (v. 43). The establishment always knows how to defend itself, and how to intimidate that large group of men in the middle, men who can follow the argument, so long as following it doesn't lead to any unpleasant consequences. So men remain quiet at presbytery, lamenting the injustice being done, but unwilling to stand.

Laziness

And for a few too many, the ministry is an indoor job with no heavy lifting. Jesus spoke of the hireling who flees (John 10: 12–13), and one of the prophets spoke of shepherds who feed only themselves. Sometimes these men are insightful enough to see their main chance might lie in going with a new reforming movement, but usually this mentality likes the quiet the status quo provides, a quiet in which a man may butter his bread, and not have to read any books.

WHEN WAS ABRAHAM CONVERTED
MARCH 30, 2005

It seems to me that this is a very important question, on two fronts. First, it is important to note that Abraham was in fact converted from idolatry. He, like all sons of Adam, was dead in his trespasses and sins and needed to have the righteousness of another granted or imputed to him. He was an idolater and had no righteousness of his own. We know he was an idolater from the account we are given in Joshua: "And Joshua said unto all the people, Thus saith the LORD God of Israel, Your fathers dwelt on the other side of the flood in old time, even Terah, the father of Abraham, and the father of Nachor: *and they served other gods.* And I took your father Abraham from the other side of the flood, and led him throughout all the land of Canaan, and multiplied his seed, and gave him Isaac" (Josh. 24:2–3).

So Abraham was not just an uncircumcised Gentile when God first called to him, he was an *idolatrous* Gentile. But a second point also needs to be emphasized. Although he clearly needed to be converted, Abraham was *not* converted in Genesis 15. When did Abraham first respond to the true and living God in genuine faith? "*By faith* Abraham, *when he was called to go out* into a place which he should after receive for an inheritance, obeyed; and he went out, not knowing whither he went. By faith he sojourned in the land of promise, as in a strange country, dwelling in tabernacles with Isaac and Jacob, the heirs with him of the same promise: For he looked for a city which hath foundations, whose builder and maker is God" (Heb. 11: 8–10).

So when Abraham left Ur of the Chaldees, he was responding to the word of God *in faith* (Gen. 12:1–2). He built several altars to the Lord in Canaan, calling upon the name of the Lord there (Gen. 12:7–8). He is clearly a faithful believer, father of all faithful but uncircumcised Gentiles (Rom. 4:11).

A few chapters later, God reiterates His promises to Abraham, promises that Abraham has already heard and already believed. And it says, well into Abraham's life of faith, "And he believed in the LORD; and he counted it to him for righteousness" (Gen. 15:6). St. Paul quotes this as a hinge in his argument in Romans 4. In Genesis 17, God reiterates the promise yet again, and grants the sign of circumcision. Abram is renamed Abraham.

Now, here is the question that may make all the participants on all sides of the Federal Vision discussion unhappy with me, but here goes anyhow. *When* was Abraham given a new heart? *When* was he converted? *When* was he raised out of his condition of Adamic death and brought into a living relationship with God? *When* was the righteousness of Christ imputed to him in the theological sense? I am not asking *whether* these things happened, for I affirm that all of them happened. I am asking *when*.

The answer that exegesis demands is that he was converted when he left Ur of the Chaldees, and he was not converted in Genesis 15. But that means that the language of imputation in Genesis is not as narrow has some have assumed. And on the other side, it appears just as plain to me that what the New Testament teaches about heart regeneration can and must be applied to Abraham in Genesis 12.

GOD PROMISES US OUR CHILDREN
APRIL 5, 2005

A few days ago, I wrote about how I became a paedobaptist. I attributed that change to a connection that was shown to me between the promises of God for our children and the practice of infant baptism. That connection stirred up a reasonable question out there, which I would like to try to answer here.

When God promises us our children, how are these promises to be understood? Head for head, each baptized child of the covenant will be saved? If that is the case, then why is God not keeping His promises? But if his promises are for *this* group of Christian parents and not *that* group, then exegetically how do we determine what our response should be? Exegetically, how do I know what group I am in?

The answer is that this is *a covenant promise.* The promises concerning the salvation of our children should be understood the same way that promises of answered prayer are to be understood. We know that God promises to answer our prayers—whatever we ask in Christ's name. The language of some of these promises is, frankly, quite exuberant and over the top. The promises are for every Christian; they apply to every Christian. No Christian has the right to say, "no, that promise is not for me. No sense in me praying." Nevertheless, some Christians do not pray as they ought to, and faithlessly they do not ask God for those things they have every right to ask for. The promise is still good, but all God's promises are always apprehended *by faith.*

It is the same with God's promises for our children. The promises are ours; they are part of the terms of the covenant. God promises that our children will serve Him faithfully, but He does not promise that they will serve Him *automatically.* We are summoned to believe these promises, and our faith in what He has declared is His instrument for bringing the promises to fruition. For those who believe the promises, the unbelief of others does not negate the promises. God promises things for His people, and some of His people do not believe Him. What else is new? Christian parents who do not believe these promises, who explain them away, or who throw them away, will often find that their homes contain the very sad results of a self-fulfilling prophecy. The just shall live by faith, from first to last, and this includes our life of bringing up children. We bring up our children in the Lord by faith, and not by works. One of the strangest charges I have had to deal with in the Federal Vision controversy is the charge that I deny the centrality of faith through my insistence that we must believe God's promises in this regard. But believing God is no work, and not believing God is not faith.

At any rate, there is no theological or doctrinal problem with the position that God promises us our children that could not be urged equally against God's general promises to answer our prayers. And a biblical answer to one supplies the answer to the other.

PETTY TRADITIONS
APRIL 22, 2005

John Robbins continues to display one of his chief polemical attributes, which is kind of a bad attribute for a rationalist to have, to wit, his inability to follow an argument. He has recently said that one of our tactics is that of quoting John Calvin, who said "some foolish things about the sacraments." He goes on to say that we know that we "can dredge up foolish statements from Reformed theologians that support or seem to support [our] heretical view."

Robbins then counters by citing some (*genuinely*) foolish things that B.B. Warfield said about evolution. But then Robbins says, in a brief and aberrant burst of charity, that Warfield's status as a Reformed theologian is "without challenge."

I am afraid he has missed the point of the citations of our Reformed fathers. The fact that the Westminster Shorter Catechism calls the sacraments "effectual means of salvation" does not make that statement *right*. The only ultimate and infallible court of appeal on such things is the Scriptures. Robbins is exactly right on that score. But this quotation *does* mean that I should be able to say that I believe the sacraments are effectual means of salvation without being told that my expression, as it stands, is contrary to the Westminster Standards.

Robbins himself exercises the kind of discretion we are looking for, only not with us. He proves that Warfield gave away the store on evolution, and yet Warfield retains Robbins's respect as a Reformed theologian. I would say Warfield gave away other important things too (e.g., his doctrine of the *autographa* being the only inerrant Bible we have, only unfortunately, we don't actually have it), and yet my respect for Warfield is still quite high. I differ with him on some important issues, but I know that he represents an important part of the Reformed tradition, and the caliber of his work on a number of issues was quite good.

The same with Calvin. I don't agree with Calvin on everything. But what I reserve to myself is the right to *agree* with Calvin and not have that agreement be used as the reason for denying that I am a Calvinist.

So my question for Robbins is this. Why can the Reformers say such "silly things" and retain your respect? Why can Warfield say genuinely silly things and still be honored by you as a great theologian? Robbins concludes by saying, "We Protestants are not traditionalists. We are radicals for Christianity, and that Root is Scripture alone." But what is a Protestant? Robbins in effect has said that "we in the Protestant tradition do not have a tradition." Unless, as I am beginning to suspect, Robbins believes that true Protestantism began with Gordon Clark and will end with John Robbins. But even *that* is a (very short) tradition. And not only is it short, it is also petty.

EXCEPT FOR PRISMS
MAY 11, 2005

Been a while since I wrote anything about the Auburn Avenue stuff. So why not? says I. A gentleman named Paul Manata has written a detailed and very fine refutation of Cal Beisner's claim that the root of the Auburn Avenue teaching was our embrace of Van Til's apologetic. Manata's post is called "The Root of The Problem With Auburn Avenue Theology?" and can be found somewhere on this site*.

In his discussion of this issue (in *The Auburn Avenue Theology: Pros and Cons*†), Cal says this, "Federal Vision theology will continue to be unstable and plagued with error so long as its adherents continue to resist the universal application of logic to theology—which is, in the final analysis, all that is meant by *systematic theology*." (pp. 323–324).

He chastises me in particular, because I co-wrote a logic textbook, and consequently ought to know better. But it is precisely because I have taught logic that I can identify a straw man fallacy. Cal made much of the fact that I spoke about the need for recognizing differences between "levels of discourse." John Robbins has done some tub-thumping on this point as well, acting as though by "levels of discourse" I meant some sort of irrationalist leaping about. Cal took it similarly, as though I was ignoring the warnings given by Francis Schaeffer about upper-story/lower story dualisms. But actually, I was simply restating in other words what Cal himself argued in a footnote in this very section. "Whether McNeill knew it or not, Calvin knew that affirming something *in one sense* and denying it *in another* was not a contradiction. He distinguished between God's (secret) will and His moral (revealed) will . . . Consequently he could affirm that God could will decretively what He forbade morally."

Now before I have some fun with this, let me speak distinctly into the microphone and say that I am making fun of something that I agree with *completely*.

* presstheantithesis.blogspot.com, no longer available.

† E. Calvin Beisner, ed., *The Auburn Avenue Theology: Pros and Cons* (Fort Lauderdale, FL: Knox Theological Seminary, 2004).

That's because I like levels of discourse, and let it never be said that I am an unjust or unfair maker of fun. Cal makes this point on p. 321. Then on pp. 322–323, he chastises me for wanting to distinguish levels of discourse. But Cal had just finished saying that we should distinguish between God's upper story will and His lower story will. When answering McNeill, we *must* distinguish levels of discourse. When answering Wilson, we must *not* do so. This is not a contradiction on our part because we must distinguish levels of discourse. Different levels of discourse do not represent a contradiction, he argues, unless Douglas Wilson tries it. Then it is creeping irrationalism, and is built on the errors of Van Til who made all the same careful qualifications about logic that I have. But these careful qualifications are not made by the rationalists, unless answering Barthians named McNeill. This must be some A–M, and then N–Z thing. And which part of the alphabet has to obey *modus ponens*?

For the record (again): All creation was brought forth from nothing by the self-consistent triune God. All reality is therefore self-consistent. No contradictions. To deny the law of non-contradiction (to use the pagan name for it) is to open the door to Trinitarian heresies that maintain that Father is also not the Father. Nobody around here wants to do that, and we would be abandoning the faith if we did. But we do need to learn how to ground the way we speak of these things on the revealed triune nature of God, instead of on some of Aristotle's preliminary sketches. So I am not against the use of reason in studying and sorting out what God has given to us. I am in favor of *reason*, and am therefore opposed to arid *rationalism*. As the poet said, beware of all *isms*, except for prisms.

Now, when we come to the promises of God for our children, here is the issue. The promises are just like God's promises to answer prayer. There are sweeping statements in Scripture that promise to grant anything to any believer if the prayer is made in Jesus's name. At the same time, we know from the rest of Scripture that not all Christians will believe these promises; not all Christians pray in faith the way they ought to. But they are invited to do so by the promises. If Cal were to argue that a man should never pray in faith until he has some kind of *a priori* determination from the decrees of God that his prayers were decretively determined to be among those that are answered, he would be arguing in *exactly* the same way he is arguing with regard to God's promises for the salvation of our children.

God gives general promises——for many things, not just our children. Those for whom the promises are intended are those who hear and believe. Faith sorts things out, not a deductive argument, the premises of which are filled out because we have pried into the secret decrees of God. So, when I referred to levels of discourse, I was saying that believing the promises of God is a moral duty (which not all Christians fulfill). God decretively has determined the names of those who will believe Him in this way. But in order to believe Him, all I need is His Word, and not access to the decrees. And if I start casting sidelong glances at others, and say, "But what about them? The promises don't seem to be fulfilled in their case," the answer comes back clearly——"What is that to you? You follow Me."

THE LAWS OF THOUGHT
MAY 12, 2005

I mentioned in the last post that I had co-written a logic text. The following is a draft of something that will be going into the next revision. Here tis:

In order to reason well, we have to assume certain things that never show up as particular items in our argument. They are simply (and quietly) assumed. For example, if you were putting together an argument about light bulbs or tricycles, it is very important that they not turn into something else (like a toaster oven or catcher's mitt) halfway through the argument. If they did, the argument would just have to lie down and sob quietly. It could never get anything done.

Traditionally, these assumptions have been called the "laws of thought." There is nothing wrong with the specific *content* of these assumptions, but for Christians, there is a significant problem with *another* deeper assumption lying beneath them. That assumption is that you can have laws without a lawgiver, and ultimately, that you can have reason apart from the triune God of Scripture. All you need to do, it is thought, is postulate some laws of thought, and off we go.

Because this is the case, we are going to begin by showing how these correct assumptions are actually grounded in the nature of the triune God, and how He revealed Himself in Jesus Christ. After we have done that, we will then be able to discuss the traditional terminology. The reason for doing this is that many modernists have been guilty of thinking that impersonal "laws" have authority in themselves, which of course they do not.

In order to deal with this, we will start with the basic Christian confession, which is that *Jesus is Lord*. When God reveals Himself in Christ, the decision that everyone has to make is whether to believe it or not. These are the only two options-faith or unbelief. This means that the statement Jesus is Lord must either be true or false. A faithful person confesses that it is true. An unfaithful person denies it as false. But God does not leave open the option of saying something like, "I believe that the higher reality of the lordship of Christ cannot be contained in our paltry categories of true and false, and so I cannot say whether I believe in Him or not." Such a response is simple dishonesty masquerading as humility.

The fact that *any statement is either true or false* is one of the three basic laws of thought, upon which much of logic is based. This law of thought is called **The Law of Excluded Middle**, because it excludes the possibility of a truth value falling somewhere in the middle between true and false. Statements are either one or the other. If a statement is not true, then it is false, and vice versa.

As Christians we confess that God is triune. If asked, we would say, "Yes, that is true. God is triune." Now if it is true that God is triune, then it must be true that God is triune. For ordinary people, in ordinary conversation, such rules are not thought to be necessary. But when people are fleeing from God, they will often take refuge in any folly. This assumption keeps people from changing the meaning of a term in the middle of an argument. If you are seeking to show from Scripture that God is triune, it is important that the word *triune* not take on the meaning of "six persons" halfway through the argument. Honesty requires the meaning of the word to stay put. In its traditional formulation, this is called **The Law of Identity**. This law simply states that *if a statement is true then it is true*. This law may be employed to answer the unbeliever who says, "Christianity may be true for you, but not for me." No. If the Christian faith is true, then it is true.

The third law says that *a statement cannot be both true and false.* This is called **The Law of Noncontradiction**. Without this law, we could not argue for the exclusive truth of *any* statement which we hold. We could try to assert, for example, that "Jesus is God." But our opponents could respond, "Oh, I agree that what you say is true. But it is also false." We see that if we deny these laws, we lose even the possibility of rational discourse.

Think for a moment what would happen to our faith if we were to allow someone to deny these fundamental assumptions. If we confess "God in three persons, blessed Trinity," someone who denied the law of the excluded middle could say that this wonderful confession is not true, and it is not false. It is just wonderful, and perhaps even a little inspiring. The one who denied the law of identity could say that "yes, it is true that God is a Father for you, but *my* truth is that She is a Mother." And one who denied the law of noncontradiction could say that God is our Father, and, also, in the same way and in the same respect, He is not our Father. In other words, denial of these bedrock assumptions would make a hash out of the simplest Christian confession like the Apostles' Creed.

Having said all this, there is an important warning. The Bible does assume that the Father is the Father, and not the Son. The Spirit is the Holy Spirit and not the Father. The Father is not "not the Father." At the same time, the Bible *also* teaches that the Father perfectly indwells the Son, and the Son indwells the Father. Statements about the Father are not detachable from statements about the Son. Jesus said that if you had seen Him you had seen the Father.

Through a wooden application of these "laws" some logicians have gotten to the point where they cannot understand or appreciate poetry, metaphor, sacraments, or marriage. The world is full of "indwelling" and mutual partaking because this is *also* what our God is like. In our study of logic and reason, we must always leave room for mystery. We know that the Father is Father, and no one else. We know that the Father is not the Son. But we should also know that the Father revealed Himself perfectly in the Son.

Summary: Faithful reasoning assumes these three laws of thought. The Law of Identity says that if a statement is true, then it is true. The Law of Excluded Middle says that a statement is either true or false. The Law of Non-contradiction says that a statement cannot be both true and false.

OUR HERETICAL HAIR
MAY 19, 2005

A friend pointed me to a new master's program at Knox Seminary, which actually looks pretty good. Click here*. But that Auburn Avenue heresy stuff is like an insidious gas that permeates *everything*, up to and including this new master's program at Knox. In bold-face type (no less), they say the following: "We need to publish the reality that cultural choices have eternal consequences in salvation or judgment: character determines destiny." Jumping Jehoshaphat *and* Land of Goshen! Just imagine if Rich Lusk had said this. In the space of a few short words, we have rabid Arminianism (*choices* have eternal consequences), we have worldliness (*cultural* choices have eternal consequences), and we have a particularly egregious example of John Robbins's euphonically named Neolegalism (*character* determines destiny).

Of course, we know that if we were to ask the orthodox brethren at Knox about it, they would qualify these comments carefully. And when we heard their qualifications, we would believe them as brothers in Christ, and put our doctrinal revolvers back in the presbyterial holster. But when *we* say things like this (and we do, honestly), our qualifications after the fact do not matter. To extend the metaphor, the doctrinal bullets continue to whistle through our heretical hair. Oh, well.

On the bright side, Knox Seminary has realized the cultural issues are central to the future of the Reformed faith and have devoted a non-Gnostic program to it. And good luck to them on seriously engaging with these cultural issues without getting in trouble with the Internet Wardens of Doctrinal Precision.

* Information on Knox's master's in Christian and classical studies is currently available here: knoxseminary.edu/programs/maccs.

DOING IT RIGHT
MAY 21, 2005

Dr. Bryan Chapell of Covenant Seminary has written a very reasonable treatment of the New Perspective on Paul, which can be found here†. He distinguishes things that need to be distinguished, he knows what central issues of the faith need to be defended and preserved, he criticizes without hysterics, and his admonitions to all parties are worth listening to prayerfully, even if you initially think you might differ. This is an example of the kind of interaction that actually might get us somewhere.

SOME PING-PONG
JUNE 1, 2005

When I was in junior high school, I used to play a lot of ping-pong. Occasionally, in the course of these bouts, one of my friends would hit a lofter—a slow ball about three feet above the table, just on my side of the net. I confess that when this happened it brought certain feelings to life in me, feelings that could probably be characterized as ungodly. The works of the flesh are manifest, St. Paul says, and one of them no doubt would include the desire to drill a hole through the other side of the ping-pong table with your slam, and then to whoop and dance in an unseemly way around your friend's basement, which is where the ping-pong table was located.

Anyhow, what brought these thoughts to mind was the most recent edition of *The Trinity Review*. John Robbins therein reviews the book recording the Fort Lauderdale colloquium on the Auburn Avenue theology, which book was edited by Cal Beisner. Anyhow, in these brief comments, I will attempt to restrain myself,

In the first place, since Robbins belongs to the "ready, fire, aim!" school of thought, he takes issue with our debating partners on the other side of the table, who were seeking honestly to determine *what* we were saying before they decided whether or not they needed to oppose it. This gracious behavior was too much for Robbins, who spends a good deal of time denouncing *them* for

† The link on Covenant's site is no longer viable, but this article on the Ligonier Ministries site appears to be the one in question: ligonier.org/learn/articles/explanation-new-perspective-paul.

not denouncing *us* in the manner which Robbins has determined is meet. This kind of indiscriminate approach has been tried in the history of the Church before—"Kill them all and let God sort it out"—but to their credit our discussion partners did not do anything like that. I do think they got us wrong at some significant points, but they conscientiously sought to get what we were saying. I am grateful to be able to say that none of those who differed with us at the Knox colloquium belong in any way to the extremes pursued by Robbins.

But my point here was to briefly respond to some of the howlers that John Robbins directed at me personally, so let me get to it.

1. "Wilson claims, 'One of our fundamental concerns is this: we want to insist on believing God's promises concerning our children.' Unfortunately, neither he nor any other proponent of Neolegalism ever quotes those promises." The problem for this thesis is that I wrote a little book called *Standing on the Promises*, the first part of which is dedicated to a discussion of many of promises God has given us in Scripture concerning our children.

2. Robbins says (of Acts 2:39), that "the last clause of the verse, 'as many as the Lord our God will call,' modifies and limits all three referents: 'you, your children, and all who are afar off.' And to this assertion I cheerfully agree, and further assert that the grammar demands it. But if Peter, in preaching to the crowd at Pentecost had said something like: "for the promise is to you, to those in your neighborhood who live in blue houses, and to those who are afar off, as many as the Lord our God will call," there would be two comments worth making. The first is the realization that not all who inhabit blue houses in my neighborhood need be elect. On this point, Robbins is correct (and ironically, so am I!) But the second point is that blue houses must be important to this process *somehow*, otherwise why mention it? Children *are* singled out. Why? Peter is referring to the promise of the Holy Spirit of God in the Old Testament, which I treat in detail in *Standing on the Promises*. And those promises graciously invite Christian parents to believe God for the salvation of their children. But they do not do this by giving a list of names for all the elect children that will be born in the history of the church. Herein lies the fundamental flaw in Robbins's epistemological approach.

Oddly, earlier in the essay, Robbins says that many Christians have a lack of courage in opposing the likes of us because of "a lack of belief in the promises of Scripture." All right—let us talk about the promises of God in Scripture, and talk further about the problem of specificity. God promises salvation to Abraham directly. He does the same for a handful of other saints in Scripture. But *most* Christians who believe the promises of God unto salvation do so even though their names are not mentioned anywhere in the Bible.

If I can only believe what is propositionally revealed in the Bible, and if my name is not propositionally revealed in the Bible as one who believes the promise of salvation rightly, then how can I believe the promise? How can *I* believe any promise there? Do I have direct warrant? No, not at all. I can, however, believe indirectly, but I must supply one of the missing ingredients (which I cannot do apart from grace). Christ promises to give rest to all those who labor and are heavy-laden, and who come to Him (Matt. 11:29–30). I can believe (on Robbins's terms) that He will do this for a particular group of people. But how can I insert *myself* into that group? Following Robbins's logic, I cannot.

Christ promises salvation to those who repent and believe. But what warrant do I have for saying that this promise applies to *me*? God promises to answer prayer. But how can I proceed to pray on the assumption that the promise applies to *me*? Shouldn't I wait until after the day of judgment to see if I should have taken God up on it? It is the same with God's promises to us concerning our children. He promises, on the basis of His covenant, that our children will serve and worship Him. This promise, like all God's promises, is apprehended by faith only, by faith alone, by faith plus nothing else, by faith apart from works, and by faith all by its own self. (Incidentally, I do understand how this kind of language is confusing to Robbins who sees in it a display of a dangerous mixture of faith and works.)

Why are some children of the covenant lost then? For the same reason that some prayers are unanswered—the prayers were not offered *in faith*. The children were not brought up in the faith that God would fulfill this promise.

The thing that closes the circle is always faith. This particular faith cannot be based on propositional warrant from Scripture, because Scripture says nothing about *my* prayers, nothing about *my* children, nothing about whether *I* am elect. I close the circle *by faith.* God gives the *general* enscriptured promise. He then works in me specifically through the person of the Holy Spirit to bring *me* to the conviction that these general promises are *mine*, and so that I may enter into rest. Not only do I have reason to believe the promises, I am *commanded* to believe them.

But when I believe these promises about children, someone could hand me an exhaustive concordance and demand to see my descendants' name in there. And when they do, I would just smile, shake my head, and hand it back. "I will show you my grandchildren's names in Scripture when you show me Gordon Clark's name there." "Gordon Clark believed the gospel," the reply would come. "Yes, he did, without any *specific* warrant to do so. Just like my grandchildren."

3. Robbins charges one of our debate partners (Fowler White) with not really believing in the inerrancy of Scripture, and then indicates that I agreed with the general point that Dr. White was making. This treatment shows once again how Robbins (for all his vaunted rationalism) cannot really follow the simplest of arguments. Of course I affirm the absolute infallibility and absolute authority of Scripture. Because I do, I reject the idea that Robbins has picked up somewhere that Scripture must submit to every last stipulated definition of a modern logic text. Now don't get this wrong (as Robbins easily might do). I am not denying that all reality, grounded as it is in the nature of God, must be internally consistent, and I heartily assert there no such thing as an absolute contradiction. That said, there are uses of "all" in Scripture which do not conform to the standards of *All P are Q* statements. This is not an embrace of irrationalism, not even a little bit. In a strict A statement, all Ps are Qs, head for head, and every last stinking one of them is distributed, as the logicians say. But in the world inhabited by regular English speakers, the word *all* admits of a whole bunch of variations. For example, God wants all men to be saved.

Because Scripture is the absolute authority, we must submit to *its* usages. And when Paul addresses those "called to be saints" in Corinth (1 Cor. 1:2), he is not intending to make the claim that everyone within the boundaries of the visible Corinthian church was necessarily elect. He is not using the vocabulary that way here, because there are a number of places in the same epistle where he warns the saints at Corinth against the danger of falling away, just like the Jews in the wilderness did (1 Cor. 10).

Related to this, John Robbins did not understand my point about levels of discourse at all. So here it is again, in another form. When Paul tells us about the cup of *blessing* which was the cause of many Corinthians getting sick and dying, is he intending to tell us that it is a blessing to get sick and die under the judgment of God? Or is he speaking about blessing at one level, and then when we get to the specific problems at Corinth, he addresses the situation at another level? When I am preaching to a group of Christians, I address them *as saints*. I address them as Christians because that is what they are. In the call to worship, I do not welcome the saints to the worship of God, and then in an aside comment on the fact that it is a shame about the reprobates who got in. I address them all as saints because it is a Christian worship service. That is one level of discourse. Later in the week I may be counseling one of the members of the church who is completely defeated by some sin in his life and may come to the conclusion that he is not regenerate. And I would be bound to try to lead him to the understanding that he needs to be born again to God. That is another level of discourse. It is not a matter of truth shifting—it is rather a matter of avoiding the fallacy of equivocation, where terms admitting of different definitions are used with those different definitions in the course of the same argument. As in: *Stevie Wonder is blind. Love is blind. God is love. Stevie Wonder is God.* This is a fallacy because the words have different uses and definitions, and they are being treated in the argument as though they did not. The same thing happens with words and phrases like *saints* and *cup of blessing*. To recognize that such words have different uses and applications in different settings is to master a basic part of a basic logic course. And to be unable to do this, as Robbins appears to be unable, indicates that he cannot master the logical point (which is unlikely), or that he is too proud to admit that he has attacked me for teaching heretical things that I don't actually teach.

COMMON HERITAGE
JUNE 15, 2005

Phil Johnson has an interesting entry entitled "Machen Speaks From the Grave,"* and I am in sympathy with much of what he notes there. In an era of postmodern and relativistic mush, we ought to be wary of all ecumenical common-causers who think that moralism is the most important thing about religion. But while Machen was a staunch Protestant, as noted in Phil's post, he was no sectarian Protestant—and there is a difference. I would be interested to know how many of Phil's readers, who were able to say amen to that quote from Christianity and Liberalism, would be able to say amen to this one as well.

> Yet how great is the common heritage which unites the Roman Catholic Church, with its maintenance of the authority of Holy Scripture and with its acceptance of the great early creeds, to devout Protestants today! . . . The Church of Rome may represent a perversion of the Christian religion; but naturalistic liberalism is not Christianity at all. (Christianity and Liberalism, p. 52)

Common heritage? Was Machen wobbly?

WHITE HORSE INN
JUNE 27, 2005

I just got a chance to listen to an interview I did for the White Horse Inn with Michael Horton, along with their follow-up comments to that interview. For those who are interested, they can find it here†—although it costs a few bucks to download.

As far as the interview went, it was pretty much how I remember it. But the follow-up comments were new, and so I thought I should give just a few responses here.

* phillipjohnson.blogspot.com/2005/06/machen-speaks-from-grave.html

† Currently available here for White Horse Inn partners: whitehorseinn.org/show/an-interview-with-doug-wilson.

Before responding to particulars, I was reminded yet again how grateful I was for the opportunity to have the discussion in the first place. Despite the disagreements that remain, there was at least the recognition that this was an in-house Reformed discussion, and that the issues we were talking about were not matters of heresy. Compared to much of the debate thus far, this was a distinct improvement, and I'll take it. For that, my continued thanks go out to Michael Horton, and his discussion partners.

That said, there are three issues that were raised in the discussion after the interview that call for a response. First, while the movement of generic evangelicals toward the historic Reformed faith was applauded (and it really was), the downside of this trek to Geneva was described as the tendency of some newly-arrived Reformed folk to start rearranging the furniture as soon as they move in. For those who have lived in these Reformed habitations for some time, this can be more than a little unsettling. Of course, I am sympathetic with this concern in principle, and I am sure there *have* been refugees from goo-evangelicalism who have tracked all kinds of things in, which can be distressing to the curators of that great Persian carpet of Calvinist soteriology. But other interesting things can happen as well. For example, to change the image we are using, the new guy who starts to hang around the great and vast library of Reformed thought might find himself taking dusty books off the shelf and reading through them. He then says something like, "Hey, did you know that Calvin said thus n' such?" To which he hears a great deal of harrumphing and is told in solemn tones that the only authoritative thing Calvin actually said can be found in the glass display case in the hall outside. In other words, sometimes the new guy comes in because he is attracted to some feature of historic Reformed thought, and he then discovers to his dismay that there are many contemporary Reformed folks who are not aware that "Calvin said that." Not to put too fine a point on it, a man might be rejected by the current folks at Banner of Truth because he teaches things that he learned from a Banner of Truth book.

Secondly, I don't know how one of the commentators came away with the idea that we have some kind of "nervousness about affirming the confessions."

I explained in the interview that Christ Church was in the process of adopting a book of confessions, the doctrinal screen of which was the Westminster Confession. The vast majority of CREC churches have a historic Reformed confession of faith. I think this was an instance of us talking past each other.

And last, I think we were criticised in the discussion for two opposite and inconsistent faults. In the first place, we were dinged for what seemed to them to be convoluted and Byzantine explanations of doctrine, e.g., lack of clarity, and then, just moments later it was asserted that we should not be trying to do "theology by blog," meaning that detailed study, seminary, graduate studies was necessary. Now I am quite prepared to believe that my teaching is opaque, murky. And I am quite prepared to believe that my teaching is pithy, cogent, memorable, and succinct. Being a sinner, I would like to flatter myself on which it is. But I also have certain limitations, and Aristotle's observation that a toaster oven cannot simultaneously be not a toaster oven in the same way and in the same respect is one of them.

Anyhow, there it is.

HERETICAL COOTIES
AUGUST 5, 2005

I recently wrote to Steve Wilkins, saying that it was almost time for him to come up to Moscow again, bringing some of his heretical cooties with him. We were almost out, I said. He wrote back, somewhat too triumphantly I am afraid, with something about him having been declared fully orthodox by the Louisiana Presbytery, along with something else about me being a smarty pants. I am disconsolate. Who am I going to hang with now?

Seriously, the presbyterian form of church government is doing its work, which you can read about here*. And I have been examined by the presbytery of the CREC as well†. This kind of careful examination, deliberation and judiciousness is bad news, but only for rogue internet presbyterians (RIP).

* louisianapresbytery.com/AAT-FV_final.htm—The Louisiana Presbytery's report on Auburn Avenue Theology/Federal Vision, no longer available online.

† Currently available at wordmp3.com/details.aspx?id=1158.

ANTHONY BURGESS
SEPTEMBER 8, 2005

Anthony Burgess was one of the delegates to the Westminster Assembly, and was one of the men who helped to write that puppy. A very helpful correspondent wrote to me to note that in his defense of the covenant of works, Burgess repeatedly denies the idea of merit. He put it this way—"though it were a Covenant of works, it cannot be said to be of merit." (*Vindiciae Legis*, 1647, p. 129).

Maybe this can help us reach some common ground in our contemporary discussions. Should it be within the Reformed pale for someone to deny any covenant of merit, while affirming a covenant of works? If so, then we are making some headway. If not, then we have a problem with Burgess——a voting member of the Westminster Assembly. Could Anthony Burgess be ordained by the Mississippi Valley Presbytery?

SECURITY GUARDS AND BOUNCERS
OCTOBER 16, 2005

I appreciate Frank Turk's comments and input from time to time, and would commend his discussion[‡]of my recent posts on the minimum of orthodoxy required to get one through the pearly gates. I commend them, not because I agree, but because it is a pleasure to interact with someone who at least gets what you are saying, or is obviously making diligent efforts to do so. This, on any issue within a stone's throw of Auburn Avenue, is quite an achievement.

That said, let me toss a few more carrots into the crock pot of truth. Conscientious paedobaptists and credobaptists are both concerned about the purity of the visible church, and are both concerned about the practice of biblical discipline in the church. But the two groups go about trying maintain this purity in two different ways, which I may be able to illustrate with (what else?) an illustration. Godly credobaptists hire security to guard the front door. Godly paedobaptists hire bouncers.

‡ This seems to have been a reference to a few posts that can be found in Frank's October 2005 archives at centuri0n.blogspot.com/2005/10/.

Before getting to the question of which one is biblical, let us at least admit that each position is faced with peculiar temptations and challenges. The obvious concern is that the bouncers might not do their job well enough, leaving people inside the road house of Christendom who shouldn't be there. The other concern is that the security guards might exclude from the nightclub of Christendom individuals who had been specifically invited by the one giving the party.

In addressing which approach is more biblical, I offer the suggestions below with the recognition that I have been a participant in both approaches. I have been a *neck-deep* participant in both approaches, and when I abandoned the credobaptist position for the paedobaptist I was in principle abandoning the security guard approach for the bouncer approach. This took some time for me to sort out but the two approaches to discipline are implicit in the positions on baptism themselves.

As I consider the condition of the church as described in Scripture, I have to come to grips with the fact that God seems to like riff-raff. We are to invite all kinds to our banquet and not worry too much about the silver. This is not because God wants us to *remain* riff-raff—He has big plans for this motley collection of forgiven adulterers and winos, and so He cares very much for the qualifications of those who run His soup kitchen (to alter the metaphor). Training of His ministers is very important, along with a godly family, and a fierce love for orthodoxy. These are all crucial. But—and this is the glorious thing—God does not have high standards for the winos. "But I am all screwed up." "That's great! You qualify!"

I am not accusing conscientious adherents of the security guard approach of having evil motives, but I do suspect an element of safety-consciousness and prudence in all this that I think should be missing from our evangelism and ministry. Let's live on the edge for a bit. Let the tares grow too. The servants in Christ's parable (Christians) were more conscientious about wanting to weed the field than the farmer (Christ) was. This is the way it frequently is. We confuse our constant inclination to be fussy-mussy with diligence in rightousness. We have a hard time with taking Christ's teaching straight up the middle ("And the Lord said, 'Aw, what can a few weeds hurt?'") and so we tidy it up a bit.

EXPRESS WARRANT FOR PAEDOBAPTISM
OCTOBER 18, 2005

With regard to the baptism of infants, I no longer accept the requirement for "express warrant" that I used to hold to when I was baptistic in my convictions. The "express warrant" hermeneutic winds up prohibiting way too much—worship on the Lord's Day, women taking communion, and so on. At the same time, when I was baptistic I really wanted the question to be settled by an express statement of the Scripture. It would be really cool, thought I, if there were only a verse recording Paul baptizing an infant from the household of Demetrius.

When I was working through the material for my book on infant baptism, I came across what I believe is express warrant for infant baptism (by good and necessary consequence). Those who want the fuller development can find it in the book, but here is the outline of the argument. Like I said, I don't believe express warrant from the New Testament is necessary, but it turns out we do have express warrant. Gravy.

The New Testament identifies believing synagogues as churches. James identifies the two in his letter. If a man in filthy rags comes into your *synagogue* (James 2:2), don't do thus and such. And if anyone there is sick, let him call for the elders of the *church* (James 5:14). Now when Paul came to Jerusalem (where many of these believing synagogues were), he went out of his way to reassure everybody that he was *not* teaching Jews to discontinue circumcising their infants. This means, in the short form, that there were New Testament churches that had infant members. A circumcised infant in a believing synagogue was a member of that church. Now if Jewish churches/synagogues had infant members, on what grounds could we exclude infants from membership in Gentile churches? We could not exclude them. But we could say that circumcision was not required for them, because the sign and seal of the covenant was in the process of being changed to baptism. "For as many of you as have been baptized into Christ have put on Christ. There is neither Jew nor Greek . . . And if ye be Christ's, then are ye Abraham's seed, and heirs according to the promise" (Gal. 3:27–29).

The question for our baptistic brethren is this. Are you prepared to maintain that an infant brought to your congregation (formally and covenantally excluded) is in the same position as an infant brought to a believing synagogue in Jerusalem in AD 52? Not only would the believing synagogue not exclude such an infant, I believe that they would have difficulty even comprehending the concept of excluding the infants. And if there was such a generation-long uproar over the inclusion of the Gentiles, what would the commotion have been if the apostles really were teaching the Jews that not only must you start admitting the Gentile adults, but you must start excluding your own children? I have trouble believing that this would not have caused the Mother of all Theological Controversies. But there is not a word about such a controversy in the New Testament.

OBJECTIVITY AND EMERGENCE
DECEMBER 4, 2005

Frank Turk raised a question about the objectivity of the covenant and emergence, but at least had the presence of mind to realize it was a baptist question. This is not a detailed answer to the question, but it provides the initial outline of an answer.

I believe emergent errors need to be identified and opposed, just as I believe Roman Catholic errors need to be identified and opposed. This is a separate question from whether or not emergents or RCs have a covenantal obligation to abandon their errors, which they do. If they are baptized in the triune name, then they have an obligation to follow Jesus in true truth.

Now suppose someone came to our church from Brian McLaren's church, baptized by McLaren himself, and requested membership here. Would we require rebaptism? The answer—in line with the objectivity of the covenant—is absolutely not. I do not deny that McLaren has the authority to perform valid sacraments.

I will return to my standard illustration, which is that of the covenant of marriage. A man who is married to a woman is obligated to be faithful to her. But if he is not faithful to her, this does not mean that he is not "really" married to her——because that would mean, ironically, that he was not really being faithless to her. You have to be covenantally obligated to be covenantally faithless.

People who chase after various winds of doctrine should stop it, regardless of what they are. They should remain true to the faith once delivered to the saints. But if they do not stop it, this does not change the objectivity of their obligation. So, to take an easier case than McLaren, let us consider an overt infidel who happens to be baptized. He is a Christian in one sense (in terms of the objectivity of his covenant obligations) and not a Christian in another (because of his faithlessness).

If a cheating husband repented and came home to his wife after years of infidelity, and she forgave him, and said to him, "Today, you have become my husband," we would all know what she meant. He had to have been a husband before his repentance in order to cheat, but when he repented of cheating, he "became a husband." A lot of faithless covenant members have "become Christians" the same way.

A lot of the problem is caused (in my view) by the evangelical absolutizing of the noun *Christian*. But the word can be used in more than one way.

JANUARY–JUNE 2006

PAUL AND JAMES
JANUARY 3, 2006

Not that I want to beat a dead horse or anything, but I would be interested in feedback from any critics of Auburn Avenue stuff on the following statement. Would you all be comfortable with this expression of the relationship of faith and works, Paul and James?

> What are we to do with James's apparent contradiction of Paul? In James 2:14–26 the writer is apparently in direct conflict with Paul. According to Paul, justification is by faith alone and not by the works of the law-see for example, Gal. 2:14–21; according to James, a man is justified by works and not only by faith (James 2:24). Upon closer examination, however, the contradiction is seen to be one of form and not of substance; and like other apparent contradictions in the Bible it serves only to reveal the Scripture combination of rich variety with perfect unity.
>
> So what is meant by faith? According to James faith without works is dead; according to Paul faith is all sufficient for salvation. But what does James mean by faith? The answer is perfectly plain. The faith which James is condemning is a mere intellectual assent which has no effect upon conduct. The demons also, he says, have that sort of faith, and yet evidently they are not saved (James 2:19). What Paul means by faith is something entirely different; *it is not a mere intellectual assent*

to certain propositions, but an attitude of the entire man by which the whole life is entrusted to Christ. In other words, the faith that James is condemning is not the faith that Paul is commending.

The solution of the whole problem is provided by Paul himself in a single phrase. In Gal. 5:6, he says, "For in Christ Jesus neither circumcision availeth anything, nor uncircumcision; but faith working through love." "*Faith working through love*" is the key to an understanding both of Paul and James. The faith about which Paul has been speaking is not the idle faith which James condemns, but a faith that works. It works itself out through love. And what love is Paul explains in the whole last division of Galatians. It is no mere emotion, but the actual fulfilling of the whole moral law. "For the whole law is fulfilled in one word, even in this: Thou shalt love thy neighbor as thyself" (Gal. 5:14). Paul is fully as severe as James against a faith that permits men to continue in sin. The faith about which he is speaking is a faith that receives the Spirit who gives men power to lead a holy life.

And so what is meant by works? Moreover, as the faith which James condemns is different from the faith which Paul commends, so also the works which James commends are different from the works which Paul condemns. Paul is speaking about "works of the law"-that is, works which are intended to earn salvation by fulfilling the law through human effort. James says nothing in chapter 2:14–26 about works of the law. The works of which he is speaking are works that spring from faith and are the expression of faith. Abraham offered Isaac as a sacrifice only because he believed God. His works are merely an evidence that his faith was real. Such works as that are insisted upon by Paul in every epistle. Without them no man can inherit the kingdom of God (Gal. 5:21). Only-and here again James would have been perfectly agreed-such works as that can spring only from faith. They can be accomplished not by human effort, but only by the reception of the power of God.

> We see then the value of James. If James had had the epistles of Paul before him he would no doubt have expressed himself differently. He might have said not that faith without works is dead, but that faith without works is not true faith at all. This is what he clearly means. But the expression of his thought is all the more poignant because it is independent. His stern, terse insistence upon moral reality in religion, of which the passage just considered is only a typical example, provides a valuable supplement to the rest of the New Testament. Of itself it would be insufficient; but taken in connection with the Gospels and with Paul it contributes a necessary fiber to the woven cord of Christian character.

CHARGES AND SPECIFICATIONS
FEBRUARY 9, 2006

It is about time that somebody realized the *source* of all the trouble. High time we brought old Jean Calvin of St. Peter's Reformed Church in Geneva up on charges*. Somebody had to do it. HT: Peter Leithart

THE SCARECROW'S HAT
MARCH 23, 2006

One of the regular charges leveled against Auburn Avenue types is that we are paving the way for our folks to go over to Rome, or, mayhap to the *other* church, farther to the east, that has apostolic credentials going all the way back. Unless you count the Copts. And the Armenian Orthodox. Bunch of others too. Keeping track of all the groups that go all the way back is almost as hard as keeping track of all the Presbyterian microbrew continuing church movements that go all the way back to Thomas Chalmers. Oh, and I forgot the Baptists. Their trail of blood goes all the way back.

But I got distracted. One of the charges we have to answer from our critics is that our Calvinistic sacramentalism (say) necessarily sets a course for Rome. In vain do we point out what Jean Calvin himself taught, and that he did it coming *out* of Rome. In vain do we quote the Westminster Catechisms on the

* invicemindeo.blogspot.com/2006/02/presbytery-memorial-to-ga.html

subject (in which those sturdy divines apparently took time out from their pilgrimage to the Holy Father in the Vatican to call the sacraments effectual means of salvation).

I got distracted again. We have to answer this charge, right? And every once in a while, somebody in *our* ranks buys the argument and bolts for Rome, or parts farther east. The fact that this happened is then trumpeted by those who are alarmed by us as evidence for the claim, and we have to answer the charge again.

This requires a lot of further development, but allow me just two brief observations here. We recently took a poll in our congregation, and from the significant number of those who responded, it appears that about ten percent of our congregation is made up of former Roman Catholics. I know, Evangelicals and Catholics Together deplored sheep stealing and all that, but I do not intend to try to keep people away from a genuine relationship with Christ for the sake of ecumenical dialogue. The dialogue is fine, but we must understand what it can and cannot do, and not stop preaching the gospel in the meantime. As much as the evangelical cliche of having a "personal relationship with Jesus" is overdone and wrongly done in our circles, the fact remains that many thousands of Protestants today grew up God-fearing Roman Catholics but became acquainted with God for the first time in a personal way when they went off to college and wound up rooming with a kid who was with Campus Crusade.

We rejoice that Roman Catholicism and Eastern Orthodoxy are still robustly Trinitarian. These two one true, holy apostolic churches do have many things going for them. But at the same time, they are encrusted with a *lot* of man-made traditions which have supplanted the Word of God and obscured the gospel. Consequently, the Reformation must never be considered as a ghastly mistake, but a necessary, Spirit-led *reformation* of the life and liturgy of the Church. And so, as much as we hate to lose anyone to these groups, and treat it as a significant back-sliding (even when not exacerbated by other factors) on the whole, taking the long view, the "balance of trade" is still heavily in favor of the Protestants.

My second point needs to be said some time, and so I will say it here. When one of our guys converts to Rome or the East and says that an essential part of their pilgrimage was the stepping stone of Auburn Avenue theology, the line goes something like this: "Couldn't have made it here without those Federal Vision guys!" My one request is that somebody get me the name of this fellow's new parish priest so I can call him up and warn him. "Hey, heads up. We are sending over a guy *who pays no attention at all to what his teachers try to tell him*." In fact, one of the guys we lost to Rome wasted very little time in denouncing John Paul II as a heretic and discovering that the papal throne was empty. All such things remind me very little of classic Roman Catholic doctrine and remind me a great deal of bottle-rocket anabaptism.

There are, of course, thoughtful converts from Geneva to Rome (wrong, in my view, but still thoughtful). But headstrong men who won't receive instruction are not in that number. Those who accept the wooden analysis offered by baptistic antisacramentalists, only to embrace the caricature instead of running from it in fear as was intended, are demonstrating one thing beyond any reasonable doubt. They cannot faithfully represent or follow out what they clearly never understood. All they do is provide our adversaries a few extra snatches of straw for the scarecrow's hat.

DOCTRINALLY BILINGUAL
MAY 8, 2006

I have come to a conclusion. I have been in the midst of doctrinal fraci (what's the plural of *fracus*?) because I am bilingual. I speak both TR *and* FV. When I talk with others who are bilingual, we get along famously, and I feel like peace is going to break out across the Reformed world any minute now. There are TRs who are bilingual, and there are FVs who are bilingual, and God bless 'em all. Group hug! But there are, alas, members of each party who speak their own provincial dialect, and that is it, and you had better pronounce shibboleth *right*, darn it. The TRs who are like this can hear Calvin quoted and think it's the pope on a bad day. And FVs who are like this forget that it was dispensational baptists who kept the Christian faith *alive* in our nation over the course of the last century.

PRESBYTERIANS AND PRESBYTERIANS TOGETHER MAY 11, 2006

I would like to direct your attention to an important statement here*. A group called *Presbyterians and Presbyterians Together* has drafted a statement, and they are inviting you to attach your signature to it. I would strongly encourage the same thing.

The importance of this can hardly be overstated. This is not an abandonment of necessary debate within the Reformed world, but rather a commitment to conduct theological and doctrinal debate (within our confessional boundaries) in a particular way. The bottom line of that "particular way" is a commitment to avoid rash and intemperate judgments concerning those who share a commitment to the historic Reformed faith. In other words, don't drop the H-bomb on your brother.

As I have argued elsewhere, the Reformed tradition has contained diverse elements from the beginning. That continues down to the present—which is why we have the URC, the OPC, the PCA, the OCRC, the CREC, and so on. We can have our various distinctives, and even think that they are important enough to guard during presbytery exams, without consigning any of those who differ to Dante's fifth level. So please, check this site out.

WELL, AT LEAST SOMEBODY UNDERSTOOD US MAY 14, 2006

I finally got around to reading Joseph Minich's paper† on the Federal Vision and the New Perspective on Paul. Maybe you heard about it too. I ran it off when it first came out, and then after that I threw it in my briefcase and

* presbyterianstogether.org/home.html, no longer available.

† Minich's paper, "Within the Bounds of Orthodoxy? An Examination of *Both* the Federal Vision and the New Perspective on Paul," is currently available here: joelgarver.com/docs/Within_the_Bounds_of_Orthodoxy.pdf

hauled it around for a while (trying to earn me some of that seductive medieval merit, which I actually did, but then the whole thing fell through because Westminster West wouldn't accept the credits), and I then finally got around to reading it. What a delightful business.

Reading this paper was timely too, because I have to get myself spiritually prepared for when Guy Waters's book‡, *The Federal Vision and Covenant Theology: Which Shall It Be?* comes out. Actually I made up the subtitle, but not by much.

BEYOND THE FIVE SOLAS
MAY 26, 2006

It is important for us to consider recent events in our town and around the country in the light of God's Word. The Lord has been very kind to us thus far, but part of our responsibility is to *understand* His kindness, and not just to receive it. The Lord has given us the great privilege of holding a contested part of a field of battle, but part of our duty lies in understanding what has just recently transpired and understanding it in all wisdom.

> Would to God ye could bear with me a little in my folly: and indeed bear with me. For I am jealous over you with godly jealousy: for I have espoused you to one husband, that I may present you as a chaste virgin to Christ. But I fear, lest by any means, as the serpent beguiled Eve through his subtilty, so your minds should be corrupted from the simplicity that is in Christ. For if he that cometh preacheth another Jesus, whom we have not preached, or if ye receive another spirit, which ye have not received, or another gospel, which ye have not accepted, ye might well bear with him. (2 Cor. 11:1–4)

> And they continued stedfastly in the apostles' doctrine and fellowship, and in breaking of bread, and in prayers . . . And they, continuing daily with one accord in the temple, and breaking bread from house to

‡ Currently available on Amazon: amazon.com/dp/B004K6MO0O.

> house, did eat their meat with gladness and singleness of heart, Praising God, and having favour with all the people. And the Lord added to the church daily such as should be saved. (Acts 2: 42, 46–47)

The gospel is not overengineered. Consider what we learn in these passages. Paul sarcastically notes that adultery and treachery are complicated, but fidelity and loyalty are simple. The serpent came to Eve in all subtlety, and this is contrasted with the "simplicity that is in Christ." Other Christs, other gospels, other spirits are easy enough to put up with (in this fallen world), but they are *complicated.* Rationalizations are always tangled, and sin breeds rationalization. But true simplicity does what the early Christians did. They accept what the apostles taught, period, they fellowship with one another, period, they take the Lord's Supper together, period, and they pray together, period. This brings the glorious result—gladness and simplicity of heart, praise to God and favor from outsiders. And God uses this to bring salvation to those who are being saved.

So what is at issue? One of the obvious concerns that we should have before us is whether all the controversies that the Lord has brought to us over the course of the last few years have anything in common. And the answer is *yes*, they do. In fact, at bottom *they are all really the same controversy.* Whenever the Spirit moves in the history of the church, He does so in a way that sweeps away all our carnal complications and restores that primitive and apostolic sense of gladness and simplicity of heart. But, in the meantime, the slogans of a previous period of simplicity have often been transformed (in the hands of trained professionals) into something that only a scribe could love.

We need to get beyond the five *solas.* Initially some might worry that this entails an abandonment of the glorious revival that came in what we call the Reformation, but nothing could be further from the truth. But it *is* an abandonment of much of jargon that has grown up around the *solas.* Loving the original ship does not mean loving the barnacles. Over against the errors of so many false religionists, we still affirm what the *solas* originally meant. Salvation is by Christ alone (*solus Christus*), not by Christ and some kind of creaturely help. Salvation is by grace alone (*sola gratia*) and not some mixture of grace and merit, grace and works, grace and ungrace, or grace and brownie points. Salvation is received through faith alone (*sola fide*) and not some mixture of faith and works. We understand all this through ultimate reliance on Scripture alone (*sola Scriptura*) and not through some combination of the Word of God and the words of men. And all this comes together to glorify God alone for all that He has done (*soli Deo gloria*). All of this is most important, and most cool.

But all glorious confessions of faith can be attacked in two ways. One is the assault from without (persecution), but the other is corruption from within. In the grip of Enlightenment individualism, pietism, sentimentalism, and so forth, in our day the meaning of the *solas* has been turned aside from their earlier and more glorious meaning. Now they are *solo Christus* (just me and Jesus), *solo gratia* (narrow, sectarian grace), *solo fide* (when I "prayed the prayer"), *solo Scriptura* (just me and my Bible), and *solo Deo gloria* (God gets all the glory for saving me, and *maybe* somebody else). Now please realize that the word *solo* here constitutes a bad macaronic pun, and not a serious attempt at matching gender, number, and case. No letters from the Latinists, please.

The need of the hour is to restore the five *solas*, and get them up out of the narrow crevice some folks have pushed them into. We need the five *totas*. Our answer to such things must be simple, and not complicated. The claims of Jesus Christ, Lord of heaven and earth, are necessarily and always total, never partial. The *solo* tendency always tends to restrict the work of God to just a *part* or *portion* of reality, and this makes the rest of reality incomprehensible—and obviously complicated, with great "subtlety" required of those who seek to understand the godless part of the universe. But there is no godless part of the universe, and so to all this we reply with *totus Christus* (all Christ and *all* His people), *tota gratia* (to be a creature is grace, to be saved is more grace), *tota fide* (we are saved by faith from first to last), *tota Scriptura* (we do not pit the Old Testament against the New, or law against grace), and *toti Deo gloria* (all the glory for all things goes to God). God save us from all partialism.

THE OPC REPORT ON THE FEDERAL VISION
JUNE 18, 2006

The OPC report on the Federal Vision is being considered at their General Assembly this week. Because of this, I want to say just a few things for the record. It is not that my opinion matters all that much, but I feel free to make these comments because I am labeled as one of the players in this report, where it says, "Though a number of men have come to be identified as FV advocates, it is the Auburn Avenue speakers, together with those who have published essays in *Backbone of the Bible* and *The Federal Vision*, whom we have identified as those chiefly representing the FV and whose works we address herein." And because I show up in the footnotes here and there in this report, it should not be considered out of line if I respond briefly.

The committee qualifies its critique of my positions *somewhat*. "Perhaps the most fruitful interaction between an FV proponent and his critics has occurred on the part of Douglas Wilson, who, in being examined by his judicatory (at his request), affirmed the covenant of works, with some qualifications, as well as the imputation of the active obedience of Christ in our justification" (p. 1659). And a little later, they allowed that I was one of the "more moderate FV men" (p. 1684). But given the fact that they were aware of my examination at the CREC presbytery, some of the direct critiques they offer in the body of this report seem a little bit strange.

Right near the end of the report, we have a summary of the OPC's critique of the FV. Speaking only for myself, I would like to hold this template up against my own positions, as I actually hold them, in my own words, in my native habitat. As I do this, I think it is fair to say that my position on virtually each of these points is clearly laid out in my published writing on this subject, indicating that I do think the OPC committee should have been a little more careful.

The committee summary is below, and my brief comments are interspersed in italics.

> The committee believes that the following points that are held by some or the other advocates of FV are out of accord with Scripture and our doctrinal standards:

1. Pitting Scripture and Confession against each other.
No. Christ Church in Moscow incorporates the reading of the Heidelberg Catechism into each Lord's Day service. The doctrinal stand of our church is a Book of Confessions which includes the original Westminster Confession of Faith. The WCF is the standard that is used in case of doctrinal disputes. As part of our doctrinal and liturgical growth and development, we adopted the HC in worship and the WCF as the doctrinal standard after the beginning of the FV controversy.

2. Regarding the enterprise of systematic theology as inherently rationalistic.
No. Systematic theology is inescapable, unavoidable, and it is not inherently rationalistic. Doctrinal Euclidianism is a possibility, but the temptations in that direction are always present because systematics cannot be avoided. The only question is whether our systematics will be obedient and subservient to Scripture or not.

3. A mono-covenantalism that sees one covenant, originating in the intra-trinitarian fellowship, into which man is invited, thus flattening the concept of covenant and denying the distinction between the covenant of works and the covenant of grace.
No. I see two covenants made with man, one that is prelapsarian and the second postlapsarian. I maintain that the covenant of life in the Garden did not depend on Adam's raw merit, to be sure, but this is not the same as saying that there is only one covenant. Any covenant that God makes with man will reflect His character, and so the question of one or two covenants is logically separate from whether or not the intra-trinitarian fellowship is covenantal. The committee acknowledged my position on this.

4. Election as primarily corporate and eclipsed by covenant.
No. Corporate election is primarily corporate. Individual election is primarily individual.

5. Seeing covenant as only conditional.

No. God's covenant decree to save the elect is unconditional. The covenant as it is manifested in history is conditional (as seen by us), but this must be sharply distinguished from our affirmation (as believed by us) that the salvation of God's elect is an absolutely monergistic affair.

6. A denial of the covenant of works and of the fact that Adam was in a relationship with God that was legal as well as filial.

No. The covenant of life (works) was filial and gracious, and it was also legal. "The day you eat of the fruit of the tree in the midst of the Garden you shall surely die." The committee acknowledged my position on this.

7. A denial of a covenant of grace distinct from the covenant of works.

No. I affirm the existence of a covenant of grace distinct from a covenant of life (works). The committee acknowledged my position on this.

8. A denial that the law given in Eden is the same as that more fully published at Mt. Sinai and that it requires perfect obedience.

Yes. I do deny this. The WCF identifies the law that was published at Sinai as part of the administration of the covenant of grace. But I also believe that the "righteous that is of the law" (a certain religious mentality) distorted the Mosaic code and turned it into a system of self-salvation, which of course, God being who He is, would require perfect obedience.

9. Viewing righteousness as relational not moral.

No. These do not exclude one another. My relationship with my wife is both relational and moral. It cannot be moral unless it relational, and it cannot be relational unless it is moral.

10. A failure to make clear the difference between our faith and Christ's.

No. I insist that we keep this distinction clear. But at the same time, because I affirm the imputation of Christ's life of perfect obedience (both active and passive) this would include the root motivation of His obedience, which would be His perfect faith. This is part of what is imputed to us, is it not? My faith is derivative from Christ's faith, and distinct from it, but it is entirely dependent upon it.

11. A denial of the imputation of the active obedience of Christ in our justification.
No. I affirm the imputation of Christ's active obedience in our justification. The committee acknowledged my position on this.

12. Defining justification exclusively as the forgiveness of sins.
No. I do not define justification exclusively as forgiveness of sins. Justification has the eschatological element of adoption. It also involves vindication. It involves resurrection. It includes the Gentiles in Israel.
13. The reduction of justification to Gentile inclusion.
No. And incidentally, note the contradiction between #12 and #13. My interest is to broaden our understanding of justification without taking away anything from the historic Reformed understanding of an individual's justification. That I continue to affirm.

14. Including works (by use of 'faithfulness,' 'obedience,' etc.) in the very definition of faith.
No. To include faithfulness in the very nature of living faith is not to intrude works. Faithful faith justifies. Faithless faith does not.

15. Failing to affirm an infallible perseverance and the indefectability of the grace.
No. I affirm an infallible perseverance for the elect, and I affirm that the effectual grace given to the elect is indefectable.

16. Teaching baptismal regeneration.
Yes, but only in the sense that the WCF plainly does. My argument for this is laid out elsewhere, but let me just make the point from a quotation from the Directory of Worship cited in a footnote to this report. "The prayer following baptism is particularly noteworthy, beseeching the Lord that if the

infant should live 'and attain the years of discretion, that the Lord would so teach him by his word and Spirit, and make his baptism effectual to him.'" The report goes on to say that the Directory asks the Lord to effectuate "in the baptized that which was signified in their baptism." But that is not what the prayer asks for. It asks that the baptism be made effectual, not that which was signified by the baptism to be made effectual.

17. Denying validity of the concept of the invisible church.
No. I do not deny the validity of the visible/invisible church distinction. I affirm it. But I do question its sufficiency as a solitary description of the Church.
18. A overly-objectively sacramental efficacy that downplays the need for faith and that tends toward an *ex opere operato* view of the sacraments.
No. I do not downplay the need for faith. I jump up and down on the need for faith. If you die without faith in Christ, you go to Hell. The efficacy of the sacraments for blessing depends entirely on faith. The sacraments are only efficacious apart from faith in the sense that they increase the condemnation of faithless covenant members. To whom much is given, much is required.

19. Teaching paedocommunion.
Yes.

20. Ecclesiology that eclipses and swallows up soteriology.
No. Ecclesiology is of course the study of corporate soteriology. But ecclesiology does not swallow up the study of what happens in what might be called individual soteriology. How could it?

So, taking these twenty points, and assigning them five points each, if this were a test that the OPC committee took on what my views actually were, I am afraid they only scored a thirty-five percent out of a possible one hundred. I don't know how they did with the other FV guys, but that is frankly not very good.

JULY 2006

GUY WATERS

JULY 13, 2006

Well, the time has finally come. I have received my copy of Guy Waters's new book, entitled *The Federal Vision and Covenant Theology: A Comparative Analysis**. It is my intent to blog my way through this book, offering my thoughts on this general subject for the edification of a bemused Christendom, and to do so whenever one of three conditions pertain: a. I am amused b. I am about to burst a blood vessel on my forehead, or c. I need to set the record, as they say, straight.

I will begin with the Foreword by Cal Beisner. Cal says that when it comes to soteriology, the FV is a "hybrid of three components." Those three components he identifies as a modified Amyraldianism, a modified Arminianism, and a modified Roman infusionism.

> Original Amyraldianism posited a hypothetically universal atonement; the Federal Visionists hold that the atonement is hypothetically for all in the historical-objective covenant but effective only for the "elect" . . . Original Arminianism affirmed that Christ died as a substitute to pay the penalty for the sins of all people. The Federal Visionists will affirm that Christ died to pay the penalty for the sins of all in "the covenant," including some who wind up in hell . . . . The third is a modified

* Guy Prentiss Waters, *The Federal Vision and Covenant Theology: A Comparative Analysis* (Phillipsburg, NJ: P&R 2006).

> Roman infusionism. We are "justified" at first by grace through faith but at last by the merit . . . of the works produced in and through us by God. (pp. viii-ix).

So let me say what I think about those three things. No, I insist. With regard to the atonement and Amyraldianism, I believe that Jesus Christ, by His death on the cross, absolutely *secured* the salvation of an innumerable host, each member of that host being known by name to God before the foundation of the world. I believe that the number of those so known and numbered by God can neither be increased or diminished by anything conceived by the mortal mind of man. With regard to the atonement and Arminianism, I believe that when Christ died to pay the penalty for someone, the penalty for that someone is actually paid. As a result, there is no one in hell for whom that redemptive penalty was paid. With regard to modified Roman infusionism, I hold that justification results from a legal declaration from God, as a result of which the righteousness of Jesus Christ is imputed to me and Cal both. Since this is an accurate summary of my positions, the conclusion is inescapable. With respect to this modified Amyraldianism, modified Arminianism, and modified Roman infusionism, I have modified them all right—modified them right into Reformed orthodoxy.

I hold that, before the heavens and earth were created, God freely and unalterably ordained whatsoever was to come to pass, and this would include every aspect of every man's salvation. I have my theological toolbox right here. What phrase could we use to describe this position? I know! Modified Arminianism! That won't confuse *anybody*.

On to the next problem.

> In sacramentology, Federal Visionists offer a modified sacerdotal sacramentalism that borders on affirming the Roman Catholic doctrine of *ex opere operato*. The sacraments are objectively effective means of *converting*, not only of sanctifying, grace because they are administered by properly ordained people in the community of the faithful. (p. ix)

Now I have to confess that I am not as gifted as some writers are in detecting juxtaposed ironies. But then, sometimes things are just handed to you on a platter. Just a few pages later, Guy Waters writes in the Preface:

> My daughters are, through my wife, descended from men and women who sat under and, I trust, profited from the ministries of Solomon Stoddard and Jonathan Edwards. It is my fervent hope that the biblical doctrine preached from that pulpit in Northampton will, by the blessing of the Holy Spirit, thrive in the Reformed churches of my own and my young daughter's generations. (pp. xv-xvi)

Solomon Stoddard. Solomon Stoddard. That name rings a bell. Who was he? I am wandering around here among these tombs that somebody built for the prophets, trying to make out the inscriptions on the plaques. Here it is!—he was that Reformed minister who believed that the Lord's Supper was *a converting ordinance.* And comes now Guy Waters, praying that the biblical doctrine preached from that pulpit will once again be preached in Reformed churches to his daughters' generation. Well, okay. We're *trying.*

And lest I get into more hot water than I already am, this is as good a time as any to say that the previous line was an attempt to be funny, and not a serious attempt to align myself with the Halfway Covenant. Lots of problems there, created by over-scrupulous Reformed types. But I will say this—is it okay to read what our Reformed fathers wrote and preached back in the day? And learn from them? Or must we simply invoke their names with pious looks on our faces?

We got distracted there. Let me also point out that I do not understand what it might mean that we "*border on*" affirming something. If a black swatch and a white swatch are placed on the table side by side, does the black "border on" the white? If I *deny* the RC doctrine of the *ex opere operato* efficacy of the Mass (which, actually, I do with enthusiasm), does this denial "border on" affirming it? Apparently so.

Now, if we are allowed to radically redefine the phrase, I believe that there is an *ex opere operato* aspect to the Lord's Supper. Whenever someone comes to the Supper, *something* happens(either blessing or condemnation). But I deny the Roman doctrine with regard to what happens (as Cal defines it in his footnote 4). But both Cal and I affirm that when an unworthy recipient comes to the Table, such a person is, by his "unworthy coming thereunto . . . guilty of the body and blood of the Lord, to their own damnation" (WCF 29.8). *Something* happens. And, as we have just now learned, if we think something (anything at all) happens, our denial of Roman *ex operate operato* efficacy somehow borders on affirming it. These things are hard to follow, but it would appear that Cal is now in trouble too, right along with us.

He continues. He was recently reading a book on developments in Catholic/Protestant relations, and while reading one section, he kind of free associated.

> In ecclesiology, the Federal Visionists are more nearly Roman Catholic than Reformed. (p. ix)

What sorts of things were in that quotation? What brought this about? Well, for example, there was the sentiment that no one can have God for a Father who does not have the Church as Mother. This is the problematic doctrine taught by that pestilent troublemaker Calvin in his *Institutes* (4.1.1), and . . . wait a sec. Did we get the sides switched again?

> . . . so also the Federal Visionists' ecclesiology, by taking the metaphor of Christ and the church as Head and body literally rather than metaphorically, nearly equates Christ and the church and so is the foundation of both their soteriology and their sacramentology. (p. x)

So now I confess that I am now officially lost. Take *Head* and *body* literally? What is that supposed to mean? As opposed to metaphorically? Is Cal saying that we are supposed to believe that Jesus is a literal head, neck up, and the body of Christ is the rest of the body, literally, neck down? I do not know where he got this, but I am confident he never got it from anything I wrote, said, thought, or dreamed in a pizza dream. It is not a literal bond. It is not a metaphor. The bond between the Bridegroom and the Bride is a *covenant* bond.

Okay, so Guy Water's book is not exactly off to a roaring start.

> But it isn't clear just what it means to the Federal Visionists to remain faithful. One thing is crystal clear: it doesn't just mean one believes the gospel, or, in the words of the Westminster Confession, that he rests 'upon Christ alone for justification, sanctification, and eternal life, by virtue of the covenant of grace," for faith*fulness* means something other than faith. (p. x)

One comment more, and I am done for the day. First, faith rests upon Christ alone. Amen. Faith rests upon Christ alone for justification. Amen again. Faith rests upon Christ alone for sanctification . . . now wait just Romanist minute! What is sanctification doing in here, right inside the defintion of saving faith (WCF 14.2)? One of the *principal* acts of *saving* faith is to rest upon Christ alone for *faithfulness*, I mean, *sanctification*? John Robbins, call your office.

MOSES THE BLENDER
JULY 16, 2006

Chapter Two of Waters's book is on covenant and biblical history. This post will not go on and on, but for two cents, it could.

> What is clear is Wilson's emphasis upon grace as the hallmark of the first covenant and as the principle that unites the first and second covenants. (p. 31)

This is true enough. I believe that God is a gracious God, and that all His dealings with His children are necessarily gracious. This emphasis is on grace from first to last, grace above and grace below, grace before the fall and grace after, grace to the uttermost and amen, and this is an emphasis that needs a name. Why not neolegalism?

But the fact that God is gracious if He makes a gracious covenant with unfallen Adam, which Adam broke, and then another gracious covenant with fallen men in the second Adam, which Christ kept, does not mean these two gracious covenants have to be the same thing. If I graciously give ten dollars to Smith, and twenty years later, I graciously give twenty clams to Murphy, does it follow from this that I am somehow trying to flatten the differences between Smith and Murphy? If I graciously rent one house on Elm Street to Smith and then five years later rent one to Smith's kids on Maple, am I trying to flatten the differences between the houses? I deny it, but what do I know?

Waters quotes me saying that faith is necessary in both covenants (the covenant of life, and the covenant of grace). And this is accurate. I said it. I believe it. "The condition is always to believe God" (p. 32). But then this is the inference Waters draws from this:

> Wilson, therefore places great emphasis upon continuity, not contrast, between the first covenant and subsequent covenants. (p. 32)

Well, if we are talking about the presence of God's grace and the need for man to respond in faith, I do. But if we are talking about the presence of sin, I don't. Note that Waters says that I place "great emphasis" on continuity. Why? Because I said the "condition is always to believe God." But then, just a little bit later, Waters says this: "No Reformed theologian has denied that Adam was to exercise faith in the covenant of works . . . covenantal blessing would come by obedience to the moral law and to the command not to eat of the Tree of Knowledge of Good and Evil" (p. 43).

So then, Adam was supposed to have been obedient to God's requirement (which I hold), and he was to have done so by means of exercising faith (as I hold, along with all other Reformed theologians apparently). So what is the beef? If all Reformed theologians hold that Adam had faith in his covenant, and we have faith in this one, how is that not flattening the differences between the covenants. Both have faith in them there. Strong element of continuity!

Waters even acknowledges that I stress the radical distinction between the older covenants and New Covenant.

> While Wilson stresses that the movement into the New Covenant was as bold and as radical as a movement from death to resurrection . . . ." (p. 33)

True enough. I do. And I stress that the covenant with Adam was a distinct covenant from the covenant that God established to secure *our* salvation. But stress these things as I may, it all avails for naught. Least around these parts. Because this is how Waters summarizes my take on the covenants, and he does this with virtually no argumentation.

> In summary, then, we have a flattening of a confessional understanding of the relationship among the covenants. (p. 33)

He says that I flatten the covenants because I maintain that both of them were exhibitions of the grace of God. But he acknowledges that Adam had to have faith. And he acknowledges that there were *aspects* of grace in the covenant of works. I simply have one question for Waters. If Adam had withstood the temptation offered by the serpent in the garden, would he have had an obligation to thank God for his deliverance. If he had been delivered from the fall, would God have done it?

One other thing. Waters acknowledges that the Mosaic law was gracious, and not a flat-out recapitulation of the covenant of works. This is something he pretty much has to do, seeing how the Bible describes it that way. But he needs to get a recapitulation in there somehow, probably because of the people he is hanging out with.

> Does this mean, however, that he could not have spoken of the covenant of works surfacing in some sense in the law—to which his opponents looked to establish the grounds of their justification? (p. 47)

In other words, the covenant of grace is there on the surface, which is what the Westminster Confession says that law of Moses was——an administration of the covenant of grace. But, from time to time, there are sightings of the covenant of works, like the Loch Ness Monster. These sightings enable Paul's opponents to establish the grounds of their justification on some other basis than grace, because they saw the monster.

Now I ask you. Who is flattening covenants around here? I hold the covenant of life was made with Adam, was contingent on his perfect obedience, and he forfeited the blessings promised in it by his disobedience. Because of that sin, and completely new state of affairs ensued, and God (whose gracious character had not changed) makes a new covenant through which He promises to redeem man from the wreckage he made of the first covenant. One gracious God, two covenants, separated by a definitive moment in time——when Adam took the prohibited fruit. Easy to keep them distinct.

But Waters has the Mosaic covenant, the covenant of grace, just sitting there all placid like, and this covenant of works keeps *surfacing* in it, scaring and misleading the Pharisees. This is not just a cute debating trick. Waters is the one who has flattened the covenants. The law of Moses, what is it? If he says that in one sense it is the covenant of grace (which the WCF says) and in another sense it is the covenant of works, who is the flattener?

My point, which Waters interacted with and dismissed, was that the law of Moses was the covenant of grace. But the legalistic hearts of the Pharisees insisted upon seeing another kind of covenant in there, a covenant of works. This was an error God anticipated, and typified in the person of Hagar. She was a type of those who would break covenant by seeing the covenant with Moses as being anything but gracious. Waters dismissed this as "subjectivist," which means that he must hold that the covenant with Moses is simultaneously the covenant of grace in one way and the covenant of works in another, and is both kinds of covenant together *objectively*, all in one big confusing bundle.

I of course deny that I have flattened these two covenants. But I go further. I assert that Waters himself has gone out of his way to jumble the two covenants all together. And he has done so while accusing others of getting these two covenants mixed up. What would he accuse us of if we affirmed a covenant of works with Adam, but said that the covenant of grace kept mysteriously "surfacing" in it?

Now frankly, I don't mind that much if Waters and others mysteriously make Moses the blender in which the covenant of grace and covenant of works are pureed. I have more pressing things to get worked up about. But if he does this in the chapter where he is charging us with this very offense, and it is being done in such a way as to propagate *a completely unnecessary controversy in the Reformed world*, then I have to say that I do mind. And I do.

THREE EXTRA EGGS IN THE PUDDING
JULY 26, 2006

After nine days on the road, occupied with this and that, I have just now had opportunity on the plane back to Idaho to comment on Guy Waters's next chapter, the chapter on "covenant and election."

In order to work through this, we should begin by taking note of what it really means to read election through the lens of the covenant, as opposed to reading the covenant through the lens of election. It appears to me that a great deal of the confusion in this debate is confusion at just this point. For example, after lengthy analysis, Waters chides John Barach for his quasi-Arminianism:

> It is in this sense, notwithstanding his profession of the Reformed doctrine of (decretal) election, that we may say that Barach's overall doctrine of election is Arminian or at least semi-Arminian. (p. 120)

And this, *after* Waters *quoted* Barach saying this: "God has eternally predestined an unchanging number of people out of the whole world to eternal glory with Christ" (p. 112).

To see election through a covenant lens does not mean to define decretal election as though it were identical with covenant election. The *fact* of decretal election is affirmed by every FV spokesman that I know of, as indicated by the quote from Barach above. But we do not drag the decrees down into our understanding of history—we let God unfold His unchangeable decrees throughout the process of all history. The content of the ultimate decrees is none of our current business, although we cheerfully acknowledge that the decrees are really there and that they *have* an unchanging content. Our connection point to these decrees is the covenant, given to us to use in this way. Because of the promises of the covenant, we may deal with election on our end, which is covenant election. The decrees are on God's end. It is important for us to know that God does what He does on His end, but we only know *that* He is doing it, not *what* He is doing. What He is doing will only be fully manifest on the Last Day. Until that Day, we walk by faith, not by sight.

Now Waters says of the FV that "we find a reticence in grounding the marks or evidences of election in anything inward or subjective" (p. 111). He says this despite the fact that I devoted a full chapter to the subjective marks of assurance in *"Reformed" Is Not Enough* (pp. 125–130). Not only that, but the next chapter of Waters's book indicates that he actually read that chapter, and comments on it. But here in this chapter, where my chapter on assurance contradicts his summary of my position, he goes on to describe my position *this* way:

> In this sense, that which in part the doctrine of the invisible church is concerned to guard—the existence of a body of sincere believers who are discernible to God and to themselves by certain infallible marks (marks that hypocrites do not and cannot possess)—is functionally neglected in Wilson's ecclesiology . . . the practical distinction between the sincere believer and the hypocrite is not ontological (they possess different types of grace) but historical in nature. It is the sincere believer's perseverance that Wilson will stress to be what identifies him as a genuine believer . . . It is simply not the case that Wilson is offering us the same doctrine but new terminology. (p. 123)

But, clean contrary to Waters's assertions, I have taught in multiple places that there is an ontological difference between what the sincere believer experiences and what the hypocrite experiences. When the grace of God effectually converts one covenant member, enabling him to persevere in holiness subjectively experienced, and does not convert another in the same way, what else can you call it?

To pummel the point (if I may), I have taught (in very clear and divers ways) that the grace given to the decretally elect at the point of the effectual call is grace that is *qualitatively* different than the common operations of the Spirit enjoyed (for a season) by the unregenerate covenant member. I have heaped this point up in a rumpled pile and have danced around it, gesticulating with enthusiasm. I have made a big building out of this point and put a blinking neon sign on top of it. If this point were an overpass, I have spray-painted my agreement with it in bright green letters at least eighteen inches high. With my white chef's hat on, I have wheeled this point out of the kitchen on a cart, poured brandy all over it, and set it on fire. If the point were a pudding, I would have added three eggs beyond what the recipe called for. To summarize briefly, this is not something I have somehow neglected to say.

What Waters has done here is a real travesty of scholarship. He is free to argue that what I have written on this is not consistent with what some of the other FV fellows might say. But this would require far more argument than he is presenting thus far. And if all I had to go on for my understanding of the other guys' positions was Waters's take on what *I* have written, I frankly have no confidence that he is representing them fairly at all. He is not free to mangle my position this way, to pretend that I have not qualified what I have in fact qualified, to invert my meaning as he has. This really is a disgrace—does P&R employ fact-checkers?

FEDERAL VISION ASSURANCE
JULY 28, 2006

The first half of chapter five in Waters's book addresses the question of assurance of salvation. After recognizing that I had dedicated a full chapter to this subject and granting that I emphasized a number of subjective aspects to assurance, Waters goes on to doubt the whole deal. Because I concluded that chapter with a call to look away, to look to Christ, to ground assurance in objective certainties, Waters concluded that I was backing away from what I had said earlier. But this is simply a category confusion. Waters says this: "We might recall that Wilson's ecclesiology, specifically his insistence upon covenantal objectivity and his questioning of the classical Reformed doctrine of the visible and invisible church, appears to render it practically impossible to frame the question of assurance in any traditional subjective sense" (pp. 142–3).

He says, at best,

> Wilson has outlined in this chapter a doctrine of assurance containing two unreconciled components, namely, subjective and objective assurance. (p. 143)

So how is this a category confusion? By definition, *assurance* is not objective. It is a *subjective* response to an *objective* reality. Every pastor knows what it is to deal with introspective souls who struggle because they try to have faith in their faith, instead of faith in Christ. Faith in Christ works this way. Subjective faith rests in an objective (outside the self) Christ. Subjective faith looks in faith to objective (outside the self) means of grace, like Word and sacrament. Now when I tell someone to look away to Christ, there are two elements in this—subjective and objective. There is the looking away (subjective) and there is Christ (objective).

Everyone understands this if we are talking about a Bible verse. "Don't torment yourself this way," the wise pastor says. "Look away from yourself. Look to Christ. Look to the text. See? All you have to do is look."

Now if I were listening to an evangelical say this, I would not catch at words, and tell him that he was teaching false doctrine because he said all that was necessary was *to look*. "Really? That's all? Just look at the ink on the paper?" Of course, we know that this means to look in true evangelical faith. But true evangelical faith does not have its origin in a hunt for true evangelical faith. The seed that germinates is the imperishable word—objective. The life that springs up is subjective. These are not two alien principles that need to be reconciled—not unless faith and the object of faith need to be reconciled.

The covenant is objective. Means of grace are objective. Grace itself is subjectively experienced, of necessity. Faithfulness to the covenant is *not* objective. But covenantal faithfulness is only possible if there is an objective covenant *there*. Marriage is objective. Fidelity is personal and subjective. Trying to reconcile these two things is like trying to reconcile ham and eggs.

And so this assessment by Waters radically misrepresents my views on this. My understanding of assurance is in no way at variance with the classical Reformed understanding of this. Not only so, but I wrote a chapter explaining this in detail. Why on earth would Waters think there was a contradiction between the subjective experience of faith and the objective ground of faith—and not understand the perfectly uncontroversial idea, advanced in that chapter, that faith flourishes when it looks, not at itself, but rather at the Faithful One, who has promised to meet us in His means of grace? What *is* the problem?

YOU BETCHER
JULY 28, 2006

In the second part of chapter five, Waters goes on to misrepresent me on some other issues, particularly on the subject of the perseverance and apostasy: "While Wilson admits the existence and presence of hypocrites within the covenant community and stresses the necessity of the inward operations of the Holy Spirit for an individual's salvation, his ecclesiology is weighted toward defining the Christian in an undifferentiated way" (p. 147).

Actually, I argue for defining Christian in two different ways. I define quarter as a coin in my pocket, and I define quarter as a fourth of something. I don't "weight" my definition of quarter one way or the other. Why is this so difficult? I hold that a Christian is someone who is born again of the Spirit of God—"Paul's statement is blunt—he is *not* a Christian who has only the externals" (*RINE*, p. 18). And then, *in a completely distinct sense*, a Christian is anyone who is baptized in the name of the Father, Son and Holy Spirit: "they were baptized in infancy or when they were ten in a Baptist church, they sang in the choir and went through catechism class, and they are not Buddhists" (*RINE*, p. 17).

When it comes to sorting out the sheep and goats before the eschaton, Waters tries to argue that I make no distinctions within the church and make no distinctions within the Word.

> In preaching and pastoring, Wilson counsels against attempting to raise explicitly the question of hypocrisy. 'Pastorally, you don't need to flush these people out by probing and doing private detective work of a pastoral nature. What you need to do is just back God's truck up to the pulpit and unload it.' This is not, Wilson stresses, defaulting on one's pastoral duties. Ministers preach the Scriptures, Wilson argues, which 'have all these severe warnings in the New Testament.' He seems fairly confident that hypocrites, under such preaching, will generally choose to leave rather than 'to slug it out.' And undifferentiated word (at least in terms of its application to various groups within the church delineated according to the doctrine of regeneration) is therefore to be preached to an undifferentiated church (pp. 147–8).

I don't know where he gets this idea, but I do not hold to it. In fact, I deny it *in the quotations* that Waters produces to prove that I do too hold to it. Look at the citation just past. After I say that the New Testament contains many warnings for the hypocrites (making the point that the Bible differentiates between hypocrites and non-hypocrites), Waters cites this as proof positive that I do not believe the Bible differentiates between covenant members. And so why did I have two separate chapters on sons of Belial and false brothers (chapters 17 and 18)? If the Bible differentiates between faithful covenant members and faithless covenant members, *then so must we*. But Waters has got this idea in his head and it will not be dislodged. He says again that I do not believe in doing this. "First, Wilson's pattern of preaching (preach an undifferentiated Word to an undifferentiated church) is not in keeping with

Scripture" (p. 152). I agree. It isn't. That is why I don't believe in doing it. I had just said, with Waters quoting me on it, that the Word differentiates, and that if you preach the whole counsel of God (the biblical expression behind my phrase about backing God's truck up to the pulpit and unloading it), hypocrites will scram. If we unload it, we unload it. The Word differentiates. The Word winnows. The Word is a hammer that breaks the rock in pieces. And why Waters would say that my confidence that the Scripture preached will establish this differentiation within the church (causing hypocrites to flee) is actually proof that I hold there is no such differentiation to be made, is a matter quite beyond my capacity to explain.

He says,

> The pattern of biblical teaching and preaching in both the Old and New Testaments, then, respects and addresses the distinguishing heart conditions found within the visible church. (pp. 152–3)

To which I reply,

> You betcher.

But wait, there's more, on a different subject. Waters maintains that I *deny* a qualitative difference between regeneration as experienced by the faithful covenant member and the faithless covenant member.

> Wilson, then, refrains here from defining apostasy in qualitative terms—that, apart from considerations of the grace of perseverance, the grace given to the elect is qualitatively different from that given to the reprobate. Rather, apostasy is defined temporally: the apostate is one who simply does not persevere. (p. 151)

Having said this, he then quotes me saying precisely the *opposite*: "'The grace experienced by the apostate and the persevering grace experienced by the elect *differ* . . . regeneration extends (or not) to every covenant member'" (quoted on p. 152, my emphasis in the original). In that quote, Waters cites my *agreement* on this point with Carl Robbins, a FV critic in the Knox colloquium book. Then he says this:

> Wilson's comments, however, do not substantially alter our analysis above. His affirmations regarding the necessity of individual regeneration are appreciated, but do not resolve the issue at hand . . . The question at hand is whether apostate members of the covenant were ever at all properly said to be regenerate. (p. 152)

If Waters is objecting because he thinks I might believe regeneration to be reversible, then he has radically misread my position. Regeneration (in the effectual call sense) is not reversible. And if he is objecting because he thinks I might use the word regenerate of the apostate covenant member in *any* sense, however distinct from effectual call regeneration, then he has radically muddled my position. When talking about apostates, and talking about effectual call regeneration, I *deny* that said apostates can be properly said to have ever been regenerate.

As I said in *"Reformed" Is Not Enough*, "This might be called regeneration, theologically considered. A man is either regenerate or he is not. When the word *regeneration* is being used in this sense, we are talking about an invisible operation performed by the Spirit of God, who does what He does when and how it please Him. And when we are talking about what might be called this 'effectual-call regeneration,' we have to repudiate every form of baptismal or decisional regeneration" (*RINE*, p. 19).

In addition, I have written an extensive series of posts on this blog in order "to offer a defense of the historic evangelical understanding of regeneration" (6/16/04). Here is a small sampling from that series*:

> In order to take all baptized covenant members as participants in Christ in the "strong sense," we would have to distinguish what is objectively given in Christ, and not what is subjectively done with those objective

* The "Life in the Regeneration" series of blog posts formed the basis for *Against the Church* (Moscow, ID: Canon, 2013).

benefits. Perseverance would, on this reading, be what was subjectively done with what God has objectively given. In this view, the person who did not persevere was not given less of Christ. But this necessarily means that persevering grace is not an objective gift or grace. God's willingness to continue "the wrestling" would depend upon what kind of fight we put up, or cooperation we provide, and because no one's fundamental nature has been changed, those natures remain at "enmity with God." In this view, whatever total depravity means, it is not ontologically changed, just knocked down and sat upon. The Spirit pins one snarling dog, but not another. But this in turn leads to another thought—eventually at some time in the process we stop snarling and start cooperating (if we are bound to heaven), and what do we call this change or transformation. The historic name for this change has been regeneration, and I see no reason to change it. (7/24/04)

Affirming the absolute need for personal regeneration is the *sine qua non* of historic evangelicalism. Affirming that the gates of hell will not prevail against the Church is the *sine qua non* of historic catholicity. Deny the former only, and the end result is the deadly nominalism found in many quarters of the institutional Church. Such saintlings need to be told that God can make sons of Abraham out of rocks. Deny the latter only, and you have the endless splintering sectarianism that has come to characterize American pop evangelicalism. This comes about when Christians cease affirming the need for an invisible work of the Spirit of God, and presume to be able to see exactly how and when that regeneration happens.

But the moment of regeneration is never visible to us. Lack of regeneration, however, is visible over time because the works of the flesh, Paul tells us, are manifest. And the fruit of the Spirit manifest themselves publicly as well, and Jesus tells us to make our judgments on the basis of fruit. But it must be noted that biblical judgments of this sort are mature, and are based on the mature outcome of a person's way of

> life. All this to say that genuine discernment is based on the video, not on the snapshot (8/5/04).

Not to put too fine a point on it, Waters represents me as holding a view that is 180 degrees out from what I actually hold. Not only do I not hold the views he attributes to me, I have argued energetically against them in print. There must be a *qualitative* difference between unregenerate baptized hypocrite and the faithful covenant member.

From overt misrepresentations of my position, we may now move to disagreements and interactions of an ordinary kind.

> Second, Wilson's doctrine of new covenant curses raises certain questions. How then may we affirm Paul's declaration that Christ has borne the curse of the law for believers (Gal. 3:13)? How may we say, with Paul, that believers no longer fall under condemnation (Rom. 8:1)? (p. 153)

Well, the point would be that *believers* within the covenant know that Christ has bore the curse for them. But covenant members who do *not* believe this are thereby identified as *unbelievers*. Because they are unbelievers, and all the promises of Christ are apprehended by faith alone, and because there is a fundamental differentiation within the covenant during the course of history, *unbelievers* within the covenant receive the curses of the covenant, and not the blessings of the covenant.

> One may agree in principle with Wilson that 'covenant members in the new covenant were judged more severely than the covenant members in the old were,' but Wilson's explanation of Hebrews 10:26f. in terms of specifically covenantal curses is a dubious one. When we consider its likely connection to Wilson's doctrine of covenant election, we are further inclined to be skeptical of its merit. (p. 153)

This quotation above may serve as a sampling of how Waters undertakes to refute something. Note that this is under a section labeled "Critique."

One may agree with me in principle about how curses in the New Covenant are more severe than those of the Old, but he says my explanation of Heb. 10:26 is a "dubious one." Furthermore, my explanation has a "likely" connection to my doctrine of "covenantal election" and so Waters is further inclined to be "skeptical of its merit." Oh? Might there be any reasons? This is just academic handwaving. He says nothing more than that he doesn't buy it, which is fine, but ought not to be confused with offering reasons for not buying it.

We now come to the last point, which is the problem of sap in John 15.

> Third, it is gratuitous, that is, baseless to say that Jesus's analogy in John 15:1–6 teaches that the broken branches partook of the sap of the vine. Jesus does not use the term sap in this parable. That metaphor is an inference that Wilson has drawn. As Beisner has rightly commented, 'It is dangerous enough to draw doctrines from parables; it is more dangerous to draw doctrines from details within parables; it is exegetically fatal to draw doctrines from details that are even there!' There is no hint in this parable that the broken branches ever existed in any vital, living relationship with Christ. Far less is it clear that the broken branches sustained the same relationship to Christ as those who prove to be decretally elect. Wilson's argument fails to overturn conventional Reformed readings of this passage, which see branches that are outwardly and inwardly related to Christ. (pp. 153–4)

Excuse me if I have just a little bit of fun with this one.

First, the point of the sap illustration was not to turn John 15 into a complex allegory, with the sap representing the internal motions of grace or something. The point of mentioning the sap was to emphasize something that Christ's metaphor says explicitly, and which Reformed exegetes consistently run away from (in the best tradition of an Arminian in Romans 9), which is to say, the *branchness* of the branches that were broken off. Christ says nothing of sap, or bark, or leaves. But He does say *that branches in Him were cut out of Him, and were then taken away and burned.* He does say *that.* So, Mr. Reformed, what does it mean? What is taken away from the Vine which is Christ? They are branches, which had a *branchy* connection to Him. All I mean by sap in the branches is to say that they are true branches. A branch can be fruitless and still be a true branch—a branch that needs to be pruned. A branch cannot be sapless and still be a true branch. That was my only point in talking about sap, which leads to this next point.

Waters chides me for mentioning sap in my discussion of this (although every branch I have ever seen has had sap), and then moves blithely on to talk about branches that are "outwardly related" to the Vine and branches that are "inwardly related." Now I have never in all my born days seen a branch that is merely outwardly related to a vine or tree. We have never seen it in nature, and Christ makes no mention of it. But it is responsible Reformed exegesis to have *outwardly* related branches and *inwardly* related branches, but exegetically fatal to have branches with sap in them, that is to say, branchy branches.

And third, Waters says, "Far less is it clear that the broken branches sustained the same relationship to Christ as those who prove to be decretally elect." Well, of course not. They were cut out because they did not have the same relationship; one was fruitful and the other not. But in some sense, at some level (not in every sense, not on every level), they did have the same relationship to Christ. How's that? They were both BRANCHES.

SALTY DOGS AND CRUSTY LUTHERANS
JULY 30, 2006

The first part of chapter seven in Waters's book is dedicated to my views of sacramental efficacy and baptism. And so, here we are.

He begins by saying that I misread B.B. Warfield definition of sacerdotalism and seeks to establish that I misread it by simply stating *why* Warfield said what he did (p. 199). But this does not change the fact that Warfield defined sacerdotalism as the notion that God uses *any means* to accomplish his saving purposes (as I said he did). Warfield holds that the evangelical position is that God's saving action is never mediated. So Waters's response here is simply beside the point. Suppose I say that Smith believes that we ought not to be fighting in Iraq. Waters says that I have misread Smith because he holds this position because the war is too expensive. How would I be misreading Smith's position?

Waters notes that I quote the WCF (28.5) and that I draw a certain inference from the way they talk about baptism there: "Although it be a great sin to contemn or neglect this ordinance, yet grace and salvation are not so inseparably annexed unto it, as that no person can be regenerated, or saved, without it; or, that all that are baptized are undoubtedly regenerated."

Waters says (accurately) that I argue from this expression that grace and salvation are *ordinarily* annexed to water baptism, although not inseparably annexed. Waters responds by saying that the "paragraph says nothing about *who* among the baptized will be saved." This is quite true, but it is also not the point of my argument. Let's just consider the structure of this sentence from the WCF, changing the topic completely: "Although it be parental neglect not to enroll your kid in a good Christian school, yet a good education is not so inseparably annexed unto it, as that no person can be educated well without it; or, that all who are enrolled are undoubtedly educated well."

Now what is this speaker claiming about Christian education? He is saying that not enrolling your kid in a good Christian school is a big negative deal. He is saying, however, that it is *possible* to get a good education without doing so, and he grants that to claim that all who are so enrolled are educated well would be an overstatement. It would be fair to say, however, that the speaker is saying that a good education is the ordinary result of enrolling your kid in such a school. It would be nothing to the point for Waters to say that the speaker was making no claim about *who* among the students would receive a good education. This is quite true, but it is also not the subject under discussion. A man can be convinced that a school is ordinarily good for the kids without making any particular claims about who will be educated well. But this is structurally the same argument the Westminster divines advance concerning baptism.

Waters then says that I believe that baptism seals what it signifies, and that it is not a "front operation." Good enough. He then says of me that "Wilson does not qualify here the objects of the redemptive sealing of the sacrament as those who have saving faith. It may be that he understands the redemptive sealing operation of the Spirit in the sacraments to transpire, at least sometimes, *in the absence of faith*. This suspicion is heightened . . ." (p. 200). Thus far Waters on my view of baptism, emphasis mine.

Here is my take on my view of baptism, the first of which is just a few pages after the citation Waters quoted.

> Of course this baptism does not automatically save the one baptized; there is no magical cleaning power in the water. (*RINE*, 99)

> The blessings are appropriated *by faith*, not by water, and the curses are brought down upon the head *by unbelief*, against which curses the water provides no protection whatever. ("A Short Credo on Baptism,"* emphasis added)

> An *unbelieving* covenant member incurs all the curses of the covenant, while the *believer* appropriates all its blessings *by faith alone*. ("A Short Credo on Baptism," emphasis added)

Now I ask you . . .

The next section of Waters's chapter is worth quoting in some detail. He says this:

> Fifth, Wilson conflates Westminster Larger Catechism 161 and WCF 27.3 to read as follows: 'Worthy receivers of the sacraments of baptism and the Lord's Supper are effectually saved by these sacramental means through the working of the Holy Spirit and the blessing of Christ.' This, however, is what neither statement affirms. The Standards are careful to say that the sacraments are 'effectual means of salvation,' but this is a far cry from saying that 'worthy receivers . . . are effectually

* Can't remember for sure where this was published, but we suspect *Credenda*.

> saved by these sacramental means.' Wilson's latter statement places a far greater emphasis on the necessity and importance of the sacraments to one's salvation than the Standard's statements do. (p. 201)

This is simply unbelievable. The difference between Waters's summary ("The sacraments are effectual means of salvation for worthy receivers" and mine ("Worthy receivers are effectually saved by these sacramental means") really amounts to a difference of voice. But "The ball hits John" is apparently a "far cry" from "John is hit by the ball." Bill, a worthy receiver, is effectually saved by these sacramental means" is a "far cry" from "These sacramental means save Bill, a worthy receiver." Sometimes I really am at a loss for words. How are you supposed to debate people like this? Waters says that my summary "places a far greater emphasis on the necessity and importance of the sacraments." Why? How? In what way? What on earth is he talking about?

Waters then reproduces another argument I advanced from the Westminster Confession.

> Sixth, Wilson takes Westminster Shorter Catechism 92 ('wherein, by sensible signs, Christ, and the benefits of the new covenant, are represented, sealed, and applied to believers') to mean that 'the benefits of the new covenant) are *applied* to a man *through the sacraments* when that man has faith.' Wilson certainly intends to be provocative by this statement . . . Is he saying that baptism and the Lord's Supper are instruments of justification? If so, they he most certainly would be out of accord with the Standards. Is he saying that a believer's sense of his justification may be built up by improvement of his baptism and by a right use of the Supper? If so, Wilson is saying nothing new. (p. 202)

This is the same kind of thing as an earlier point made about persevering grace, a question that is sometimes legitimately directed against some FV expressions. If a baptized individual receives all of Christ's benefits, then how can we account for such a person not having persevering grace? Isn't that part of Christ's benefits, and doesn't he have them all? A reasonable kimd of quesion, I think, and so now I present it back to Waters.

The Shorter Catechism teaches that Christ and the benefits of the new covenant are *applied* to worthy receivers by means of sensible signs. Waters wants to see this as the relatively uncontroversial notion that a man's *sense* of his justification can be built up by improvement of his baptism and through a right use of the Supper. But no, that can't be it. The Shorter Catechism says, "Christ and the benefits of the new covenant" are applied by sensible signs, not my "sense of Christ, and my sense of the benefits of the new covenant." And so my question for Waters is whether he believes this. If so, what is his beef with what I have been saying? If not, has he taken an exception to the WCF at this point? Spelling it out, justification is one of the benefits of the new covenant, is it not? Just like persevering grace is.

Put this another way. If *I* were to be so foolish as to say that Christ and the benefits of the new covenant were applied to a man (a worthy receiver guy) by means of the sensible signs given in the sacraments, would Waters interpret *me* as saying this meant nothing more than a man's *sense* of these benefits being strengthened as he rolls these propositions around in his brain? Not a chance. He would interpret me as a roaring sacerdotalist, as he has done. How about if Wilkins said it? No, wait . . . what if *Lusk* said it?

For misrepresentations, Waters is setting a record in this chapter. He then says this:

> Wilson's doctrine of sacramental efficacy is intriguing in that it conceives of redemptive sacramental efficacy in the case of an unconverted recipient (the 'nominal Presbyterian, baptized in infancy'). As SC 92 and many other passages state, however, the Westminster Standards conceive of redemptive sacramental efficacy in the presence of a faith that embraces what the sacrament holds forth to it. (p. 204)

Well, of *course*. That was the whole *point* of my illustration. The Westminster Standards clearly teach that the grace conferred by means of baptism is not anchored to the moment of baptismal administration. Someone is baptized in infancy, grows up a hellion, lives in unbelief for a time, and is then converted. When he is converted, he comes to "a faith that embraces what the sacrament holds forth to it."

I say, "By means of baptism, this efficious grace is *conferred* on the elect at the appropriate time, the time of conversion, and it is the *applied grace of their baptism*." And yes, I said that, because that is what the Westminster Standards teach. Waters summarizes this as saying the exact opposite of what I said. "We may speak, then, of redemptive baptismal efficacy quite apart from the subjective condition of the recipient" (p. 208). Okay. So I say that the applied grace of baptism is conferred on someone at the time of their *conversion* (e.g., when they are brought by God to a subjective condition of repentance and faith), and Waters represents this as me saying that this baptismal efficacy occurs quite apart from "the subjective condition of the recipient" (p. 208). Now I am no salty dog, or crusty Lutheran, or anything like that, but this really is a "what the hell?" moment. Maybe I should start typing words like CONVERSION or REPENTANCE or FAITH in all caps so that scholars can find them.

Waters ends his section dealing with me by saying that "Wilson's understanding of precisely what is conveyed to the recipient in baptism is not at all clear" (p. 210). Well, not at all clear to some people's children.

AUGUST 2006

CONFESSIONAL LAXITY OVER AT MISSISSIPPI VALLEY
AUGUST 1, 2006

In my previous Auburn Avenue post, in the comments section Mark Horne supplied the following quotation from Turretin. The emphases are Mark's, and Turretin was da bomb.

> The question is not whether faith alone justifies to the exclusion either of the grace of God or the righteousness of Christ or the word AND SACRAMENTS (BY WHICH THE BLESSING OF JUSTIFICATION IS PRESENTED AND SEALED TO US ON THE PART OF GOD), which we maintain ARE NECESSARILY REQUIRED HERE; but only to the exclusion of every other virtue and habit on our part . . .. For all these as they are mutually subordinated in a different class of cause, CONSIST WITH EACH OTHER IN THE HIGHEST DEGREE. [16.8.5]

I bring this up because I just finished chapter seven of Waters's book-length material. I don't have much to say here because in the second part of that chapter, Waters was taking other fellows to task. As I said at the beginning of this series of posts, I will let my compadres answer as the fit takes them, and their wives are unable to restrain them. But a few things in this were too delicious to pass up, and the Turretin quote provides a good springboard for just a few comments. Waters says

> By way of preface, we may note that Lusk's argument is filled with quotations from Calvin, other sixteenth-century Reformers, and certain seventeenth-century divines. He points to these quotations as evidence that his position has some pedigree and precedent in the Reformed tradition. To engage each of these quotes *seriatim* would distract us from our primary concern . . . ." (p. 211)

I dare say it would. Nevertheless, Waters does give a general hand-waving response to the quotes, though it is nothing quite so magisterial as a *seriatim* response.

First, he wonders aloud what the context of those pesky quotations might be. Of course, this is reasonable as a general point (context always matters), but the substance of these sorts of quotations would only be seriously affected if the context of the above quote (say) had an intro like this from Turretin: "Here I summarize the position of my opponent, that hardy blasphemer Sergius Smith. He maintains, and we deny, that . . . ." It is not really an appropriate response to muse thoughtfully that it is *possible* that some contextual clues in the original setting might possibly "bail my position out. Let us prayerfully hope that it is so."

Second, he grants that it sometimes sure *looks* like Calvin and all those other home boys of ours were saying the same thing that Lusk is. But were they advancing "that statement in service of of the same theological ends for which Lusk as adduced it"? (p. 211). Hmmm? Maybe not, and so there we rest our case.

Third, Waters wonders if certain qualifying or balancing statements have been left out. Oh? Sort of like how Waters has left out all *my* qualifying or balancing statements? When talking about the same things? I have to grant that this argument from Waters is the most persuasive. This sort of thing *does* happen.

And last, Waters and his readers have "bypassed these quotations and have restricted ourselves to a single argument, the argument from the Westminster Standards" (p. 212). But to do this is to miss one of the central historical and theological arguments that the FV guys are advancing. And for a critic, to miss it is fortunate because if you miss it, you don't have to answer it. To read the Westminster Standards in the light of Dabney, Hodge, Miller, and Thornwell is to read the document in the light of theologians (to whom all praise!) who, despite all their signal strengths and virtues, cannot be said to have had an impact on the theological climate that *led* to the writing of the Standards. This is because they all lived a long time later. This is not the case with Calvin, Beza, Knox, Turretin, et al, men who lived, wrote, and reshaped the continent of Europe *prior* to the writing of the Standards. The Westminster Standards are not a confessional standard that fell from the sky. It was composed by men who were self-consciously doing theology in the Reformed tradition, and a battery of quotations from the fathers of that tradition would seem to be to the point. A battery of quotations from those men from whom the Westminster divines *learned their theology* would seem to be pertinent. The issue is not what can be read back into the Standards in the light of subsequent developments in anabaptist America. *That* is anachronism. The issue is what the Standards meant to the generation that first adopted them. And in order to understand *that*, a grasp of 16th and 17th century Reformed thought would be, shall we say, screamingly relevant. Waters cannot simply say that to study the context of the Confession would take him far afield, far away from his attempts to interpret a pristine Confession of faith that mysteriously showed up (in a place of honor)on his bookshelf.

To this point in his book, Waters has quoted (a number of times) that portion of the Westminster Confession (28.6) that says that the efficacy of baptism is such that, by a right use of it, the grace promised in it is not only offered, *but really exhibited and conferred.* He has done this, and yet he himself cannot bring himself to say that baptism confers the grace promised in it. He objects to Lusk's argument from this portion of the Confession. "He does this by isolating such terms as *confer*, *sign*, *seal*, and *exhibit* from their confessional qualifications" (p. 231). Okay, let's not do that. Let us not fall into the Error of Lusk (just because Lusk didn't doesn't mean that we *should*). Let's qualify it like Zeus distributing thunder, lightning and blue ruin. Worthy receiver, repentance as deep as David Brainerd on steroids, evangelical faith sloshing out the ears. Dr. Waters, has there ever been a Christian in the history of the Church to whom you believe this sentence applies? One who used his baptism rightly, and who, as a consequence, had the grace of salvation promised in that baptism, not only offered to him, but also exhibited to him and *conferred* upon him? Has this *ever* happened? If you think it has, then lay off us already. If you think it has not, then when will you notify your presbytery that you have to take exception to this portion of the Confession? I don't think you need to worry because Mississippi Valley is kind of lax when it comes to this kind of thing. They overlook this particular discrepancy *all the time.*

A TULIP FROM CALVIN'S GARDEN
AUGUST 2, 2006

The last chapter of Waters's book gives him an opportunity to wrap up. But although I will interact with some elements of this chapter, I am not going to wrap up, not just yet anyhow. Nossir. I am going to go through the *footnotes* too.

First, Waters charges me with a "misuse of logic." Were it true, 'twould be serious, for it might affect sales*. He quotes me arguing the following: "Branches can lose their position on the tree. You can be on the tree, someone can be on the tree right next to you and he is as much on the tree as you, he's as much a partaker of Christ as you are, he is as much a member of Christ as you are." After saying this, I then respond to a criticism that says this cannot be reconciled with election. I say, "Well, first it is reconcilable, that is the first thing. Secondly, if you can't reconcile it, it's not your problem. What does the Bible say?" (quoted on pp. 268–269).

Waters then says,

> In fairness to Wilson, he believes that his doctrines of election and apostasy *can* be reconciled. He argues, however, that there is no burden

* Link is no longer viable, but this was probably directed to Canon Press's *Introductory Logic* curriculum, which was co-authored by Doug and is available here: canonpress.com/products/new-introductory-logic-complete-program.

> on the interpreter to reconcile what he perceives the Bible to teach. We are "just [to[take the Bible at face value." Logical reconciliation is not necessary for the student of the Bible. (p. 269)

Once again, is not accurate at all. *No* burden on the interpreter to reconcile disparate elements in the text? No. God gave us minds for a reason. I believe we should use them to harmonize various passages of Scripture, whenever possible. *The temptation that comes with this*, and the one I was addressing, was the temptation to do violence to the text for the sake of a "harmonized system." Don't be like the fellow who got the wrong box top on the wrong jig saw puzzle, and who wound up having to put some pieces in with a mallet. It is all consistent in the mind of God, and if we submit to the plain teaching of Scripture, at the end of the day we will have a much fuller (and harmonized) sense of what God has revealed to us. The alternative is to be like the guy who has a sailboat that was supposed to be a lighthouse.

Later he says that I have contributed with a vote of "no confidence" with regard to logic as a means of "assessing and attaining to the truth." (p. 272). This is simply not true. But it is true that I *would* register a vote of no confidence in slipshod reasoning and dogmatic bluster masquerading as tough-minded orthodoxy. But the problem I have with it is that it is unreasonable . . . illogical. One of my complaints against Waters is that he is unwilling to follow certain arguments that proceed by good and necessary consequence. If baptism exhibits and confers a certain grace on those who use the sacrament rightly, it follows, by good and necessary consequence that baptism exhibits and confers a certain grace on those who use the sacrament rightly. I am using a straightforward example here. He who says A must say A.

A second criticism that Waters offers concerns the matter of curses in the new covenant. Water says of my handling of 1 Cor. 10:1–14 that I have a certain interpretive assumption, which is true enough.

> Observe now the interpretive assumption behind Wilson's argument. It is that the national blessings and curses that pertained to Israel under the old covenant now pertain to the church under the new covenant.

> This speaks a much stronger conception of covenantal continuity than most nontheonomic Reformers interpreters have allowed. (p. 286)

Two problems here. Have *allowed*? Is St. Paul not allowed to say certain things? This leads to the second problem. Where did my interpretive assumption come from? How did I get the idea that the national blessings and curses pertaining to Israel under the old now pertain to the Church under the new? Who comes up with this stuff? Well, maybe it was because of what the apostle Paul expressly *said*. "Now these things were our examples, to the intent we should not lust after evil things, as they also lusted" (1 Cor. 10:6). I think it is plain enough on the surface, but I have also argued for this position in some detail. Some interaction with the arguments would be nice, and then Waters would not have to resort to saying that I have come up with a stronger covenant continuity than I was allowed to.

A third criticism in this last chapter returns to the question of differentiation in preaching to the covenant people.

> We have also seen Wilson's concern that we not preached in a differentiated manner to the covenant community. We are to preach the promises and the warnings of the covenant and presume that most hypocrites, not tolerating such preaching, will leave the church. (p. 293)

I have a hard time figuring out what Waters means by undifferentiated preaching. If I preach that the covenant tree contains fruitful branches and fruitless branches, and I also preach the promises and warnings that apply to each, what else does he want? Egg in his beer? Is it undifferentiated preaching unless and until (from the pulpit) I nail Smith, three rows back, for being a shoddy tither, intermittent Sabbath-breaker, and grumbler, all the result of his unconverted heart? "Yes, *you*, Smith! Don't act surprised, you whitewashed tomb!"

Waters also returns to the question of what happens to the nominal Presbyterian, baptized as an infant, but who lived in a wild and unconverted way until his conversion. When he is converted, Waters describes my position this way:

> It is, we may note, to this man's baptism that Wilson will ultimately attribute the man's conversion, whatever proximate causes and means may have intervened between his baptism and his conversion. (pp. 293–4)

According to Waters, the "doctrine of saving faith" is already being "outshone by baptism" (p. 294). Now the Westminster Confession says that the efficacy of baptism is not tied to the moment of its administration. That means, good and necessary consequence again, that the efficacy of baptism is not tied to the moment of its administration. *That* means, in its turn, that when a baptized person is converted later in life, he is coming into true evangelical faith. He is becoming a worthy receiver, to use the description of the Standards. That being the case, what happens as a result of his newly-given "right use" of the sacrament later in life? The grace promised in it is not only offered (as it has been throughout his whole unconverted life), it is *now* exhibited and conferred. It can be conferred later in his life because the efficacy of baptism is not tied to the moment of its administration. This really is a tight argument, and I would be interested if someone like Waters interacted with it. I am not a doctrinal imperialist. All kinds of wonderful Christians don't subscribe to the Westminster Confession, and that is fine. But I do subscribe to it, and I take my vows seriously. And at this point, like it or not, Waters is out of conformity with the Standards and I am not. This is not a cute debating ploy. I have advanced a serious argument here. There is a difference between believing that the efficacy of baptism is not limited to the time of administration and believing the impotence of baptism is not tied to the moment of its administration.

Waters concludes his book of failed criticism with this hope:

> It is my sincere hope that FV proponents will recognize this discord and return to their first love. Barring that, may the souls of believers be spared, to borrow Samuel Miller's phrase, from the 'poisonous exotic' that the FV offers to the Reformed church. (p. 300)

In order to issue this kind of pastoral warning to the Church, there are a few prerequisites. One of them is that you have to do your homework. You have to know what you are talking about. The plant that Waters is pointing to is not a poisonous exotic at all. It is a tulip, right out of Calvin's garden.

MAKING THE NECESSARY QUALIFICATIONS
AUGUST 3, 2006

One of the things that became obvious throughout this review of Waters's book on the Federal Vision was the extraordinarily sloppy job done by Waters in representing my views fairly or accurately. Unfortunately, this pattern continues in the footnotes and bibliography.

An astonishing omission in the bibliography is the doctrinal examination I took before my presbytery in order to address these question. That examination can be found here*, under the heading of Ecclesiastical Issues.

Another striking example of sloppiness is the following summary of my contribution to the Knox Colloquium on sacramental efficacy. Waters says,

> Wilson charges the modern Reformed church with compromising the "sacramental theology found in the Westminster Standards," and proceeds to elaborate precisely what he understands that sacramental theology to mean. In so doing, he advances a doctrine of baptismal efficacy *that neglects needed confessional qualifications*. He thereby transgresses the very Confession that he professes to espouse. (p. 363, emphasis added)

My point here is not to dispute the doctrinal issue itself—that is forthcoming in response to a footnote from Cal Beisner's Foreword. My point here is simply to illustrate Waters's critical methods. I want to simply quote from the article in question, in order to see if I in fact neglected "needed confessional qualification."

Remember, the issue is not our disagreement over what we believe baptism does. Later for that. The issue is whether I qualify what I believe it does in

* Currently available at wordmp3.com/details.aspx?id=1158.

accordance with the Confession's qualifications. Waters says that I neglected this important task. Read the following, and see if you agree with this assessment:

> Let us grant that the *Catechism* here is *not* maintaining that all those who are baptized with water are automatically and inexorably saved. Let us grant that it is *not* saying that individuals are watertight jugs and that baptism pours an 'effectual call fluid' into each and every one of them. Let us grant that those who are baptized but who remain in unbelief are worse off for having been baptized, not better off. Of course the *Confession* is not teaching baptismal superstition (and, incidentally, neither are *we*). **The Confession is talking about worthy receivers**, who in the broader context of the *Confession* should be understood as the elect. (*The Auburn Avenue Theology: Pros and Cons*, "Sacramental Efficacy in the Westminster Standards," p. 236, italics original, bold added)
>
> So positively, what *is* the *Confession* saying **about such worthy receivers**? (p. 236)
>
> Spiritual blessings work the way they do because of the involvement of God in them. God is always the one who gives the increase—**not water, not bread, and not wine**. He works through His instruments, but it is His involvement that gives the increase for blessing. (p. 237) Those who come to the sacraments **with true evangelical faith in God** are those on whom this blessing of salvation is bestowed. (p. 238)
>
> In the words of the *Confession*, a sacrament . . . is a holy ordinance that uses sensible signs to represent, seal and *apply* the benefits of the new covenant **to worthy receivers. Who are worthy receivers? The elect.** (p. 240) [Note—I am aware that an elect individual who is foreordained to be converted next year is not *yet* a worthy receiver. I am telescoping here.]

In my quotation of the Shorter Catechism 91, I italicized the phrase from the answer that says "in them that by faith receive them." (p. 238). I did this in order to jump up and down on it.

> Now faith is **the only instrument** *that occupies this place.* We cannot intrude works, or good looks, or willing, or running *here*. But there are multitudes of *other* instruments, used by God, that occupy *other* places in the process of salvation. (p. 244)

So then, the Standards limit the efficacy of the sacraments (for blessing) to worthy receivers, to those who use the sacraments rightly. Do I agree with this? Did I say so? Why would Waters say that I had not made these qualifications? Beats me. The whole thing is beyond weird.

TALMUDIC LAYERS OF REVIVALISM
AUGUST 4, 2006

In the footnotes of Waters's book, Cal Beisner makes this statement: "The Westminster Standards present the sacraments solely as means of *sanctifying* grace, not as means of *converting* grace" (p. 302). In his response to my essay on sacramental efficacy in the Westminster Standards, Rick Phillips makes a similar point:

> In reading Wilson's paper I find that a single issue or question determines the whole, namely, 'What is the nature of the grace conveyed via the sacrament?' Is the grace of the sacraments limited to edifying or sanctificational issues, or do the sacraments regenerate or enter the recipient into a new relationship with God, conveying a grace not previously received through faith alone? (*Auburn Avenue Theology: Pros and Cons*, p. 245)

I have already argued on behalf of the sacramental teaching of Westminster in several places—in *"Reformed" Is Not Enough* (pp. 103–107) and in "Sacramental Efficacy in the Westminster Standards" in *Auburn Avenue Theology: Pros and Cons* (pp. 233–244). My purpose here is not to rehash all of this, multiplying words unnecessarily, but rather to provide a simple summary of the argument. There are additional questions or qualifications that I would want to make beyond this, but at the heart of *this* issue, I subscribe to what the Westminster divines taught in the following:

1. The grace that we are talking about here is limited to what Westminster calls "worthy receivers," those who have been graciously given (by God) a "right use" of the sacrament. I take this to mean evangelical faith as evidenced in the one being converted at the moment of his or her effectual call. And that evangelical faith is a gift of God, lest any should boast.
2. Baptism and the Lord's Supper are both sacraments, but they signify different aspects of the overall process of salvation. Baptism is about *entry* and the Lord's Supper is about nurture.
3. There is *a sacramental union* between the sign and the thing signified in baptism (WCF 27.2) Baptism in water is therefore *united* in this sacramental way to what it represents.
4. So what does Christian baptism represent? Baptism represents solemn admission of the party baptized into the visible Church; it is a sign and seal of the covenant of grace, it represents the baptized individual's ingrafting into Christ, it represents regeneration, it means remission of sins, as well as surrender to God, through Jesus Christ, to walk in the newness of life. There is therefore a sacramental union between water baptism and all these things. Note that baptism means or represents a number of things on this list which we would normally associate with *conversion*, and not with sanctification——things like ingrafting into Christ, regeneration, remission of sins, and so on. This is the language of conversion, not surprisingly, because baptism is the sacrament of initiation.
5. The sacramental union between the sign and the thing signified is not tied to the moment of time when it is administered (WCF 28.6). The union is a sacramental union, not a temporal union.
6. If this converting grace promised in baptism (and sacramentally united to it) belongs to someone (one of the elect), then by a right use of the sacrament (remember what right use means), then the promised grace is, by the power of the Holy Spirit, not only offered to this individual,

but exhibited to him, and *conferred* upon him (WCF 28.6). What is conferred? Remission of sins, regeneration, ingrafting into Christ, etc.

7. This baptismal grace is not limited to those who are "of age," but can also belong to infants. This means that the Holy Spirit can offer, exhibit, and confer this baptismal grace upon infants. Notice what this does to Rick Phillip's alternative, where baptism only conveys a grace *previously* received through faith alone. If someone restricts faith only to those who can knowingly give their assent to propositions, then they are out of conformity with the Standards. If baptismal grace is possible for infants (who die in infancy, say), and evangelical faith is the only way to have a "right use" of the sacrament to receive this blessing, then the Confession teaches that infants can have evangelical faith. Right? Great—glad that's settled.

Such is the teaching of the Confession. I subscribe to it *and* agree with it. Guy Waters does not. Cal Beisner does not. If the Confession gives a detailed description of a sacramental union between water baptism and converting graces (which it plainly and unambiguously does), then what do you call it when guardians of the Confession just wave their hands over it, and pronounce (*ex cathedra*) that is doesn't mean what it says? When this kind of inversion happens, then only one thing can follow it—accusations must be brought against those who still hold to the original meaning of the Confession at this point. And that is what is happening. The rabbis are cracking down lest the original sacramental Calvinism of the Confession break free from the talmudic layers of revivalism that have been imposed upon it.

It is like the Second Amendment to the Constitution. If you maintain, with a straight face, that the right to keep and bear arms means that you don't have the right to keep and bear arms (as many solons and political chin-scratchers do), then what is to be done with those raving lunatics in Idaho who think that they somehow have the right to keep and bear arms? When you twist the original intent of words like this, then only one thing can be done with those who remain faithful to the original intent of those words. *Attack them as innovators*, which is exactly what Beisner and Waters have done in this book.

Incidentally, just for the record, I don't put Phillips in the same category. He shares the same paradigm with the other anti-FVers, but has in a number of instances shown a fair-minded willingness to hear his opponents out in a judicious and nonpolitcal way. I differ with him as much as I ever did, but it is (as far as I can tell) a straight-up doctrinal difference. I can't say the same thing about some of the high-octane weirdness elsewhere. And I hope this doesn't get Rick into trouble with any of his friends, but there it is.

LAST POST ON WATERS
AUGUST 5, 2006

Okay, one last comment, and I am done reviewing Waters's book. In the bibliography, Waters says this about my lecture on heretics and the covenant at the 2002 Auburn Avenue Pastors Conference.

> Wilson calls for a "covenantal approach to heresy," one that recognizes the "objective . . . covenantal obligations" of the heretic, who, if "lawfully baptized," must be "received[d] . . . as a fellow Christian." Such an individual must then be treated as a covenant breaker. This lecture well illustrates the overwhelmingly external cast of Wilson's ecclesiology. (p. 361)

I won't take long with this. Jesus teaches us that it is out of the abundance of the heart that the mouth speaks. The good man brings forth good things, and the evil man brings forth evil things. We must deal with it when it gets to the outside because we are not competent to address it at the root. I cannot convict someone of *incipient* heart-heresy—that is the way to ecclesiastical tyrannies. Only God can deal with the heart directly. I am called to deal with the person in accordance with what I can deal with—and that means what Waters calls the "externals." But there is a difference between my practice, which of necessity deals with externals, and my ecclesiology, which does not. My ecclesiology takes full account of the heart—the fact that covenant members have them, the fact that they must be transformed by the Holy Spirit, and the need for the Church to deal with external corruptions that follow when hearts are corrupt.

So it is false to say that my ecclesiology is external. If there is anyone who has gone out of his way to emphasis the absolute necessity of heart regeneration, true conversion to God, the needed for true closure with Christ, I would be that guy. In addition, I have emphasized that while the hidden things of the heart (as such) are out of our reach, the Bible teaches that the works of the flesh are *manifest*. You identify the tree by the *fruit*. And when you see the heretical manifestation of fruit that unregenerate hearts always bring forth—you deal with it.

Although Waters's clear departures from Westminster sacramentalism are not (in my view) heresy, this whole thing does provide us with a good example of this principle. I do not have any idea of Guy Waters's motivations. I have no way of ascertaining what his heart's intent was in writing this book. All I have to go on is the external product—the slipshod book he actually wrote. This does not mean that I think that there is nothing more to Guy Waters than the book he wrote. This does not mean that I have an "externalist" view of Waters. I just have an externalist view of what I am competent to deal with. I can answer the book he wrote; I cannot answer for why he wrote it.

To summarize this series of posts, I would conclude by urging the anti-FV forces to reconsider their choice of a champion. Guy Waters is clearly more than capable of reading mountains of material. He can assemble evidence in print that he has read it by using the usual scholarly apparatus. As I have shown repeatedly in this series of posts, what he cannot do is represent that material fairly, or refute it with theological integrity.

CHUGGING THROUGH THE MEADOW
AUGUST 10, 2006

What does it look like when the Presbyterian locomotive jumps the rails and finds itself chugging valiantly through a meadow? Let a recent statement from Evangel Presbytery (PCA) answer the question. HT: Jeff Meyers*

* jeffreyjmeyers.blogspot.com

> Evangel Presbytery declares that the doctrines of the "New Perspective on Paul," "Auburn Avenue Theology/Federal Vision", and teachings of Norman Shepherd, N.T. Wright, and Douglas Wilson which foster these positions, to be outside of the bounds of acceptable theological doctrine for Teaching Elders and Ruling Elders in Evangel Presbytery and are not to be believed or taught within the churches of this Presbytery; and each Teaching and Ruling Elder be charged with equipping the members of their churches to stand against these doctrines.

I don't think this is general enough yet. I think they need to back off a bit and just condemn anything we teach "to the extent that it might be in error." What do they mean, "the doctrines of"? If they are charging TEs and REs to equip the members of their churches "to stand against these doctrines," is this pronouncement supposed to be an example of how to do it?

CONSERVATIVES BLITZ ANYWAY
AUGUST 20, 2006

I believe it was Samuel Francis who said that Washington, D.C., was run by two political parties—the Evil Party and the Stupid Party. The same thing is true in contemporary ecclesiastical politics. We have the people who are selling out the "faith once delivered," and then there are those who are clueless about what is going on. A dangerous subset of this latter category is made up of those who know *that* the faith is being corrupted, but they have no idea of *how* it is being done. They don't know what play is being run. That being the case, they enthusiastically set up exactly the wrong defense. They blitz, which is what the conservatives usually do, and so then the unbelievers in the Church run a really sweet screen pass. Not only that, but it *always* works.

I am not really sure what category to put this post under——it could be any number of them. Postmodernism, Auburn Avenue Stuff, N.T. Wrights and Wrongs——this thought relates to any number of those topics, but not directly. So I am going to put it under Auburn Avenue Stuff, but please make applications elsewhere.

An uproar begins in conservative circles about the relationship between faith and works. With some parties to the dispute, it is just a matter of semantics (this is at the heart of the Auburn Avenue controversy). But outside conservative circles, there are people who really are trying to intrude autonomous works into the process of justification, which is, of course, a really bad thing to do. This is what religious man always wants to do. Conservatives react to this like it was catnip, and it does not matter that it was catnip set out especially for them. Making this observation does not mean that I am friendly to the idea of making anything-that-could-lead-to-boasting into an instrument (or partial instrument) of justification. But what is the *actual* play being run here?

Taking the broad picture in the Church today, who is most likely to be talking about the need for love, good works, missional concern, social ethics, and so on? Right, the liberals. And why do they do this? In order to seize the high ground, and to make sure that no one brings up their lack of love, lack of good works, contempt for real evangelism, and their corruption of social ethics. Conservatives don't bring up this glaring inconsistency because they don't want to play into the "works salvation" scheme. But Scripture requires us to bring up any such discrepancy.

Of course we are not saved *by* good works (Eph. 2:8–9). But we are saved *to* good works (Eph. 2:10), which God prepared beforehand for us to do. Not only so, but we are told expressly that the testing ground of true faith is true works. Show your faith by your works, man. Not mere affirmation of good works with the lips, either, but genuine, honest-to-God good works. Not good works redefined to fit comfortably into some humanist's social agenda, but good works defined *biblically*, and structured biblically on the foundation of real faith in the revealed will of God.

This is why we should be opposed to the ordination of women—because faith without works is dead. This is why it is a profanation of God's Temple to solemnize homosexual unions—because faith without works is *dead*. This is why we have no business redefining sentimentalism as love—because faith without works is dead. This is why godly Christian leaders must stand opposed to the growth of the idolatrous state (even when done in the name of the poor)—because faith without works is dead.

Nothing wrong with *sola fide*. Amen seven times over. But by emphasizing it the *way* they have done, some contemporary conservatives have done a grave disservice to the gospel. This is not because they themselves are distorting the gospel, but rather because they are unaware of how the adversary is seeking to distort the gospel at this point. Because of this, the conservatives unwittingly help with the distortion.

Many years ago, I learned (talking with Mormons) that we need to speak as though all the Bible belongs to us, and not as though we have Romans and Galatians and they have James. When an evangelical says "by grace are ye saved . . .", they say, "faith without works is dead." And there we both are, safely barricaded behind our respective passages. But suppose an evangelical said to a Mormon (I am using them for illustrative purposes because they explicitly avow a role for works), right out of the starting blocks, "You know, a central reason why I can't embrace the LDS approach is because faith without works is dead."

Faith and works (biblically) have a robust relationship—like the body and the spirit, designed to work together. Some conservatives, in the interests of keeping these two things really, really distinct, want the body and spirit separated, the result of which is death. Liberals want the body and spirit *together*, and are all about it, but on closer inspection, the spirit turns out to be an unclean spirit.

When we get to the place where it becomes apparent "what play was run," it will be seen that one kind of conservative ran a bunch of other conservatives out of their Reformed denominations, paving the way for the liberals. The conservatives who were made to feel unwelcome were those who had been trying to insist that orthodoxy and orthopraxy belong together, and that faith without works is dead. But suspicious of good works that proceed from the grace of God, other diehard conservatives prepared the way for the "good works" that proceed from the devious mind and heart of man. Instead of faith, hope, and love, we will find ourselves with the "good works" of sodomy, tolerance, and free chocolate milk for everybody. All that, and a group hug after therapy.

SEPTEMBER–DECEMBER 2006

ACTIVE OBEDIENCE AS THEMATIC STRUCTURING DEVICE
SEPTEMBER 9, 2006

And with a sexy title like that, if you can avoid being dragged in then you are beyond all hope.

I know that I have been referring to Peter Leithart a bit lately, but that is just the way it goes. This last Wednesday, Peter presented an unpublished paper to the NSA faculty forum. The paper, not surprisingly, was fantastic. But this post is different than the discussions of postmodernism—in those posts I have just been repeating and reinforcing Peter's deconstruction of faux-deconstruction. This is a little different. Peter's paper was on the life of Christ in Matthew as a recapitulation of the history of Israel. In the course of his paper, another line of application entirely bounced into my mind unbidden. I think this application is compelling, but want to ask you not to blame Peter for any weirdness you detect in it.

First, the fact that the New Testament writers saw Christ as the new Israel seems to me to be beyond dispute. In Matthew, for example, Christ was baptized in the Jordan as Israel was in the cloud and in the sea. After the baptism Christ spend forty days in the wilderness, as Israel spent forty years. During the wilderness Christ was tempted as was Israel. Christ stood, and Israel failed. After the wilderness sojourn, Christ began His "invasion" of Canaan, and Israel invaded Canaan. Beyond these obvious sorts of parallels, Peter's paper went on to show that Matthew presents the life of Christ according to the structure of Israel's history throughout the course of the entire Old

Testament. There is certainly room for discussion in the details, but Matthew is explicit in the central fact of this identification. When he quotes Hosea (out of Egypt I called my son) and applies it to Jesus, he is quoting a verse which in its original context applied to Israel and the Exodus. When Israel was a child I loved him, and out of Egypt I called my son. This is an egregious misquote . . . unless Matthew rightly sees Christ as Israel.

So then, what does this have to do with the doctrine of active obedience? This is where my jeep left the road and went bouncing across the meadow. If the history of the Old Testament can be summed up as "Israel screws up," then the story of Christ is summed up as "Israel does it right." If Christ is fulfilling all the failed promise of Israel's long story, then it is obvious that the perfect life of Christ is far more important than just a precondition for His sinless sacrifice on the cross (His passive obedience).

His entire life is obviously crucial to the justification of all Israelites (those who are in Him, the true Israel). The recapitulation of Israel's history in the life of Christ shows that the perfect life of Christ is significant to believers *in a soteriological sense.* If it is undeniable that the New Testament shows Christ as the new Israel (and I believe it is), and if this is self-evidently because He is being the true Israel *for us*, so that we can be true Israelites in Him, it follows that we are participating in His obedient life. The perfect obedience that He rendered to God throughout the course of His life was a life lived before God, *and He did it for us.* This is nothing other than the doctrine of the imputation of the active obedience of Jesus Christ. It is being stated at a broader level than perhaps some talk about it, but it is clearly and recognizably the same thing.

Some of the problems that some have with the doctrine of the imputation of the active obedience of Christ is that is our focus is too individualistic—we put the thing under the microscope. What we see is accurate, but out of context. In that setting, a glorious truth can look outlandish or surreal. We think of Christ's perfect individual righteousness being transferred to another individual, *as* an individual. This is true—that does happen at the end of day, but there is some broader context.

But if we look at it in the native habitat (say, in the gospel of Matthew), and not under the microscope of individual soteriology, we see that the active obedience of Christ is not an esoteric doctrine tucked away in some obscure part of the Bible for some Puritan divine to find in the seventeenth century. Rather, it is one of the grand structuring devices of the original writers. It is clearly Matthew's thematic structuring device.

Think about it. If Matthew structures his entire gospel around the theme of Christ being an obedient Israel, and not a disobedient Israel, and He is doing this so that we could be a restored and true Israel because of His obedience, what else can we call this?

A shorthand form of the doctrine of active obedience is that Christ's obedience throughout the course of His sinless life has been imputed by the grace of God to me. I believe this is true, but there is a fuller way to explain it, and this fuller way makes the doctrine not only true, but one of Scripture's primary truths. Christ's obedience as the true Israel has been imputed to *us*, to all of us who are the Israel of God, and therefore to me. The reason I can be an Israelite and not be destroyed is Israel is now obedient. And whose obedience was this? How did it happen? The active obedience of Christ began with His miraculous birth, and His exile in Egypt, and His restoration from Egypt. Out of Egypt God called His Son. And when God called His Son, we came too.

NO DEBATE
SEPTEMBER 18, 2006

Some weeks ago, after I finished reading Guy Waters's book on the Federal Vision, I contacted him, and offered to work with him to set up some kind of discussion/debate between the two of us. I was willing to fly to Jackson and have our interaction there. Our phone conversations were very cordial, but he was not interested in a face-to-face debate of that kind. He indicated that a written debate would be a possibility, so I wrote up a proposal and sent to him. That debate would be published in *Credenda*, and Dr. Waters would have the freedom to publish it in whatever setting he would like.

Today I heard back from him. He wrote that he had "been advised by [his] presbytery's study committee on the New Perspectives and Federal Vision that [he] not engage in this debate." Wishing to respect their counsel, Dr. Waters declined the invitation.

Unfortunately, that being the case, I would like to extend the invitation more broadly. I would like to ask any anti-FV pastor or theologian (who would be recognized as a credible spokesman for that position), and who is willing to identify with Dr. Waters's critique of the FV, to please contact me.

And it should be mentioned that the stance of the PCA study committee is curious.

BUCKETS OF BLOG WATER
OCTOBER 4, 2006

Some time ago, I posted a note on my invitation to a debate over Auburn Avenue issues. I did that here.* And now, on *The Puritan Board*, there is an ongoing discussion† of that invitation. The consensus appears to be that a debate with me would be a bad idea, with a few folks questioning the wisdom of this approach.

Just two comments. The first is that such a debate is not some crazy idea that I cooked up. "A bishop must . . . be able by sound doctrine both to exhort and to convince the gainsayers. For there are many unruly and vain talkers and deceivers, specially they of the circumcision: whose mouths must be stopped . . ." (Titus 1:7–11). If my positions actually *are* what these gentlemen claim, then that means that I qualify as an unruly and vain talker, a deceiver, a Judaizer, and one whose mouth must be stopped. Okay, then. You can't have it both ways. If I really am that kind of man, where in North America is a recognized champion of orthodoxy who will provide the valuable service of shutting me up? "Ah, but Wilson is so *slippery*," say many on *The Puritan Board*. Okay. Isn't that precisely why you have to shut such people

* This linked to the September 18 post directly above.

† Currently available here: puritanboard.com/threads/a-federal-vision-debate.15818.

up? Their slipperiness subverting whole households and all? "But he contradicts himself, morphing his positions! Hard to pin down!" That's what they say, anyway, and apparently this is so obvious a failing in me that it should be child's play to demonstrate in a debate. Right? I would wager that the first century contained false teachers who were just as much a slippery gus as I appear to be in the eyes of some. St. Paul told Titus to do something about them. St. Paul is telling the TRs, *given their premises*, to do something about it also. But if they won't debate, then they have a responsibility to ramp down the rhetoric, and to knock off calling fellow Reformed ministers "unruly and vain talkers."

The second point has to do with an *ad hom* that was offered on the board, explaining why I am desperate for this debate. Apparently, I have a career to save, networks to preserve, contracts to sandbag, a high-profile reputation to keep from tanking, and so on. Like Mark Twain, who said that reports of his death were greatly exaggerated, I really have to say a similar thing here. *Through no merit of ours*, and *by His grace alone*, God continues to bless what we are connected with, and we are most grateful to Him for it. New St. Andrews is bursting at the seams, Canon Press has a stack of new books at the printers now, *Credenda* is flourishing, our churches here in Moscow have been continuing to steadily grow, and the CREC is prospering. So my "desperation" for a debate needs to be grounded in something else, and if it needs to be nefarious, perhaps someone should suggest that I am being blackmailed. But whatever they say, the real reason for a debate is that I would like to make it plain to the broader Reformed community that Machen's warrior children don't really need another civil war.

And in the meantime, if this altar is God's, and the fire is going to fall, it doesn't matter to me how many buckets of blog water you pour on it.

ACHAIA REFORMED SEMINARY
OCTOBER 6, 2006

Scott Clark recently was critical of what we are reportedly trying to do here in Moscow.

> The culture reacted to the early Christians in official and unofficial ways. 1 Peter 4 reflects this. The apostolic Christians suffered social stigma not for trying to "take back" or "take over" the Roman empire (or small towns in Asia Minor) but for simply living quiet, godly lives. They suffered shame for worshiping a crucified Jew. They were misunderstood for eating "the body" of Christ. They were mocked for changing their lifestyles, for not getting drunk and attending orgies any more.*

Two quick comments. I am afraid that this is a little simplistic, on two fronts. The first is that there were many political undercurrents to the clash between Rome and the Christians. What was a religious issue for the Christians was a political issue for Rome. And those who had it in for the Christians knew exactly what buttons to push. "Whom Jason hath received: and these all do contrary to the decrees of Caesar, saying that there is another king, one Jesus" (Acts 17:7). But what they were *accused* of doing and what they were *actually* doing were two distinct things. Which leads to the next point.

Clark is quite right about 1 Peter 4. The Christians were attacked for living pious and orderly lives. But the *reason* for the attack and the *content* of the attack were different. They were accused of cannibalism and incest so on. So what would we say to the Christians in Achaia who were mistakenly critical of their brothers in Asia Minor? What should we say to a theological professor at Achaia Reformed Seminary who posted a stern warning to the slandered Christians of Asia Minor? "We should be persecuted for the sake of *Christ*, and not for practicing cannibalism or incest, for pity's sake!" Perhaps a letter suggesting that perhaps such charges are, to use an old-fashioned word, false? Yes, I bet a letter would fix everything.

The price of doing exactly what the apostles required of us is that unbelievers will slander us and speak of things that "we know not" (Ps. 35:11). Another cost is that fellow believers, *who ought to know better than to believe this kind of stuff*, will (for reasons of their own) accept it anyway.

* Posted at puritanboard.com/threads/doug-wilson-movie.15809/#post-202504.

JUST CALL ME TREVOR
OCTOBER 14, 2006

In the history of the Church, Christians have certainly divided over inconsequential matters before. Should you make the sign of the cross with two fingers or three? They have also divided over momentous issues, where the gospel itself was at stake. The magisterial Reformation was an example of this.

Sometimes issues arise where it is hard to categorize. There is enough confusion over theological terminology and usage to make the discussions themselves difficult, and if you throw in personal suspicions and ecclesiastical turf issues, you have yourself a perfect storm. Might the gospel itself be at stake? Maybe. Might the gospel itself be at stake *either way you go*? Maybe.

The FV controversy provides a very good example of this. How many issues are connected to it? There are quite a few, and they are all of them weighty. The relationship of faith and works, justification by faith alone, hermeneutics, sacramental theology, paedocommunion, the centrality of liturgy and worship, the exile of the Church in the Babylon of modernity, and lots more than that. So for people on both sides this is not a simple "do we baptize with heads upstream or downstream" issue.

As a bona fide guy on the FV side of things, I definitely have sharp differences with those who are on the warpath against us. But as a confessional Reformed minister who has honestly subscribed to the Westminster Confession of Faith, I am also convinced that many of the "distinctives" I am accused of promulgating are not distinctives at all, but are in fact the teaching and doctrine of the Confession. And so this means I believe our adversaries are actually out of conformity with the teaching of the Confession at a number of points.

At the same time, I believe that at the heart of the TR concerns are *some* issues that they are quite right to be concerned about, and which they have the right and responsibility to defend and make a big deal out of. On these concerns, they *do* represent the teaching of the Reformers. The systematics course in Greyfriars Hall, our ministerial training program, is a course through the Westminster Confession, and there are a number of central issues there where

I believe FV advocates have a responsibility to *emphasize* their whole-hearted agreement. As I told my students recently, there are many ways in which I consider myself a TR. Or make that a TRFVer. Just call me Trevor.

But here is the problem. I have found that for many on the other side of this fracas, the more I emphasize my agreement with certain evangelical essentials (e.g., the absolute necessity of the new birth), the more it convinces my adversaries that I am a disingenuous sneak. I have resolved to affirm any FV truths that are grounded in Scripture and the honored traditions of the Reformed faith (and there are many). In fact, *sola Scriptura* is one of our central traditions, but that is a subject for another day. But I have refused to take this stand in a glib *either/or* way. Why rush to divide? I have approached the whole deal in as catholic a *both/and* way as possible. But far from establishing my orthodoxy in some quarters, it has merely served as an clinching argument for my theological dishonesty.

And this is why I think it is necessary to turn the charge around. Catholicity in this discussion does not require that we refrain from vigorous debate. Given the state of the church, and the turmoil this whole controversy has engendered, focused debate is most necessary. To continue the accusations without being willing to debate is the real intellectual dishonesty. The broader Reformed church coming to consensus and like-mindedness on this complex set of issues will *not* be accomplished by all of us preaching to our respective choirs.

And so, again, I would like to reissue the invitation to the debate that Guy Waters declined. I would be more than willing to meet in charitable Christian debate with any credible representative of and spokesman for the mainstream anti-FV position. We would arrange a time and place mutually agreeable, conduct the debate, and make the audio and video tapes available for distribution by both sides.

In issuing this invitation, I want specifically to invite men like Ligon Duncan, Scott Clark, Cal Beisner, or Joe Morecraft. If any of you are willing, please contact us. The invitation is also open to any young, *capable* Elihu who is embarrassed by the silence of his elders.

TABLE TALK
OCTOBER 19, 2006

I have been asked to comment on the following statement, taken from the October edition of *Table Talk*.

> Other revisions or rejections of orthodox covenant theology include the so-called Federal Vision movement that not only rejects the covenant of redemption; it rejects the distinction between law and gospel and the distinction between the covenants of works and grace. According to them, every baptized person is elect and united to Christ through baptism, but this election and union can be forfeited through faithlessness.

Speaking for myself, I don't reject the covenant of redemption. I see a marked difference between law and gospel, but I find that this difference is fundamentally located in the heart of the one reading the Scriptures. Law and gospel are terrifying soteriological and eschatological realties, not hermeneutical principles. I affirm the distinction between the covenant of works and the covenant of grace, but I also affirm that the covenant of works is gracious because God is gracious. In the foregoing list, there is clearly confusion, but I think it is an understandable confusion. But the last statement——"According to them, every baptized person is elect . . ." is an appalling example of misdirection.

I am sorry to see *Table Talk* taking this direction.

LIKE A CANOE FULL OF BRICKS
OCTOBER 20, 2006

Let me recommend a post over at TeamPyro*, and let me do this for a couple reasons. The first is that I want to commend Frank Turk's post there. He is a genuine non-FV guy, a baptist, and he is the only one I have encountered (thus far) that is really capable of stating my position in terms that I would *generally* recognize and own. He then goes on to reject it, but I believe he has a good grasp of what is actually happening in all this.

* teampyro.blogspot.com/2006/10/wednesday-funnies.html

The second reason for heading over there is that Michael Metzler showed up in the comments section of the blog to do his typical thing. In his interactions with him, Frank Turk found out what it is like trying to give a tar baby a bath in vegetable oil. But I bring it up for this reason. In the course of his in interaction with Frank, Michael said this:

> You here seem to imply that I am some kind of **anonymous troll. But this is entirely not true. I always give my real name** and often give even my cell phone and email address . . ..sometimes even my PO box address. This is information advertised on my website too. As Stacey recently argued on Wilson's blog however, if Steve was Michael Metzler it is clear what the only intentions would be in using an alias; it would simply be for the purpose of being able to participate in the discussion at all. That seems like a pretty simple issue. So I'm not sure why you would make me out to have this kind of problem when **I am in fact one of the most non-anonymous guys on the internet**.

"Entirely not true." "Always give my real name." "One of the most non-anonymous guys." So this constitutes a categorical denial of internet anonymity on Michael's part. The problem with this statement is that it is entirely and demonstrably false. Michael has been repeatedly banned from this blog because of his posting under anonymous names, and this is not just a bare assertion. I am in possession of weighty proof—like a canoe full of bricks—that this is what he has been doing. And in the quote above, Michael treats Stacey and Steve as two other individuals, with photos on their very own driver's licenses. But Michael = Stacey = Steve. In other words, I *know* Michael posts anonymously, and can *prove* it, and I am using "proof" here in a sense not in vogue with postmodernists.

This means that Michael has repeatedly violated the ninth commandment on my blog, and he just now violated it on TeamPyro's blog. And for all the differences we have over FV stuff, we agree that violating the ninth commandment is not to be done. Michael really needs to remember that Pooh was an honest bear.

THE ONE AND THE MANY
DECEMBER 2, 2006

In this space I have often referred to the various controversies that blew up over the last three or four years. The controversies, in alphabetical order, were: baptism, boarders, elder qualifications, Federal Vision, new perspective on Paul, perjury allegations, plagiarism allegations, postmodernism, satiric bite, slavery, tax apportionment and assessment, and, of course last, zoning.

I have mentioned before that these fraci (is that the plural?) are really only one controversy. The many are actually one, and the one is the many. My reason for saying this is not that they all have the common denominator of me being in them, but rather because I think they are really all about the same thing. That "one thing" is the full authority and sufficiency of Scripture.

Different people want the Scripture to stay away from different things, and for the sake of those different things they will frequently band together, cheek by jowl, in order to resist a comprehensive scriptural vision of the good life. Some of them think that the increased influence of Reformed theonomic imams here in Moscow bodes ill for a lesbian foreign policy. The reason this distresses them is that we are not *really* imams—if we were, they would be appeasing us like crazy, trying to dialogue with us, and building bridges instead of walls. But really, they don't like imams, unless they *are* imams.

Others don't want the Scripture messing with their scholastic definitions of certain doctrinal items. As somebody back in the eighties put it, "can't touch this." And because of their insistence on sticking with an "under a glass case orthodoxy" they are willing to make common cause with the anti-non-imams-imams, if you can follow me here. Related to this, this means that they are willing to adopt a pragmatic and Machiavellian use of church courts, than which there is no greater form of theological liberalism. What the liberals did to Machen, their *liberal* heirs are doing to numerous godly Christians around the country. Presbyterians like to point out (and I actually agree with them on this, being a presbyterian), that the first century Jewish system of polity and governance was a representative and presbyterian one. That makes Jesus a presbyterian. But after the warm glow has worn off, we then realize that this means that the Lord was condemned by the General Assembly—moved, seconded, and spanged right into the minutes.

Then there are the folks who don't know what is going on, but they know how to boo and hiss based on the kind of music that is being played by the pianist in this Federal Vision melodrama we have going here. This is the kind of movie you throw popcorn in.

Slavery? What does the Bible say? Satire? What does the Bible say? Covenant faithfulness and obedience? What does the Bible say? Baptism? What does the Bible say? Sexual ethics? What does the Bible say? Elder qualifications? What does the Bible say? And consistently, the answer comes back that—with regard to the "precious," whatever it is—they don't *care* what the Bible says. It is easy for doctrinal conservatives to talk about the sufficiency of Scriptures. But from what I have seen, it is just as hard for them to apply as it is for anyone else.

BUILDING BRIDGES, NOT WALLS
DECEMBER 8, 2006

I saw a piece by John Piper* that Justin Taylor linked to, which I actually thought made quite a few good points. And I even believe he made a number of similar points to what I had argued here†. But then I saw Mark Horne's response to Piper, and Mark didn't seem that keen on it‡. He didn't say a lot (he promises more when he cools down), and because I respect Mark highly, I look forward to what he will say about it. But what he *did* say reminded me of some points that I made here§. So that's me. A uniter, not a divider.

A "YELLING AT MY WINDSHIELD" REPRISE
DECEMBER 7, 2006

Some time ago I listened through a set of conference tapes put out by Westminster West, and blogged on that experience, calling the series something

* Currently available here: desiringgod.org/articles/jesus-islam-pharisees-and-the-new-perspective-on-paul

† Unclear what post this was referring to.

‡ Currently available here: hornes.org/mark/2011/02/repost-the-new-perspective-on-moses

§ Unclear what post this was referring to.

like "Yelling At My Windshield." That series of posts is in the archives here, located somewhere under Auburn Avenue Stuff. I mention it now because this particular part of my *oeuvre* was alluded to in a comment to my post on the Westminster Confession's teaching on baptism. In that comment, Aaron Cummings said, "I listened to one of the Westminster West profs lambaste you, saying, 'Doug Wilson, if you're listening to this and pounding the windshield, please, give your comments on Heidelberg #21 and #60.' Would you be so kind as to fulfill this request?"

Sure. So let me say this about HC 21 and 60.

First, at Christ Church our liturgy follows the church year, and recitation of the Heidelberg Catechism is part of our worship every Lord's Day morning. Last Sunday was the first Sunday of Advent, so we have six weeks to go before the entire congregation confesses together the first of these two questions, and twenty-two weeks to go for the second. The entire congregation answers these questions, confessing our faith together.

Second, I am teaching the Lordship Colloquium at New St. Andrews this year, and one of the class requirements is to memorize key portions of the Heidelberg Catechism. As it turns out, just last week our freshman class all memorized Q60. In Jerusalem Term, they memorized Q21 (along with a number of others). This morning, before receiving this question, I just finished drafting the written portion of their final, which requires them to write out completely two of the answers that they have memorized this term. I would like to inquire of this professor at Westminster West if his students can stand at the beginning of each class period, as my students do, and recite together the most recent question they have memorized.

Third, we do this because we believe it. We are confessing our faith, learning our faith, and deepening in our love for our faith.

And fourth, lest this all be dismissed as some kind of nutso classical college parrot-drill—where it is alleged that we might know what the Heidelberg Catechism says, but we don't really believe it, as opposed to those true souls elsewhere who believe it, but don't know what it says—let me summarize each of these answers in my own words.

> Question 21: *What is true faith?*
> Answer: It is not only a certain knowledge by which I accept as true all that God has revealed to us in his Word, but also a wholehearted trust which the Holy Spirit creates in me through the gospel, that, not only to others, but to me also God has given the forgiveness of sins, everlasting righteousness and salvation, out of sheer grace solely for the sake of Christ's saving work.

I take this to mean that true faith is not just a confident knowledge that whatever God has revealed in Scripture has to be true, but also that it is a settled trust and confidence (this also a work of the Holy Spirit in my heart through the gospel) that God has not just saved other people, but that He has bestowed the grace of salvation on me also. This salvation, a sheer gift of nothing but grace, brings with it forgiveness for my sins, everlasting righteousness, and salvation. This is all done through Christ's work of obedience alone. In the work of salvation, Christ did His part and I did mine. He did the saving, and I got in the way.

> Question 60: *How are you righteous before God?*
> Answer: Only by a true faith in Jesus Christ. In spite of the fact that my conscience accuses me that I have grievously sinned against all the commandments of God, and have not kept any one of them, and that I am still ever prone to all that is evil, nevertheless, God, without any merit of my own, out of pure grace, grants me the benefits of the perfect expiation fo Christ, imputing to me his righteousness and holiness as if I had never committed a single sin or had ever been sinful, having fulfilled myself all the obedience which Christ has carried out for me, if only I accept such favor with a trusting heart.

I take this to mean that the true faith, described above in #21, is the sole instrument that God uses to declare me righteous before Him. Even though my conscience can accuse me of gross violations of God's commandments, having broken all of them, with a tendency still to veer off toward evil, nevertheless

God, without accepting or regarding any moral or ethical contributions from *me*, but rather out of unadulterated grace alone, gave and imputed to me all the perfections of Christ. These perfections included the perfect satisfaction of His death, not to mention the righteousness and holiness of His perfect sinless life. The result of this unspeakable grace is that it is as though I had never done anything wrong at all in my entire life, and also as though the perfect life that Christ actually lived had really been lived by me. All this is mine to extent that I accept such benefits with a believing heart, in true faith. And amen.

That said, let me make just a couple of concluding remarks. I believe all of this, and I believe it with a whole heart. I am even largely comfortable with the assertion in #21 that true faith accepts *everything* that God has revealed, meaning that those who deny the infallibility of Scripture are at the very least susceptible to the charge that theirs is not a true faith. Does our Westminster West friend come with me this far? Does he believe that "*true* faith accepts as true all that God has revealed to us in his Word," and that if someone holds as false something that God has revealed as true, that such faith is quite likely not a *true* faith?

AUDIO AUBURN STUFF
DECEMBER 15, 2006

The audio of Steve Wilkins's examination are now available. Session 1 is here*, and session 2 is right next to it. Three feet over we have session 3, and then, in the blue binding, we have session 4. I hope to post a few further comments on this whole subject a little bit later.

STEVE WILKINS AND THE PCA
DECEMBER 14, 2006

Here is the ecclesiastical situation with Steve Wilkins as I currently understand it. As a result of the Auburn Avenue controversy, Lousiana Presbytery of the PCA was asked to look into Steve's orthodoxy, which they did by means of a committee. And, given his orthodoxy, it is not surprising that they cleared

* auburnavenue.org/mp3_exam/session1_fromCD.mp3. These recordings appear to be currently unavailable.

him. But the controversy has continued apace anyhow, and the Standing Judicial Commission in the PCA was given authority in the matter. They have asked the Louisiana Presbytery to look into the matter *again*. The cynical among us might infer from this the upspoken expectation that "they might want to get the answer right this time." If the results of the second exam are not satisfactory, my understanding is that the SJC can then assume original jurisdiction, and take matters from there. I am not familiar with the BCO in the PCA so I would invite anyone to please correct me if I have missed something important. Which several of you have done, and I have entered the corrections.

Now this second exam by the Louisiana Presbytery took place this last Saturday. Part of it included asking Steve to respond in writing to a number of questions presented to him. His written answers to those questions can be found HERE*. You can see from reading through this material that the questions were not softball questions—they addressed all the substantive issues, and Steve answered them clearly, cogently, and well. I understand that in the near future an audio version of the oral exam will be available at this site also.

As I read through this material last night I was struck by a number of things. I would like to mention the bottom line first, but then go on to draw out what is really at stake for the PCA. Reading through Steve's answers was a genuinely bracing experience. His answers were biblical, confessional, orthodox, clear, honest, historical, faithful, and *right*. I am very grateful to be a friend of his, and proud to be associated with him in this.

But a lot is at stake. The need of the hour is this. Every person who has been following this Federal Vision thing at all needs to make a point of following this particular segment of it, and *really* should read through these answers that Steve has given. Because of how everything has fallen out, it looks as though Steve gets to be the *cause celebre* of this whole thing, at least within the PCA. But this is what *that* means. When you look at the claims in the memorial against Steve from the Central Carolina Presbytery, and you look at Steve's orthodox answers, there are only a few possible explanations for what could happen here. The first (and greatly to be desired) possibility

* auburnavenue.org/documents/wilkins_presbytery_response.htm

is that honest and conscientious TRs will see that whatever differences they might have with Steve, they do not rise to the level of requiring any kind of censure or discipline. Steve is well within confessional bounds. I pray that this will happen with many honest TRs who love Christ and the Westminster Standards, and who do so in that order.

But what if strident opposition continues despite these answers? This creates several possibilities also. One of them, sadly, is that it might be driven by a high level of theological ignorance. Certain men are being asked to follow arguments that they are simply not equipped to follow. Another possibility is simply old-fashioned hostility and malice. The facts don't matter to them, and they will do whatever they do to Steve simply because they think they can. And yet another possibility is that they have been persuaded somehow that because Steve's answers are orthodox, they must be dishonest. And so they want to convict him for the heresy they know he must harbor somewhere deep in his heart.

So as I see it, the ideal situation would be for ten thousand Reformed believers to read through Steve's answers *now*, and then turn and patiently wait for the SJC to make their determination. As I see it, given this clear confession of faith, any negative assessment of Steve is only possible if the judges are 1. clearly in over their heads 2. simply vindictive or 3. prepared to admit spectral evidence. If a conviction of heterodoxy happens through any combination of these three factors, I think it needs to happen in the bright light of day, with all sorts of checked out people looking at them as they do whatever they do. This must not be a back-room deal. It is an examination of a public minister's public teaching. That teaching is out on the table. We can all read it. And we can witness for ourselves whether or not the SJC is reading the same things we are.

MORE ON STEVE WILKINS
DECEMBER 16, 2006

Now, just a few comments on why Steve Wilkins's answers to his presbytery's questions satisfactorily address all the basic questions. This will not be long and involved because the issues are *not* complicated.

First, Steve unambiguously affirms the exhaustive sovereignty of God over all things.

> 2. Do you at all deny the definition of election as given in the Standards?
>
> Absolutely not, never have, and God willing, never will. I firmly believe in the absolute sovereignty of God over all things, including the salvation of man.

Now from any affirmation of the final and complete sovereignty of God over all things, the five points of Calvinism (as traditionally defined and understood) inexorably and necessarily follow. Steve is aware of this, and affirms the absolute sovereignty of God. He is therefore embracing the consequences of that affirmation.

Now the controversy is not over this, but rather over other affirmations which some believe to be inconsistent with this one. But as long as the full system of Westminster soteriology is unambiguously and clearly affirmed, the burden is on those bringing the accusation to demonstrate the inconsistency. They are certainly capable of *asserting* the inconsistency (so long as it is a friendly crowd, and no one there to debate them), but they actually have to show the inconsistency.

This leads to the second point. Steve is clearly not asserting that the benefits enjoyed by all covenant members are identical until the moment of apostasy undergone by some of them. This is not what he says. The emphasis below is mine.

> 4. How would you distinguish between the benefits enjoyed by a (decretively) elect member of the visible Church and a reprobate member of the visible church who has not yet manifested his apostasy?"
>
> This is not an easy question to answer but it does seem to me that the benefits enjoyed by the 'decretively elect' do differ from those received by the non-elect. First, they differ qualitatively. Thus, for example, though the non-elect are brought within the family of the justified and

> in that sense may be referred to as one of the justified, the elect person's justification in time is not only a declaration of his present acquittal from the guilt of sin but also an anticipation of his final vindication at the last judgment. The non-elect church member's "justification" is not. His 'justification' is not the judgment he will receive from God at the last day. Second, the blessings conferred differ in their duration. The elect person perseveres and remains in a state of grace until the end of his life. The non-elect believer eventually forsakes the faith and falls away from the state of grace. There may also be other experiential differences between the elect and the non-elect, but these differences may not be discernible (to the individuals themselves or to others) until the non-elect person displays his unbelief in some very explicit and concrete ways.

In other words, Steve is not affirming a tautological definition of perseverance (e.g., those who persevere are the ones who persevere). There is a *reason* for the perseverance of the decretively elect covenant member, and there is a *reason* for the apostasy of the non-elect covenant member. Part of that reason is qualitative and is seen by God throughout the entire course of their lives. God sees the apostasy coming, and, furthermore, going back to the first point, the whole thing is within His sovereign control.

This goes back to my first post on the Steve Wilkins thing. Those who have read through this material and cannot see that Steve embraces the heart and soul of the Calvinistic system are not qualified to be guardians of that system. There may be various reasons why they cannot see it. I mentioned three earlier—ignorance, hostility, or suspicion of personal dishonesty. I would be willing to consider other options if anyone wants to suggest them.

I don't want to seem rude to observers like "Johnny Redeemed," but it seems to me that his comments betray a real naivete when it comes to historic Reformed theology. I appreciate his caution, and would encourage him to continue, but the basic issues here are really *clear*. If I were talking to a pastor friend—say a Wesleyan Methodist or a Lutheran—and he affirmed in the course of our lunch discussion that he believed that God sovereignly decreed whatsoever comes to pass, including the salvation (or lack of it) for all individuals, and that he affirmed that God knew His elect from before the foundation of the world, and that He knew His elect throughout the course of their lives as they mingled with non-elect covenant members, my eyebrows would go up and I would say, "Friend, you had better be very careful. You're a *Calvinist*."

KICKING THIS PARTICULAR CAN DOWN THE ROAD
DECEMBER 18, 2006

All right, then. More on Steve Wilkins.

Actually, this is more on the sociology and demographics of the thing. From where I sit, in the Idaho nickel seats, this is what the lay of the land looks like.

I have urged every Reformed believer who has had any interest whatever in the Federal Vision controversy to follow this particular chapter of the story very closely. The early indicators show that this is exactly what is happening. Each day, the web traffic for this site averages between three and four thousand visitors (and between 16,000 and 19,000 hits). Last Thursday, when I posted the first of this series on Steve, I had over six thousand visitors that day—in short, a spike unheard of in these parts. There were almost 25,000 hits. *Lots* of people are following this.

On paper, the folks involved with the Standing Judicial Commission can do whatever they want to do with Steve. Their decision would be final; there is no appeal to GA. They don't have to have their action approved by GA—all they have to do is report what they have done, and the GA would say *oh*. This is a body that carries the full authority of the entire PCA. Whether *that* was a good idea is a discussion for another time, but right now that is just the way it is.

This being the case I am urging everyone with a dog in the fight to watch these developments very closely, and it is important for the SJC to know that they are being watched closely in this way. And more people have a dog in the fight than you might think. Ministerial candidates who are under the care of various presbyteries need to follow this. Seminarians need to be following this.

Ministers in the PCA need to follow this because everything that is happening to Steve could happen to them—with no charges ever having been brought and no appeal possible. Nice set up if you can arrange it. These guys know their onions. This could happen even if a minister jots and tittles his way through the entire Westminster Confession of Faith.

If this travesty happens (as it certainly could), it needs to happen with many thousands of informed observers looking straight at it, in the broad light of day. From what I have gathered thus far, *thankfully* that is what is happening.

As I have written earlier, this is not at all inconsistent with what I have urged people to do in other judicial situations (e.g., the RC Jr. situation). When a judicial body is charged with sorting out a host of did-too-did-nots, the last thing that needs to happen is for Internet-land to form a committee of the whole, with the loudest quadrant of that committee being made up of anonymous and scurrilous railers. This is because the nature of the dispute has to do with particular situations and about what happened, or did not happen, at a session meeting last August, say. But this situation with Steve is a public dispute about doctrine, a public dispute about what Steve teaches and has taught in public. What does he affirm? What does he deny? In this situation, Christ's words to the high priest are far more apropos. "Go ask the Temple crowd about that parable. *They* heard me."

Steve holds to the Westminster Confession of Faith. If we are talking about original intent, he is far more in conformity to the Westminster than are his accusers. Ask any of those who are worked up about his teaching if they believe the two sacraments are effectual means of salvation. They will respond that they believe the sacraments are means of grace, but they are means of *sanctifying* grace, not saving grace. So then ask them why the Catechism question put it the way it did, instead of asking how the two sacraments are effectual means of sanctification. You will get a reply that amounts to them having an interpretive wand that they wave over certain words to make them mean, a la Lewis Carroll, what they want them to mean. They will perhaps add that this is why nobody wants to debate you. You keep getting off the point, which is that you are a heretic, and keep gravitating to extraneous material, like how the early Reformed fathers made almost all the same points you guys are making. "Like, man, who cares?" This is a postmodern era, and the TRs are now going in for advocacy history—the cheap and easy way of being historic and confessional. But they would rather not know about this because they still like believing that they are genuine conservatives.

I got distracted. The central point remains this: read Steve's written responses* to the questions put to him by presbytery. Listen to the audio† if you need to. Without any judgment on these responses having been made by any judicial body, make up your mind on what Steve is teaching and saying. And then wait for the decision of the Lousiana Presbytery next month. After that wait and see what the SJC does, if anything.

HONESTLY. I ASK YOU.
DECEMBER 20, 2006

The problem with the word *conservative* is that it leaves open the question of what it is you are conserving exactly. It can refer to Kremlin KGB types, Saudi Muslims, polygamous Mormons, and men like J. Gresham Machen. And a conservationist is someone who derives his ideological identity from wanting to conserve *other* stuff.

So different kinds of conservatives want to conserve different kinds of things. Big government conservatives want to conserve the victories of their fathers' enemies. Small government conservatives want to conserve the memory of a kind of thinking that made its last public appearance during the administration of Grover Cleveland. So different kinds of conservatives want to conserve different things. They differ in the direct object.

But they can also differ in the adverb—*how* do you conserve things? One kind of conservative tries to do this woodenly. He doesn't want

* Available here: auburnavenue.org/documents/wilkins_presbytery_response.htm.

† auburnavenue.org, resource no longer available.

anything to change, period, and so he insists that every candidate at presbytery take a vow to uphold the original Westminster, in exactly the form it came down from Allah in the original Arabic. But the mushy liberals are no better. They want candidates to appear at presbytery like they were guests on Ophrah. "Tell us what the Westminster Confession has meant to you in times of trouble."

But strict subscription does not uphold the Westminster Confession. It is a flagrant *denial* of it. Synods and councils have erred, and do err, including *this* one, chump. Loose subscription is no help either. What good is a fence around the vegetable garden of truth that makes sure there are holes every ten feet big enough for the average erroneous rabbit? But there is an alternative to strict subscription, which necessarily elevates the Confession to the level of Scripture, and loose subscription, which lowers the Confession to the level of the 9th and 10th amendments to the U.S. Constitution.

This alternative is called honest subscription. A confession is a form of doctrinal shorthand. I can communicate a great deal in a short space of time by saying that I hold to the Westminster Confession, with "the following exceptions." The person taking the exceptions, and the presbyters hearing him, are dealing with the material honestly. If he says that he subscribes to the Confession, but that he doesn't buy all "that Trinity stuff," he is a heretic, but at least he is being an honest one. And when the presbytery rejects him, they are doing so because they know exactly where he is coming from. But if he says that he believes the Westminster is overly restrictive in its statement of what is required on the Lord's Day (as I did when I subscribed to the Westminster Confession), they know that this exception does not strike at the innards of Calvinism. Indeed, many of them would agree that this actually strengthens sabbatarianism; it does not weaken it. But the key is to let the presbytery *know* that you agree with the whole thing, with the exception of "this, this, and that."

Now when a man subscribes to the Confession and his beliefs are not in conformity with what the Westminster theologians intended when they adopted it, there are two possibilities. One is that he is a dishonest man, saying that he believes things he does not believe. This is the way of liberalism——the same liberalism, incidentally, that prides itself on openness, transparency, and honesty. This is confessional rot, and it is a character issue. It is dishonest subscription.

But there is a "conservative" way to do this also. The problem is in the adverb, as I pointed out earlier, and it is usually done through ignorance, not dishonest malice. But ignorance can get you as far away from the original intent of the Westminster Assembly as dishonesty can. If a man gets off the right road and is barreling along in the wrong direction at 75 mph, his speed is not affected by whether the choice to get off the right road was deliberate or accidental. In either case, his car still has eight cylinders.

And this brings us to Steve Wilkins. Steve really believes that through a right use of the ordinance of baptism, the grace of that baptism is really exhibited and conferred on those who whom it properly belongs (Westminster 28.6). He subscribes to this portion of the Confession intelligently and honestly. To speak in theological categories, he *agrees* with it. His opponents *say* they subscribe to this, but they really do not, and they do not give any kind of reasonable explanation for how they can take these words. They don't need to give an explanation because we, on the other side of this divide, would like to *debate with* them, not *prosecute* them.

So why the crisis then? Their problem is that if they don't prosecute us, they will eventually have to debate, and they don't have the answers that such a debate would require. They cannot answer the simple confessional questions that would be put to them in a debate. "Dr. Waters, do you believe that in salvation a worthy receiver, one who is such by virtue of the evangelical faith given to him by God, is receiving the salvific grace of his baptism? Or do you take an exception to 28.6?"

And this is the conclusion of the matter. Honest subscription is a moral necessity, one that requires diligent, hard *work*. Of course. liberals need to learn how to be honest with their own hearts, and with us. But there are many "conservatives" who need to learn how to be honest *with the text*. There is a difference between honest subscription to an oral tradition of American revivalism and honest subscription to the Westminster Confession. And as recent events have indicated, this is not a minor difference.

NO, NO. THE GOOD KIND OF LYNCHING
DECEMBER 21, 2006

Scott Clark has called the treatment that Steve Wilkins is getting an ecclesiastical lynching*. But before you start scratching your head over this puzzlement, he does say this like its a *good* thing. HT. Mark Horne†

Land of Goshen! if I may exclaim here with more than my usual vehemence. Or looking at it from another angle, *hush my puppies!* The entire post needs to be read in order to be believed. And so, as you can see, because Dr. Clark's concerns have apparently not been addressed satisfactorily, I would like (*again*) to cordially extend an invitation to discuss/debate these matters to:

> R. Scott Clark, D.Phil
> Associate Professor of Historical and Systematic Theology
> Westminster Seminary California
> "For Christ, His Gospel, and His Church"
> Associate Pastor
> Oceanside URC

But I honestly don't know why he thinks *our* theology is lax, with him sharing an office with Dr. Phil like that.

MORE TO BEING REFORMED THAN BELIEVING IN JESUS AND SMOKING CIGARS
DECEMBER 23, 2006

Most weeks we have a Friday morning men's prayer meeting, followed by a breakfast. The discussion at breakfast is frequently rowdy, and this last week

* Currently available here: puritanboard.com/threads/steve-wilkins-presbytery-examination-and-response.17769/#post-223946

† hornes.org/mark

it turned to the events surrounding Steve Wilkins—what Scott Clark might want to style as a Westminster necktie party.

In the course of the discussion, I made the point that this was nothing more than a simple continuation of the theonomy fracas in the Reformed world a couple decades ago. As a continuation, there are some differences, of course, but there it is.

First allow me to point to some points of continuity, seen most clearly in some of the players. Theonomists, because of their emphasis on the continuing validity of God's law, were frequently accused of undermining justification by faith alone. Norman Shepherd was slated to be one of the original Auburn speakers until he was providentially hindered by the tragic death of his wife and was replaced by John Barach. But had he been one of the speakers, the whole thing would have blown up, just like it did, only probably quicker. During the original Shepherd controversy, he had strong support among the theonomists—Greg Bahnsen and Gary North, to mention two. North even devoted an entire book—*Westminster's Confession*—defending Shepherd. Other supporters of Shepherd included such notables as Cornelius Van Til.

A number of other people who were involved in the theonomy movement are still around and pushing some of the root assumptions into the corners. From the front rank of the original theonomists we have Jim Jordan. From the second tier (of that day), we have men like Wilkins and Leithart. An exception would be someone like Joe Morecraft, who decided to bail. In short, when you look at the scorecard, and take in the names of the players, you see a lot of the same names. In addition, one of the central disputes (over justification) is the same, then and now. This is not a straight up debate over whether *sola fide* is true, but rather a debate over whether other assertions are consistent with *sola fide*. Now, just as then, confusion has caused certain Reformed believers to be accused of denying *sola fide*, when they claim they have done nothing of the kind.

Now, what's different about this episode and the theonomy episode? I do not mean to claim that the theonomists have learned nothing or have not modified their emphases. They most certainly have, and I actually believe that this is why the conflict has become even more intense. In the first round, the theonomy movement was an ideological movement, fueled largely by book publication. Once in a conversation with Greg Bahnsen, when I had explained to him why I was not theonomist, he made a helpful distinction for me. He said there was a difference between a movement and a school of thought. A movement is ideologically driven, has an explicit agenda, requires a movement leader, and so on. A school of thought encompasses people who share a broad number of assumptions but are not necessarily in the same revolutionary cell group. When we say that Descartes and Spinoza were both rationalists, this doesn't mean that they put out a newsletter together.

To apply this distinction, what has happened is this. The hardcore theonomy movement morphed into a broad theonomy-lite school of thought, and from there began to settle into particular communities, with a specific cultural embodiment. So there have been significant changes, but they have been the kind of changes necessarily introduced when you move from abstract idea to concrete application. The concrete application has included scores of classical Christian schools around the country, a college (New St. Andrews), church communities that emphasize parish life together (Monroe, Moscow, and numerous others). At the center of all of this is the practice (not just the idea) of the covenant renewal worship model. It is important to note that one of the changes has included turning away from the idea of political lobbying to the idea of cultural transformation through the potent leaven of worship.

In short, we have moved from the time when a handful of outrageous men were saying crazy things on paper (the Old Testament is still in the Bible, the gospel will conquer the world, etc.) to a time when a number of thriving communities are being built on the pastoral assumption that all of God's truths are designed to be *lived* and lived in community.

In our breakfast discussion, it was around this point that Roy Atwood offered a helpful breakdown of the Reformed world, as recalled from an article by Wolterstorff in the mid-seventies. Wolterstorff, talking about the CRC, broke that tradition down into three main streams—the doctrinalists, the pietists, and the Kuyperians. What he said there applies to the whole Reformed world, in spades. The doctrinalists are rationalistic and are concerned about getting the doctrines right on paper. The faith once delivered is a giant math problem, and they want to get a gold star on the top of their assignment when they turn it in. The pietists are concerned about whether they pray enough, whether they are going to heaven when they die, and whether or not they have witnessed to Uncle George in the right way. The Kuyperians hold that the lordship of Jesus Christ must be affirmed, and the cultural mandate fulfilled by extending the crown rights of Jesus over every last aspect of life. Now, it has to be emphasized here that for the first two options here, these choices present some kind of either/or choice. Either doctrinal purity or an upright life. Either an upright life or political engagement. Either doctrinal purity or But to accept this kind of dichotomy is to reject the Kuyperian option. The third option (of necessity) includes the need for personal piety and the need for doctrinal integrity. *The Kuyperian option includes the other two in a way that is not reciprocated.*

The failure to reciprocate is also the reason why these two truncated positions *cannot* understand how an embrace of the cultural mandate, driven by covenant renewal worship, is not, at some basic level, a fundamental compromise. This is because they do not recognize doctrinal faithfulness when it is out in the world, getting dirty. Nor can they see faithful Christian love and piety when it is out in the marketplace, sleeves rolled up and working hard. Some people can only recognize the five *solas* when they are pinned on a poster board, under the basement light of personal soteriology, like so many butterflies, now deceased. Take that thing out in the back yard and look at it in the sunlight. What have you changed? *Nothing.* There is no heresy here. What have you changed? *Everything.* There *is* a reason for the conflict.

Put another way, I am not being attacked because I deny *sola gratia* and *sola fide*. I affirm them, and with about the same level of enthusiasm as a Cossack dancing. But the backyard sunlight that I am looking at these truths in causes me to affirm *also* that this salvation, by grace alone, appropriated by evangelical faith alone, is a salvation that will cover the earth, as the waters cover the sea. Included in that salvation will be the Muslim world, Hollywood, Thailand, the National Academy of Sciences, and, *mirabile dictu*, the United States Congress. It is not through law that Abraham will INHERIT THE WORLD (Rom. 4:13).

So bring this all back to my friend Steve Wilkins. He is being attacked by a certain doctrinalist faction within the PCA. The pietists are not attacking him but are in no position to do anything other than feel bad about the whole thing. He is being defended (and prayed for) by the Kuyperians. To appeal to another set of distinctions (Neibuhr), the Christ-against-culture faction (the doctrinalists) is trying to make the PCA safe for the Christ and culture faction (the happy-clappys) by running out of the denomination one of their leading representatives of the truth that the Lord Jesus Christ is the transformer of culture.

DEATH IN THE POT
DECEMBER 26, 2006

Open Door Community Church is in the Little Rock area, and is pastored by an open homosexual, as you can see.* If you scroll down on their front page just a bit, you can see the enthusiastic endorsement of that church from Peggy Campolo, wife of Tony Campolo. If you look here†, you can see Brian McLaren in the course of his visit to that church.

Now if you look in the comments section of the recent post "More to Being Reformed Than Believing in Jesus and Smoking Cigars," you will see (our good friend) David Bahnsen's take on when the use of satire is appropriate. He has no problem with it when we are dealing with out-and-out unbelievers and secularists but does not believe it is appropriate when dealing with fellow believers.

But this lands us right back in the Auburn Avenue definitional difficulties. Define *believer*. If you believe in the objectivity of the covenant, as I do, then

* sherwoodopendoor.org/pastor-randy-and-gary/

† sherwoodopendoor.org/gallery2006.html, no longer available, but here's McLaren receiving the church's "2014 Peggy Campolo Carrier Pigeon Award for his work in support of LGBTQ Christians": sherwoodopendoor.org/open-door-2014-fall-conference.

these people are in the covenant. They are covenant-*breakers*, and they are the kind of people who in the Old Testament would receive fierce visits from prophets bringing a covenant lawsuit against them. And the words used in such a visit—polemic, challenge, rebuke, preaching, and satire—are not banished by the terms of the new covenant.

I am no kind of baptist, as my Federal Vision opponents well know. But if there were a corollary to the expansion of the objective boundaries of the covenant, and the corollary was that we had to leave impudent and over-the-top sin like this alone, then no, thanks. Deal me out. I'd rather be a baptist. I'd rather be a faithful sectarian than an unfaithful churchman.

But this is a false alternative. It is possible to be a faithful churchman. Being in the new covenant does not mean that you cannot be a high-handed covenant breaker. And it does not mean that covenant-keepers are somehow prevented from pointing out what is going on—with all appropriate adjectives involved. Although one of my critics could not see this in my review of McLaren's book, it was quite apparent to those who know how to read these signs where he (McLaren) was going. Well, now he is openly there.

That being the case, does anyone seriously think that Tony Campolo and Brian McLaren and others like them will suddenly feel that the broader evangelical world is unwilling to identify with them at all? That the book deals will dry up? That the speaking invitations will all go away? To ask the question is to answer it, which is to say, *ha*.

Now this is how it lands us back in the Federal Vision stuff. If you apply David's rule, you have to apply it as a baptist or as an objective covenant guy. If you do the former, then you can go after McLaren and Campolo on obvious grounds—they are not Christians, and this is why you can have at them. If they were Christians, they would not be endorsing sodomy as somehow "within the pale." This solves the problem (for conservative baptists) of lesbian Eskimo bishops, but it leaves them with the problems of genuine sectarianism—they successfully excised the skin cancer on the knuckles by cutting off the whole right arm. They get rid of problems like this, but they also cut themselves off from vast numbers within the healthy church.

But if you apply the rule as an objective covenant guy, then the whole thing becomes a vehicle of compromise. As the pressure to expand our ecumenical cooking increases, there needs to be an assistant to the prophet (me), looking over the rim of the kettle in which we are cooking our ecumenical stew, whose job it is to cry out, "There is death in the pot!"

As the evangelical church continues to disintegrate, it is *most necessary* that Federal Vision advocates be in the forefront of identifying immoralities, follies, rebellions, stupidities, blasphemies, and monkeyshines. If that does not happen, and happen on a prophetic basis, all the good that the Federal Vision promises will be squandered.

JANUARY 2007

SCOTT CLARK GEARING UP TO UNCHURCH EVERYBODY
JANUARY 2, 2007

Before the final round of bets, Scott Clark is pushing *all* his chips out into the middle of the table. He has recently gone over* the *notae* of the church, which in itself is not a problem for anyone following the Reformed understanding of the Church. So, okay so far. But then, as one commenter on his blog notes, he is applying these standards so tightly that he is excluding from the Church people that he himself is associated with in the Alliance of Confessing Evangelicals. His tight definition does enable him to say that the CREC is not a true Belgic church (sniff), but apparently unbeknownst to him, it also *requires* him to unchurch vast acres of the contemporary Reformed and evangelical world.

In particular, if Steve Wilkins is upheld by the Louisiana Presbytery later this month, and if the Standing Judicial Commission realizes that they ought not discipline an orthodox minister in good standing (without charges and without appeal), then Scott Clark will be seen standing in the corner, paint can and brush in hand. The professor of systematics at Westminster West will have unchurched the PCA. And he will have done this while believing that the *CREC* is sectarian! But sectarian is as sectarian does.

FEDERAL VISION HAIKU POETRY CONTEST
JAN 4, 2007

In the spirit of whatever it is, I thought I would offer a short cycle of Federal Vision haiku poems. Anyone who feels similarly inspired can make their

* dannyhyde.squarespace.com/the-heidelblog/2007/1/1/when-is-a-church-not-a-church.html, no longer available.

contributions in the comments section. Once it is apparent the creative springs have dried up, or perhaps never got started, as the case may be, I will announce a gold, silver and bronze winner. In the spirit of fair play, and to keep my adversaries from shelling out good money to pay for blogs exposing the haiku-gate Wilson scandal in all its tawdry griminess, I am humbly removing my poetry (see below) from consideration.

Just teaching the word,
Surprise from the conference,
Whud I say this time?

Long months had gone by
Then internet turmoil from
Samurai Robbins.

Peach petals floating,
Now drift down on the water,
Ah, presbytery!

Words from the Bible,
And not in the Confession,
Caused a commotion.

Big books full of words,
Blogs earnestly publishing
Their crinkum crankum.

With seasons turning,
Presbyterian nobles
Lift their steel gaze to

The whole PCA
Standing Judicial
Commission Report.

INVISIBLE AND ESCHATOLOGICAL
JAN 5, 2007

The Westminster Confession of Faith defines the invisible church as "the whole number of the elect that have been, are, or shall be gathered into one" (XXV.i). Some of you may know that over the last several days, I have been commenting on Scott Clark's blog, and trying to carry on a discussion there, albeit not very successfully. But one of the matters that came up from some of Clark's defenders was the idea that the invisible church was made up only of those who are *already* effectually called. In other words, regeneration was necessary to membership in the invisible church. This definition is obviously out of line with the Westminster definition, which includes the "whole number of the elect." But this novelty got me hunting around, and one of the things I discovered was that it is not a *complete* novelty.

Berkhof says that citizenship in the invisible church is "determined by regeneration" (*Systematic Theology*, p. 569). But he earlier says that "good definitions of the visible and invisible church may be found in the Westminster Confession" (p. 567). The first comment is in tension with the second, and part of the reason for this is that timelines keep getting in the way. Election happens outside human history, and regeneration happens within history. In his discussion, Berkhof also gives a list of ways the phrase "invisible church" has been interpreted, the second of which amounts to what I have been calling the eschatological church—"the ideal and completed Church as it will be at the end of the ages" (p. 565). Berkhof prefers to place his emphasis elsewhere, but this definition is consistent with the standard Reformed understanding.

For Dabney, the visible church is simply that entity which carries the same name as the invisible church "by accommodation." For him, the *true* church is the invisible one: "Let us remember then, that the true Church of Christ is invisible, and consists of the whole body of the effectually called" (*Systematic Theology*, p. 726). The visible church is an approximation; the action is in the invisible realm. Dabney's view is representative of a tendency in the American church, in which the visible church consistently receives shorter shrift.

Turretin, in proving the invisibility of the church, says that it consists "of the elect and believers alone" (*Institutes of Elenctic Theology, Vol. III*, p. 35). But, as mentioned earlier, the question is *when* does it consist of the elect? Having said this, I learned a long time ago that no question in theology can arise but those which Turretin has already gone over quite thoroughly. He says this a bit earlier. For him, the invisible church

> is taken for the mystical body of Christ constantly and intimately united to him as its head according to eternal election and efficacious calling . . . . This is the catholic church which we acknowledge in the Creed. It may be regarded either universally and all together (*kath' holou*) with respect to the whole multitude of believers (of which it is composed of whatever place and time) or particularly and as to its parts (*kata meros*) (now concerning that which reigns gloriously with Christ in heaven; then concerning this which labors and pursues its journey in the world and inasmuch as it is distributed into various particular churches which are designated by the same name as the whole). (p. 8)

As we saw at the first, the Westminster Confession defines the invisible church in accord with Turretin's *first* sense—"the whole number of the elect." And I think we could allow for Turretin's second use by synedoche, where you speak of the whole in terms of a part, or vice versa. This is close to what the other commenters on Clark's blog were saying, if I understand them right. Thus we could speak of the invisible church of this or that generation, speaking of those who are effectually called in that generation. But in order for this to be done with any kind of clarity, however, it has to be done *loosely*—because it is a rolling definition. At any given moment, in any generation, numerous saints are going to be with the Lord, and numerous unbelievers are coming to true faith. Thus the invisible church of January 5, 2007, is quite a different roster of names from the invisible church of March 5, 2009. Add to this the oddity that Smith, who is elect, but not yet converted, is a member of the invisible church in the Westminster definition, but not yet a member of the earthly invisible church. And because of this rolling change, I think it is best to follow Westminster here and define the invisible church in a way that doesn't keep moving around.

This is how A.A. Hodge handles it, following Westminster: "Our Confession teaches in these sections . . . that there is a collective body, comprising all the elect of God of all nations and generations, called the Church invisible" (*The Confession of Faith*, p. 311). He adds that "this entire body . . . has been constantly present to the mind of God from eternity" (p. 311). This is the sense in which Steve Wilkins affirms the invisible church, as do I. Defining the invisible church this way does not exclude affirming that at any given moment, there are a fixed number of effectually called people alive on the earth. I have always believed there is such a body—but it had never occurred to me to call that body the invisible church. In my mind, the invisible church has always been defined in the Westminsterian sense, the "whole number of the elect" sense.

Hodge then makes a statement that shows that what he is calling the invisible church is identical to what I call the eschatological church. "This body, thus seen in its absolute fulness and perfection by God from eternity, will be at last revealed to the universe in all its completeness and glory, so that it will transcend all the other works of God in its visible excellences" (p. 311).

Exactly. The entire company of the elect, the whole number of them, invisible now to everyone but God alone, will be made manifest to everyone at the eschaton, and that church will be without spot or wrinkle or any other blemish. And that eschatological church I define as the "whole number of the elect."

AUBURN AVENUE 2007 IN THE CAN
JAN 10, 2007

Sorry for the paucity of posts, and the reason for this is that I have been on the road. More specifically, I have been delighted to have been (once again) a guest speaker at the Auburn Avenue Pastors Conference. Just finished at noon today. As always the singing was stupendous, the hospitality top drawer, and the fellowship was the kind you get when you put a bunch of happy people together. The talks by Jeff Meyers, David Field, and Steve Wilkins were really, really good. Not only that, but Auburn Avenue now has a media center where you can download this stuff right away. If you want to take a look, go here.* They also have various podcasts, interviews, etc. Check it out.

THE POSTMILL CULPRIT?
JAN 5, 2007

In a discussion this morning at breakfast, some of the men in our gathering were talking (not surprisingly) about the Federal Vision controversy that has recently heated up again. One of the things that was noted is that there are some issues that are not currently part of the controversy, but which are real indicators of where someone would be in that controversy.

I mentioned one of those issues and suggested that I thought it was the real culprit, the issue being postmillennialism. I know there are a handful of exceptions, but it is striking to me that the Federal Vision side of things is overwhelming postmill, and the anti-fv side is overwhelmingly not. Is this just an oddity, or might there be a causal connection?

If there is a causal connection, here is how it might work. Postmillennial thinking is the type of view that gets into everything. Postmillennialism proper requres us to believe that God is intent on saving the world, all the nations of men. At the end of the process, the world will in fact be saved, and the number of the saved will vastly outnumber those who are lost. This, in its turn, commits the one who believes it to a certain optimistic frame of mind. Peter Leithart's recent book *Deep Comedy* goes into this in a wonderful way.

What does that optimistic frame of mind do when it encounters other issues? First, what does the alternative do, the pessimistic frame of mind? If your worldview could be summed up with "where are we going, and why am I in this handbasket?" the end result will necessarily be a certain wariness, an expectation that Murphy's Law will govern everything. If something can go wrong, it will—in the sacraments, in admitting young children to the table,

* auburnavenue.org/media/mp3.html

in teaching Christians from the law, in having a high view of the church, and so on. A hermeneutic of suspicion gets into everything.

Going the other way, the postmillenialist does not approach everything he does with the idea that the wheels are all about to fall off. Having become convinced that God is lovingly engaged with human history in order to ensure that everything will *turn out right*, this affects how we approach our everyday tasks. It affects how we approach our congregations, our spouses, our children, our studies, our theologies of everything else. This is not a dogmatic belief that nothing can ever go wrong, but it does help set the general orientation in a positive way. And everything that does go wrong is doing so in a broader, comedic context. When a nation rejoices because they have just won a war, the grief of the widow whose husband was killed the day before the armistice was signed is a very real grief. But it is grief in a context of broader joy.

God is love, and He is demonstrating that love throughout the course of history. His love will not be revealed in a surprise move at the last day; His love is shed abroad in our hearts now. This means we can afford to extend grace more liberally than we used to, without fear of that grace being abused. We now have a more potent view of what God is actually up to with that grace.

A TARGET RICH ENVIRONMENT

JAN 11, 2007

Obviously, since I am in Monroe (still) for the now finished Auburn Avenue Pastors Conference, the "situation" in the PCA has been much on my mind. And the guys have talked about it in various ways, and from various angles.

As I was reflecting on it this morning, I thought that I should write about one aspect of all this that I do not believe I have mentioned before. Steve Wilkins is accused of some kind of incipient Arminianism in his alleged departure from the Confession. (Incidentally, Steve's last talk at the conference was on the Westminster Confession, in which Steve clearly demonstrated his fundamental allegiance to the Reformed understanding of the role of creeds and confessions.) Now this confessional "departure" of his has to be pretty subtle because, for the life of me, I can't find it. Steve is a straight-up predestinarian, and he acknowledges that this sovereignty on God's part encompasses all things, including the salvation of individuals coming to faith in Christ. If this is all true, then it has to be said that Arminianism is really different from what it was when I was a kid.

Anyhow, this is all happening in a denomination in which there are scads of genuine, *bona fide* Arminians running around in ministry. The PCA does not have any shortage whatever of man-centered contemporary evangelicalism. Happy-clappy goo churches are plentiful, and in many of them, the extent of their acquaintance with Calvinism is that the pastor once read a book about it in seminary, which book he won't publicly admit to reading. Now, in *this* setting, a group of predestinarian TRs have set about to get predestinarian Steve. Anybody who believes that there isn't something personal about all this just isn't paying attention. Why go after a minister whose "Arminianism" is so implicit as to be non-existent, and leave alone those countless ministers in the PCA whose compromises with contemporary Arminianism *are* explicit? If that is what you want to do, the PCA should be a target-rich environment. But the PCA pragmatism (that does not take the Bible seriously) is not the target in all this, and the Federal Vision (which takes the Bible *and* the Reformed faith very seriously) *is* the target. What is the explanation?

Steve has been examined by his presbytery, twice. If later this month, on the basis of the second exam, the presbytery declares him to be A-OK, then the Standing Judicial Commission of the PCA has the option of picking up original jurisdiction on this. Technically, they would be reviewing or evaluating the actions of Louisiana Presbytery, not Steve, but given the procedures they have been willing to violate to get to *this* point, it seems pretty clear that they could "get Steve" if they so desired. If they do, I believe it is important for them to have to do it in broad daylight, on the fifty-yard line, with the stadium full. Hence these posts.

What is happening here is all in Girard. A victim has been selected, and the courts of respectability want to draw a veil of respectability over the process of dispatching the victim. The more the victim protests that this is all an abuse of the church courts and procedures, the more this enflames those who want the justice they dispense to be self-evidently "righteous." But it is not—it is nothing of the kind.

Imagine a classroom where students are standing on their chairs, throwing spitballs, yelling at one another, and so on. One student is sitting in the back, quietly. He shifts his feet, and accidentally brushes the desk in front of him, moving it two inches. Suppose the teacher ignores all the other students and busts this one. If the teacher really cared about classroom decorum, he has other things to address first. But if he does not, then we are justified in thinking that what is happening is more a matter of settling some personal score, than a matter of protecting the classroom.

If the TRs out to get Steve defend themselves by saying that "you have to start somewhere," and if they succeed in using the SJC to accomplish what they want, then this should strike fear in the hearts of all the other rowdy students. There should be a "chilling effect" across the PCA, where every minister who is running some Finney-inspired seeker service should think to himself, "Oh no! The PCA will deal with us *next*!" But there will be no chilling effect at all. No one will even slow down. The rowdy students will continue their classroom riot, while the quiet student is cooling his heels in the principal's office. And this is because everybody involved knows exactly what this is about. We also know what it is not about. Why pretend otherwise?

FAITH IS MEDIATED
JAN 12, 2007

When someone says that God foreordained the conversion of Smith, and that the conversion of Smith was therefore made necessary, a denial of this would include the view that the conversion of Smith was contingent, not necessary, and that God's foreordination took up some percentage of the whole deal that was less than 100%. In other words, if the conversion weighed ten pounds, God carried nine and Smith one, or God eight and Smith two. This kind of thing is a *denial* of God's sovereignty in salvation.

But if someone says that God does it all, and that His foreordination does not need the cooperation of any other agent in order to make it effective, but that it is *also true* that Smith is not a puppet, and that God uses various instruments in layered hierarchies, all subordinate to the sovereign use of God, who is directing it all, this does not amount to a denial of God's sovereignty in salvation.

Now a fundamentalist Calvinist, if we may postulate such a one, could say that all this theologizing makes his head hurt, and that as soon as we starting saying things "how will they preach unless they are sent?" we are threatening to undermine pure Calvinism, as he understands it. But by pure Calvinism he means invisible lightning bolts from heaven, converting souls in a willy-nilly and inscrutable fashion, and connected in no way to Christian literature, preaching, prayers, Christian nurture, or any of that stuff. But this is not Calvinism—it is a caricature.

The same kind of thing is going on with this Auburn Avenue business. If I were to say that we are saved by the instrumentality of faith alone (which I in fact do say), this does not commit me to deny God's use of secondary instruments. These secondary instruments are subordinate to the sole instrument used by God when a man is justified . . . by faith alone. Where does this faith come from? Faithfulness to *sola fide* does not require us to say that it comes from that invisible lightning bolt. God uses means, and He uses primary means (faith) and secondary means (preaching, baptism, nurture, etc.). Faith comes by hearing, and hearing by the Word of God. St. Paul does not say "faith comes by lightning bolts."

Put another way, faith is *mediated* to us.

A RESPONSE TO RICK PHILLIPS
JAN 13, 2007

As the Wilkins controversy continues to give off fumes, I would like to refer you to three places before we begin our next installment of comments. The first is to reiterate that Steve's written responses to his presbytery exam can be found here*. The second is a response to *that*, written by Rick Phillips, found

* auburnavenue.org/documents/wilkins_presbytery_response.htm

here†. And the third is a first-rate response by Jonathan Barlow to Rick's piece, found here‡. I'll give you a few minutes to work through all that.

Okay, here is the problem. In my response here I am simply reworking or amplifying Jon Barlow's central point, which was outstanding, and hoping all the while that I do not obscure it for anyone. What we have here is a linguistic controversy, which many have mistaken for a substantive doctrinal disagreement. While there *is* a doctrinal disagreement involved in all this, it is *not* located where the FV critics want to locate it, and it does *not* involve a denial of the Westminster Standards.

But also, before responding to Rick's critique of Steve, I want to register a personal note. At various times in this imbroglio, it has been more than a little obvious to me that agendas and motives other than what has been publicly claimed have been driving this whole affair, and I believe that I have noted this on more than one occasion. I bring it up here simply because I want to make it absolutely clear that in my mind Rick is emphatically not in that category. I believe that Rick is honestly interested in preserving and protecting the truth of the Reformed faith, and I do not believe that he is playing ecclesiastical politics. I have solid grounds for saying this, and my respect for his personal integrity is high.

Having said this, I believe he is badly misconstruing what Steve is saying, and I hope to be able to show why I say this. First, let me list a battery of quotes from Rick's article, with my comments marked in bold. Then I would like to conclude this point with a counter-example, and a question.

> As TE Wilkins's answers consistently show, he affirms the teaching of the Westminster Standards and then proceeds to argue that the Bible teaches otherwise. [Wilkins actually says that the Bible teaches the same doctrine as the Standards, but that it does not always use the same words in the same way.] But this is not to affirm the Standards.

† This response was posted at groups.yahoo.com/group/bbwarfield/message/24434, but appears to be no longer available,.

‡ barlowfarms.com/barlowphillips1.pdf, no longer available.

It is not sufficient, I would argue, to affirm the scriptural doctrines as taught in the Confession unless one agrees with the meaning of the terms. [Agreed] TE Wilkins states that his reading of Scripture yields "broader" definitions of doctrinal terminology. [Broader definitions in Scripture are not the same as contradictory definitions. More on this anon.] I will argue that the true effect of these broader definitions is that TE Wilkins teaches different definitions of key terminology that appears in the Confession in such a way that his teaching is out of accord with the Confession's summary of biblical truth. **[This would only follow if Steve were *substituting* the different definitions found in Scripture *into* the Confession. But in the Confession, for Steve, elect means decretally elect, the way the Confession means it. And in Scripture, he argues, the word elect is sometimes used in a sense other than this precise meaning. But the more precise meaning remains *true*.]**

But the question pertains to the acceptable consistency of certain of TE Wilkins's published teachings with the Confession's doctrine of election. **[As mentioned above, the issue is *verbal* consistency, not *substantive* consistency.]**

But the point of his question is to reconcile the [***verbal***] difference between the Confessional doctrine and the biblical doctrine—yet the Confession maintains that its doctrine is the biblical doctrine. **[Steve maintains that the Confession's doctrine is the biblical doctrine too. But he also says that it is not the *only* biblical doctrine, and that the Bible uses some of the same words with greater latitude than a Confession of Faith can or ought to.]**

He is, in effect, declaring that the Standards define and use the key doctrinal term "election" in a way that is at odds with the Scripture definition and usage of that term. **[Something may be different without being "at odds."]**

> His answers to the LA Presbytery's questions serve primarily to argue that the Standards are out of accord with Scripture. **[A better way of putting this would be: 'His answers to the LA Presbytery's questions serve to argue that the Standards employ a technical theological vocabulary in places where Scripture does not. Which is fine, both places.]**

My counterexample is this: There are few theological words that are as important as *hypostasis*. The three persons of the Trinity are described with this word, and the ancient Standards also teach us that there is a hypostatic union between the divine and human natures of Jesus. For more on the problem of definitional ambiguities surrounding this word, please see at Robert Letham's wonderful book on the Trinity. I am currently high-centered by an ice storm in an airport, and therefore do not have my Greek stuff. But if you look it up, you will discover that the Bible uses the word *hypostasis* in a very different way than the later fathers did. This later use, a stipulated, theological meaning does not intend to contradict the scriptural uses, nor does it actually do so in fact. Nevertheless, they still set a precise, theological definition for particular purposes which I applaud, and I wholeheartedly subscribe to Nicene and Chalcedonian orthodoxy. Not only so, but I would take it amiss if someone were to suggest that my statement that there is a "broader" or "different" use of this word found in the Bible was being advanced by me in an attempt to show that Nicene orthodoxy was somehow "unbiblical."

The Bible uses *hypostasis* in a particular way, and the task of exegesis is to find out what that meaning was in its original context, and then to believe and teach it. The fact that a later creed uses the word *hypostasis* to describe a *different* biblical reality, but which reality is not described in the Bible with the word *hypostasis* creates a minor problem . . . but it is a problem which can be resolved by spending ten minutes with Jon Barlow's essay. These uses *are* different, but they are not contradictory. The fact that I believe the Bible to teach that there is a fixed number of people to the decretally elect, which number cannot be augmented or diminished, just like Westminster teaches, does not obligate me to assert that every use of the word *elect* in the Bible has to carry the same decretal denotations and connotations.

And so here is my question for Rick. It is a version of a "have you stopped beating your wife yet?" But no need to worry—this is for illustrative purposes only, and I do not intend to accuse Rick of being anti-Trinitarian. But if the reasoning being employed against Steve is legitimate, then I think a series of questions like this would have to lead to such charges. "Do you believe that *hypostasis* is used in the Bible in the same way it is in the Nicene formulations? If so, could you please demonstrate this lexically? And if not, could you please defend your denial of the Trinity and Incarnation?"

One more quick thing. Rick takes Steve to task on the subject of the invisible church because Steve says that except in the mind of God, the invisible church "does not yet exist." Rick says that this is out of conformity with the Standards, but then astonishingly quotes the Standards where they say that the invisible Church consists of the "whole number" of the elect. But if a goodly portion of that whole number does not yet exist, then how can an entity which requires their presence exist? I can't make a present omelet with future eggs. Rick skates quickly over this, which is a good thing, because the ice is pretty thin here. He says, "What TE Wilkins sees as an eschatological fulfillment growing out of the visible church, the Confession sees as a past, present, and future reality in overlap with the visible church."

But what do you mean, exactly, by "future reality?" If you mean that it is settled by God's decrees, and is therefore known to God, then I could go for that, and Steve would too. In fact, in his written answers, he *did* go for that. The whole number of the elect, by name, *does* exist in the mind of God. So we affirm that it exists this way, but Rick rejects this formulation. He rejects it while saying that the invisible Church is a "past, present, and future *reality*," and so he must mean this in some *other* sense than that God simply knows who the future elect are. The entire Church invisible has to "exist" in some important sense *distinct* from existing in the mind of God. Since the invisible Church is made up of the whole number of the elect, which includes members not yet born, this means that the future exists in some sense *other* than in the mind of God. And this must be a very important doctrine, because to deny it gets this kind of controversy going. So my question to Rick here would be this: "What specifically do you mean by the invisible Church existing as a past, present, and future reality? Where? How? When? And most importantly, where does the Bible teach this?"

Enough for now.

Okay, I read over this before posting, and need to point out one other thing. To subscribe to the Westminster Confession (as I do) does not obligate me to affirm that the Confession represents the doctrine of Scripture exhaustively. The Westminster is not a summary of the entire Bible. It is a summary of the Bible's teaching on the subjects that it addresses. I affirm that it represents Scripture accurately, as far as it goes, but I deny that the Confession represents the Bible exhaustively, and also deny that it ever intended to. For example, Jon Barlow mentions missiology as a missing subject, to which I would add my beloved postmillenialism. *Now* that's enough.

LAYERED DEFINITION
JAN 17, 2007

One undercurrent beneath the Federal Vision business is a hidden difference in epistemological assumptions. The Hellenistic method strips accidents away from the thing, looking for essences. The Hebraic way of definition adds layer upon layer, looking at the thing from as many different angles as possible, and in as many situations as possible. Peter Leithart talks about this latter way of knowing in his book *The Kingdom and the Power*, and there is also a section on it in *Angels in the Architecture*.

This leads to an assumption on the part of the former that once you have a "definition," it is time to stop, and defend that orthodox definition against all comers. We can see this tendency in the definitions of the visible/invisible Church, or with statements about "outward" Christians and Christians "inwardly." But I have no trouble with these distinctions, as far as they go. Yes, there *are* Christians outwardly and Christian inwardly. But I then want to take this matter under discussion and look at it from numerous other directions, trying grasp the whole *by means of addition*. In contrast, the Hellenistic approach to definition (and I am not using this pejoratively; there is an important place for this kind of definition) seeks to understand *by means of subtraction*. How much can we take away and still have the thing we are talking about? But the temptation is then to disallow other approaches, approaches that may operate with a different set of descriptive rules. The Hebraic way gives us man worshipping, man playing, man eating, man making love, man working, man sleeping, and man writing poems. The Hellenistic way gives us a featherless, bipedal carbon unit.

For the Hellenistic approach, a true Christian is one who is one inwardly, period, stop. *And this is true*. But I also want to say that we have inward Christians and outward Christians, faithful Christians and adulterous Christians, temporary Christians and Christians forever, slaves and sons, wheat and tares, sons of Hagar and sons of Sarah, washed pigs and washed lambs, fruitless branches and fruitful branches, Christians who die in the wilderness and Christians who die in Canaan, and so on.

Now if someone of the other party thinks that I am essentially doing the same thing he is doing (that is, picking one and one only out of this list in order to make it the "true" definition), he has every right to be concerned. For example, if we are limited to one, then inward/outward is one of the best metaphors. But it is a *metaphor*, and needs other metaphors. If I were to isolate "fruitless branches and fruitful branches" to the exclusion of all others, and make it "*the* definition," then I have become an Arminian. I think that this is what our critics are worried about. But we are not seeking to substitute; we are seeking to *layer*.

OUTSIDE GALLIO'S HOUSE

JAN 19, 2007

Someone over at Reformation21 thought of a funny*, and twisted it like a washcloth until it was dry enough to serve as pulpit supply in some churches that could be mentioned.

* reformation21.com/Reformation_21_Blog/Reformation_21_Blog/58/pm__114/vobId__5069, no longer available.

But in the course of his *excursus* into humor, the writer developed a new accusation that merits some response, however brief. Speaking in the faux-guise of an advocate of the "foetal vision," he says this:

"if it becomes clear that we have a majority in the church courts, I would say to our opponents "Yo, you bunch of spineless apostate losers! Charge us if you think you're hard enough. And Ligon Duncan—if you're out there, just bring it on, man, BRING IT ON!!!!!" If, on the other hand, it emerges that we don't seem to have a majority in the church and might lose our jobs as a result of unconfessional practice and belief, I would plead with our brothers, in the love of Christ, to show forth Christian love in unity, to acknowledge the rich diversity of the Reformed tradition, and to walk together with mutual care and respect, and live at peace for the sake of the kingdom.'

In other words, the Federal Vision folks, who have brought charges against no one, and are currently trying to drive zero opponents from their pulpits, and who are blocking no candidates at all in presbytery exams, are *nevertheless* to be blamed because that is no doubt what they *would* do if ever given the chance. Thus we see the doctrine of hypothetical retaliation and justification, which really is a problematic use of that last word. This kind of "justification" sees launching an unprovoked attack as "retaliatory in *principle*" because, "even though they didn't do this unto us, they *will* do it if they ever have the chance." To the pure all things are pure, and so it makes sense that to the aggressive all things look aggressive.

What this kind of thing does is blur the difference between offense and defense, between which team has the ball and which one doesn't. The suggestion is made here that we in the Federal Vision are only making nice because we don't have the upper hand, but, when we do, then the TRs will all be hauled off for a little presbyterial bastinado. The problem with this little thesis is what the Federal Vision folks have actually done. The catholicity of the Federal Vision (which is an important and under-reported emphasis in it) is not merely hypothetical; it is no temporary ploy. And, for the record, that catholicity *has to include TRs*. It makes no sense to try to develop ecumenical bridges to other distant communions while starting fights with your next door neighbor.

We understand this. For just one example, the CREC, which is accused by some of being a haven for Federal Vision refugees, is *also* a denomination of Reformed churches which allows the London Baptist Confession as one of its six reformed confessions. For those not following the details of this, baptists are generally un-federal-visionish, if that's a word.

It is one thing for our adversaries to decide that a fight is necessary for the sake of "the truth." If that what someone's conscience demands, then that is what he should do. But the fight should be justified on the basis of the *facts*, examined in the clear light of Scripture, and not on the basis of an imaginary scenario in which is it assumed that the other side wants the fight just as much as you do, and in the same way. This latter approach, far from demonstrating the robust insight of Athanasius dealing with the snaky charm of an Arius, rather indicates the reluctance born of a bad conscience, that of a decent guy maneuvered into beating someone up outside Gallio's house, and all over "words, and names, and your own law."

THANKS FOR THE OPPORTUNITY TO RESPOND
JAN 22, 2007

Editor,

In your last issue of *The Confessional Presbyterian*, I read an article by R. Scott Clark entitled "Baptism and the Benefits of Christ." There are many issues here, but I would like for reasons of space to limit myself to two.

The first has to do with Dr. Clark's straw man representation of the position he critiques throughout the course of his article, that of the Federal Vision. You would think that he would be especially careful in stating the views that he ascribes to this position—in that he concludes the article by calling for "confessional Reformed and Presbyterian churches to begin disciplining those pastors, elders, and teachers who teach the Federal Vision doctrine of baptismal benefits" (p. 19). This is no place for "ready, fire, aim!"

The focus of his article has to do with Dr. Clark's claim that the Federal Vision denies the internal/external distinction for members of the covenant of grace, and the closely related issue of the visible/invisible church distinction.

He says, "A group of writers, some of whom are ministers in confessional Reformed and Presbyterian churches, known collectively as the 'Federal Vision' are, however, either denying or calling into question the distinction between the church visible and church invisible and with that they are proposing that there is no distinction between those who in the covenant of grace externally and internally" (p. 4). I am cited in his footnote nine as one who is "expressing doubts" about the visible/invisible distinction (p. 4). He identifies me as a Federal Vision writer, and later sums up our position this way: "The *Federal Vision denial of the internal/external distinction* and their doctrine of baptismal union with Christ necessarily conflate the substance of the covenant of grace with its administration (p. 15, emphasis mine).

Yes, that would follow, if the premise were correct. But it is radically inaccurate. Not only do I affirm the internal/external distinction between regenerate and unregenerate covenant members, but I have done so repeatedly, in print, and in ways that are pretty hard to miss. I have done so in pieces that Dr. Clark apparently read and in pieces that he ought to have read. In my essay from *The Federal Vision* that Dr. Clark cites, I say this: "As an historic evangelical, in no way have I altered my conviction that a man must be converted to God in order to see the kingdom of heaven" (p. 263). In that essay, which Dr. Clark describes as a vehicle for "expressing doubts" about the visible/invisible church distinction, I actually said something more nuanced. "At the same time, the historic Reformed terminology can be applied in such a way as to cause some problems of its own. While it was a valuable distinction, it was still not an inspired distinction. I say this *while embracing the distinction*, as far as it goes" (p. 266, emphasis in the original). In my lexicon, "embracing" and "expressing doubts" are not interchangeable. In that same essay, I show my agreement with the internal/external differences between regenerate and unregenerate covenant members in various ways and places. I referred to "unconverted professing Christians" on p. 268. I refer to "false professors" on p. 269. I refer to "baptized hypocrites" on p. 266. All this in the essay that Dr. Clark actually cited.

But there is more. In my book on the Federal Vision controversy (*"Reformed" Is Not Enough*), I make the same point over and over again. I *embrace* the internal/

external distinction, and this is something that Dr. Clark had a responsibility to know and acknowledge before writing an article like this. For example:

> Circumcision was a sign of the covenant, but Paul points out that the mere possession of the external sign was not sufficient to guarantee a genuine spiritual reality. We can reapply these truths this way: 'For he is not a Christian who is one outwardly; neither is that baptism, which is outward and external. But he is a Christian who is one inwardly; and baptism is that of the heart, in the spirit, and not in the letter; whose praise is not of men, but of God." Paul's statement is blunt—he is *not* a Christian who has only the externals" (*RINE*, p. 18)
>
> In short, we can say that God knows those who call themselves Christians and who take upon themselves the marks of discipleship. Their lips are close to God, but their hearts are far from Him" (*RINE*, p. 19)
>
> Does this mean that anyone so baptized is a Christian in the other sense—one who is born of the Spirit of God? Not at all" (*RINE*, p. 19)
>
> The lips draw near while the heart is far removed from God. But such snakes within the covenant have the worst lot of all" (*RINE*, p. 21)
>
> Simply put, the objectivity of the covenant does *not* mean that a man does not have to be born again" (*RINE*, p. 33)
>
> First, *the new birth is a reality*. To be born again separates those who love darkness and those who love the light" (*RINE*, pp. 35–36, emphasis in the original)
>
> When the word regeneration is being used in this sense, we are talking about an invisible operation performed by the Spirit of God, who does what He does when and how it pleases Him. And when we are talking about what might be called this 'effectual-call regeneration,' we have to repudiate every form of baptismal or decisional regeneration" (*RINE*, p. 39)

Lest this become tedious, I will not quote very much from the three whole chapters later in the book that I dedicated to a detailed discussion of different aspects of the internal/external distinction, which I clearly and plainly hold and teach. Chapter 16 is on "Heretics and the Covenant," Chapter 17 on "Sons of Belial," and Chapter 18 on "False Brothers." I close these chapters by quoting, with approval, from Calvin. ". . . we therefore distinguish the true from the spurious children, by the respective marks of faith and of unbelief" (as quoted in *RINE*, p. 155).

But as an announcer on television might say, with regard to the fantastic vegetable steamer he is trying to sell us, "Wait! There's more!" In a collection of Credos, found in *Credenda* 15/5, I say this: "I believe that God in His sovereign and secret decree has elected by name a countless number to eternal salvation (Eph. 1:11). Each of these elect are justified individually, and irreversibly, at the point of their conversion, when God imputes to them all the righteousness of Jesus Christ (Rom. 8:29–30)" It sounds like whoever wrote that (to wit, *me*) holds to a pretty robust view of the internal/external distinction, which view, if it got any *more* robust, the Evangelical Theological Society would have tested for steroids.

In short, to put it mildly, Dr. Clark's article is not a reliable guide on whether Federal Vision advocates like myself deny the internal/external distinction. Given this problem, it is not surprising that his paradigm blinders cause him to say *other* inaccurate things in the course of this article as well.

This is not intended to be an exhaustive refutation, so let me close with just one example. In his discussion of Romans 9, Dr. Clark says this: "Paul knows nothing of any sort of historically conditioned or contingent election. He views redemptive history as populated by two classes of people, those who are unconditionally elect and those who are reprobated" (p. 13). This is yet another situation where someone's ship of dogma, under a full sail, runs aground on the shoals of the text. Paul knows nothing of a historically conditioned or contingent election? "As concerning the gospel, they are enemies for your sakes: *but as touching the election*, they are beloved for the fathers' sakes. For the gifts and calling of God are without repentance" (Rom. 11:28–29, emphasis mine). Beloved enemies on account of *election*? Paul's profound discussion of decretal election in these chapters *arises* out of the problem created by the historical election of Israel. After Paul's rhapsody at the end of Romans 8, a natural question would arise. If all this is true of the elect, then why was the elect nation of Israel trying to kill Paul? And that is why Paul goes on to distinguish between different kinds of election, distinguishing between the historical, contingent election of Israel, and His sovereign decretal election than reveals itself in a glorious way throughout human history, culminating at the last day. This is why Paul began chapter nine with a discussion of the status of Israel, who had the adoption, the glory, the covenants, the law, the service of God, the promises, and the fathers. But this historical election, by itself, was insufficient, because they are "not all Israel, which are of Israel" (Rom. 9:6). All Israel was elect in *one sense*, while those who were of Israel were elect in *another*. And I cannot fathom how someone who stumbles over equivocal uses of the same word like this can ever hope to interpret faithfully the teaching of someone like the apostle Paul.

Calvin did not have this trouble. "Therefore Paul skillfully argues from the passage of Malachi that I have just cited that where God has made a covenant of eternal life and calls any people to himself, *a special mode of election is employed for a part of them*, so that he does not with indiscriminate grace effectually elect all" (*Institutes* III.xxi.7, emphasis mine). Peter Lillback has shown convincingly that Calvin distinguished a general election from a secret, special election. "Calvin denies that those who fall from the covenant were never in the covenant in the first place. Rather, they were in the covenant, but only from the vantage point of a corporate election or adoption . . . General election is not automatically efficacious in imparting spiritual benefits because God does not always give to all in the covenant the spirit of regeneration that enables perseverance in the covenant" (Lillback, *The Binding of God*, p. 216).

Why is this so hard?

Cordially in Christ,

Douglas Wilson

MORE ON LOUISIANA PRESBYTERY
JAN 25, 2007

I am grateful to be able to announce that Steve Wilkins has been cleared (for a *second* time) by his presbytery.

> Louisiana Presbytery, after thorough examination and investigation of TE Steve Wilkins as per the SJC directives regarding allegations made in the Central Carolina Presbytery Memorial, finds no strong presumption of guilt in any of the charges contained therein and exercises its prerogative not to institute process regarding those allegations. [Clerk's note: See BCO 31–2.]*

My understanding is that according to the process the PCA has set up for this, the Standing Judicial Commission has the automatic authority to review this decision. They are meeting sometime next month, and we shall see what they decide to do. If they take it up, their focus is to review the action of the presbytery, not the views held by Steve. But there is no way for them to do this without bringing into the picture what some are alleging that Steve teaches and holds. So this action by Louisiana Presbytery is an answer to prayer, but there is still something to pray about.

In this situation, the more public accountability the better. If the tangle is now resolved, then thank the Lord. But if it continues (through parliamentary chicanery, old-boy-network-pressure, or other means), then at some point there will be a stopping point, a trial. At that point, the accusers will have to make a case that depends on more than just bare assertions. If and when *that* happens, it would be good to have all eyes focused on the accusers, and for said accusers to have the mike turned on, and the tape running. Perhaps they have not thought this far out, but I don't see why they are pressing for this. Those hostile to the FV have also been equally hostile to *any* setting where verbal exchange or cross-examination would be possible——debates, etc. Given what some of them have been writing (e.g., Scott Clark, Guy Waters), this coyness is not surprising.

* This linked to auburnavenue.org, but here's a more current URL: auburnavenue.org/federalvision/index.htm

Perhaps the goal has just been to "make things hot" for Steve, so that he voluntarily leaves the PCA. Then they could explain the heresy in detail to various bought-and-paid-for crowds, with no theological debate necessary, and no robust interchanges in the Q&A. The problem is that Steve is a churchman and has no plans to make it easy for them by acting the part of a radical individualist. He is going to make them prove what they are saying, and this will prove awkward for them *because they can't.* If they could, they would be the ones eager for debate, right? And I hereby extend my offer yet again . . .

OPENING PLAY OF THE END GAME
JAN 29, 2007

Scott Clark, big surprise, has written some more about the Federal Vision here.*

But in the course of his litany of ecclesiastical entities that have in various ways rejected the Federal Vision, he then goes on to say something very important—something that gives the end game away, incidentally. This, I predict, will be the basic content of their two-minute drill.

At the conclusion of his post, Dr. Clark says this:

"I'll tell you what I don't understand is why these folk don't align themselves with CREC where they will be 'understood'?"

Look for this question that Dr. Clark raises to become a constant drumbeat in the weeks to come.

"Why are you disrupting the PCA? Why don't you just go where you're wanted?"

"Why are you making all this trouble? Don't you care about the peace and purity of the church? Why don't you just join the CREC and make everybody happy?"

"Why do you have to be so disruptive? Why won't you just leave quietly?"

"If you just left voluntarily, we could avoid a *lot* of trouble, Wilkins."

Now the accusation that Steve Wilkins is making trouble in the PCA is a little bit like Ahab calling Elijah the one who troubled Israel (1 Kings 18:17). Steve has brought charges against no one, he is attacking no one, he is blocking the

* dannyhyde.squarespace.com/the-heidelblog/2007/1/29/siouxlands-presbytery-pca-rejects-federal-vision.html, no longer available.

ordinations of no one, and so on. But that does not keep him from being the bad guy in the story that some are industriously trying to tell. He is simply the one that some TRs in the PCA have dubbed the designated villain. He is to be blamed for all *kinds* of things, and these pressing problems would all be solved if he would just agree with their negative assessments, and put himself into exile. Not only must he be at fault for all the current troubles, but he is being intransigent by refusing to do their dirty sentencing work for them. If he *really* had the peace and purity of the PCA in mind, he would just slip away quietly and allow his opponents time for a little touchdown dance. But he isn't going anywhere, and by remaining it is beginning to appear that his opponents may soon have to start *proving* what they are saying, and *that* is an outrage upon their dignity. The ones attacking always feel victimized by the one they attack. It's all in Girard, man.

So this is the drill. The last thing in the world that the anti-FV people want is any kind of open forum where questions get to be asked in both directions. They don't want this in a voluntary set-up, as in a debate. They don't want it in a judicial setting, as in an open trial. They don't want it in a box; they don't want it on the floor. Not in the closet either. We piped but ye would not mourn; we played the bass line from "Play That Funky Music, White Boy," and ye would not dance.

They want to *chase* Steve Wilkins from the PCA into the CREC, and they then will return to their home churches, still breathing hard, and will wonder aloud where he went. And however sheepish they will be over a move so transparent, that sheepishness would be *nothing* compared to what they would have to deal with if they are ever required to prove these assertions with all the Reformed folk in the English-speaking world looking on.

AH, THE BITTER, BITTER WORMWOODS!
JAN 30, 2007

Scott Clark has posted a form letter, here†, for repentant FVers to sign off on. As has been my wont in times past, I would like to repost that letter here, with

† oceansideurc.org/the-heidelblog/2007/1/29/a-form-for-penitent-ex-federal-visionaries.html, no longer available

some editorial comments sprinkled throughout. I have put my comments in brackets and in **bold**, so that you can tell where it is exactly that I am speaking. The bold also helps to signify the blackness of my Federal Vision heart. Some of this is tongue in cheek, but some of it is as serious as it gets.

> To all whom this these presents do come **[eh?]**,
>
> I hereby declare that I really and heartily believe in form and substance what the Reformed churches confess, that God declares sinners righteous *sola gratia, sola fide*, only on the ground of the imputation of the whole and perfect obedience of Christ. **[Amen. *Preach* it. This might not be so bad.]**
>
> I also confess that being caught up in the fever of the moment, I was attracted to the anti-revivalist rhetoric of the Federal Vision movement and my enthusiasm for their anti-revivalism and anti-subjectivism lead me to embrace doctrines and practices I now recognize to have been mistaken. **[Oh, here it comes. Okay. I further confess that I was seduced by the trinkets and other shiny objects they gave me.]**
>
> I confess now that I embraced the movement without fully understanding the implications of their theology and practice. **[In fact, I confess that I do not fully understand much of *anything*. I am slow of wit, and dim-witted of bulb. Ah, the bitter, bitter wormwoods!]**
>
> I hereby repent of failing to distinguish the law and the gospel as Reformed folk have done for four-hundred years, **[But I *do* distinguish them. Not for four hundred years, certainly, but for quite some time now. Year after year of distinguishing them.]**
>
> of denying the covenant of works, **[Did I do that? When did I do that? I am not saying this has to be wrong, but I have always tried to affirm this, preferring to call it the covenant of creation . . . Okay. If you say so. Okay.]**

of confusing it with the covenant of grace, **[But . . . but . . . but . . .]** of teaching viz. the *ordo salutis,* a temporary, conditional election alongside the eternal unconditional election **[But didn't Calvin teach this in his Institutes, referring to a general election, and . . . no, no, not the thumbscrews! Sorry for teaching a temporary, general election. Sorry.]**

and of sometimes conflating the two, **[Whatever you say. Sorry.]** of teaching temporary possession of baptismal benefits such as union with Christ, adoption, and justification that are said to be conditioned upon my faithfulness and thereby implicitly denying the doctrine of the perseverance of the saints. **[Okay. I just want to get this straight so's I don't mess up again. I don't want to deny perseverance of the saints, no way. So when did I say that anything was *conditioned* on my faithfulness? That would be really bad if I had done it. Can you cite a place where I did?]**

I hereby repent of denying the visible/invisible distinction, **[But I don't deny it! I *qualify* it! Whatsa matter witchoo? Michael Horton made the same point . . . John Murray . . . Banner of Truth *Collected Works* . . . look, I'm sorry. I love you guys. I am trying to see your point. I think I kinda do. I think the Stockholm thing might be starting to kick in. About time.]**

of denying that there are two ways of being in the one covenant of grace, **[But I *affirm* there are two ways of being in the one covenant of grace. Are you sure you got the right guy? Yeah, that's my picture. But I never signed *that* statement. That's not my signature. Is my lawyer here yet? What do you mean "you are interrogating him in the next room"?]**

of attempting to revise the definition of faith in the act of justification to include Spirit-wrought sanctity. **[I see it all now, and I do repudiate my former errors with enthusiasm. I now agree with you that**

saving faith must be unholy and rebellious. I don't know why I didn't see this before. Irony? What makes you say that?]

I repent of trying to smuggle into the doctrine of justification the doctrine of condign merit whereby God reckons me righteous partly on the basis of Spirit-wrought sanctity, **[I don't remember thinking this thought anywhere in my natural born head. I hotly deny it. Now what do we do?]**

and of trying to smuggle into the doctrine of justification the doctrine of congruent merit whereby God is said to approve graciously of my best efforts to cooperate with grace toward justification.**[I hotly deny this one too. Not that anybody listens.]**

I repent of equivocating about justification as present and future in the same sense. **[How can you equivocate about something in the same sense? Isn't equivocation using different senses? Not trying to be difficult here. Just trying to understand.]**

I admit that all believers are fully justified now and shall be vindicated as such at the judgment. **[I actually agree with this! *Without* the iron boot!]**

I repent of trying to enlarge faith in the act of justification to be more than simply "receiving and resting" on Christ and his finished work, of trying to include fruit and sanctity in the act of justification in either faith or the ground of justification rather than simply allowing them to be fruit and evidence of justification. **[But if repentance and faith are the fruit of *regeneration*, which is *not* justification, that coming later, and regeneration is a type of sanctification (something wrought *in* me), then aren't we *all* saying that faith is the fruit of a change of heart in me? Leastways, all of us who hold to the traditional *ordo salutis*? You do hold to the *ordo salutis*, don't you? Since regneration is first, and justification later, we all agree that something is wrought *in* me before anything is imputed *to* me. Right?]**

I repent of confusing baptism and the Lord's Supper as signs and seals of initiation and renewal and thereby trying to commune infants and others before their catechizing and credible profession of faith. **[In all seriousness, if you really want to keep your kids away from Christ until they have passed one of your blinkered ordination exams, then why don't you just say so? You don't want your kids to tolerate condign merit or congruent merit for a second, but you *demand* cognitive merit from them. Now kids, when you score 100 percent on this comprehensive exam covering the *tota gratia* portion of the syllabus, then you will have *earned* the right to participate in God's free grace. Don't ever make the mistake of thinking that God's free grace is just lying around for *anybody*. Gotta ace the *test*. Gotta clear the *bar*. Gotta convince the *session*. Grace is only for those who understand, as *we* understand, which is to say, perfectly.]**

I repent of troubling the churches before bothering to learn the rudiments of Reformed theology, **[Hey, now you are getting a little personal.]**

before learning the basic distinctions of the Reformed confession, **[This appears to be as good a time as any for me to re-extend my invitation to a debate. Since I don't know the rudiments of Reformed theology, and don't know the basic distinctions of the Reformed confession, it will be the work of mere moments for you to pull my shirt over my head and roll my socks down. The crowd will go wild, and orthodoxy will rest comfortably that night, for the first time in years.]**

of wasting the time of the church courts and assemblies, **[I like *that*! Let's make this guy buy the rope before we lynch him. That way we won't be wasting *our* hard-earned money.]**
in forcing them to teach me in committee reports what I should have learned in seminary had I paid attention. **[Didn't go to seminary. All I got is these committee reports.]**

Most heartily of all I repent of being confusing about the one thing about which a minister should never ever be confusing, about which our confessions are completely and utterly unambiguous, about which the entire Protestant Reformation agreed: how sinners are right before God. **[And that should be obvious by this portion of the letter of confession, shouldn't it? According to what this letter asks us to affirm, sinners are right before God by means of their theological prowess. Sinners are right before God by intellectual achievement. Sinners are right because they aced the exam and had the teacher put the gold star of grace on the top of their paper. We have to use the word *grace* lest any should boast, but we still do.]**

Mea culpa, mea culpa, mea maxima culpa. **[Isn't this a Latin thingy that papists say? This isn't a trick, is it?]**

EVEN WARRIORS FOR TRUTH HAVE TO FUDGE THE FACTS A LITTLE

JAN 31, 2007

In the "Bitter Wormwoods" post below*, I appreciated a comment by David Gadbois, an FV critic, and thought I should respond to it here. He said, "I think Dr. Clark is right in his statement about the FV in general, although I think only 2 of the points would apply to Wilson at all (paedocommunion and the nature of justifying faith)."

And there are three responses, two of them brief qualifications, and one that I think is really central in the continuing controversy.

The first is that I obviously would differ with Mr. Gadbois over whether Dr. Clark is accurately representing my friends in FV circles. At the same time, it is fair to say that I have gone out of my way—for the sake of ecumenism, believe it or not—to state my convictions in ways that I believe an honest TR could immediately accept. I know my FV friends are telling the truth when they clearly state that they are not denying the system of doctrine

* The previous entry, January 30, 2007.

taught in the Westminster Confession. But I have sought to go one better, and actively and openly *teach* the doctrines of the Westminster Confession. It is this, in my view, that accounts for the difference in *perception* between Federal Vision lagers and Federal Vision amber ales. But for anyone who doubts our substantive agreement, Canon Press has a recorded discussion between me and Rich Lusk that should be helpful.

Second, my difference on the "nature of justifying faith" is clearly a difference I have with Dr. Clark, but I would deny that it is a difference that I have with the Westminster divines at all. By "obedient faith" I mean nothing more or less than "living faith." I do not mean in any way, shape or form, some kind of merit found in the creature that would ingratiate him with the Almighty. Obedient faith is the only kind that God ever gives, and when He gives it, this justifying faith *obeys the gospel*, obeys the truth, obeys His salvation. Faith that does not obey the gospel is not justifying faith. This faith is qualitatively different than the "yeah-uh-huh" kind of faith that even devils can have. This qualitative difference (if you wish, its *sanctity*) arises from the fact that, in the traditional *ordo* which Dr. Clark is apparently denying, living repentance and living faith are the fruit of regeneration. Regeneration is *prior*. This regenerate heart is (in the traditional *ordo*, if measured with a stop watch) an unjustified heart. The order is effectual call, regeneration, repentance, faith, justification. Now the obedience of Christ is imputed *to* me at the *end* of this process (if you *must* call it a chronological process), but something is done *in* me at the beginning of it. Because my heart was changed from hostility to submission, the repentance and faith that arise out of this new heart share this new quality of submission. Faith cannot but partake of the qualities of its source. Dr. Clark is free to deny this traditional *ordo* if he wants, but he is not free to accuse people of heterodoxy for no other reason than that they hold to it.

The last point is the one that I was glad was obvious to Mr. Gadbois, a critic of the Federal Vision generally, and that is the fact that I gladly hold, teach, embrace and love the vast majority of Dr. Clark's doctrinal affirmations (to be distinguished from his slanderous assertions about what other people are supposed to believe). And I am glad that this is obvious to men like Mr. Gadbois. But here is the problem. Over the years of this controversy (five years now), it has been apparent to a number of my Federal Vision friends that my extra efforts have in this regard have done minimal good. How can I answer them? If one were to say to me, "Wilson, why do you do all that extra work? I agree with everything you have said, but I haven't done the work of saying it. But, at the end of the day, you aren't believed any more than I am. Why don't you save your breath for cooling your porridge?"

And this is because this is a battle of ecclesiastical *politics*, and not, as has been ostensibly claimed, a battle for the *truth*. If it were a battle for truth, then people would be willing to acknowledge plain truth, even if it seemed contrary to their current political advantage. But they are not at all willing for this. I have heard, through back channels, that there are leaders in the anti-FV movement who would acknowledge *privately* what Mr. Gadbois says here about me. But they will not say anything like that publicly because warriors for truth have to fudge the facts a little if they are to keep up the political pressure.

The ninth commandment requires us to speak the truth. We are prohibited in Colossians from lying to one another—we have put off the old man, with its practices. We serve and worship the one who *is* the Truth. But in defiance of this obvious scriptural requirement, we have gotten to that point in this controversy where pressure, politics, more pressure, fear, and selfish ambition make it all but impossible for anyone to say something *obvious*, if it goes contrary to his party's interest.

So let us talk for a moment about the tenet of Dr. Clark's that I agreed with, the one without the iron boot. "I admit that all believers are fully justified now and shall be vindicated as such at the judgment." I agree, Dr. Clark, and one of the things I will be vindicated from in that day will be *your* false charges.

"For to this end Christ both died, and rose, and revived, that he might be Lord both of the dead and living. But why dost thou judge thy brother? or why dost thou set at nought thy brother? for we shall all stand before the judgment seat of Christ . . . So then every one of us shall give account of himself to God" (Rom. 14:9–10, 12)

We, all of us, will stand before Christ. You, me, Norman Shepherd, Rich Lusk, Peter Leithart, Cal Beisner, John Robbins, Ligon Duncan, all of us. We are (*all* of us) going to give an account of ourselves, down to every idle word, every motion at presbytery, and certainly down to every blog post. Because you have been justified by the free grace of God in Christ, this means that your misrepresentations of my position have been as forgiven as it gets. The judgment seat we will all stand before will not be *that* kind of judgment seat—we will (*all* of us) have to walk past the altar where Christ sprinkled His blood before we get to this seat of evaluation, where Christ sorts out our tangles. But *when* He sorts out our tangles, as He promises He will, you will shake hands with me, brother, and we will be able to chat in true fellowship while the angels are passing out the sheet music.

FEBRUARY 2007

THE KIND OF EYEBALL THAT SEES
FEB 2, 2007

Scott Clark is at it again.* He misrepresents my views (again) by saying this: "Mr Wilson's doctrine of justification through 'living' or 'obedient' faith is the very doctrine that we rejected in the Reformation. He makes faith efficacious, not because it looks to Christ alone, but because it looks to Christ and is obedient."

The only problem with this is that he doesn't cite any place where I say that faith is efficacious on account of its sanctity. I didn't say that because I don't believe it, and not only do I not believe it, I stoutly deny it. *I teach the opposite.* To say that God looks at the holy quality of my faith and pronounces me justified on account of it would be a distortion of and denial of the Protestant doctrine of *sola fide*. The problem for Dr. Clark's fixed notion is that I reject it, and I do so *clearly*.

The thing that makes this misrepresentation mind-boggling is that Dr. Clark began this post by quoting this from me: "By 'obedient faith' I mean nothing more or less than 'living faith.' I do not mean in any way, shape or form, some kind of merit found in the creature that would ingratiate him with the Almighty."

I deny that God looks at my faith and says, "Whoa, look at that holiness! Better justify *him*." The faith that is the instrument of justification *is* holy, and *is* alive, and it is necessary for it to be holy and alive. But those qualities are not the reason or the ground that God has for justifying me. The ground is the obedience of Jesus Christ. I have not taught or said anything contrary to

* oceansideurc.org/the-heidelblog/2007/1/31/doug-wilson-is-right.html, no longer available.

this, and since Dr. Clark is confident that I do in fact deny it, I would appreciate it if he would produce some evidence to this effect. If he cannot produce an example of me saying that God reckons the good qualities of my faith to me as righteousness, then I believe he owes me an apology.

The fact that my faith is alive makes it possible to see Christ, the sole basis or reason for anyone's justification. If my faith were dead, it would be blind also, and incapable of looking to Christ as the sole ground of justification.

So, Dr. Clark, let me spell it out for you. Do I believe that God justifies me through the instrumentality of a living and holy faith? *Yes*. Do I believe that God in any manner whatever reckons that sanctity *as part of His reason or ground for justifying me*. As God is my witness, *no*. What is the ground for my justification? The living obedience of the Lord Jesus, plus *nothing*.

True faith is an eyeball and cannot look to itself. True faith sees Christ alone. But unless it is is a living eyeball, it cannot see. Dead eyeballs have no vision. So this life is necessary but is in no fashion meritorious. God does not give living faith so that it might admire itself in the mirror. If Dr. Clark would like me to say this any more clearly—I don't know, throw in some more adjectives or something—I will be happy to do it. As I as said in my post, we do have disagreements, but whether God reckons any of my virtues into His calculations as He justifies me is not one of them.

MORE STUFF ON CLARK
FEB 2, 2007

I just posted this as a comment on Scott Clark's blog.

Dr. Clark,

Late Wednesday night, you posted this on your blog. "Mr Wilson's doctrine of justification through 'living' or 'obedient' faith is *the very doctrine* that we rejected in the Reformation" (emphasis mine).

After saying I follow the Romanist *ordo*, you also say, "Mr Wilson agrees in principle with Rome. I don't mean to say that he intends to agree with Rome, but I do mean to say that he can't help it. He, like the rest of the Federal

Visionists, has set up a system of justification that is (they think) guaranteed to produce the desired result, sanctity." So here you say I unwittingly follow the Tridentine *ordo*.

After this was challenged by a number of individuals commenting on your blog, some of whom asked you to produce any citation where I had said anything of the kind, and after I again denied holding to this in any manner whatever, yesterday you said, "Mr Wilson is on the fence. He wants to fiddle with orthodoxy without being tagged for doing it."

Earlier I was denying, and now I am just fiddling. Are you able to produce a quote where I am doing *either*? And does this statement from you that I am on the fence amount to a retraction of your earlier statements of my position?

SOUP TO NUTS
FEB 2, 2007

My conversation with Dr. Clark goes on. I asked him to cite some examples of where I have said that God considers the moral quality of my faith (as having been formed by love) as the basis or foundation for justifying me. I deny teaching this. To his credit, Dr. Clark acknowledges that I am at least *trying* to deny it, but that I am haplessly falling into error on this subject anyway.

At any rate, when I requested a "for instance," Dr. Clark replied this way:

> I did, in fact, quote Mr Wilson and I'll do it again: "Faith cannot but partake of the qualities of its source." To be sure, this statement would be true if it were referring to the function of faith in sanctification, but because Mr Wilson does not make this distinction and because it is the role of faith in the act of justification that is in question, I understand him to be referring to the role of faith in the act of justification. Nothing he has said since, by way of complaining gives me any reason to change my opinion.

Now it is quite true that I was talking about faith at the moment of justification. But I was talking about the *nature* of this faith when I said that it partook of the qualities of its source (the regenerate heart). I was not talking about the *role* of faith in the eyes of God when He justifies me. Dr. Clark quotes this sentence, points out things that I failed to include in that sentence, and assumes certain things about the reasons I must have had for failing to include them. *This is not quotation.* It is not responsible. It doesn't establish *anything.*

I also used the example of the eyeball, and I thought Dr. Clark's response to this was very telling. I had said,

> True faith is an eyeball and cannot look to itself. True faith sees Christ alone. But unless it is a living eyeball, it cannot see. Dead eyeballs have no vision. So this life is necessary but is in no fashion meritorious. God does not give living faith so that it might admire itself in the mirror. If you would like me to say this any more clearly—I don't know, throw in some more adjectives or something—I will be happy to do it. As I as said in my post, we do have disagreements, but whether God reckons any of my virtues into His calculations as He justifies me is not one of them.

Dr. Clark responded to this:

> All analogies break down and in this context, the analogy has the same problems as the language above. The analogy fails, because, in this case, the one should have to say that it is the object of vision that makes the eye function as it does, but I think an eye is an eye and it's alive or not whether it has an object of vision or not.

The object of vision creates the eyeball first, which means that the object of vision is active in this before it is seen. God gives us eyes and *then* we see. He, being gracious, gives us eyes that function, that are alive. That is the first thing. Then the living eyeball blinks a couple times (repentance) and secondly it sees (faith). What does it see? The object *out there*, which in this case is Christ. This should not be difficult.

Let me explain what I think is going on here. "About time!" somebody cries. Dr. Clark has made a big point out of the uses of words like *because* and *is*. And I keep trying to agree with him, at least on this point. Our justifying faith *is* alive. God does not reward with justification *because* we have an alive faith. Okay? Amen.

But there are different uses of the word because. If a mother said to her son, "I am going to give you ice cream *because* you were a good boy today," this is a merit system. He could have been otherwise, but he wasn't, and so he got the ice cream. Some people want to go to heaven this way but they can't.

But what about this? "I saw Christ in His glory *because* God gave me a faith that could see Him." Now what? If someone thinks this means he was justified "on account of what a fine boy he was for having living faith," then he deserves whatever the Reformed confetti-counters do to him. But if he simply means that had God given him any kind of faith other than the living faith that He did give, and that he was justified *because* he had been given *that* kind of faith (instead of the other kind), this is simply Reformed orthodoxy. This is the difference between necessity and merit. It is necessary for me to have living faith, for if I do not, I will be blind to Christ, the sole ground of my justification. But there is no merit in my faith that God uses as a *reason* for justifying me.

Now notice how thinly Dr. Clark has to slice it here. He admits that faith partakes of the quality of its source when we are talking about sanctification, but he says that to admit that faith partakes of the quality of its source in *justification* amounts to a denial of the Reformation. But this is like saying that the eyeball is dead and blind when it looks to Christ in justification but mysteriously alive again when it looks to Christ in sanctification. This makes no sense; it is all the same faith. The faith that is the instrument of justification is also the faith that is the instrument of sanctification. I don't get one kind of disposable faith in order to justified, and then a replacement faith in order to be progressively sanctified. The entire Christian life, soup to nuts, is from faith to faith (Rom. 1:17). The just shall *live* by faith. But Dr. Clark is insisting that justifying faith has to be considered as ontologically distinct from sanctifying faith. For if you say that it partakes of the nature of its source (while justification is occurring), then you have denied the Reformation. This means that faith at the moment of justification, according to Dr. Clark (if he were consistent), has to be unholy, blind, and dead. For if it were holy, it would be partaking of the holiness of the new heart which produced it.

One other thing. To say that all our sanctity is "evidence only" has a serious problem with the traditional Reformed *ordo*. What does this do with definitive sanctification? When a man is given the new heart that produces a holy repentance and an (unholy? Dr. Clark?) faith, this happens when he is in an unjustified state. But *somewhere* in there, love and repentance and holiness are going on, and they are not proceeding from the man's justification, which according to the traditional *ordo*, has not happened yet. So all *post*-justification acts of love are "evidence only" and nothing else. But what are the pre-justification stirrings of love? You can't deny their existence without denying the reality of regeneration. The new heart hates sin and loves God. That love is not meritorious, and God does not reward it when He justifies a man. But it is sure enough *there*.

Dr. Clark's dilemma is not resolved by taking Dr. Gaffin's solution (although I appreciate what Gaffin says on this point) because even if the *ordo* is not taken as a chronological business (measured with a stop watch), it still represents the *logical* order of things as the Reformed have historically understood it. The *ordo* rightly protects monergism in salvation, and, to borrow a phrase, Dr. Clark is "fiddling" around with this.

A WEE BIT MORE
FEB 3, 2007

A couple of very reasonable posters have urged me to spend my time on more fruitful endeavors than trying to persuade Dr. Clark of my orthodoxy. While I have no intention of conducting a debate like this *ad infinitum*, I do believe it is fruitful now. While it would be wonderful to persuade Dr. Clark, the exchange of views can be entirely successful otherwise. If it persuades a significant number of people in the audience of the true state of affairs, it will have been worth it. This is what Luke says about the debating prowess of Apollos. He vigorously refuted the Jews in public debate. And what was the result? He was an encouragement to those who through grace had believed. I am convinced that there are many in the Reformed community who are still making up their minds on Federal Vision issues, and this kind of exchange can be very profitable for them. So I don't intend to debate this issue world without end. But I am going to keep it up for a wee bit more.

SAVING FAITH IS A BUSY BEE
FEB. 3, 2007

All right, let's recap.

Dr. Clark says that I have unwittingly denied the Reformation because I hold that saving faith is holy. I say that when God calls us effectually and regenerates us and gives us a new heart, this new heart turns away from sin (in repentance) and turns to Christ (in faith). Because I have said that this faith "partakes" of the qualities of heart that produced it, Dr. Clark says I am therefore necessarily saying that God considers these qualities to be meritorious. But I deny that God considers the merit of these qualities in any manner whatever as He justifies me.

But what options are left for Dr. Clark if he wants to avoid denying the Reformation like me? He must *either* say that the faith that "rests and receives" is an unholy faith (no works here!), *or* he must say that faith somehow comes in detachable modules, so that it can be holy in this part, but in the part that does all the resting and receiving, no qualities of holiness are to be found anywhere in *that* module, which is sealed off from the others. For otherwise, if he grants that the faith that does the resting and receiving is also holy, then he has agreed with me, and will not simple souls conclude from all this that prayers to Mary are appropriate?

Now, with this said, let us turn to what Dr. Clark says is the definition of what it means to be Reformed—the confessions. We will content ourselves this morning with the Confession that I am in submission to, the Westminster.

But the principal acts of saving faith are accepting, receiving, and resting upon Christ alone for justification, sanctification, and eternal life, by virtue of the covenant of grace (WCF 14.2).

A great deal has been said by Dr. Clark about "resting and receiving" alone. But in Westminster, this is all part of a larger sentence. The principal acts of *saving* faith are accepting, receiving, and resting upon Christ alone for justification, sanctification, and eternal life, by virtue of the covenant of grace. Notice that the accepting, receiving and resting are not isolated. They are directed toward certain defined ends. Three of them are mentioned. Justification is one of the things that saving faith looks toward. *Sanctification* is the second thing that *saving* faith looks toward. Get that? Saving faith has something on its mind other than just getting past the moment of justification. And the third thing that saving faith thinks about is eternal life. Saving faith proceeds from a heart that is interested in personal holiness, and it looks forward to the personal holiness that sanctification brings. If Dr. Clark doesn't like it, he can take it up with Westminster—the Confession, not the seminary.

So is this *all* that saving faith does? No, those were just the *principal* acts of saving faith. These are the central things that saving faith does, but the Westminster divines do not believe for a moment that saving faith has to be stripped bare of everything around it in order to become a naked assent that would make the Escondido Lutherans happy. No, for them, saving faith is a busy bee.

By this faith, a Christian believeth to be true whatsoever is revealed in the Word, for the authority of God Himself speaking therein (John 4:42; 1 Thess. 2:13; 1 John 5:10; Acts 24:14); and acteth differently upon that which each particular passage thereof containeth; yielding obedience to the commands (Rom. 16:26), trembling at the threatenings (Isa. 66:2), and embracing the promises of God for this life, and that which is to come (Heb. 11:13; 1 Tim. 4:8). But the principal acts of saving faith are accepting, receiving, and resting upon Christ alone for justification, sanctification, and eternal life, by virtue of the covenant of grace (John 1:12; Acts 16:31; Gal. 2:20; Acts 15:11).

So what are some of the *other* things that saving faith does, misbehaving as it does right here in a Reformed confession? *Saving* faith believes whatever God has revealed in His Word, and that would include, incidentally,

Genesis 1–2. Note that the point is not that saving faith affirms the generic inspiration or inerrancy of the Word, but that it believes as true the *content* of what is revealed there. *Saving* faith has a sound hermeneutic, acting differently according to the nature of the passage before it. Saving faith yields *obedience* to the commands of God. The problem here for Dr. Clark is that the Westminster was written in English, and so in a crisis like this we can't resort to Greek word studies. Saving faith yields obedience to God's commands, and what Dr. Clark is doing is declaring unconfessional a number of Reformed ministers who have the temerity to believe the confession in places *where he doesn't.*

Saving faith trembles at the threats. Saving faith embraces promises for *this* life and the next. But the principal acts of saving faith are to accept, receive and rest upon Christ for three things. Those *three* things are justification, sanctification, and eternal life.

Now, however saving faith does this, it is clear that it does not do it detached from all love, sanctity, and holiness.

A new heart is given, one that loves God, and submits to Him. That new heart detests sin now and turns from it in repulsion. We call that motion repentance. This new heart loves Christ and turns to Him, seeking Him out. We call that motion faith. Dr. Clark says that if I allow the motive of love into this motion of turning to Christ then I am somehow diluting it with Romanism. Yikes. *It is not Romanism to love Jesus from the first moment of the effectual call.*

Lest anyone who specializes in taking quotes out of context see this (and I know you're out there!), and point to it, saying that Wilson is clearly mixing "works" into the moment of justification, let me slice it as thinly as you do. In a thought experiment (I am out of my mind to talk like this), if God were to stop the process of an individual's salvation just *before* the moment of justification, but *after* the effectual call, and if He were to judge that individual on the basis of the loving qualities of the person's new heart, what does Wilson think would happen to that guy? Is this question esoteric enough for you? I believe that if God were to interrupt the moment of someone's conversion with judgment this way, the person concerned would go straight to Hell headfirst. If God were to mark iniquities, would could stand?

The new heart is different from the old one, but still sinful and fallen. The repentance is genuine, but still imperfect. The faith in Christ, and love for Him are not hypocritical, for they are gifts of God, but they still fall short of the glory of God. They have turned away from sin, and have turned to Christ, but they have not done so perfectly—and a holy God requires perfection. Being a loving God, what He requires of us in this respect He also gives to us in the perfections of Jesus Christ. But we are still in our thought experiment. So the individual is *not* declared righteous, sinless, acceptable, or holy on the basis of how good he was being for that nanosecond before justification.

But because his heart was quickened, his eyes opened, his faith stirred into life, the one thing that this person can do *is see Jesus Christ.* To argue against this is unscriptural, unconfessional, and incoherent. To push Dr. Clark's logic out to the end requires us to say that a blind and dead eye sees Christ and can rest in Him, receiving Him. But wait . . . is it not obedient, and holy, to rest in Him? Maybe saving faith has to do this while snarling and sullen. No popery *here.*

To refute all this from the Scriptures would be easy, but we have come to the point in this controversy where if I were to do that, the response would be something like, "Yeah, well, Jehovah's Witnesses have Bibles too, and they appeal to them too. We need the confessions."

You have appealed to the confessions, and so to the confessions we have gone. Saving faith yields obedience to the commands of God. Among many other activities, saving faith trusts in Christ alone for sanctification.

LIKE A FEATHER BOA
FEB. 5, 2007

A shrewd observer of my exchanges with Dr. Clark contacted me privately and made a point that I think is well worth repeating here.

I would urge anyone who needs the refresher to read through our respective posts, along with the comments. You can look through the Auburn

Avenue Stuff on this blog for the last week, and look at Dr. Clark's blog* for the last week. Prior to our exchanges, one of the things that Dr. Clark was very adamant about was just how *clear* the issues were. The Federal Vision is *plainly* heretical, this was *obviously* headed to Rome, and so on.

When Dr. Clark agreed to our indirect debate, one of the things it did was put two representatives of these positions side by side, talking about the same issues. And all of a sudden the only thing that was clear was that the Federal Vision is not clearly heresy. This point does not depend on the FV being right. Let's suppose for the sake of this illustration that FV is just one more mainstream Reformed mistake, like amillennialism—erroneous, but no way heretical.

Dr. Clark was maintaining that FV is slam-dunk heretical. Our reply was that if this is the case, a debate should make the clear even clearer. But we just had our debate, after a fashion, and in the aftermath of this debate everybody could plainly see that I hold to a Westminsterian soteriology, and that I wear the traditional Reformed *ordo* around my neck like it was a feather boa. Where did all the plain heresy go?

Further, by the end of the exchanges some of Dr. Clark's supporters were calling on *me* to lighten up. To which I reply, please remember that every word I have written in this controversy has been on defense. We are responding to charges, we are not making them. We are defending our callings and vocations in ministry; we are not trying to challenge the ministry of our fellow ministers in the Reformed faith. This is the season when another slate of books attacking us have been, are being, or will be released. I was asked to remember that Dr. Clark has a doctorate from Oxford. Given his credentials, which I do respect, it seems to me that one of the things that Dr. Clark should know how to do is represent his opponents in a polemical exchange accurately and clearly. Read through our exchanges again. Has Dr. Clark represented my views fairly?

The exchange has made certain things very clear. But they were not the things that Dr. Clark maintained beforehand as plain and clear.

* oceansideurc.org/the-heidelblog, now at heidelblog.net

MR. SANDEMAN, BRING ME A DREAM

FEB. 8, 2007

Here* is a short audio snippet from John Piper's talk on Fuller. This is the section where he references my recent discussion with Scott Clark on Heidelblog.† I think Piper is exactly right about the relevance of this discussion. As he points out, the handles are in slightly different places than they were in the 18th century, but we are trying to pick up the same thing.

INTERESTING

FEB. 7, 2007

In his talk on Andrew Fuller at the 2007 Desiring God pastors conference, John Piper had this to say: "I just tuned into the debate between R. Scott Clark and Doug Wilson over at Scott's blog, Heidelblog, and there were elements of it that relate directly to Fuller's response to Sandemanianism (though no one there would be in the category of a Sandemanian)."

I would be interested to hear from anyone who listens to the audio whether or not John Piper amplifies this comment at all.

OH

FEB. 10, 2007

Well, I have listened to an interview‡ with Guy Waters on the Federal Vision (HT: Mark Horne). In a nutshell, I agree with Mark's response here§. How is it possible for the same teaching to create false assurance and no assurance? How is our preaching and teaching putting them to complacent sleep in their covenantal pew and at the same time dangling terrified parishioners over the abyss? This is a theological problem with his critique. What exactly

* The link to the clip is dead, but the full lecture is available here: desiringgod.org/messages/holy-faith-worthy-gospel-world-vision.

† heidelblog.net

‡ callingfortruth.org/loggeraudio/CFT-02-08-2007.mp3, no longer available.

§ There was no link in the original post, but Mark's comments are available here: hornes.org/mark/2007/02/is-faith-sufficient-to-justification.

is the bad thing we are doing to the people of God? Are we taking assurance away or trucking in great amounts of undesired surplus assurance? That is the *theological* critique.

Here is the *ethical* critique. In this interview, Guy Waters did the same thing that he did in his book, and which I have already refuted section by section. He says we don't say things we very clearly say, he says that we obscure things we don't obscure,and in short he grossly misrepresents us (to an unsuspecting Christian audience). I would refer him to the Larger Catechism's treatment of the ninth commandment, and ask him to adopt an attitude of strict subscription.

Here is one glaring example from the interview. Dr. Waters said that assurance is simply not to be found in FV preaching and teaching. Not to be found. Okay, what about *the whole chapter* on assurance in my book *"Reformed" Is Not Enough*? And this was not a chapter on how assurance is bad, but rather a standard, straightforward pastoral treatment of assurance, in line with our confessions, and in complete harmony with what I was arguing in the rest of the book. We know we have passed from death to life because of our love for the brethren. We know we are God's children because He chastizes every son whom He receives, and so on. John the apostle wrote 1 John so that we might *know* that we have eternal life.

But if I were a member of that unsuspecting Christian audience, listening to this stuff, I would be alarmed. If I were alarmed enough to form an opinion, but not so alarmed that I actually went and got a book by an FV author, or listened to a downloaded sermon from one of them, I would walk away from hearing this interview with a *false* opinion of Christian brothers, and I would have gotten that false opinion directly from Guy Waters.

Given the line that is being spun about us, it is plain as day why there will not be any debates anytime soon. Hypothetically, we could find ourselves hearing something like this. Dr. Waters: "Nowhere in FV preaching and teaching will you find anything on assurance." Wilson: "I just finished a short series of sermons on the important subject of assurance, which can be obtained from Canon Press." Dr. Waters: "Oh."

YOU HAVE TOUCHED THE THING WITH A NEEDLE
FEB. 12, 2007

I would like to pass on to all of you some questions posed by a correspondent in Australia. He has been observing us toiling away here in our FV swamps and sent on some questions that I thought were just grand, going right to the heart of the matter. If I were speaking to this correspondent right now, I might resort to a felicitous Latin phrase (the kind I learned from Wodehouse, not Wheelock), which is to say, *rem acu tetigisti*—you have touched the thing with a needle.

Here they are:

1. Are the children of believers in covenant with God?
2. If so, which covenant are they in? (Are they in the covenant of works, grace, new, privilege, other?)
3. Are they fully in that covenant?
4. Were such children who have grown up to final unbelief ever really in that covenant to begin with?

Because this is not a gotcha game, but a sincere set of questions, I think that I should answer them too. So here goes.

1. Are the children of believers in covenant with God? **Yes.**
2. If so, which covenant are they in? (Are they in the covenant of works, grace, new, privilege, other?) **The covenant of grace.**
3. Are they fully in that covenant? **With regard to membership and the attendant obligation to live by faith alone, yes. With regard to enjoyment of all the blessings of the covenant, that depends on whether or not they are elect.**
4. Were such children who have grown up to final unbelief ever really in that covenant to begin with? **Yes, they were.**

Now since it should be obvious that these questions cut right to the heart of the issue, it would seem to follow that FV critics would have to answer these questions differently *somewhere*. But where? My money is on #3, but they have to be careful. If they answer too robustly, they will find themselves out of accord with the Westminster Confession.

THE JOHN CALVIN MEMORIAL ARCHIVE AND BOOK STACKS

FEB. 14, 2007

Mark Horne has posted a quotation from Calvin on Deuteronomy. I reproduce the quote below, but the comments on Mark's blog* are worth reading also.

> For, since the fall of Adam had brought disgrace upon all his posterity, God restores those, whom He separates as His own, so that their condition may be better than that of all other nations. At the same time it must be remarked, that this grace of renewal is effaced in many who have afterwards profaned it. Consequently the Church is called God's work and creation, in two senses, i.e., generally with respect to its outward calling, and specially with respect to spiritual regeneration, as far as regards the elect; for the covenant of grace is common to hypocrites and true believers. On this ground all whom God gathers into His Church, are indiscriminately said to be renewed and regenerated: but the internal renovation belongs to believers only; whom Paul, therefore, calls God's "workmanship, created unto good works, which God hath prepared, etc." (Ephesians 2:10.). Calvin, Deut 32:6

I want to draw attention to a number of things here, and then follow up with an observation on the authority of Calvin for Calvinists.

Notice first that Calvin says that the grace of renewal is *effaced* in some. It is effaced in those who have afterwards *profaned* that grace of renewal. In order to profane something you have to come into some sort of contact with it. As a result of this profanation of renewing grace, it is proper to speak of the Church as God's work and creation in two different ways. The first is general,

* Currently available here: hornes.org/mark/2007/02/calvin-on-the-covenant-of-grace.

and has to do with outward calling. The second is special, and has regard to *spiritual* regeneration of the elect. Calvin goes on to say that the covenant of grace is common to hypocrites and true believers, and both kinds of people in the covenant are appropriately said to be renewed and regenerated. *Internal* renovation, however, belongs only to genuine believers.

In case anybody missed this, Calvin says here:

1. The grace of renewal can be effaced;
2. It is effaced by those who profane it;
3. God's work and creation in the Church can properly be spoken of two ways: general and special;
4. The general work is the outward call;
5. The special work is the spiritual rebirth of the elect;
6. The covenant of grace is common to hypocrites and true believers both;
7. Both hypocrites and true believers can be said to be renewed and regenerated;
8. And heart renovation belongs only to genuine believers.

Now this is all straight from Calvin, and I guess we all know who will not be speaking at Westminster West conferences any time soon. In fact, Calvin hasn't been invited to speak there in *years*. We shouldn't make too much out of that though—I think it is an internal faculty/politics thing.

Now a comment on the authority of Calvin for Calvinists. The fact that Calvin said it doesn't make it right, and I think it is fair to say that a man could be a conscientious Calvinist and think that Calvin got a lot of things wrong. But that is not the point. I think it should be safe to say that for Reformed, Presbyterian, and Reformed Baptist believers, Calvin's errors, whatever they were (take paedocommunion, for example) were not the kind of errors that should get him labeled as a flaming heretic at RTS Jackson.

But here is the kick in the teeth. The sentiments above, run through a syntax scrubber to hide the 16th century origins, and advanced to Waters, Clark, Duncan, et al. in the name of Lusk or Leithart *would* get labeled that way.

There is no better way to illustrate how out of touch with the reformational tradition these men have become.

Note, the point is not that Calvin is right and these men are wrong. Their revivalistic version of the Reformed faith might be the Reformed faith come into its own. They could be right on all points, but if they want to consider themselves Reformed, they can't be saying that they are "Calvinists except for those parts where Calvin is always denying the gospel."

Calvin might be talking through his hat on this point. But if he is talking through his hat, he is obviously saying the same kind of thing that the FV people are saying. And that means *we* are talking through our hats as well. The fact that "Calvin said it" should not be followed with "I believe it, that settles it." If Calvin was silly for saying it, so are we. But it is a bit thick for the "heirs of the Reformation" to be drumming John Calvin out of the corps of the orthodox like this. If this is an error, it is an error within the Reformed pale—we share the error with no less than ol' Jean himself. If it not an error, then certain schoolmarm librarians at the John Calvin Memorial Archives and Book Stacks need to do a little less shushing and a little more reading.

The ancient pagans had their myths of the gods coming down incognito, and finding out how everybody treated them that way. The Messiah of Israel did something similar to the custodians of the Torah, and found out what they *actually* thought of Moses, who had warned them that this would be happening.

This leads to an edifying thought experiment. Bring Calvin back, shave his beard, get rid of that kamikaze hat, make him a young man in his twenties, and send him before classis (or presbytery would do just as well) to get his little French hinder parts *examined.*

> RSC: What do you understand by regeneration?
>
> JC: The word can be used differently . . .
>
> [Whispering on the panel]
>
> RSC: What do you mean "differently?"
>
> JC: Well, in one sense both the hypocrite and the true believer can be properly said to be renewed and regenerated, but . . . excuse me?

RSC: I said *what*?

JC: The covenant of grace encompasses both kinds of covenant members, but regeneration can only be used in a special sense if we are talking about the internal grace that belongs only to the elect.

RSC: Where did you go to seminary?

JC: Well, actually I went to law school.

RSC: Have you ever been to Auburn Avenue Presbyterian Church?

JC: No, sir.

RSC: Have you listened to the CDs?

JC: What's a CD?

MH: Mr. Chairman, I think we are getting off the point . . .

RSC: Quite right. You say that the covenant of grace includes the reprobate?

JC: Yes, with regard to the outward call. So they are truly members of that which they profane, and the renewing grace that comes to them is something they really efface. But there is a qualitative difference between them and the . . .

RSC: Do you really want us to vote on you?

JC: I really wish you would. I was warned what would happen, but I had to come see for myself.

Enough fun. I am on the road right now, but just before leaving I got my copy of *Covenant, Justification, and Pastoral Ministry*, edited by Scott Clark. I have only had a chance to look it over and haven't gotten grace or time enough to read it yet. But to show you what we are dealing with, the somewhat breathless copy written on the cover says that the gospel today is "under assault." Heavy word, *assault*, especially if you are talking about language like what Calvin uses above.

All modern and educated Calvinists know various places where they take issue with Calvin. But leave it to Westminster West to develop the line of thought that makes Calvin a heretic, assaulting the gospel. Land of Goshen.

PERSONAL LOYALTY
FEBRUARY 19, 2007

A few weeks ago, I made the point that leaders among the anti-FVers have been extremely reluctant to admit the obvious, which is that I hold to the historic Reformed view of justification and so on. The reason for this, I suggested, was political. In other words, to admit publicly that I had a clean bill of health would do damage to the political campaign against FV now under way.

It would do damage to their cause in two ways. First, it would undercut those on their side of the fence who have already gone on the record about me—e.g., someone like Guy Waters. To recognize my orthodoxy would make these guys out front to be the anti-FV equivalent of guys on the beach at the Bay of Pigs—"Where's the air support, man?" The second way it would undercut the current crusade is by making people make distinctions when they are in no mood to make distinctions. If they start doing *that*, it might set an unedifying chain of thought in motion. "If Wilson is okay," someone might muse, "after years of hearing that he *isn't*, maybe some of these other guys are okay too."

So I made this point about the politics of the thing, and one poster here raised the question of whether I was "playing politics" also. Can the tables of this argument be turned? I don't believe so, but here is how the argument would go. If I am as orthodox as all that, then why haven't I denounced my friends and ecclesiastical homies whose language makes people more nervous than my language does? Am I not circling the wagons for political reasons, just like I say the folks on the other side are doing?

No, and here is why. There is a difference between partisan loyalty and personal loyalty. Personal loyalty obviously has limits, but the biblical principles of justice define what those limits are. Here is how it works. The first thing to remember is that ministers in good standing should be considered (especially by their friends) to have done nothing wrong unless someone establishes that they have done something wrong. Second, when accusations are raised against a group of men, it is reasonable and prudent to judge the reliability of the accusers by holding their charges up against the positions you know best, which in this case would be my own positions. I am not an expert in everything my friends have written or said. I am an expert in what I have written and said, and if people are saying outrageous things about my views, what motivation do I have to tunnel through everything Rich Lusk has written in order to "prove him innocent"? Rich can do that better than I, and I already *know* his accusers are out to lunch. Remember, they came over to my house first, and said some crazy things. Third, when trouble arises the first reaction of a friend ought not to be that of backing away and coming back sheepishly later when things look safer for *his* sorry idea of a friend. And fourth, using theological language that is not typical for provincial presbyterians is not the same thing as heresy. I know enough about how my friends express themselves to know that they don't always put things the same way I would. So why, when someone starts trying to whoop up a heresy trial, don't I join in the general frenzy and acknowledge publicly that "some of this language is troubling"? The reason is that there is a difference between operating outside the well-worn grooves of theological clichés and heresy. Yes, some of my friends speak differently than I do. So does Calvin. So does Turretin. So do a bunch of other Reformed fathers. This has been the point of the various Calvin citations I have used. The point is not that I would put things the same way that Calvin would. For example, I do not use the word *regeneration* the same way Calvin does. That is no reason for me to douse my hair with lighter fluid, set it off, and run around in tight, little circles. Men can use different theological vocabulary without disagreeing in substance. If it appears that this is what is happening (as it does to me in this situation), then cooler heads ought to prevail until the thing is sorted out. Different terminology is a standard technique used by damnable heretics to conceal their pernicious errors, but it is affirming the consequent to say that the presence of different terminology is equivalent to heresy. All dogs have four legs, but that does not turn cows into dogs. Heretics use different terminology for their unrighteous purposes, but James and Paul used different terminology for their *righteous* purposes.

So then,

1. Innocent until proven guilty;
2. Evaluate the unknown in terms of the known;
3. A brother is born for adversity;
4. And the Reformed faith should be big enough to encompass different streams or traditions within it. But at the very least, it should be big enough to include those who established it.

Put all this together and you can see why I felt no pressure whatever to ditch my friends just because someone started yelling. This refusal to budge is not an example of me playing politics on this issue; it is actually an example of me declining to do so. In contexts like this one, personal loyalty—to men like Wilkins, Lusk, Leithart, Horne, Schlissel, or Barach—is simply what Christ calls for.

LIKE A MAN DRAGGING A ROPE
FEBRUARY 21, 2007

I am afraid that Westminster West is disgracing itself. I finally had a chance to begin reading *Covenant, Justification, and Pastoral Ministry*, edited by R. Scott Clark, and released by Presbyterian and Reformed, proud publishers of Norman Shepherd's *Call of Grace.*

The first essay in this new bucket of fruit is by Clark, and is set up to answer the question "how we got here?" "Here" would be that controversial point where we have two sides within the Reformed camp, each claiming to be orthodox. Here is Scott Clark's summary of the points at issue.

> One side tends to argue that genuinely Reformed doctrine teaches one covenant before and after the fall, the imputation of Jesus's passive obedience only, and faith that justifies because it obeys. The other side in contrast holds that the Reformed doctrine denies those very things. Without equivocating, both sides cannot be correct. (p. 5)

Here it is in a slightly different form.

> To conclude that in justification faith justifies *because* it obeys or that Christ did not perform vicarious active obedience or that Paul's

> doctrine of justification was not primarily about right standing before God has the most serious implications for the historic (and confessional) doctrine of justification. (p 4)

A slight difficulty arises because, as readers of this blog know full well, I hold that there are two covenants, one before the fall and one after. I hold to the imputation of the active obedience of Christ, and I do so with robust gesticulations. And I deny that faith justifies because of any boy scout qualities it may have. Strike *three*. At this point, Clark needs to hand his bat to the bat boy and respectfully take his seat in the dugout. But he does nothing of the kind. He just assumes the stance again and looks at the pitcher with a steely gaze. "That all you got? Three pitches? I'll hit one eventually. C'mon." Okay. I also affirm that justification is primarily about right standing before God. Strike four.

Observers of this debacle, who are sympathetic to the concerns of Westminster West, but who are clear-headed enough to see what's going on, will no doubt say, "Yeah, but you're an anomaly, Wilson. Shepherd does deny the imputation of the active obedience of Christ, and rumor has it that some of your friends are squishy on the other two." But denying the active obedience of Christ wouldn't have prevented Shepherd from being a delegate to the Westminster Assembly, would it? And neither would the "squishiness" of insisting that God's dealings with man are always gracious, or the view that faith has to be living and not dead. And faith is living because it *obeys* the command to rise and walk. All these positions were found participating in the work at Westminster.

But in my case, that dodge won't work anyway. Here is how I fit into this scheme, according to this book. I show up, for starters in a footnote in the second essay (p.52).

> For a summary of the convictions of the Federal Vision by one of its most vocal advocates, see Douglas Wilson, "Union with Christ: An Overview of the Federal Vision," in *The Auburn Avenue Theology, Pros and Cons: Debating the Federal Vision* (ed. E. Calvin Beisner; Ft. Lauderdale, FL: Knox Theological Seminary, 2004), 1–8.

I am one of the most vocal advocates of the Federal Vision, and I deny all four of the characteristics of that vision as kinda assigned by Clark. These are strange doings. Somebody doesn't know what he is talking about. Either I am not in the Federal Vision at all, or the Federal Vision is not what its opponents claim, or it is not monolithic as its opponents claim. In any case, this book is out of line.

One of the criticisms that I have had to field is that we have an innovating spirit about us, fiddling around with the Reformed heritage that our fathers bequeathed to us. "Why mess with the fathers?" the cry goes up. "We must hold mindlessly to the tradition of rejecting mindless papist traditions." But that is a subject for another time.

We are considered impudent movers of ancient landmarks. But I learned a bunch of this stuff *from* these fathers. I became a Calvinist in 1988 and began reading stacks of books published by Banner of Truth, P&R, Soli Deo Gloria, and so on. And a bunch of the current controversy was already in print, *in those books*, and circulating peacefully in Reformed circles—almost as though these issues were an intramural set of differences within the bounds of Reformed orthodoxy. But now, becoming aware of this problem, Clark is preparing himself for a purge of the history books.

He appears to be preparing us to say that John Murray was at the headwaters of this mischief (p. 6). Cornelius Van Til, despite his stalwart support for Norman Shepherd, is still considered a good guy (p. 7), but we can put this down as another manifestation of the tombs-of-the-prophets phenomenon. It would be impolitic to touch Van Til just yet, or Richard Gaffin for that matter—for blurbing Shepherd's book. But Clark is ready to throw Melanchthon under the bus because at least for a time he thought that good works were necessary for justification (p. 13). And we also have to rid ourselves of Richard Baxter because he "taught quite clearly that faith justifies because it obeys" (p. 15). So when is Banner of Truth going to repent of publishing *The Reformed Pastor*?

The intent is apparently to bury the truth under a rock pile of footnotes.

> These essays are not intended to be popular. The faculty held a conference in 2003 in which we presented some of this material in a way

> that is accessible to Christian laity. Those lectures are available from the Westminster Seminary California. Some of the essays in this collection do arise from that conference, but they have been significantly revised to speak to a more academic audience. (p. 23)

You betcher. This is the kind of book that has footnotes like *this* in it:

> Seeberg, *History of Doctrines*, 2.364. See also Robert Kolb, "Georg Major as Controversialist: Polemics in the Late Reformation," *Church History* 45 (1976): 455–68; idem, *Nikolaus von Amsdorf (1483–1565): Popular Polemics in the Preservation of Luther's Legacy* (Nieuwkoop: DeGraaf, 1978), 123–71.

I for one find myself almost persuaded. You would think that with all this firepower they would be able to get the basic facts of the case right. But they have not. I responded to the Westminster West conference referred to above, and I did so back at the time. This means there is *no excuse* for not getting the basic positions right. Robert E. Lee was not a Yankee. The Dutch have not conquered Holland. Maybe referring to a series of blog posts entitled "Yelling at my Windshield" would not have enough of a scholarly patina to be included in *these* footnotes.

One last thing for now. Clark objects that the "word *Reformed* has come to mean *predestinarian*" (p. 11). The problem here is that if you believe in heaven and hell, as all of us in the Federal Vision do, and if you are predestinarian, as all of us are, and as Clark acknowledges, then all five points of Calvinism follow from this, inexorably, like a man dragging a rope. Not only so, but *sola gratia* and *sola fide* also follow, like a second rope. This is something we all know, acknowledge, and affirm. He who says A must say B. We know that. So, Dr. Clark, for the record, *again*, "B."

KIND OF TACKY TO POINT OUT
FEBRUARY 22, 2007

In Chapter Two of *Covenant, Justification, and Pastoral Ministry*, David VanDrunen continues to sound the alarm. The doctrine of justification is "under fire" (p. 25), being attacked (p. 25), there are "three distinct lines of attack" (p. 26), and he concludes that "justification is indeed under attack" (p. 57).

He desires to describe the views of the attackers "accurately and fairly" (p. 26), and in some cases, he may have done so. The three lines of attack he mentions are modern ecumenical movements, the New Perspective on Paul, and Federal Vision stuff. I don't have a lot to say about his treatment of the first two, but I do need to say something about the third.

He categorized those of us in this third "line of attack" as "self-styled Reformed church leaders" (p. 26), and we are leaders of the "self-styled Federal Vision" (p. 52). I am not sure what this means, but it sounds like we got our theological education in night school after teaching ourselves to read off of milk cartons. Kind of tacky to point out, even if it *is* true.

When he gets to our line of attack, he starts with Norman Shepherd. My point is not so much Shepherd's position here as it is VanDrunen's idea of refutation. Watch closely.

> First, Shepherd's teaching denies, or at least redefines, the idea that justification is *by faith alone.* (p. 49, emphasis his)

And how is that? How does Shepherd deny this?

> In his book, Shepherd repeatedly stresses that justifying faith is an active, living, obedient faith. Given the context of debates over justification, such language is inherently ambiguous. (p. 49)

Then apparently the only way to get through ambiguous justification debates is to insist that we are justified by an inert, dead, and disobedient faith. That way all the glory goes to Christ, and nobody gets the wrong idea.

> In short, whereas Reformed theology teaches that faith alone, defined as an extraspective trust in Christ and his atoning work, justifies and that obedience, which is never to be confused with faith itself, inevitably flows from justifying faith. (p. 49)

Okay, let's talk for a moment about this "flows from" business. The Bible teaches in multiple places that the nature of the source determines the nature of that which comes from the source. You don't get pineapples off bramble bushes. Fresh springs don't produce brackish water. Out of the abundance of the heart, the mouth speaks, and so on. If obedience flows from justifying faith, then obedience has to have had something to do with that justifying faith. Like begets like. God does not intrude the obedience a nanosecond later in a work of special creation. No—God establishes *life* with regeneration, and that life continues to manifest itself through the entire life of the believer in question, including in his justifying faith. God does not justify anyone because of what a fine job they are doing with their life, but He never used a dead faith to justify anybody.

VanDrunen continues to represent Shepherd this way:

> Furthermore, "a living and active faith is the fruit of the regenerating and sanctifying work of the Holy Spirit." Whereas the Reformation doctrine has always taught that sanctification is a fruit of justifying faith, here Shepherd says just the opposite—that faith is the fruit of sanctification. (p. 50)

Two responses. The first is to just quote Calvin. Work through what Calvin says here, and see if you can find in it what VanDrunen says the Reformation doctrine "has always taught." The emphasis in bold is mine.

> Why, then, are we justified by faith? Because by faith we grasp Christ's righteousness, by which alone we are reconciled to God. **Yet you could not grasp this without at the same time grasping sanctification also**. For he 'is given unto us for righteousness, wisdom, sanctification, and redemption' (1 Cor. 1:30). Therefore Christ justifies no one whom he does not **at the same time** sanctify. These benefits are joined together by an everlasting and indissoluble bond, so that those whom he illumines by his wisdom, he redeems; those whom he redeems, he justifies; those whom he justifies, he sanctifies. But, since the question concerns only righteousness and sanctification, let us dwell upon these. Although we may distinguish them,

> **Christ contains both of them inseparably in himself.** Do you wish, then, to attain righteousness in Christ? You must first possess Christ; **but you cannot possess him without made partaker in his sanctification, because he cannot be divided into pieces** (1 Cor. 1:13). Since, therefore, it is solely by expending himself that the Lord gives us these benefits to enjoy, **he bestows both of them at the same time, the one never without the other.** Thus it is clear how true it is that we are justified not without works yet not through works, since in our sharing in Christ, which justifies us, **sanctification is just as much included** as righteousness. (Calvin, *Institutes*, III.xvi.1)

Calvin is dealing with this topic in a sensible, pastoral, Christocentric way. He is doing so in a way that avoids the stopwatch problems with the traditional Reformed *ordo salutis*, if that *ordo* is conceived of in a clunky way. Calvin's approach here harmonizes nicely, in my view, with Richard Gaffin's treatment of the ordo in his book on the subject. (Have I mentioned that Gaffin blurbed Shepherd's book, and that P&R published it?) The *ordo* is an illustration, a metaphor, meant to preserve a right understanding of God's sovereignty in salvation. It is like a paper-mache model of an atom, hanging above a fifth-grade classroom. There is a point to the illustration, which must be grasped, but, once it is grasped, you ought to stop thinking of the atom as a teeny solar system.

That said, those who insist on living by the *ordo* will die by the *ordo*.

> For example, Shepherd reasons that because regeneration is the beginning of sanctification, hence saving faith (which is subsequent to regeneration) is produced by sanctification and, therefore, sanctification begins prior to justification. (p. 50)

VanDrunen mentions this argument which, given the *ordo*, is actually unanswerable. Regeneration (a change of heart) is prior to justification. The initial change of heart (definitive sanctification) is prior to the on-going change of heart (progressive sanctification), and justification is the meat in this sanctification sandwich. First comes a form of sanctification, a change of heart, which enables me to repent and believe. Because I have been changed in my heart, I repent and believe, and God imputes the righteousness of Christ to me (justification). Now, given the constraints of the *ordo*, how is it that all subsequent sanctification must flow from justification only? Why can't it flow from the earlier sanctification? And why are you not willing to say that the faith that is the instrument of justification in some sense flows from definitive sanctification?

The only response VanDrunen gives to Shepherd's question is that of a twofold denial. First, he says that Shepherd clearly denies that good works are "entirely" the fruits of justifying faith. And second, he says that Shepherd clearly affirms that "sanctification actually *precedes* justification." No. Shepherd is not saying this. Shepherd is simply pointing out that the traditional Reformed *ordo* says this. And it does, in kind of an undeniable way. It is simply astonishing to me that in a book like this, a writer could mention a potent argument like this, presented by his opponent, and then proceed blithely on without answering it, or even attempting to answer it.

If you go with the *ordo*, the model of the atom, *some* form of sanctification comes first. If you don't like that, then don't yell at Shepherd. Ditch the ordo, and declare that William Perkins, or whoever came up with it, crept into the Reformed camp four centuries ago to spy out our liberty. But if you keep it, don't get upset with the people who pay close attention to what it *says*. But if you acknowledge that the *ordo* has some problems, then that leads to descriptions like Calvin's above. But notice that Calvin doesn't have good works flowing from a justification that is made of some completely different stuff. He has sanctification and justification simultaneously coming to the sinner from an undivided Christ. So you need to keep an eye on Calvin, along with that Perkins fellow.

One other quick point before I am done with this chapter. As I have said many times, I enthusiastically embrace the doctrine of imputed righteousness, and I affirm that the righteousness that is imputed to the believer is *all* the righteousness of Christ. What is imputed to me? Everything Jesus said and did, as well as His life of faith that was the spring of everything he said and did. I am justified by Jesus believing, by the faith of Jesus Christ (Gal. 2:18). That faith was the source of His sinless life and His sacrificial death. All of this is ours, imputed to us. His active and passive obedience both are credited to the believer, and to all His people. I trust that is clear enough.

But I reject, as enthusiastically as Rich Lusk does (p. 54), the idea of merit. If you want to maintain that Christ's obedience belongs to His people, and is imputed to His elect, I am right with you. Not only do I agree but would be willing to preach six sermons in a row on it, and I would have plenty of texts and to spare. If you want me to preach on "the Lord our righteousness," it is the same, and I would gladly do it. Not only is it right, it is the need of the hour. But if you want me to preach a series of sermons on *merit*, then you are going to have to help me out. Where are the texts?

JOHNNIE, M'BOY
FEBRUARY 22, 2007

The book I have been commenting (*Covenant, Justification, and Pastoral Ministry*) on makes it very clear that the imputation of the active obedience of Christ (which I hold) has to be considered a *sine qua non* of Reformed orthodoxy concerning justification (which I don't hold). If you would like to read a very short article which shows how John Owen demolishes this assumption, then click here*. HT: David Field

NOT EXACTLY JOY UPON JOY
FEBRUARY 24, 2007

The third essay in *Covenant, Justification, and Pastoral Ministy* is by Iain Duguid, and is entitled "Covenant Nomism and the Exile." It is really quite good overall, and my critical comments will not be extensive at all. There is one place where he has a superb interaction with N.T. Wright's confusion about courtroom imputation. In a famous passage in *What St. Paul Really Said*,

* This link, motherkirk.blogspot.com/2007/02/imputation-of-christs-active-obedience.html, is no longer publicly accessible.

Wright says that "righteousness is not an object, a substance or a gas that can be passed across the courtroom" (p. 98). In his treatment of Zechariah 3, Duguid shows that it *is* an object that can be passed across the courtroom—it is a clean cloak that replaces the filthy cloak that Joshua had been wearing previously. The first 87 pages of this book has not been joy upon joy, but that one argument has made it worthwhile. Everything can go downhill from here, and I am still okay.

So, then, my two critical comments. On page 73, Duguid says this:

> [The Lord] will sprinkle his defiled people with clean water, making them clean and able to stand in his sight . . . "justified," to use the language of systematic theology. The subsequent inner transformation, "sanctification," flows out of that prior act of God as its fruit.

But the person who is justified is already regenerate. That regeneration is an inner transformation. What need is there for a subsequent inner transformation? There is need for an *ongoing* transformation, but this process does not start immediately after justification—not if we are going to follow the traditional Reformed *ordo*. And we are going to do that, aren't we?

When Duguid implies that all forms of inner transformation are *subsequent* to justification, he is departing from the historic Reformed understanding of this business. That doesn't make him wicked, or a heretic, but it does mean that those among the Reformed who have actually noticed William Perkins's *Golden Chaine* ought not to be accused by R. Scott Clark of tinkering around with the ancient landmarks. As good old Monergism.com* puts it, "In the Reformed camp, the ordo salutis is 1) election, 2) predestination, 3) gospel call 4) inward call 5) regeneration, 6) conversion (faith & repentance), 7) justification, 8) sanctification, and 9) glorification. (Rom 8:29–30)" Notice how "inward call" and "regeneration" (a renovation

* This resource appears to be no longer available at Monergism, but if you search for the quote, you'll find the article, "Ordo Salutis," by David Brown, reprinted in *The Saving Grace of God*, by J.A. Hubner (pp. 51ff), which you can preview on Google Books.

of the heart) *precede* justification. And it will not do for those who say that all sanctification is *subsequent* to justification to try to get off the hook by saying that temporal terms are not strictly accurate and are to be held provisionally. If you are going to follow the chronological, then follow it. If you are not going to follow it, then don't upbraid us for chronological reasons. And for those who want to pursue this further, a very helpful discussion of some important aspects of this can be found in John Murray's marvelous article "Definitive Sanctification."†

The second point I want to make here is that Duguid is arguing "that human unfaithfulness cannot annul God's covenant commitment" (p. 81). I think this is good, and an important point to make. But there is an additional qualification that desperately needs to be made. Human unfaithfulness cannot annul God's covenant commitment *for the elect*. But since we are dealing with a covenant people which also contains within her ranks members who are not elect, we have to be careful how we navigate between corporate and individual realities. Today, if you hear His voice, do not harden your hearts as you did in the wilderness. Covenant branches are cut out. Bodies are scattered across the desert. The old Jerusalem the great harlot that God puts away in divorce but does so in such a way as to marry the New Jerusalem. For the elect, nothing can separate us from the love of God which is in Christ Jesus. But for non-elect covenant members, it is quite possible to fall from grace.

SOME HEADWAY, MAYBE
FEBRUARY 25, 2007

Green Baggins is reviewing a new book on the Federal Vision, and, if you check out the comments section of this entry‡, you will find that an ecumenical dialogue of sorts has broken out. Well, not exactly, but I think the exchange was more productive than not.

† the-highway.com/definitive-sanctification_Murray.html

‡ The link was missing from the original post, but probably refers to the comments here: greenbaggins.wordpress.com/2007/02/23/by-faith-alone-part-9

IN WHICH I GIVE MERIT DEMERITS
FEBRUARY 26, 2007

I honestly do not see how it can be considered possible to separate Christ from His benefits. So when I speak of the imputation of the active obedience of Christ, this means that I am ultimately speaking of the imputation of Christ Himself, and there is no way to understand this apart from the Pauline idea of union with Christ. We may *distinguish* Christ and His benefits (as the Bible frequently does), but if we try to *separate* them, we are guilty of a very serious mistake.

We can see this clearly in Ephesians 6, where the apostle tells us to put on the full armor of God. Every piece in that panoply is given a separate name, as though it were a discrete thing. The breastplate is righteousness, the belt is truth, the helmet is salvation, and so on. But Jesus is our righteousness, Jesus is the truth, Jesus is our salvation. Putting on the armor of God is another metaphorical way to speak about putting on the Lord Jesus Himself, which we are told in numerous places to do. This is even clearer when we see the passage in Isaiah (59:16–21) where this image comes from——the Lord Himself is the one who puts on the armor. The Lord saw that there was no man, and so equipped with His own righteousness, He stepped into the breach. Paul then tells us to do the same thing, to put on that same righteousness. But it cannot be *our* own righteousness——the Lord is our righteousness (Jer. 23:6; 33:16).

After I wrote last week about the passage in Zechariah where Joshua the priest was clothed in a clean garment that was transferred to him (across the courtroom), I received an email from a friend, a fellow FVer. He said, "I don't have a major objection to reading Zech. 3 as an 'imputed righteousness' passage . . . [but] it seems more fitting to see the rich robes with which Joshua is clothed as Christ himself, per Gal. 3, rather than merely Christ's righteousness." And my response to this is, "Well, certainly. Of course it is Christ Himself." Honestly, it is has never occurred to me that the benefits that flow from Christ could ever be enjoyed outside His presence, or apart from Him.

And this leads me right back to the discussion of *merit*, and why I object to it. But further, lest I create more confusion in an already confused situation, let me say that my following description of merit is what I am objecting to, and if someone doesn't hold to that which I am describing, but wants to use the word merit anyway, let's shake and be friends. I don't want to get into a wrangle over words merely.

At the same time, I believe there is a genuine substantive confusion going on here, and having this debate is a reasonable price to pay in order to get this confusion out of our system. I don't ever want to use the word *merit* in a way that lends itself to the continuation of that confusion. In the medieval system (which continues down to the present in some quarters), merit was a quantifiable substance. In Roman Catholic theology, it is possible to have a reservoir of merit, into which the "merit" of works of supererogation can go. Merit is therefore a stackable, fungible and transferable substance, detachable from the persons who initially generated it. Merit is awarded to any action that is "above and beyond the call of duty." In Roman Catholic theology, this reservoir can be drawn on by us, and can be contributed to by Mary, the saints, and other volunteers. In the world of good deeds, or so it is thought, it is possible to run a surplus and have a bunch left over—which other people can then use.

I imagine there are any number of criticisms that can be brought against this, and the central one of course is that it is not in the Bible. But I would like to bring a particular criticism that may help shed some light on this internal Protestant debate we are having. Works of supererogation depend upon a particular bookkeeping mentality, one that *depersonalizes* the whole idea of obedience. *My* good works are in principle detachable from *me* and could therefore be eventually put down in someone else's account. Now we all agree (good Protestants all) that none of us gets any merit from Mary or the saints. But one of the FV concerns is that some Protestants have kept the medieval definition of merit itself, while limiting (in an important biblical direction) the number of people who are allowed to contribute to the pile of surplus merit. In this particular Protestant view, only Jesus generates surplus merit. Now if you must cast the debate this way, I am with them rather than with the other guys. We are saved by Christ alone, *solus Christus*. But further questions beg to be asked. Can we really detach Jesus from the merit of His obedience like this? I don't believe so. This view (whether Protestant or Catholic) presupposes *that merit can somehow be impersonal.*

If you believe that in the life, death and resurrection of the Lord, God was operating a divine distillery through which He extracted the *merit* of Christ's obedience from that obedience, storing it in a separate container in a separate place, then you hold to the view of merit that the FV is rejecting. If you don't hold that, there is no need to get irate and post a hot comment, because if you don't hold that, we are not rejecting it. If you hold that every blessing received by us is on the basis of God's gift to us of Jesus Christ Himself, then you are in sympathy with one of the central FV concerns (whether you are comfortable with that sympathy or not).

One other thing. Union with Christ *does not exclude* the more traditional expressions of imputation. Rather, in my view, it provides a platform from which such expressions of imputation make better sense. This is important when we are talking about the differences between elect and non-elect covenant members. If I hold that non-elect covenant members can have union with Christ (in some sense), then is there a sense in which the elect covenant members receive something of Christ that the non-elect covenant members don't? The answer that I would give here is an unambiguous *yes*. This is where the language of imputation (found in Westminster) gets pushed into the corners. A regenerate covenant member is justified (personally and individually) in a way that a non-elect covenant member is not, just like the Confession says. But I would also want to say that the justification of the elect covenant member is profoundly connected to his union with Christ. The imputation is personal, forensic, judicial and declaratory——all of that. But the imputation does not occur across an infinite distance. It is for someone, though once far off, who has been brought near.

Go back to the Jeremiah passages cited earlier. "The Lord our righteousness." The prophet doesn't say "The Lord *has* righteousness, better get some from Him." The Lord, the Lord Himself *is* our righteousness. And in Him, we find all is ours (1 Cor. 3:21–23).

A REGULAR GUN SHOW
FEBRUARY 28, 2007

The next essay in *Covenant, Justification, and Pastoral Ministry* is by Bryan Estelle, and is entitled "The Covenant of Works in Moses and Paul." Estelle is plainly acquainted with a vast amount of theological and biblical studies literature, and his close handling of that literature is obviously competent. If footnotes were biceps, this thing would be a regular gun show.

Even so, I am not going to respond in point-by-point detail for one basic reason. Like many scholars, Estelle tends, frankly, to miss the point. He spends a great deal of time establishing and proving things that no one in this controversy would dispute. One of the things that ancient rhetoricians taught well was the ability in a polemical exchange to identify the *stasis*—the issues that were actually in dispute, and upon which the whole debate turned. As it is, this article argues up and down the waterfront and never actually engages with the central arguments that have been raised against the traditional concept of the covenant of works. I certainly don't dispute that Adam was in a probationary state in the Garden, that he was being tested, that his fall was entailed upon all his descendants, and that the last Adam's obedience brought about the great reversal of this disaster. We all agree, so why couldn't we just start there and go on to discuss whether or not the covenant of works was *gracious*, whether the covenant of works was recapitulated at Sinai, and whether the Bible teaches that the merit of obedience can be extracted from obedience? That would have been a genuine advance in the discussion.

That said, there are a couple things I do want to point out. One was a place where the scholarly persona rubbed a little thin, and something else peeped out. "Lusk reaches the pinnacle of his vitriolic criticism of the covenant of works when he says: 'In short, the doctrine of a meritorious covenant of works has a dangerous Gnosticizing tendency on theology as a whole'" (p. 92). I know . . . I hate it when Rich flies off the handle like that.

The second thing is this. Estelle says that he does not plan to get into a discussion of the recapitulation of the covenant of works at Sinai, but then he devotes a major part of his argument to Galatians 3:10, applying it (without missing a beat) to the covenant of works. But Paul is quoting Deuteronomy 27:26, the culmination of the words of self-malediction spoken from Mt. Ebal by Reuben, Gad, Asher, Zebulun, Dan, and Naphtali. Deuteronomy 27:26 was not spoken by Adam in the Garden.

This covenant [of grace] was differently administered in the time of the law, and in the time of the gospel: under the law it was administered by promises, prophecies, sacrifices, circumcision, the paschal lamb, and other types and ordinances delivered to the people of the Jews, all foresignifying Christ to come; which were, for that time, sufficient and efficacious, through the operation of the Spirit, to instruct and build up the elect in faith in the promised Messiah, by whom they had full remission of sins, and eternal salvation; and is called the old Testament (WCF 7.5).

The book of Deuteronomy is all about this aforementioned adminstration of the covenant of grace, and the people of Israel bound themselves to the covenant of *grace* on Mt. Ebal with a series of curses. Huh, says you. As well you might.

This is probably the central complaint I have about the prelapsarian covenant of works. I believe there was such a covenant but why call it by that name? The name throws just about everybody off, including Estelle. In the Pauline vocabulary works and grace are antithetical. So when you say works, you don't think Adamic probation, you think of your standard issue Pharisees. And when you think of *them*, you think of their distortions of the Old Testament grace into their Ishmaelite system of works. And then you read their distortions of Sinaitic grace back into the Old Testament, and then you read *that* back into the Garden. How else could Galatians 3:10 get applied so easily to the pre-fall Adam?

Put another way, if the warp of the Old Testament law is the covenant of grace, and the woof is the recapitulated covenant of works, may I make a humble request? May I ask anyone who believes that to swear off (for the rest of their natural lives) any accusations they might want to make against *others* for blurring the important distinction between the covenant of grace and the covenant of works? Thanks.

Estelle concludes:

> This essay demonstrates, however, that the innovators and innovations suggesting revision to the covenant of works have been weighed in the scales of classic Reformed orthodoxy, modern biblical scholarship, and modern linguistics and have been found wanting. (p. 135)

But I conclude differently—it does nothing of the kind.

UPHILL FROM HERE
FEBRUARY 28, 2007

I thoroughly enjoyed the next chapter in *Covenant, Justification, and Pastoral Ministry*. This was the chapter by S.M. Baugh, and was entitled "The New Perspective, Mediation, and Justification." In it he tackled the central confusion of E.P. Sanders, along with some of the resultant muddles, and does an effective job with it.

One particular thing worth noting is that in his discussion of *pistis Christou* in Galatians 2:16, he correctly sees that to identify this as the fidelity of Jesus Christ Himself (as I do, if allowed to see it *also* as fidelity proceeding from His faith) is simply another argument for the imputation of the active obedience of Christ. Baugh prefers another rendering for exegetical reasons but says that to render it as the fidelity of Jesus is not a revolutionary concept for the Reformed at all. This is exactly right.

I bet this essay means we have turned the corner. All uphill from here.

MARCH 2007

MERIT ISN'T ONE OF THOSE WORDS

MARCH 2, 2007

The next chapter in *Covenant, Justification, and Pastoral Ministry* is entitled "The Covenant Before the Covenants," and is written by Scott Clark and David VanDrunen. In the course of reviewing it, I intend to quote Ambrose Bierce not once, but twice.

The first citation is of a more general nature. The topic of this chapter is the *pactum salutis,* the intra-trinitarian covenant between the Father and the Son before the creation of the world, and whenever theologians get into such rarified atmosphere I am always afraid that someone will have forgotten their oxygen mask. But then it turns out that at least half of them did. While there are sound scriptural grounds for holding to such a covenant, there are also grounds for being concerned that arcane speculations about the internal workings of the triune mind might intrude themselves unhappily into the discussion. If they do, then the whole thing begins to resemble the debate between infralapsarians and supralapsarians, which Bierce summarized as a debate over whether Adam fell down or Adam slipped up. In this kind of debate, unless everybody involved watches his step closely, things can get pretty stupid—like a couple of dogs, neither of them very smart, debating quantum physics. "No! *Arf,* arf."

That said, two observations. The first is that that pest *merit* keeps showing up. This is another chapter that misses the *statis,* the basic point at issue. *Merit* is the thing that needs to be talked about, that needs to be established, and yet it is the thing that is always getting assumed.

The *pactum salutis* is "the eternal covenant of redemption" (p. 167).

> In Reformed theology, the *pactum salutis* has been defined as a pretemporal, intratrinitarian agreement between the Father and the Son in which the Father promises to redeem an elect people. In turn, the Son volunteers to earn the salvation of his people by becoming incarnate (the Spirit having prepared a body for him), by acting as the surety . . . of the covenant of grace for and acting as a mediator of the covenant of grace to the elect. In his active and passive obedience, Christ fulfills the conditions of the *pactum salutis* and fulfills his guarantee . . . ratifying the Father's promise, because of which the Father rewards the Son's obedience with the salvation of the elect. (p. 168)

The issue for me is not the *word* merit, but the medieval conception of it. And my point is that someone can reject the idea of merit, root and branch, and yet hold to the definition above.

If we conceive of the Father and Son conducting a raw, legal transaction, akin to the sale of a mule, then there are some fundamental problems with this scheme. But if we see it as promise and promised blessing, more like a king promising his daughter's hand in marriage to any knight who slays the dragon, I am good with it. *Worthy* is the Lamb that was slain, and with His blood He purchased men from every nation. That purchase price was settled before the creation of the world, and it was settled within God's eternal counsels. It was not settled by two adversaries in the marketplace, but rather by the Father, Son and Holy Spirit, all of whom indwell one another everlastingly in love. God *is* love, and the context of this *pactum salutis* has to be this love. *This is what God is necessarily like*, in all that He does. As I said, I don't want to quibble over words, but I think that more than words is involved.

According to this chapter, this eternal covenant is a straight, legal business. God is acknowledged to be gracious, but that is off to the side, and doesn't enter into the definitional nature of *this* transaction. "For the Son, the *pactum salutis* is a legal/work covenant of obligation, merit and reward" (p. 168). To parse the legalese like this, in my view, obscures the graciousness of *all* that God does. It makes me think of someone at a car rental counter, with a long line behind him, trying to read and grasp every word of the 4 pt. font contract he is signing.

When Christ came into the world, He came to do the will of His Father. He obeyed. He was promised the nations of men, and He gloriously fulfilled the conditions attached to that promise. So in discussing this, words like promise, blessing, obedience, submission are straight out of the Bible, and we should stick to them. Merit isn't one of those words, and the sooner we get this gum off our Reformed shoe the better.

My second criticism of this chapter is of another nature entirely. The first one had to do with the nature of the theological claims; the second has to do with what I take to be a serious scholarly lapse. And here is my second Bierce citation. In his definition of valor, Bierce tells this anecdote.

"Why have you halted?" roared the commander of a division at Chickamauga, who had ordered a charge; "move forward, sir, at once."

"General," said the command of the delinquent brigade, "I am persuaded that any further display of valor by my troops will bring them into collision with the enemy."

This volume is offered to the Christian public because the gospel is purportedly under attack. The historic Reformed faith is being frittered away, and it is time for someone to take a stand. Okay, take a stand then. Elsewhere in this volume, specific threats are mentioned and, after a fashion, dealt with. But here, in a chapter dedicated to a discussion of the *pactum salutis*, in the context, remember, of Federal Vision threats, there is no interaction with Ralph Smith's book *Eternal Covenant*. The book was published in 2003 by Canon Press, and, given the subject, it would be hard to imagine a more relevant book to interact with than this one. But no, nothing.

LIKE SCARSDALE
MARCH 5, 2007

So here I sit in the Chicago airport, exercising the patience of Job, or at any rate thinking that I *ought* to be exercising the patience of Job. No, nothing to do with the flights. I just finished reading Michael Horton's contribution to *Covenant, Justification, and Pastoral Ministry.* I was seriously disappointed—I think because I really was expecting more.

This was a significant and atrocious misrepresentation. Horton sets out to show that Sanders, Wright, Shepherd, and the Federal Vision advocates are *all* advocates of "covenantal nomism."

> Not only Second Temple Judaism *but all of these* somewhat diverse challenges to the evangelical doctrine of justification *may be accurately described as* 'covenantal nomism.' This pattern of religion is united by three principal theses: [1] our personal obedience is a condition of justification, but but that this does not mean that justification is strictly merited; [2] there is no qualitative distinction between law and gospel or a covenant of works and a covenant of grace; and [3] we 'get in by grace, but stay in by obedience' [Sanders]—that is, a final justification by works. (p. 198, emphasis mine)

You know, I don't know why I bother anymore, but here it is again. [1] When it comes to conditions of personal and individual justification, our personal obedience, all forms of merit, whether condign, congruent, purple or green, and all individual strivings to be shiny, clean and good, can all go to Hell. I capitalize Hell because, as Fulton Sheen once said, it's a place, like Scarsdale. [2] There is a qualitative difference between the covenant of life with Adam and the covenant of grace with his fallen heirs. There are two covenants, not one. [3] The view that we get in by grace and stay in by obedience really is a form of semi-Pelagianism. This means that everyone tagged in this essay for believing it is a semi-Pelagian, except for me, of course, because I don't believe it. But then *that* means that this essay might not be a reliable guide to who is and who is not a semi-Pelagian.

In his conclusion, Horton says this: "If we are to recover a genuinely Reformed covenant theology, it will require patient exegesis, not reactionary and dismissive polemics that derive from false dilemmas, reductionism, and caricature" (p. 227). *These* words, at the conclusion of *this* essay, were right out of a Twilight Zone episode. No false dilemmas, no reductionism, no caricature? Okay, you guys go first. Show us how it is done.

Please note that this is not a Federal Vision whine about being misunderstood in some nebulous and generic way. Horton has said that Federal Vision types think the sky is green, and here I am, maintaining that it is blue, just like I always did. This chapter was really unfortunate.

Two theological comments. A lot of the confusion about faith and works in this debate depends upon the idea that the Fall did not radically distort the relationship between the two. But it was the introduction of sin that introduced all the tension. In this chapter, Horton rightly points out that Christ was exalted *because* of His obedience. But as the perfect man, Jesus did not divide what God had first joined together in the creation. Put it this way. Did Jesus live His perfect sinless life (which, remember, people, was *imputed* to us) by faith in God? Or by works? Which was it? When His life and His death are imputed to us, was the foundation of this life faith in His Father or not? Was Christ's obedience faithless or not? Now I agree that Christ's obedience was imputed to us, but where did this obedience come from? Did Jesus gut it out for us on a works principle, or was His obedience grounded in His absolute trust in His Father? The answer is simple. It was perfect obedience, right? That meant that it was not grounded in the actions of the first successful Pelagian.

Secondly, Horton makes plain his rejection of the Westminster Confession's identification of the Mosaic covenant as an administration of the covenant of grace (e.g., p. 212). He tries to justify this by some kind of discussion of Galatians, but I don't know why he is messing around with *that* when we have the Standards.

CHRIST AND THE LIFE OF FAITH
MARCH 7, 2007

In my previous post on the Auburn Avenue business, I said something that I think requires a bit more amplification.

I believe that the unfallen Adam was under a covenant that obligated him to obey God completely and entirely. He broke that covenant, and God promised him a redeemer through another kind of covenant, a covenant of grace and forgiveness. The entire remainder of the Scriptures is about the outworking of that covenant of grace—this second covenant is *not* a recapitulation of the broken covenant of Eden, except in the hearts and minds of the sons of Hagar, who deliberately misread the Mosaic covenant of grace as though it were according to the principle of works. *That misreading continues down to the present.*

I have objected to the use of words like *works* and *merit* to describe all this because such usage tends to obscure and confuse the gracious nature of all God's dealings with man, whatever covenant we may be talking about.

As with the first Adam, so with the second. But the reason some of our critics get so worked up over this is that if all consideration of merit is excluded from the obligations of the first Adam and the achievements of the second Adam, it is assumed that the merit (which is thought to be inescapable) must be coming from somewhere. And if we are denying that we are justified by Christ's merit, we must be affirming (somehow, someway) that we are justified by our own merit. But none of this follows—we simply deny that merit can be extracted from a virtuous act and stored on shelves. Christ's obedience is ours because He is the father of the new humanity, and His obedience is ours through covenantal imputation.

The division between grace and works is a post-Fall division. It is the result of sin. Sin and rebellion introduced all such fragmentations, and the perfect Man, Jesus Christ did not come into our world in order to participate in our fragmentations, but rather to overcome them. When we confess that Jesus was without sin, this does not merely mean that He never stole, or lusted, or worshipped idols. It also means that He never accepted or lived by false categories. He was the perfectly integrated personality.

I deny that God dealt with unfallen beings on a raw merit principle, and then, after we demerited His favor, extended it to us on a grace principle. Rather, grace and works were not fragmented or divorced prior to the Fall.

Adam was expected to obey, certainly, but there is no reason to think that this obedience, had it occurred, would not have been motivated by faith, hope, and love, sustained by the grace of God. As I have pointed out in many places, if Adam had withstood the tempter, it would have been necessary for him to thank God afterwards. This means that this covenant was fundamentally a gracious one.

And as with the first Adam, so with the second. When Jesus obeyed the Father perfectly, this was not raw obedience, teeth gritted, with no motivation of love. In John 17, Jesus made it clear that He and the Father were one, and they loved each other perfectly. Now, this love—did it have anything to do with Christ's obedience? Any relationship to His willingness to trust His Father? We have no scriptural reason, apart from the demands of a particular systematic schema, to picture Jesus gutting out His obedience to the Father for the sake of a pristine merit.

In a similar vein, after Jesus successfully completed His life and death of perfect obedience, what did He do? He paid his vows to God (Ps. 22:25). "In the midst of the congregation will I praise thee" (Ps. 22:22). "The pleasure of the Lord shall prosper in his hand" (Isa. 53: 10).

But with all this said, there is still good reason for being extremely wary about any admixtures of faith and love together in our justification. But this is not because faith and love don't go together (they did in Adam, before he fell, and in Christ throughout His life), but because *they don't go together in sinners.*

When we are presenting the gospel to fragmented sinners, we have to be very careful not to give or allow for any kind of self-righteous "out." C.S. Lewis says somewhere about good writing that it is like driving sheep down a lane—you have to keep all the gates closed on both sides of the lane, for if there is any way for the sheep to veer off, the sheep will enthusiastically do so. It is the same sort of thing with any allowance at all being made for the religiously smug. All grace all the time is the only thing that can possibly restore us. Self-righteousness, earning, and merit are all in our bones—detached, divorced, and separated from love. If we give any opportunity for the sinner to boast in himself, then he will do so. Telling him about how his faith needs to work itself out in love is a great way to get inveterate self-saviors to attempt just that. This is not because it is wrong for us to do, but rather because it is *impossible* for us to do. What is wrong is to kid ourselves after the fact, saying that our faith actually did work its way out in us in love, and that God was tremendously pleased with it, and with us for being so clever as to help out with our justification.

Adam could have obeyed, and had he done so it would have been by grace through faith, and it would not have been detached from any other virtue. Christ did obey, trusting His Father, and neither was this obedience detached from any other virtue. Sin destroyed the possibility of any such integration for us, and *sola fide* is the only safe way back. But even here we have to be careful—believing in *sola fide* the wrong way can be a soul threatening error. In this sense, not only is it a work, but it is a tiny and impudent work—considered *as* a work. But we are forgiven, not because we believe in justification by faith alone, but rather because justification by faith alone is *true*.

Much more can be said about all this. And I am convinced it needs to be, because in this understanding we can find a full harmonization of the *currently* discordant elements of the TR and FV visions. But I can find no reason why this should necessarily be so.

TAKE THE GRILLED CHEESE SANDWICH AWAY
MARCH 9, 2007

The next chapter in *Covenant, Justification, and Pastoral Ministry* is by Scott Clark, and is entitled "Do This and Live." In it he argues for the active obedience of Christ as (an essential part of) the ground of our justification. Okay, I agree with that. So how hard could this be?

But alas. On p. 234, Clark says this in a footnote.

> Since the proponents of the so-called Federal Vision seem to affirm both an eternal, unconditional election and a historical, conditional election that can be lost without perseverance, it is difficult to see how they escape the strictures of the Synod of Dort on at least half their position.

Now this is a fine way of doing theology! If we only get credit for half our theology, or we get blamed for the unbalanced half, which is unbalanced precisely because that half (in isolation) is condemned by some council or other, what shall we then do? The half position was condemned because the initial bad guys had not affirmed the balancing portion, but now along comes these new fellows who *do* affirm what they need to. What now?

One time Scott Clark walked into a diner and ordered a grilled ham and cheese. When it came to his table, he complained to the waiter because he didn't want a grilled cheese. The waiter (helpfully, he thought) pointed out the ham that was in there, big as life. But Clark had a riposte at the ready. "I am not counting the ham. And I would like a ham and cheese." The waiter hadn't been to seminary, so he was a little bit disoriented. "You are not counting the ham?" "No," said Clark. "And if we don't count the ham, this is clearly a grilled cheese sandwich. Grilled cheese alone was clearly condemned at the Synod of Dort. The ham is really necessary." "But the ham is right there," the waiter said. "I mentioned this before," Clark replied stiffly. "I am not counting the ham."

Let's use a theological example. The Calvinist position is to affirm the exhaustive sovereignty of God over all things as well as human responsibility. Both and. God freely and unalterably ordains whatsoever comes to pass *and* He gives free agency to His creatures. Clearly each half of this by itself is a grievous error, and so this must mean that balanced Calvinism which affirms both must be unbalanced both ways by denying each, provided we don't count their affirmations of each. We are not counting the ham, and we want the grilled cheese sandwich taken away. It displeases us.

This is simply astonishing. Clark would have a point if Federal Vision types affirmed eternal unconditional election and historical conditional election as applying to the same people in the same way. That would be an attempt at A/not A, and in such circumstances to highlight one of the contradictory principles is fair game. But we do nothing of the kind. Decretal election applies to the elect, and only the decretally elect. Historical election applies to the Church in history, all the baptized. Where on earth can Clark find any kind of A/not A business in there? The Federal Vision affirms two positions, each affirmation being necessary to the orthodoxy of the other. Clark detaches one of them, carries it off, and then says, "Huh. Looks heretical to me. Where's the necessary context?"

We are not very far into this chapter, and things are looking pretty grim.

> Despite his discomfort with the traditional and confessional doctrine of the covenant of works, John Murray (1898–1975) affirmed the imputation of active obedience repeatedly. (p. 237)

I am glad that Clark recognizes that someone can differ with the traditional language of the covenant of works, and yet affirm repeatedly the imputation of the active obedience of Christ and be cited positively by Clark. This being the case, I have to wonder why Clark has been unable to publicly recognize that I too have repeatedly affirmed the imputation of the active obedience of Christ. My personal goal is to make it into one of Clark's footnotes, clutching a position I actually hold.

In this chapter, the closest he comes is this. Clark says "*some* federal-vision proponents also reject the imputation of active obedience. Rich Lusk argues . . . ." (p. 241, emphasis mine). Now leaving aside for the moment whether Clark understands Rich Lusk's argument, even on his own terms, this formulation means that some Federal Vision proponents *affirm* the imputation of active obedience. But how does this fit with Clark's larger criticisms of Federal Vision theology as a whole? Why wouldn't it have been helpful for Clark to list the Federal Vision proponents who affirm the imputation of Christ's active obedience? He appears to know that they are out there. Might it be that this would sort of make the current campaign against us a little bit more difficult?

This leads to another curious point in this chapter. And by curious, I mean *really* curious.

Clark, to his credit, acknowledges that there were delegates to the Westminster Assembly who denied the imputation of the active obedience of

Christ. This would place them in disagreement with ME, be it noted. I place ME in all caps here so that scholars in future generations can pick up on this particular nuance, to wit, that I AFFIRM the imputation of the active obedience of Christ. But my position is similar to the majority of the Westminster theologians in *two* respects here, not just one. Not only do I affirm the imputation of the active obedience of Christ, but I also affirm that it would be okay to include (as fellow Reformed colleagues) men who denied it. The roof of that deliberative chamber did not fall in when the assembly allowed the 17th century equivalent of Norman Shepherd to join with them in their important ministry.

What Clark does not really note about the behavior of the Westminster Assembly is how they tolerated this minority view within their ranks. Actually, Clark does note it, but inadvertently. He notes it, but he doesn't *notice* it.

> Reformed resolve would be tested by the opponents of the imputation of active obedience, eventually forcing a verbal compromise at the Westminster Assembly, but the center held, and the language of the confession remained sufficiently strong. (p. 235)

And again, he says

> I agree and am suggesting here that the Westminster Divines removed the more explicit language (i.e., 'the whole obedience of Christ') regarding active obedience to allow the opponents of the imputation of active obedience (Twisse, Vines, and Gattaker) to subscribe the confession while providing language sufficient for the preservation of the doctrine. (p. 235)

And then, near the conclusion of his chapter, he says this.

> That the Westminster Divines graciously formed the confession to allow a small minority who denied the imputation of active obedience to

> affirm it should not blind us to the external evidence (from the minutes) that the majority held and understood the Westminster Standards to teach the imputation of active obedience. (p. 264)

This is a big deal, and so let us discuss what it means. In the first quote above, Clark says that a verbal compromise was "forced" by the opponents of the imputation of the active obedience of Christ. But in the last quote above, he says that these opponents were a "small minority." How does that work? The small minority was actually accommodated because the vast majority at Westminster *was far more conciliatory on this point* than Clark is currently being. They held to the doctrine, as do I, and yet they deliberately framed the language to accommodate men who denied the doctrine. Clark says that they kept the substance of the doctrine, but note that he also says that the verbal formulation was *intended* to accommodate men like Norman Shepherd, who denies the imputation of the active obedience of Christ. So, if Twisse, Vines, and Gattaker subscribed the Confession would it be appropriate to then call them liars? Did the majority frame the language in such a way as to be able to give Twisse the right hand of fellowship afterwards? Clark says *yes*, and he says further that if we imitate them in this then we are compromising the gospel. But the men who showed us *how* to compromise the gospel in this way were not guilty of compromising the gospel *themselves*, because they, after all is said and done, were Westminster divines.

Speaking of the law/word of God in the Garden, Clark says:

> In this case, the formal "doing" required by the law was abstinence, but the material obedience was loving God and obeying him completely. Those who lived under the Mosaic system will be judged accordingly (2:12–13), and those who did not (2:15) shall face judgment on the basis of the "law written on their hearts" . . . but they are substantially identical. All human beings live under the same law: "do." (p. 244)

Now *yikes*, as the apostle Paul might say. Again, I say *yikes*.

First, notice that Clark is again confounding the Mosaic covenant with the covenant of works, despite the fact that the Westminster Confession clearly says that the Mosaic covenant was an administration of the covenant of *grace*.

And notice another way that Clark is sailing a little close to the wind here. By saying that our first parents were to fulfill the material obedience of "loving God and obeying him completely," he is allowing us to mix a little love in with the merit. And what kind of merit is that? At Westminster West, they take their merit raw. In the past, when *we* have said, as many Reformed theologians before us have said, that the covenant of life in the Garden was essentially gracious, we are accused of all kinds of horrendous things. But Clark says something like the above, and then says (in a footnote, to be sure, but *still*) that this is an opinion upon which the Reformed tradition has been divided.

> After Dort, the Reformed orthodox spoke of God's grace in making the covenant of works, and some (e.g., William Bucanus, John Ball, Anthony Burgess) said grace was necessary for Adam to complete it, but others (e.g., Caspar Olevianus, Robert Rollock, Johannes Wollebius, Amandus Polanus, James Ussher, John Owen, Johannes Cocceius, J.H. Heidegger, H. Witsius, W. a Brakel) said that Adam, by virtue of his creation, had natural ability to meet its terms. (pp. 257–258)

This is the second time in this chapter that Clark has established and shown the existence of a Reformed catholicity *that he himself is refusing to imitate*. Look again at what he just said. Some said that God was gracious in making the covenant, others that grace was necessary for the fulfillment of it, and others say that Adam had natural ability (from *God* via the creation) to fulfill the covenant. I call that last option grace, by the way, but my point here is not to debate with the third option. Back then if you took the second option, you could be a father in the Reformed faith and be in print down the present day, thanks to Banner of Truth. But if you take the second option today, then the folks at Westminster West hold conferences and publish books about you, saying that you are attacking the gospel.

One last point. I am beginning to think that Clark has a particular kind of tunnel vision that afflicts some scholars. He can nuance the heck out of a particular position, provided the problematic position needing the nuanced massage was held by a man who has been dead and deep, lo, these three and a half centuries. But if the person in question is alive today, has an email address and a phone on his desk, and is willing to talk about it at any time, there is a curious inability to get even the simplest things straight.

Here is an example, and then I am done for the evening.

> The federal-vision advocates suggest that we are justified so long as we are united to Christ, but we retain that union partly by cooperating with grace. (p. 262)

This is simply a screwy and irresponsible misrepresentation. Our position is NOT that we are justified by our cooperation with grace. I don't maintain my union with Christ. How could I possibly do that? I am fond of a Spurgeon story, where his suspicions were aroused one day when a man said something like "in my salvation, Christ did His part and I did mine." "What do you mean?" was the obvious question. And the suspicions were eliminated when the man replied, "Christ's part was to do the saving, and I got in the way."

When Clark says some like "federal-vision advocates suggest," and then follows it up with some fruity and heretical comment, he really ought to cite some examples. For my part, I flat deny it. Don't believe anything of the kind, and never have. Scott Clark needs to learn how to be as careful with living authors as he appears to be with some dead ones.

THE SCREAMING MORALISTIC FANTODS
MARCH 10, 2007

Taking one thing with another, Robert Godfrey's contribution to *Covenant, Justification, and Pastoral Ministry* was really quite good. Entitled "Faith Formed by Love or Faith Alone?" Godfrey summarizes the original Reformed response to the medieval definition of faith (made complete and salvific when formed by love) and discusses the grounding of the Protestant response in the teaching of the apostle Paul. With just a few blemishes, the chapter was outstanding, and I had no problem signing off on virtually everything he wrote.

But first a quibble, and then a quibble with larger aspect. The first quibble is that in reproducing an argument from Calvin, Godfrey points out that Abraham was a follower of God before Genesis 15 but makes the point that until he was justified by faith alone in chapter 15, he was considered to be a "wicked" man by the apostle Paul. This wickedness is meant to emphasize just how imperfect the works of even the best of men are. The problem with this is that we are told in Hebrews 11:8 that Abraham's life of faith began when he first left Ur of the Chaldees. In short, it is too simplistic to say that Abraham lived by "inadequate good works" until Genesis 15, when he was finally converted. The author of Hebrews describes his responses of faith before and after Genesis 15 in exactly the same terms. But of course, I do not raise this point in order to dispute the theological point being made by Calvin and Godfrey. This is simply an exegetical point.

The larger quibble is this. Godfrey doesn't really get into the current fracas, only referring to it a few times. In these three places Godfrey registers his disagreement, but unlike some of his colleagues, he never moves into high slander mode. Here is the first statement. "Calvin anticipates the great error of many contemporary critics of the Reformation doctrine" (p. 276). That's not so bad, and, depending on who he is talking about (he doesn't say), it is actually quite accurate. Calvin *does* anticipate the error of many contemporary critics of the Reformation doctrine.

The second place shows that Godfrey believes that what he is writing is relevant to the current debates and belongs in this volume. He is more specific here:

> This misunderstanding of Paul suggests a crucial question for some of his interpreters. Would anyone ever read the federal-vision writers or Norman Shepherd or the new perspective on Paul or Thomas Aquinas or the Council of Trent and come with the question to them: Should

> we sin that grace may abound? That question would never, could never, arise for anyone who has read these teachers. (p. 280)

First, actually reading what we write has not thus far appeared to be a prerequisite to any number of critics. The accusation of teaching "sin that grace may abound" is not an accusation that would have arisen for anyone who had *read* the apostle Paul either—but he generated the accusation anyhow. In these situations, something else is always going on. Our circumstance is no different.

And second, this kind of accusation *is* raised in the current debates, particularly when we are talking about the objectivity of the covenant, the sacraments, and so on. What is the accusation of tending to nominalism (an accusation we have fielded numerous times) but a variant of this? "If you buy what Wilson is saying, what is to prevent an 'I'm baptized, I'm good' attitude?" And anyone who reads through my homilies on the Lord's Supper will know that I emphasize free grace well past the point that would have given Paul's unknown interlocutors the screaming moralistic fantods.

And third, not only have I been accused of antinomianism, I have been accused of being a hell-bound graceless sociopath. Shoot, in other settings, having to do with Westminster West, I have been accused by Scott *Clark* of being, ahem, the opposite of a prim Pelagian moralist—leader in a cult-like organization, sectarian, advocate of slavery, and so on. So I don't really think that the "these-guys-inexplicably-fail-to-generate-slander" argument is one that Godfrey really wants to mount at this point in the discussion.

The third statement is this:

> The new perspective on Paul and the Federal Vision are not really new, but a reiteration of medieval theological errors. (p. 284)

Since he doesn't give particulars, I can only say that, as concerns myself, and a bunch of people I know, I don't think so. And since I agreed with so much of this chapter, I can only conclude that talking past each other at this point of the controversy is now politically mandatory. Doesn't make it healthy, but there it is.

RECAPITULATION DRIVES OUT GRACE
MARCH 12, 2007

The next two essays in *Covenant, Justification, and Pastoral Ministry* are by Hywel Jones, and are tightly related, and so I will treat them together. As with Robert Godfrey's contribution, there is not a lot to disagree with here. The bulk of what is written here is good, sturdy Reformed stuff.

At the same time, there are some minor problems, and there are also some larger questions generated. In the category of the former, for example, Jones apparently misidentifies John Armstrong as a Baptist (p. 286), which he was at the time of the 1996 footnote, but not now. And his occasional interactions with Norman Shepherd appear to me to be based on differing definitions of the same terms. Does *obedience* (in the context of justifying faith) mean *works*, or does it mean *life*? If the former, then mixing it into justifying faith is death warmed over. If the latter, then leaving it out is death stone cold. But at the same time, I am not really an expert in *The Call of Grace*, a 2000 publication of Presbyterian & Reformed, a respected publisher of material that is always genuinely Reformed. Perhaps questions could be referred to Richard Gaffin?

For the rest of Jones's writing, I would like to content myself with addressing certain questions that he raises, either directly or indirectly.

Jones makes a very good point with regard to James and Paul, noting that these two men were not strangers to one another. He says that those who confound their messages have done so in such an insistent manner "that anyone who is not familiar with the New Testament might well be pardoned for thinking that those men never had the opportunity of talking to each other" (p. 289). Even though their stipulated definitions of certain terms are clearly not the same, they agree in substance nonetheless. "What is clear is that they did not disagree with each other" (p. 290). I think this is very true, and it highlights the need that certain parties in the current conflict have to visit with their adversaries. Perhaps men who have talked with each other in person can come out of it agreeing—even though their usage of certain terms is varied. Verbal differences do not necessitate substantive disagreement, as Paul and James show.

On another point, I want to emphasize again that the Westminster Confession describes the Mosaic economy *as an administration of the covenant of grace*. I do so because Jones (on p. 298) brings that economy up in a way that demonstrates what might be called the Pauline corollary to Gresham's Law. Gresham's Law is an economic principle that says bad money drives out good. Those who want the Mosaic law to recapitulate the covenant of works from the Garden need to be aware that *works will always drive out grace*. To mix the covenant of works into the Mosaic administration of grace will ensure that the grace of the law will be entirely supplanted. It is astonishing that, throughout this book, the recapitulated sense of law and condemnation has almost entirely effaced the Westminsterian understanding of the graciousness manifested at Sinai. For a sampling, consider this:

> Up to the coming of Christ, Jews had been 'held captive under the law' (3:23 ESV) or under its disciplinary function (3:23). Something similar was also true of Gentiles because they were 'enslaved to the elementary principles of the world (4:3 ESV) and to 'those that were by nature no gods,' that is, to idols (4:8). Life before Christ was therefore life 'under law' for Gentile as well as Jew. There was a universal obligation to obey however much of God's law that had been made known, by whatever means it had been disclosed, and on pain of awful penalty if it was not fully kept (Rom. 1:18–32; 2:14–16; 3:9–20).*

God had brought the Jews out of the land of Egypt, out of the house of bondage, but apparently the hosts of recapitulation had not been drowned like Pharaoh, but chased them out into the wilderness, caught up with them, and

* Whoops. We don't have an exact page number on this one, but we guess it'd be 298 or thereabouts.

subjected them again to a yoke of slavery. A very striking thing in this book so far is that the writers never speak of Moses the way that Westminster does.

In his second essay, on the preaching of *sola fide*, Jones says many good things. But he brings up several issues that (I believe) reveals the hidden engines of our controversy. The first has to do with pastoral ministry directly. Speaking of "a local Christian congregation," Jones addresses how we are to preach to them.

> Those who have not yet believed are to be *regarded* as "under the law" and "outside of Christ" thought they have a promise that God will be gracious to them if they turn to him. They are covenant children by birth and holy (1 Cor. 7:14), and baptism incorporates them into the covenant community (visible church)—but not necessarily into Christ. (pp. 325–326)

This is the heart of all the troublesome business. Note that baptized members who have not yet believed are *outside of Christ*, and *under the law*. What are they inside then? They are *inside* the *covenant community* or *visible church*. Put these two things together and what do you get? This means, at the very least, that (potentially very large) portions of the visible church or covenant community are outside of Christ. What kind of ecclesiology is this?

Far better to say that the entire visible church is joined to Christ covenantally. The entire congregation is in Him in that objective sense. But there is a subset within the first group that is joined to Him with fruit to eternal life. As John 15 and Romans 11 plainly state there are two classes of branches. One kind of branch is in Christ temporarily and the other permanently. What distinguishes them is how long they are in the trunk. They are *not* distinguished by one being in the trunk and the other not.

Another interesting point is raised by Jones. Speaking of those who die in infancy or those who cannot understand the gospel because of mental incapacity, he says (wonderfully) that they . . .

> will be admitted to heaven because they are "regenerated and saved by Christ through the Spirit, who worketh when, and where, and how he

> pleaseth." Two things, however, need to be remembered at this point. The first, by way of necessary implication, is that such persons were born in sin and were destitute of spiritual life. Another way of salvation is not therefore being taught, but *sola gratia* is being reinforced in that the one group cannot properly be said to act and the other cannot be said to understand. Here, perhaps, lies the rub of the debate over *sola fide* in every age—no capable and knowledgeable adult likes to have to admit being as helpless in spiritual things as those described. (pp. 326–327)

Now I agree with Jones completely that such infants are saved, but I need to point out that he has completely confounded *sola fide* and *sola gratia* here. He begins well by saying that the salvation of dying infants or those otherwise impaired is "one exception" to the "connection between Christ's worth and human faith" (p. 326). Okay, so then we have an exception to *sola fide* in a large category of saved individuals. How then is it faith alone? Faith alone for whom? At the day of judgment, could we ask for a show of hands? "How many of you were saved by grace through faith alone?" All who had come to years of discretion would raise their hands. "How many were saved by grace alone through some other instrumentality of God's sovereign devising?" Many millions of hands would go up. So what do we mean by faith *alone*?

We have been told elsewhere in this volume that our emphatic agreement with *sola gratia* is insufficient for us to keep our Reformed credentials up. But now we have *an acknowledged exception* to *sola fide* found in a book edited by R. Scott Clark. Either somebody was asleep at the switch editorially speaking, or Clark needs to be brought up on charges for denying *sola fide* . . . or the question is perhaps more complex than the current sloganeering might allow. Why are they allowed to say there is "one exception" to *sola fide* while we must sign all the talking points blindfolded, no questions permitted?

One last thing. Speaking of Paul's use of the phrase the obedience of faith, Jones says this:

> The apostle is using the term *obedience* to describe faith as submission to what Christ did (by way of his obedience) and not to refer to anything the sinner is to do by way of contribution to Christ's work or even by way of appreciation of it. (p. 328)

I am amening my way along here, but then am suddenly arrested by that last phrase. The obedience of faith is simply submission to the gospel. Okay, I buy that. It does not refer to anything a miserable sinner might do to improve upon Christ's work. Okay, I buy that too. But then comes this—"or even by way of appreciation of it." I confess myself nonplussed. I can understand how obedience is used in Scripture as a synonym for faith. We not only believe the gospel, but we also obey the gospel. And this belief or obedience is knowing, assenting, and trusting. But how can someone obey the gospel in this sense without appreciating it? All the other verbs are stronger—why would *appreciation* of the gospel introduce a works principle where trusting, obeying, and believing did not? Just curious.

Enough for now. Only three more chapters. Stand fast.

DO THIS AND LIVE, OR LIVE AND DO THIS
MARCH 13, 2007

The next chapter by Scott Clark begins oddly, but the latter part is just a standard discussion of the law/gospel issues. First the oddity. We have heard a great deal about how the gospel itself is under attack in this controversy. This is because certain settled Reformed shibboleths have been pronounced funny, and anyone who has been paying attention knows that the sibbolethians have been represented as a grave threat to the gospel as it is in Christ Jesus. But what then shall we do with all those Christians who lived before these formulations came to be? Guys like Augustine? And this is where Scott Clark says some truly odd things.

> The fathers in the postapostolic church spoke frequently about the gospel, but there is disagreement over the degree to which one can find

> a clear, developed expression of what confessional Protestants would recognize as the gospel. (p. 333)

I dare say. Clark tends to side with Torrance, who says "that what one tends to find in the fathers is confusion of law and gospel" (p. 334). All this is to be expected, and follows necessarily from Clark's premises. But here comes the odd part. In an inexplicable lurch into catholicity, Clark says this:

> This is not an indictment of the fathers. To criticize the fathers for failing to use Luther's (or Calvin's) language is rather like criticizing Aquinas for not using Einstein's physics. (p. 334)

Putting all this together, to confound law and gospel is to confound the issues of salvation and damnation itself, with the eternal destiny of eternal millions at stake. But if you do this before 1517, that's really okay because it is simply a theological development that has not yet happened, like the discovery of relativity theory. But if you do it after 2002, then you are a threat to the gospel. Paul could understand the gospel, but we don't have that expectation for anyone else until we get to the first Protestants. Huh. I didn't know that faithfulness to the gospel *could* be anachronistic.

And now to the issues themselves. Having read Clark's summary of the theological development of this idea of law and gospel, I want to say that I have no reason to doubt what he says. But then I remember how he has in the past represented my views, and so I will reserve to myself a little wiggle room. But assuming his representation of the pre-Reformation fathers is correct, not to mention his take on the Reformed fathers themselves, I can happily say that, once again, I turn up as a robust Protestant, cheerfully grinning.

There *is* a difference between how I talk about law and gospel and some of the quotations that Clark assembles here. But this difference does not touch any issue of substance, as I hope to show in a moment.

Clark speaks of a law/gospel hermeneutic, and some of the men he quotes speak the same way. In other words, the categories of *law* and *gospel* represent different sections of Scripture, which must be identified. They are not to be equated with Old and New Testaments respectively, because, as Clark points out, the quintessential law statement, "Do this and live," comes from the lips of the Lord Jesus, and the preamble of the Ten Commandments can be seen as gospel. So the Old Testament has both law and gospel in it, and the New Testament has both law and gospel in it. Thus a law/gospel hermeneutic is necessary for the one who comes to the Bible, hoping to understand it.

Instead of this, I prefer to speak of a law/gospel *use*, rather than hermeneutic. Just as the law is one, but there are three uses of the law, so with this. Instead of assuming that the Scriptures come in two categories, I prefer to speak of the human race coming in two categories—the regenerate and unregenerate.

For the regenerate, the entire Bible is gospel, good news. The gospel is obviously gospel, and the law falls under the third use of the law. The regenerate believer looks to Scripture and finds Christ everywhere. Christ in the manna, Christ in the water, Christ in the sacrifices, Christ in the law. He finds Christ in the promises and Christ in the law.

To the unregenerate, the law is simply condemnation. For the elect who are unregenerate, this condemnation drives them to Christ and therefore functions as servant to the gospel. For the unregenerate who are not elect, this condemnation drives them away. All this is simply standard for Reformed believers. But we have to note that for the unregenerate who are not elect, the *gospel* does exactly the same thing that the *law* does—it is the aroma of death.

> For the message of the cross is foolishness to those who are perishing, but to us who are being saved it is the power of God. (1 Cor. 1:18)
>
> Now thanks be unto God, which always causeth us to triumph in Christ, and maketh manifest the savour of his knowledge by us in every place. For we are unto God a sweet savour of Christ, in them that are saved, and in them that perish: To the one we are the savour of death unto death; and to the other the savour of life unto life. And who is sufficient for these things? (2 Cor. 2:14–16)

In other words, to the unregenerate soul, law and gospel are repulsive in exactly the same way——they both smell like the holiness of God. To the one whose heart has been transformed, he sees and understands the intent of the law, and he sees and understands the intent of the gospel, and it is all the same intent.

If the law drives me to Christ, then how is the law not servant to the gospel and part of it? And if the gospel repels a sinner with the aroma of death, then how is it not part of the law? I don't want to say that law is gospel or that gospel is law, but rather that they are *used* as such. What the law *is*, and how the law is *used* are two separate issues. What the gospel *is*, and how the gospel is *used* are two separate issues.

One other point is important to mention here. It is plain to me that anticipation of this division among men is clear in Scripture itself. Put another way, the Bible knows that some men will run away from the law and the gospel, declaring their hatred of God openly. Some men will take just the law and try to use it as a ladder to climb into heaven with. These men Paul identifies as Ishmaelites, sons of Hagar, men who have bound themselves in a covenant to break covenant. Then there are others, unfortunately not rare, who take just the gospel and try to turn that into a ladder which they can use to climb to heaven. This Marcionite approach is also to be rejected.

God is not at odds with Himself. If we personify law (as Bunyan wonderfully does in *Pilgrim's Progress*), we have a Moses who really knows how to beat us up. But a man under conviction of sin can be just as worked over by the Sermon on the Mount as by the Ten Commandments. That doesn't make it appropriate to state as a *hermeneutical* principle that Christ now has to be Moses. This is why I prefer to speak of *use*, rather than *hermeneutic*.

Now I can understand how there would be room to discuss or debate this kind of thing. But for the life of me, I cannot see how any essential feature of the standard law/gospel distinction is lost. But if it is lost, then lost it must be. And if that is the case, then I would just ask Clark to imagine my position surfacing, oh, circa 1300, in the writings of some monkish scribbler somewhere. *Then* he could praise it as a remarkable instance of prescience with regard to the coming orthodoxy, instead of the heresy it is currently being.

STUFF I HEARD IN THE HALLWAYS
MARCH 14, 2007

The next chapter in *CJ&PM* (should've done that before) is by Julius Kim and is entitled "The Rise of Moralism in Seventeenth-Century Anglican Preaching." What might this have to do with the current Federal Vision controversy? Well, nothing, but that doesn't keep it from being a fine and instructive article. A very good article, in fact, marred only by a few comments in passing that tie it in with the current hyperventilations.

The article outlined a history of the "metaphysical" preachers and the "plain" preachers of the 16th century and described the reactionary rise of Latitudinarianism as a school of preaching in the 17th century. All very good, and quite applicable today. I enjoyed the article very much.

But alas, the contemporary applications are made only briefly, and without any documentation. In a footnote, Kim refers to a certain temporizer back then who had an

> optimistic view of man's rational faculties as an alternative to the Reformation's emphasis on sovereign grace and trust in Christ's extrinsic righteousness is different that the alternative to views proposed by Norman Shepherd and those who advocate the Federal Vision . . . ." (p. 379, garble in the original, but you get the drift)

> Again, Tillotson's view here that one remains in favor with God through holy living has striking parallels with those who advocate the views of the Federal Vision. (p. 387)

> This seventeenth-century distrust and disposal of the doctrine of *sola fide* parallels those in the twenty-first century caught in the midst of the current justification controversy. (p. 396)

The problem is that there has been a clear oversight. None of these particular claims, which is the point of the *book* after all, are given the dignity of any kind of citation. Everything else in the chapter is documented front to back, not to mention sideways. But when we get to the point at issue, the *loci* of the dispute, the thing we are debating . . . nada, zilch. I think this is must be because there isn't really a theological journal called *Stuff I Heard in the Hallways at Escondido*, Vol. VI, No. 3.

ONE LAST THINGS
MARCH 14, 2007

Not a lot of complaints about the last essay in this volume, a chapter on justification and pastoral counseling by Dennis Johnson. Like some of the others, this chapter was just great also, with a sub-standard Federal-Visiony footnote jury-rigged into the argument. Like I said, not a lot of complaints about the text proper. Go, team, go.

But the footnote can't be allowed to pass without *some* comment. It provides an outstanding example of the kind of problems that have afflicted us throughout this whole imbroglio.

> Some Federal Vision advocates draw a distinction between God's 'strict' justice, which only Christ's perfection can satisfy, and God's 'fatherly' assessment, which accepts our less-than-perfect obedience, calling it 'pleasing' and 'good.' Rich Lusk, for example, asserts . . . . (p. 411)

The rest of this footnote goes on to critique Lusk for this second sense, apparently for messing around with congruent merit and such, but leaves the acknowledged sense (involving what only Christ can do) out of the discussion. But how come?

One last comment, and this book goes back on the shelf. Back when Westminster West first did their conference on this controversy (out of which this book grew), they issued "Our Testimony on Justification." Most of it is wonderful, consisting of quotations from the Reformed confessions. But the preamble tells us why they are doing this, and shows that they haven't learned anything about this issue in the last few years. And frankly, given the amount that has been written on it, this is just inexcusable.

> Such critics, called neonomians in the seventeenth century, today are perhaps better labeled covenant moralists. Our testimony is directed primarily to this third group, who claim to be genuinely Reformed. These covenant moralists teach, contrary to the Reformed confessions and/or historic Reformed conviction, some or all of the following . . . ." (p. 432)

A series of gross misrepresentations follow, which I addressed when this statement first came out. For one fruity example, consider this claim about our beliefs—"that justification is not by faith alone, but by faithfulness, that is, trust in Christ *and* obedience" (p. 432).

Westminster West, as a seminary, has put their reputation on the line in this book. They issued the statement initially, held a conference, developed this book out of that conference, and they have published this testimony again. This means that their testimony is *false* testimony.

Where does this falsehood come from? The temptation is to resort to the standard two alternatives in cases like this—this is being done because they are stupid, or because they are malicious. Incompetent or hateful? But I don't think either alternative explains what is going on here.

Tight dogma held in the wrong way can make good people do bad things. In this case, the irony is particularly thick, because the dispute is about how the free justification that is given to us all in Christ is the fount of all practical godliness. This volume has stated, more times than I can remember, how the Reformed doctrine insists that the faith alone which justifies is not a faith which *is* alone, but rather is accompanied by other gifts and graces. This is the Reformed doctrine, *and I agree with it.*

So, when are we going to *do* it? Does the free justification in Christ alone, appropriated by faith alone, naturally lead Christ's followers to state the obvious truth about one's doctrinal adversaries, regardless of the 'political' cost? Does it require men who hold to the historic Reformed doctrine on justification to pick up the phone and call a brother on the other side of the line whom they know to have been misrepresented? Does free grace allow one to refuse to "break ranks," even though he knows that an injustice is occurring? Does an orthodox understanding of *sola fide* allow justified believers to continue to publish inaccurate books, and refuse to meet the brothers mentioned in those books to thrash out the issues? And does it allow those leading the charge to refuse to debate when repeatedly invited to do so? You say you have faith? Show me your faith by your works. And if this book was an example of those works, you need to try another one.

THE BUBBLE BATH OF ORTHODOXY
MARCH 19, 2007

Scott Clark is at it again on his blog*, and since he disabled the comments feature there, it is not possible for me to comment in that venue. So I will comment in this one. My comments are bold.

> "How I am redeemed from all my sins and misery." The Heidelberg Catechism was written not just to those who profess the Christian faith but to those who actually believe the Christian faith. The writers of the catechism had to assume, for the purposes of writing the catechism, that the hearers/readers of the catechism are united to Christ by true faith (HC 21) and a vital union with Christ.

Why did they have to assume that? Didn't they know that many children in the visible church would not have true faith and that the church, in making them memorize all this glorious stuff in the first person singular, was turning them into rank hypocrites? Why did they "have" to assume true faith?

> According to the catechism, and the Reformed faith generally, there is a great difference between profession of faith and true faith. This is a distinction of the greatest importance and one which some seem bent on blurring.

I think this is quite true.

* heidelblog.net

> Some folk (who call themselves "the Federal Vision")

Uh oh . . .

> who are concerned about the ill effects of revivalism and religious subjectivism (as I am) in contemporary Christianity seek to redress the problem by turning to what they call the "objectivity of the covenant." In their scheme, all baptized persons are said to be in the covenant of grace in very same way. They speak of a "covenantal" election, union with Christ, justification etc. By "covenantal" they mean conditional and temporary.

They also speak, in numerous places, of a decretal election, settled and sealed before all worlds, in which the elect of God are named and numbered, and with a number that cannot be increased or diminished. But there is no sense bringing *that* up *here*—it would only serve to confuse people who have settled into the warm bubble bath of orthodoxy and wish to have no pounding on the bathroom door.

> They argue from the example of the temporary national covenant with Israel. Just as God chose the Israelites to be his temporary national people so he "elects" individuals today to a temporary conditional status as Christians which status is said to be retained by faithfulness (trust and obedience). "If," they say, "we keep our part of the covenant we will be ultimately righteous before God."

This would be really, really bad if anybody held to it.

> Faith is now said to have two parts: trusting and obeying. This, they say, is what God asked of Adam before the fall; what God asked of Abraham after the fall, what God asked of his Son Jesus, and what God asks of us.

Jumping Jehoshaphat *and* Land of Goshen!

> Please note how they move

Or rather, how Clark moves on our behalf. And I have never seen some of these moves before, not even during the disco years.

> from Israel's status as a national covenantal people with Israel to the baptized person today. Does Scripture do this? Not exactly. Both Paul and the writer to the Hebrews to appeal the example of Israel as the old covenant visible church.

They sure do.

> There is a distinction to be made here. Israel fulfilled a couple of roles in the history of redemption at the same time, that's because there have always been two covenants operating in history: works and grace.

I thought it was bad to blur these two things. And now Israel is doing both at the same time? Or is it like watering your lawn in a drought? Works on Monday, Wednesday, Friday, and grace on Tuesday, Thursday, Saturday, and (bonus day!) Sunday?

> By making a national covenant with Israel, our Lord re-instituted a picture of the covenant of works that he had made with Adam. Just as Adam was called to obey the law and enter into glory, so national Israel was called to obey and remain the national people of God. As we all learned in catechism class, Israel failed miserably and lost her status as the national people of God. So this re-institution of the covenant of works on a national basis served to direct national Israel to the true Israel of God who would keep the covenant of works perfectly for all the elect.

Where was this recapitulation stuff in the Westminster Confession again?

> The covenant of grace, first announced after the fall (Gen 3:14–16) was also re-published during Israel's national covenant because Israel also served as the visible church under Moses and David. The covenant of grace was unconditional. It was temporarily administered through the national covenant but which, before the national covenant, during the national covenant, and after the fulfillment of the national covenant, included folk from every nation, tribe, and tongue (Rev 5:9). This covenant is a free promise of righteousness by grace alone, through faith alone, in Christ alone.

So God publishes two covenants at once to Israel, operating on antithetical principles, and then He blasted them for getting confused.

> These are two distinct covenants operating on two distinct principles.

So which one were they supposed to do? No man can serve two masters.

> The proposed revisions of the Reformed faith, however, blur the distinction between these two covenants and between these two principles.

We blur this distinction? Compared to some in this discussion, we are but pikers and posers.

> With just a moment's reflection, you can see right away how different this proposed revision of the Reformed faith is from what the Heidelberg Catechism actually says. The catechism says "How I am redeemed from all my sins and misery." The catechism does not say that "how I am placed in a temporary relation to Christ and his salvation conditioned upon grace and my cooperation with grace."

Right. The catechism doesn't say that. Neither do I.

> It does not say, "How I could be redeemed from my all my sins and misery." The catechism speaks of our redemption as present reality. According to the catechism I am now presently redeemed.

You don't say?

> In the history of the Christian church there was a covenant theology that did place Christians by baptism into a state of grace conditioned upon grace and cooperation with grace that described faith as trusting and obeying and righteousness as a future possibility but never a present reality. The medieval church taught this system for a millennium and the whole Protestant church rejected that system as one man.

The medieval church taught what *we* teach about decretal election? Really? About how the decretally elect are saved by grace alone through faith alone on the basis of the once-for-all sacrifice of Christ alone? Limited atonement and the whole deal? They did? That's amazing. So what was the Reformation about then?

> Remember the question: "How many things are necessary for you to know that in this comfort you may live and die happily?"

I sure do.

> It is not possible to live happily in a conditional temporary covenant wherein my righteousness is contingent upon my performance of the terms of the covenant.

Amen.

> It is impossible because of our sin and misery.

Amen again.

> Because of sin we're not able or even willing to keep the terms of the covenant.

That's right. Because of our sin and misery, we can't even represent the positions of fellow Reformed ministers fairly or accurately. That's why Christ had to die as a perfect substitute. If our justification depended upon *our* actions, or even our actions limited to the course of this Federal Vision controversy, all of us (on both sides) would be condemned to Hell.

> That's why we have a perfectly obedient and wholly trustworthy Savior who performed all the conditions of the covenant of works and Israel's national for us.

Our free justification is in no way dependent on our progress in our sanctification. But precisely because of this glorious grace, we are set free to pursue a life of holiness (and all who are truly justified will do so). This liberates us so that we can diligently work on representing the views of fellow Reformed ministers fairly and accurately.

> That's why faith, in justification, is not "trusting and obeying" but "a certain knowledge and a hearty trust."

Were we *told* to have this certain knowledge? Were we commanded to have this hearty trust? If not, then why are we doing it? And if so, then how can we obey without adding obedience to the mix, thereby incurring the wrath of Escondido?

> Works and grace are two different systems (1 Cor 11:5).

Except in Old Testament Israel, where some of us at Westminster West decided it would be pedagogically helpful to smush them together. Let's recapitulate both covenants at once! And then attack other people for getting them confused!

> They are two different religions operating on two different principles.

Two different religions? God bound Israel to two different *religions*?

> The Heidelberg Catechism doesn't confuse them and it premises our assurance on Jesus's fulfillment of the covenant of works for us.

The Heidelberg Catechism didn't confuse them because it was written centuries before *this* business erupted.

FUTURE PLANS
MARCH 21, 2007

The next critical book on Federal Vision, due out soon, is *By Faith Alone**, edited by Gary Johnson and Guy Waters. I have it on order, but there has apparently been some delay according to the good folks at Amazon. The current plan is to review it thoroughly in this space. By "review it" I mean that I intend to take it apart brick by brick, and if the past is any indicator of the future, I intend to snap any flawed brick in two, and throw at least one half of that brick at the moon.

VANTAGE THEOLOGY
MARCH 21, 2007

For creatures, there is no such thing as a "view from everywhere," and this is especially true in theology. One of the problems that happens with people who do decretal theology all the time is that this can be forgotten, and we begin to assume that we do have the ultimate vantage point for our theological perspective. And so when someone says that it would be edifying to look at election through the lens of the covenant, and not just to look at the covenant through the lens of election, this is taken as an incipient denial of both election and the covenant.

But when something is much bigger than we are, we have to look at it from different angles. And when I walk around to the back of the mansion to have a look at the gardens there, I am not *denying* what I saw when I was looking at the front. Decretal Calvinism is *true*, and its towers are imposing. But the truths of Scripture can be looked at from other angles, without forgetting or denying or contradicting what we saw when considering the decrees.

The same issue of "vantage point" can help us when considering the issues of recapitulation. The apostle Paul was fond of the *reductio*, stepping into the

* crossway.org/books/by-faith-alone-tpb

assumptions of his opponents and reasoning from there. "Come now, you who depend on the law . . ." This is what I believe he is doing when he is talking about the two covenants, one with Hagar and one with Sarah. We most emphatically have two covenants, which is what the recapitulationists are arguing for. But this covenant of Hagar's, was it something we ought to look at from the vantage of a divine offer, or from the vantage of inevitable human self-righteousness? I opt for the latter. I don't believe that God made a serious "covenant of works" with Hagar, knowing that she and her descendants would not be able to keep it. But if He didn't make a covenant of works with Hagar, then how did she wind up in a covenant of works? I do agree that her spiritual descendants were in a covenant of works. How did they get there?

I would argue that the works principle is the only alternative to the grace principle, and when people break the covenant of grace, their only option to is function, somehow and someway, on a works basis. There is nowhere else to go. No one has to teach this—it is just the way it is. God made a covenant of grace with His people (and that is *all* it was), and yet the covenant of grace can be rejected and broken by the non-elect within that covenant. When descendants of Sarah rejected the covenant of grace (taking pride in their own "achievments"), this made them covenantal Ishmaelites.

Put this another way. The covenant of grace was made with visible Israel in the Old Testament, and the covenant of grace is with the visible Church in the New. Because the covenant is not limited to the decretally elect, it is possible for the covenant of grace to be broken by those in the midst of the covenant people who are not elect.

(Special reminder for theological scholars: for the elect, everything the Westminster Confession says about them, and five pounds extra to be sure, is *true*.)

But the non-elect reject God's grace. That is the distinguishing mark of the non-elect; they *cannot* live by grace through faith. But they are surrounded with the apparatus of grace—Word, sacraments, promises, fellowship, and so on. Grace is everywhere—except in their hearts. So what they do (and they always do it) is construct a covenant of works out of the materials around them. This is the high rebellion of reverse engineering. This is why people can come to the Lord's Table as though they were doing a good work, or they sign a card at the revival, or they memorize the Shorter Catechism. They can take pride in a confession of unworthiness. Who among us has not known a Calvinist who was proud of his knowledge that creatures cannot take pride in anything?

All this is contrary to the design of the covenant of grace, but the works-heart can turn absolutely *anything* into a work. I was talking to someone once about the famous question posed at the Pearly Gates, "Why should I let you into heaven?" And I said the answer was something like, "Because of the death of Jesus Christ on the cross, plus nothing." The person confessed to me that her first reaction was, "Gee, I hope I remember to say that."

WHIFFING ANOTHER SLAP SHOT
MARCH 22, 2007

Someone needs to tell Scott Clark that when you are in the penalty box for a three-hour penalty, you don't get to keep skating around on the ice. He says:

> There have been numerous attempts to resurrect the old "grace and cooperation" with grace scheme. The Arminians tried it in the late 16th and early 17th centuries and it has persisted since. Richard Baxter tried it in the 17th century. The neo-nomians tried it during the Marrow Controversy (18th century) and moralists have tried it repeatedly since and they [are] trying it again today (in the Federal Vision). Some folk even say that "grace and cooperation with grace" toward eventual righteousness is Reformed theology. Well, it isn't, not according to the Reformed confessions.

So, according to this representation, if we may use our terms loosely, the Federal Vision consists of moralists who are advancing that old-timey semi-Pelagian foolishness. According to this view, God offers us grace, and then we go on to make that grace effective by cooperating with it.

Just so everybody knows, this would be something that we would *deny*. I italicize the word *deny* there in the hopes that Scott Clark would eventually be able to pick up on it. We are rapidly approaching the time when everyone in the country will be in possession of this theological datum with the exception of the Escondido faculty, and I am trying to head off this particular embarrassment.

Any cooperation with grace that we offer, such as it is, is itself a grace or gift from God lest any man boast. Our salvation, all of it, including our responses during the course of our salvation, is from grace, in grace, to grace, on grace, under grace, and with grace. If I left out any preposition that makes good orthodox sense when combined with the word *grace*, then let us affirm that one too. I not only affirm *sola gratia*, but *tota gratia* as well. God does not do 90% and we do 10%. God does not do 99% and we do 1%. God does it all, and all that we do after the fact is entirely dependent upon what He has already done. Jesus gave the command, and *then* Lazarus came out of the tomb. This was not an instance where Jesus pulled and Lazarus pushed. Jesus did not give the command to rise from the dead so that Lazarus could then think about whether to make that particular command efficacious by cooperating with it. I mean, good grief. After Jesus gave the command to rise, all the essential life-giving work was already done, and so when Lazarus did walk around after that, his steps were not intended to be a walking embodiment of semi-Pelagianism. And it would not have helped his Calvinistic *bona fides* if he were to lie down and hold his breath.

God can bring good out of anything, and there has been a fun side benefit to this controversy. As I interact with Arminian friends (who really *do* hold to some form of "grace and cooperation with grace" scheme described above), it pleases me no end to know that they have to figure out how my brand of high-octane Calvinism has been identified by a paid theologian at Westminster West as being the same thing as what *they* teach. Heh. Hey, bro. How about that Finney, eh?

US DWARFS
MARCH 27, 2007

Full disclosure right at the outset. The Foreword to *Faith Alone* was written by David Wells, and if that man's books were orange juice concentrate, I could still eat them right out of the can with a spoon. When he is on his message (which is the exposition of the soul-destroying nature of relativistic mush), there is no one better. Thankfully, this foreword continues my opportunity to cheer and applaud, and to remain a staunch Wells man, because Wells basically tackles something other than the subject of the book.

The subject of the book was summarized on the back cover in the blurb by Robert Godfrey.

> But the recent assault on justification by the New Perspective on Paul and by the Federal Vision is particularly pernicious, cloaked as it is in apparent scholarship and piety. This important book defends the historic Reformation doctrine with better scholarship and more profound piety.

Okay. I was oriented, and I knew who the bad guys were supposed to be. Then I read the foreword. Wells divides the evangelical world into three basic groups.

> What I suggest is that there are currently three main constituencies in evangelicalism. There is one in which the historical doctrines of evangelical believing are still maintained and even treasured. There is one that is oblivious to these doctrines and considers them an impediment to church growth. Finally, there is one that is thumbing its nose at both of these first two constituencies, in the one case because its orthodoxy is too confining and in the other because its church life, glitzy as it may be, is too empty. (p. 15)

Now given the fact that I got the right book with the right title. I thought I knew right away who these constituencies were. There were the historic Protestant lovers of the Reformed standards, there were the happy-clappy seeker sensitive pragmatists, and then there were the Federal Vision troops giving both of the first two groups the raspberry. But I only got two out of three.

I was right about the first group. "The reformational doctrines, part and parcel of which is sola fide, are still preserved among churches and by individuals in the first major church constituency" (p. 15). Okay, check. And I got the second one right too. The second constituency is "made up of a generation of pragmatists" (p. 16).

> And so it was the the seeker sensitive church emerged, reconfigured around the consumer, edges softened by marketing wisdom, pastors driven by business savvy, selling, always selling, but selling softly, alluringly, selling the benefits of the gospel while most, if not all, of the costs were hidden. (p. 16)

Then we got to the third constituency, which I missed completely. Since we are what the book is about, I thought the third group had to be us Dwarfs, duly chastised for shooting at Calormenes and horses indiscriminately. But no, the third group is the Emergent church, of the Brian McLaren stripe. "The Emergent church, the third of these church constituencies in evangelicalism, is a reaction which, in effect, is saying to the other two constituencies, 'a pox on both your houses!'" (p. 17). Huh.

Again I say, *huh*. Maybe there was a mix-up at Crossway. Maybe this is the foreword to another book. But probably not. Wells concludes by saying he is grateful for the book because of what the authors believe and declare. He does not appear to know if their adversaries believe what is attributed to them and doesn't really get into that. But the Emergent church is bad.

> I am grateful for this book because I am grateful for any clarity, any light, that can be brought to bear on our situation in the evangelical world, and this particular book brings a lot. This desire for doctrinal clarity that I share with all of these authors, this yearning for biblical truth, makes me hopelessly "modern" as it does them. (p. 19)

Yeah, I yearn for clarity too. I long for the day when our adversaries will be able to write a book in which they quote us accurately *and extensively*, demonstrate clearly that they understand what we teach and what we do not teach, and interact with it in a way that is actually informative. Shooting reformational *solas* into the air is not the same thing as defending the faith. But Robert Godfrey promises more. He says in the blurb that the New Perspective on Paul and the Federal Vision are going to get their comeuppance in this book at the hands of "better scholarship and more profound piety."

How much better? All this made me wonder exactly how much interaction with the Federal Vision there was going to be. So, going back to the index of subjects and names, I discovered that Jim Jordan is mentioned three (3) times, Peter Leithart one (1) time, Rich Lusk an avalanche of five (5) times, Norman Shepherd tying him at five (5) times, Steve Wilkins getting one (1) mention, and me getting one (1) *favorable* mention—I am quoted critiquing N.T. Wright. And the Leithart and Wilkins references are on the same page, simply identifying them as paedocommunionists along with Robert Rayburn.

THE HELL YOU SAY
MARCH 28, 2007

The original Auburn Avenue conference, the font of all the trouble, occurred in 2002. The ruckus proper began the following summer, and since then, we have had another Auburn Avenue conference, a Fort Lauderdale colloquium, a book that resulted from that, a book published by Athanasius Press (*The Federal Vision*), a book by me (*"Reformed" Is Not Enough*), a conference at Westminster West, a conference at Greenville Theological Seminary, a presbyterial exam of me in the CREC, several presbyterial exams of Steve Wilkins in the PCA, and a recent flurry of critical books from the opposition. The most recent of these, *By Faith Alone*, is edited by Gary Johnson and Guy Waters. I just finished reading the Introduction to this modest volume, written by Guy Waters, entitled "Whatever Happened to *Sola Fide*?"

During the course of this controversy, extending lo, these last five years, I have been a sweet Christian boy. I haven't lost my temper once, and I haven't sent any jalapeño emails. I have not punched any holes in the sheetrock, whether at the office or at home. As the apostle Paul would say, I am out of my mind to talk like this, and he never sent any letter bombs either, just like me. I have sought to clarify my position in any way that I could do so, and I have gone the second, third, and fourth miles in offering to meet, discuss or debate. I *have* yelled at my windshield, but that was just a fun metaphor. I didn't really.

All this to say, I think I am entitled to a rant. A "rant" is, in blogospheric terms, a bit of prose written in the style of an Elizabethan pamphleteer, with color, and bite, and dash. A rant is a full-throated expression of . . . exuberant dismay. Watched carefully, a rant can occur with a rare-jewel-of-contentment smile on the face, and not break any of the Ten Commandments, or cause any of the fruit of the Spirit to rot in the bowl. But it has to be done with self-control—you can't be seeing red. Light pink at the most. At the same time, the *tactical* point is to come off the top ropes. The tactical point is to *uncork*. I think I am entitled to *that* kind of rant at least. Just a short one. Hold on. Let me shake it first.

* * *

The need of the hour is not to defend the *solas* of the Reformation the same way F Troop defended the American frontier. We don't need any more conservatives who don't conserve anything except their own sense of self-importance. Here we conservatives are in Fort Hapless, and we are surrounded by hordes of seeker-sensitive CEOs, fully credentialed entertainment engineers, and they have recently been reinforced by a bunch of postmodern hooey-mongers from France. Things are looking pretty grim for us, and so, at this critical point in the movie, when the music is really tense, some of *our* guys decide to start a fight along the ramparts over whether the sole instrument of justification is a living faith or a faith that is living.

Sincerity is not the issue. There may be some who are doing this for cagey political reasons, but I prefer to think that the problem is naivete. For some that naivete is a function of having decided thirty years ago to translate all discussions of theology into the metric system, just to keep life simple. If ten won't divide into it, then it can't be a part of the *dikai-* word group. For others the reason for the naivete is more obvious—graduate school is still a fresh memory. They are just out of the egg with bits of shell on their heads.

We don't need any more male cheerleaders for the Reformation, chest-bumping in front of the stands. We don't any more cardboard megaphones of truth, and we don't need any more slogans instead of argument. We don't need any more attempts to rouse a bewildered crowd that is proving hard to whip up. "So-LAH, so-LAH, so-LAH!"

The need of the hour is not to try to establish the Reformed faith in America through apostolic signs and blunders. What in the foggy blue morning *is* this? I feel like somebody locked me up in a Walker Percy novel.

Suppose the apostle Paul had been unable to make the confrontation at Antioch and had sent some of his seminarians instead. So off they went to confront Peter and Barnabas because they were compromising the truth as it is in Jesus. Suppose they walked up to a group at lunch to rebuke them for withdrawing table fellowship from Gentiles. That group responded with, "Nope. That's actually a false report, about us at any rate. We have some Gentiles right here at the table—here, meet Nicholas, and Stephen, and Demetrius, and Bob." The seminarians' eyes narrow. The confrontation had been going so well, and the idea that they may have gotten the wrong table is beyond their ken. "And so now you compound your corruption of the gospel with *dishonesty*?"

I am a high Calvinist. For almost twenty years, I have been standing here well past the tree line, up amongst the boulders. I am prepared to be rebuked for lots of things but living in a semi-Pelagian swamp is not one of them. Try something else. Try something *plausible*.

But never mind. This is all being done because "the truth" is under attack. The foundations of "the truth" are being undermined. The "truth" is precious and is to be defended at all costs. "Truth" is not relative, elastic, or dependent upon how we *wish* things were. The "truth" recovered at the Reformation must be preached with power and defended with courage today. The "truth" cannot be reduced to mere slogans. The hell you say.

OH, NEVER MIND
MARCH 28, 2007

Guy Waters's Introduction has three main sections. In the first, he summarizes the doctrine of *sola fide*. That section was quite good in many respects, actually. I can say this because I affirm, believe, and teach the doctrine of *sola fide*. The only place I would quibble with Waters here is that I would want to talk about the imputation of Christ's obedience, as distinct from the imputation of Christ's merits. Other than that, I was good with everything he said, with the exception of why he was saying it. "Other than that, how was the play, Mrs. Lincoln?" There was a major problem with this section in that he begins by asking how the "New Perspective on Paul and the Federal Vision" have "challenged *sola fide*?" (p. 22). Notice how things are already getting mushed together.

In the second section, he takes on the New Perspective on Paul—Stendahl, Sanders, Dunn, and Wright in four pages. It is not trying to provide an in-depth treatment, and he makes some solid points. In fact, *Credenda/Agenda*, what Waters would consider a Federal Vision magazine, made many similar points in its *Pauline Take on the New Perspective*. But mentioning this would interfere with the next point, which was to try to show how the NPP runs into the FV.

As he is discussing Dunn, he summarizes Dunn's position by saying, "Justification, then, includes the inward transformation of the sinner" (p. 27). Remember that.

He then turns to the Federal Vision and begins by noting that we (unlike the NPP) are trying to call the Reformed world, at least according to our lights, to "a more thoroughgoing commitment to the Reformed tradition" (p. 28). But then he says:

> Neverthless, Federal Vision proponents have often been supportive of Reformed efforts to embrace Wright's and Dunn's insights on matters related to justification, particularly in their efforts to recast the doctrine as primarily ecclesiological . . . One federal Vision writer has expressed appreciation for certain New Perspective(s) definitions of the 'righteousness of God' as covenantal faithfulness(rather than the righteousness of Christ imputed to the believer for his justification) at key points in the letters of Paul. (p. 28)

The footnoted one is Peter Leithart, and the reference is to Peter's essay in *The Federal Vision*. Because he is not named in the text, but only in the footnote, this particular interaction does not show up in the index of *By Faith Alone*. Waters goes on to say this about Leithart:

> This proponent consequently defines justification in terms of non-forensic, transformational categories. To put it simply, he conflates justification and sanctification. In so doing, his definition of justification cannot sustain the doctrine of *sola fide*. (p. 29)

After reading Waters, I went back and read Peter's essay *again*. It is quite clear that he wants to say more about how the Bible uses the words relating to justification and righteousness than some Protestants have said, but it is equally clear that he insists that we must not say less. Reread what Waters just said above, and then consider these quotes from Peter's essay.

> Though justification terminology has a number of different nuances in Scripture, it does not refer to an act of 'making just.' (*The Federal Vision*, p. 206)

> The Protestant confessions reflect the biblical teaching when they claim that justification is an 'act of God's free grace' by which *God* pardons and forgives and counts us as righteous. (p. 206)

> As far as it goes, the Protestant doctrine is correct; if the scene of a sinner in the dock before the Judge is put before us, and we are asked, 'What does justification mean?' or 'On what grounds is a person justified?' then the proper answer is the Reformation answer: Justification is an act of God's free grace whereby He pardons all our sins and accepts us as righteous in His sight, only for the righteousness of Christ reckoned to us and received by faith alone. (p. 209)

> First, the Protestant doctrine of justification has mainly been concerned with the question of applying the redemption of Christ to individual

> believers. While that is certainly a central part of the gospel and the apostolic doctrine of justification . . . . (p. 211)

And then Waters concludes with this turnip:

> As different as the New Perspective(s) on Paul and the Federal Vision are, they converge in this respect: they deny the doctrine of *sola fide*: justification by faith alone. rather than calling men and women to rest on the perfect righteousness of Jesus Christ alone for their justification, the New Perspective on Paul and the Federal Vision give us a modified covenant of works. They tell us 'do this (with God's help) and you will live.' (p. 31)

And I have to sit down and fan myself. When I have recovered sufficiently, I will say (*again*) that salvation is of the Lord, from first to last. The Lord is our only righteousness, and He is the only one who can impute that righteousness. We are saved by grace alone through faith alone and . . . oh, never mind.

WRITE THAT SPOT DOWN
MARCH 29, 2007

Chapter one of *By Faith Alone* is a critique by Cornelis Venema of N.T. Wright's views on justification. This chapter was very good and was admirable on a number of levels.

Readers of this blog know that I have learned a lot from Wright, and I appreciate much of what he has to offer. In this, I am in agreement with T. David Gordon, who starts chapter two of this same book by pointing out that he finds Wright's work "utterly lucid, and profoundly stimulating" (p. 61). Okay, that's me too. But at the same time, Wright misses some important things. Sometimes he misses them (I think) because of the Anglican *zeitgeist* (women's ordination), and other times because he has accepted as axiomatic some scholarly settlement that ought not to be regarded as settled yet (Sanders on Palestinian Judaism).

Anyhow, my appreciation for Venema's critique here ought not to be taken as a change of overall attitude. On many issues, I believe that Wright is top drawer. But there *are* places where he just plain whiffs it. For some reason it reminds me of a *Far Side* cartoon, where a wooly mammoth is on its back, all four feet to the sky, with a little teeny arrow stuck in its belly. Two cavemen are standing by him with their bows, and one of them says, "We really ought to write that spot down."

Venema's chapter was good in the first place because he under-promises and over-delivers. When he summarizes what he finds problematic with Wright's views on justification, his statements are measured and judicious. The most strident comment in the chapter was, "The carelessness with which Wright and other writers of the New Perspective speak of a final justification on the basis of works threatens a central point of Paul's gospel" (p. 58). For the rest, Venema says that the "New Perspective ought to be carefully evaluated before it is too quickly embraced" (p. 59), or "critical elements of Paul's teaching about the law are either downplayed or left largely unacknowledged in Wright's view" (p. 53), or "I am convinced that the older Reformation perspective more faithfully and comprehensively represents the Scriptures' teaching" (p. 51). When it comes to his rhetoric, Venema does not come into this with a flame-thrower.

At the same time, in my view some of his criticisms are devastating. This is the part where he over-delivers. His evidence far surpasses his stated conclusions. This is in sharp contrast, for example, to Waters's introduction, where his evidence was running for home plate like crazy but started its slide twenty feet early, with predictable results.

Venema takes great care (almost twenty pages) to set forth and describe the position that he is going to critique, and I believe that advocates of that position would be able to sign off on his description. He states that position dispassionately and fairly. The last nine pages are his assessment.

One criticism is worth mentioning here. Venema shows that Sander's views on Second Temple Judaism do not really overthrow the older Reformation view of Paul, but rather, rightly interpreted, lend credence to it. In short, how is covenantal nomism not semi-Pelagian (p. 51)? Getting in by grace and staying in by obedience is something that could work in the first century for some Jews and in the thirteenth for some Christians.

> However the obvious weakness of Wright's insistence that this requires a new view of Paul's teaching on justification is that he (and other New Perspective writers) does not seriously consider whether covenantal nomism could accommodate a form of religious teaching that regards acceptance with God to be based upon grace *plus good works.* (p. 52)

Agree or disagree with it, this was a chapter of argument and judicious conclusions—not sloganeering and random quotation.

FEDERAL VISION EARTHQUAKE
MARCH 30, 2007

The next chapter in *By Faith Alone* is by T. David Gordon, and it too is a critique of N.T. Wright. The bulk of the chapter is just fine. Gordon, like Venema, is not hyperventilating over this, and he brings Wright's approach to biblical theology under scrutiny and does so in a moderate and fair way. He does this as one who has reviewed Wright's work favorably in the past (p. 61), and who is not automatically freaked out by him.

Gordon mentions the Auburn theology in passing, and that is what I would like to briefly comment on.

> This explains why some associate the New Perspective with the Auburn theology—neither explicates its biblical theology with reference to the Adamic administration. (p. 62)

A bit later, he says:

> Much of the present debate in some circles is not merely, or primarily, about the relation of faith and works in justification, though it has ramifications for that discussion. The present debate is about whether

> we can properly handle the doctrine of justification apart from juridical categories, apart from God's right judgment of his creation in terms of its obedience or disobedience to his rule. (p. 62)

The phrase *in some circles* is footnoted, and Gordon says, "Regarding not only N.T. Wright, but also the so-called New Perspective on Paul, the views of Norman Shepherd, and the views of the so-called Auburn theology" (p. 62).

First, I think the comment that this is being driven by something deeper than the simple relation of faith to works is an astute one. The dirt clods on the surface aren't causing the earthquake; the tectonic plates are. But past that intial point of agreement, I think the observation needs serious modification. Put another way, what are those tectonic plates? It is not so much that downstream TR theology is explicated in terms of Adam, and downstream FV is explicated in terms of Abraham. It would be better to say that we relate Adam to the last Adam differently, but everything I have heard in FV circles is a Gen. 1:1 to Rev. 21: theology.

Here is one example. In *Back to Basics*[*], my colleague Doug Jones sets the stage of covenant theology this way.

> *The most prominent distinction that appears in God's covenant work* is that between God's covenant before the Fall and His covenant thereafter. Before the Fall, the Lord graciously condescends to covenant with Adam (and humanity) in his condition of genuine righteousness. But after the Fall, the Lord establishes a covenant to redeem rebels alienated by their sin. *These two distinct covenants* have gone by many names in the history of Christian thought, but we will call them the Covenant of Creation and the Covenant of Redemption. These labels highlight the different conditions of humanity with respect to each covenant. Regardless of the names we apply to these two covenants, the more interesting point is that the distinction between them is *prior to*, and

* David Hagopian, ed., *Back to Basics: Rediscovering the Richness of the Reformed Faith* (Phillipsburg, NJ: P&R, 1996).

> *more foundational than*, the distinction between the Old and New Covenants, which sometimes receives undue emphasis. The important distinction between the Old and New Covenants is really between anticipation (the Old Covenant) and fulfillment (the New Covenant) within the Covenant of Redemption. The intricate covenantal chain of redemption runs unbroken through both Old and New Covenants. (*Back to Basics*, p. 76, emphasis mine)

And amen. In FV circles, you will get various responses to the covenant of works. Some, like the above, insist on the language of covenants, but also insist that the Covenant of Creation was essentially gracious in character. Others, following John Murray, might want to say that there is an Adamic administration, but not an Adamic covenant. Others, like Jim Jordan, speak of two "stages" of intended human existence. Adam rebelled before getting to the second stage, and so the last Adam came to bring us into the maturity of that second stage. Now clearly something is going on here, and despite all the intramural differences in how we put things, it is distinct from a strict merit system which sees Adam as the first failed Pelagian.

And here, I would suggest, is the fundamental difference between our camps. It is not how many covenants there are, or how many administrations. This is a debate over what constitutes the necessary nature of the relationship between God and any one of His obedient servants. One side says that it is always (necessarily) a relationship of favor and gratitude. The other says that the archetypical relationship is one of requirement and obedience. This is *not* to say that the terms of each side are excluded from the other. The debate is over primacy. One side gives primacy to requirement and obedience, and within that context finds room for favor and gratitude. The other gives primacy to favor and gratitude, and within that context finds room for requirement and obedience. But there it is. In my view, these are the tectonic plates.

APRIL 2007

A MOUSETRAP GOSPEL
APRIL 1, 2007

I'll explain the title shortly. Promise.

The next chapter in *By Faith Alone* is by Rick Phillips, and in it he tackles two different challenges to the Reformed doctrine of imputation. The first is on the part of contemporary Arminians, who say that God accepts our faith in lieu of righteousness, and the second is on the part of N.T. Wright, who says that that the 'righteousness of God" has to refer to the righteousness of God Himself, and not 'a righteousness that comes from/avails with god' (p. 84). Wright denies that Paul teaches that the righteousness of Jesus Christ is imputed to or is reckoned to the believer. Rick does a good job in defending the doctrine of imputation on both fronts, and I commend the chapter to you.

Those who have followed this "Auburn Avenue" business on this blog for any length of time know that I have a great deal of respect for Rick. We have been on opposite sides of this thing, but I have a number of compelling reasons for concluding that he has not been motivated by "political" issues in this at all. One of those reasons is the fact that when I speak to an issue clearly and unambiguously, he is one of the few who is willing to acknowledge publicly that I have done so. He does that again in this chapter, where he quotes me arguing a point about imputation against N.T. Wright. He understood my point perfectly, and quoted me accurately, and I appreciate it a great deal.

That said, before I take up a few differences I have with Rick, I want to say that I agree completely with the position on imputation that he takes, over against the Arminians, and over against Wright. There will be a difference of opinion, that I will argue shortly, but the difference is not on the importance of the imputation of Christ's obedience (in His life and on the cross) to a robust and Pauline doctrine of justification. We agree on that point. And let me point to some other areas of agreement before we get to the differences.

Rick sees and acknowledges that N.T. Wright has *a* doctrine of imputation, one that follows from his larger theology. It is just not *the* doctrine of imputation.

"We should acknowledge that Wright does see a righteous status being applied to those who have faith in Christ. For this reason, it is often argued that Wright does not deny imputed righteousness. Clearly, however, Wright pointedly refutes and denies that Christ's righteousness is imputed to believers" (p. 86).

Rick also quotes Wright as saying that justification is not so much about "soteriology as about ecclesiology; not so much about salvation as about the church" (p. 86). Rick doesn't follow this up, but I honestly cannot make any sense out of it. Soteriology and ecclesiology may be different departments in a large seminary, or different chapters in a work of systematics, but how can we possibly separate the two? They can be distinguished, certainly, but outside the church there is no ordinary possibility of salvation. I put the word ordinary in so that people would know that I am being Westminsterian, and not a superstitious papist from the middle ages.

Rick also points to a misunderstanding that Wright has about the nature of a "righteousness transfer." According to Wright, "Righteousness is not a quality or substance that can thus be passed or transferred from the judge to the defendant" (p. 86). It is here that Rick quotes an argument that I posted here at *Blog and Mablog* (p. 90). No one that I ever heard of in Reformed circles has described imputation as a substantive infusion or transfer.

In another place, Wright talks about this kind of transaction as a "cold bit of business." This is another misunderstanding, and I believe it is of a similar nature to the first one. I was the foreman of a jury once, in a murder trial, and I can assure you that when the time came for the reading of our verdict, no one in that courtroom was bored or dozing off. The reading of the verdict, *especially* for the one on trial, is one of the most riveting things that a man can ever experience. We even have an entertainment term for it—courtroom drama. And for a man who is as guilty as sin, who comes to the bar of justice, and who hears the sentence of "not guilty" read out loud (by the God who will by no means clear the guilty, no less) . . . well, words to describe what this feels like should fail us. It certainly is not a cold bit of business.

Now, to a few differences that I would ask Rick to consider. The first has to do with what happened to Abraham, our father in the faith.

> Furthermore, note that in Romans 4:5 Paul adds the statement that faith "trusts him who justifies the ungodly." This can only be a reference to God justifying Abraham. If Abraham was ungodly when he was credited with righteousness, it cannot be because he did something that God considers righteous. (p. 82)

The difficulty with this argument is the time line. In order for Abraham to be ungodly just prior to the declaration of righteousness in Gen. 15, he would have had to be ungodly in Genesis 12, when he left Ur of the Chaldees. But . . . "So Abram departed, *as the Lord had spoken unto him . . .*" (v. 4). And in Hebrews 11, this action is explicitly described as an action of faith. "By faith Abraham, when he was called to go out into a place which he should after receive for an inheritance, obeyed, and he went out, not knowing whither he went" (Heb. 11:8).

My second disagreement with Rick is more substantive, but I have to qualify it, because I am not sure if Rick would disagree. One of the things that plagues our discussion of this issue of justification is that the language tends to shift back and forth between justification as it is in the plan of God and justification as it is in the heart and mind of the person being justified. When we say that something or other is "necessary to justification" (p. 77), we have to be absolutely clear what we are meaning. Do we mean "that which is revealed in the Bible concerning justification," or do we mean "that which a sinner has to understand in order to be justified"? If we affirm the latter, then we are denying the Pauline doctrine of justification apart from works of the law. As N.T. Wright has wonderfully pointed out, justification by faith alone is not by faith in justification by faith alone. Justification—apart from our works, theological or otherwise—is the sheer, gracious gift of God.

An understanding of this is most helpful in keeping debates over justification from getting ramped up unnecessarily. I have already agreed with Rick, over against Wright, on the doctrine of imputation. I think Rick is right and Tom is wrong. Now, if Wright is wrong on something as critical as this, doesn't that make him a dangerous heretic? Doesn't that mean he must not be a Christian? Absolutely not, and it is the confusion I described above that even makes us bring the question up.

Here the place where I explain the title of this post. Michael Behe used the helpful example of a mousetrap to illustrate the concept of "irreducible complexity." The illustration comes from the debate over evolution and whatnot, but I think it is helpful here. Irreducible complexity refers to a system which requires all its parts to be present in order to work at all. With the mousetrap, we need the wood platform, and the spring, and the part that snaps, and so on. All parts must be there, and if you take just one of them away, the whole thing doesn't work. Now there is a tendency among conservative Christians to want to get down to a very basic gospel, the mousetrap gospel. What is the point past which, if you take anything away, the whole function is lost?

Now the Bible rarely refers to the gospel this way, as though it were a simple machine. You could argue that the first verses of 1 Cor. 15 do this, as I believe, but this is not the normal way the word *gospel* is used in Scripture. The gospel is not a simple little machine, which can be undone by the removal of just one part. It is more like an ancient olive tree, with roots that go everywhere, and branches that have been there forever. It is possible to chop a tree like this down, but it can take a lot more interference than a mousetrap can—and keep on growing.

I agree that imputation is an important part of how this tree grows and flourishes, and I agree that N.T. Wright gums up this doctrine. I believe he is wrong at this point, and his Reformed critics are right. But this is not enough to get me yelling for his scalp because on other aspects of the *gospel*, he is right and many of his Reformed critics are wrong. We make a great deal (as we should) about how Abraham believed God and it was credited to him as righteousness. But what was it, exactly, that Abraham believed? It was that his seed would be like the stars in their multitudinous glory, and Paul interprets this as meaning Abraham was going to inherit the world——not through the law but through the righteousness of faith (Rom. 4:13). N.T. Wright believes this to be true, just like Abraham did, and (I really hesitate to say this, honestly) his amillennial Reformed critics do not believe it. This proclamation to Abraham was a proclamation of the *gospel*, and many within the Reformed camp do not believe it.

Now does this make them heretics, or unregenerate men? Of course not. The gospel is not a simple little mousetrap that we can disable that easily. Perverse men, who *intend* to disable the gospel, do have the capacity to twist it beyond recognition, to the point where it becomes an anti-gospel. But that takes a lot of work, and a twisted heart. This is not true of a Christian gentleman like N.T. Wright, who gets imputation wrong, and a Christian gentleman like Kim Riddlebarger, who wrote a very capable book on amillennialism, getting (according to my lights) the Rom. 4:13 part of the gospel wrong. If our justification were to be lost if we scored less than 100 percent on the justification test (administered by St. Peter at the Pearlies), every last one of us, yours truly included, would be headed for the bad place. We don't take the justification test for our justification. *Jesus* took that test. And no, this should not make us want to sin that grace may abound.

One last comment. Rick took a great risk in quoting me favorably, but then he went out on the limb even further, and quoted John Murray favorably also (p. 96). I point this out because a few chapters later, T. David Gordon describes John Murray as the "drunk uncle" of Reformed theology (p. 118) and wonders why nobody is willing to talk about it. Two or three more quotations like this, and Rick might find that he is falling under suspicion as well.

WHAT ABRAHAM SAW
APRIL 2, 2007

Frank Turk has made a reasonable request in the comments section of the previous post. He has asked for 200 words on why I believe that Abraham believed the expansive promises, and whether this is in tension with Christ's statement that Abraham rejoiced to see His day. So here it is, in brief compass. Remember this is just the skeletal argument. It certainly needs to be fleshed out a good deal.

First, look at the content of the promises themselves in Genesis. In Genesis 12:3, Abraham is told, among a number of other glorious things, that "in thee shall all families of the earth be blessed." In Genesis 15, he is told that his seed will be beyond numbering (Gen. 15:5.). This is precisely *what* Abraham believed (in the text) when his faith was credited to him as righteousness.

Second, this faith of Abraham's in the promise is expressly called faith in the *gospel*, and Paul does this as he repeats the *content* of the promise.

"Even as Abraham believed God, and it was accounted to him for righteousness. Know ye therefore that they which are of faith, the same are the children of Abraham. And the Scripture, foreseeing that God would justify the heathen through faith, *preached before the gospel unto Abraham*, saying, 'In thee shall all nations be blessed'" (Gal. 3:6–8, emphasis mine).

What comes out of God's mouth when God preaches the gospel to Abraham? An expansive promise concerning the salvation of the world. And, as mentioned before, Paul settles this as talking about Abraham's inheritance of the *world* (Rom. 4:13).

When Abraham believed this, he was looking for, among other things, a city with foundations, "whose maker and builder is God" (Heb. 11:10). And this is why Abraham when he saw the day of Christ, rejoiced to see it and was glad. He did not look forward to the first coming of Christ as the final fulfillment of the promise, but rather as the groundbreaking for the fulfillment of the promise. The cornerstone was laid, and this indicated that construction on the city had commenced. In a similar way, Abraham saw his Seed in the advent of Christ, and he rejoiced. But he will not see all his seed (who are what they are by virtue of their place in the Seed) until the last generation rolls in.

So, may our gracious God not only impute the righteousness of Christ to us because we receive His word the *way* that Abraham did (which we should certainly do), but also may He give us the faith to believe *what* Abraham did.

STILL NO DEBATE
APRIL 6, 2007

Green Baggins* recently posted a call for repentance for those in the FV camp. Not surprisingly, this elicted quite a few comments (279 to be exact), and among them I noticed the following comment by Gary Johnson. Gary is one of the editors of the book I am currently reviewing (*By Faith Alone*), and because he occupies a position of leadership in this controversy, I need to respond to several things he said here. So that you can follow, I will put in bold the comments I will respond to. For the rest, I think I have already responded . . . multiple times.

> Wilson admitted to Mike Horton on the White Horse Inn that he was aware that there were a number of different positions amongst the Federal Visionists themselves. He also said that his take on NT Wright was not necessarily the same as that of Rich Lusk, who has written high praise for Wright's position on justification and the 'pesty' issue of imputation. Contra Wilson public statements, Lusk, like Shepherd, dismisses the WCF on the Covenant of Works and not only throws out the doctrine of active obedience, but speaks of not even needing any kind of imputation. Like Shepherd and Wright, a number of the FVers hold to a two-fold justification with the final justification being determined by works with an appeal to Romans 2:13. These representatives of the FV likewise define saving faith as 'covenantal faithfulness' and come up with a category they call 'non-elect covenant member' or 'the believing non-elect' who, according to Lusk and Wilkins are by

* greenbaggins.wordpress.com/2007/03/29/ego-repentance-and-the-federal-vision/

> virtue of their baptism, grafted into Christ ,and for a period of time temporarily possess all the redemptive blessings (including the forgiveness of sins) the elect have—save for the grace of perseverance. When these positions are given their due comeuppance by the FV critics, Wilson goes into a rage accusing us of distortion, misrepresentation, slander and the like. In Wilson's eyes NONE of the criticisms of ANY of the representatives of the FV has any merit (pun intended). It does not matter who it is, or what kind of credentials they might have, be Guy Waters, the members of the OPC study report (which include Dick Gaffin), Scott Clark, Mike Horton, Bob Godfrey and the entire faculty of Westminster Calif along with the faculties of Greenville Presbyterian, and Knox seminaries or Lig Duncan and the study committee of the PCA - in Wilson' eyes we are all lack the ability to either understand or appreciate the insights of the FV. Furthermore, since we do not recognize the value of these innovations, and actually have the audacity to charge these men with error, Wilson carries on a scathing personal vendetta against anyone who dares question ANYTHING related to the views of the FV.

This is a textbook case of trying to stand and sit at the same time. In the first portion, Johnson helpfully outlines an instance (and there are many others), where I have made distinctions between what I believe, hold and teach, and what is believed, held and taught by other friends and acquaintances——whether Norman Shepherd, N.T. Wright, or Rich Lusk. (Incidentally, this means that, while I believe in a pre-fall covenant with mankind in Adam, and in the imputation of the active obedience of Christ, I do not believe John Murray and Norman Shepherd are heretics for differing with me on these points. Doctrinal disagreements *can* be held in a spirit of catholicity.) But *then*, after Johnson cited an example of me admitting the justice of certain doctrinal criticisms that could be made against some of my FV friends, he then goes on to make an assertion that would not seem to follow from this. "In Wilson's eyes NONE of the criticisms of ANY of the representatives of the FV has any merit." Except for the ones *he* just mentioned a few seconds before. So the real problem here is not that I have not made my position clear, as contrasted with other positions on the table. The problem is that I am part of the Reformed *faith*, and not a Reformed *sect*. The Reformed faith is the Mississippi, anywhere south of Vicksburg. A Reformed sect has a flow of water also, but it runs through a green garden hose, and we closed the valve three quarters of the way because things in the garden were getting too wet and were starting to grow.

The second thing is Johnson's gratuitous assertion that when any FVish positions, anywhere in the world, "are given their due comeuppance," my response is that of flying "into a rage." Whereas that is pretty much the only thing I *haven't* tried. I have argued, debated, conceded points, reasoned, made distinctions, offered to debate publicly, made jokes, and hired three necromancers to cast a spell on the Mississippi Valley Presbytery. Actually, that last one is just an example of the next to last one.

And third, what Johnson calls a "scathing personal vendetta" is actually something else entirely. I have no personal vendetta whatever, although I *do* understand how some of my responses would be experienced by some of the more irresponsible brethren as scathing. I am reminded of the old political anecdote about Harry Truman who responded to a cry, "Give 'em hell, Harry!" with the comment that he just tells the truth, and they think it's hell. So let me take that last statement, and edit it to something more to my liking. Compare:

1. Wilson carries on a scathing personal vendetta against anyone who dares question ANYTHING related to the views of the FV
2. Wilson carries on an effective rhetorical campaign against those who dare question anything related to the views of the FV, while refusing to allow any public and accountable cross-examination of their charges, such as would be provided in an arranged debate.

Why no willingness to debate? *Still*? Guy Waters, Gary Johnson, Scott Clark, Ligon Duncan, Cal Beisner . . . what about it?

THE TRUE CHURCH WITHIN THE CHURCH
APRIL 6, 2007

This must be national Green Baggins Day. I want to post just a few comments about an article posted at that blog by the Rev. Wes White. In this article, he critiqued what he thought to be my take on the visible/invisible church distinction. My position on the visible/invisible church distinction is represented thusly:

> We shall deal first with the error of Rome, which is repeated in Douglas Wilson . . . that the word Church in the present time should only refer to what we call the visible Church. That is, those who are baptized and members of the Church are in the Church, and we cannot apply any other sense of Church to say that unbelieving baptized members who remain in the external communion are not in the Church at this point in history. (p. 2)

A bit later, in answering a point I raise, he says that I *deny* the visible/invisible church distinction. "The answer to these problems is not a denial of the invisible/visible church distinction" (pp. 5–6). The problem with all this is that *I don't deny it.* I *affirm* it and seek to add qualifications to head off errors of application at the popular level.

For example, here is one thing I said in my short essay on the subject in *The Federal Vision*: "At the same time, the historic Reformed terminology can be applied in such a way as to cause some problems of its own. While it was a valuable distinction, it was still not an inspired distinction. I say this *while embracing the distinction*, as far as it goes" (p. 266, emphasis original).

There's a robust denial for you.

I do *not* take an exception to Westminster's definition of the invisible church as consisting of the entire number of the elect throughout all history. That same roster of names, incidentally, head for head, will be gathered around Jesus Christ at the eschaton, on the day when the invisible church will be made fully visible. My phrase eschatological church is nothing other than the invisible church on the day she is made visible. Neither do I take an exception to Westminster's definition of the visible church as consisting of those who profess the true religion, together with their children. That church corresponds perfectly to what I call the historical church——same definition. I call it the historical church, and Augustine called it the pilgrim church. The only thing that my terms seek to do is ensure that we work with these two (unchanged) definitions *within the flow of history and time.*

If someone like Pastor White wants to take Westminster's definition (all the elect) and reapply it as a stipulated definition to those who are currently regenerate, I am happy to go along with the stipulated *changes* to Westminster's definition. Honest. But I do so knowing that this will cause some dislocations that we will have to iron out, and there might be confusion in the meantime. For example, election and regeneration are two different things, and if we bring a portion of the invisible church down into history (say, on April 6, 2007), we have to recognize that to limit it to those who are already effectually called excludes those among the elect who are alive on this day, but not yet converted.

On another point, White argues that true faith is not seen by us because it is an internal heart thing. True enough. But that is not the only reason why the true faith of invisible church members might not be seen. In some cases, it is because unconverted individuals who are elect don't *have* any faith yet. In other cases, most cases actually, it is because their true faith is in the distant future. They aren't born yet.

But Pastor White says that I don't allow the word Church to be used in the present in any other way than the visible/historical church. This is glaringly, demonstrably false, and is yet another good example of how our positions are not being accurately stated before our opponents undertake to refute them. Invisible and visible? I affirm "the same doctrine" (*RINE*, p. 73). Invisible and visible? I "embrace that distinction" (*RINE*, p. 78).

God knows His elect, and He knows them *today*. He knows the true Church within His Church. He knows which branches will still be on the tree at the last day, and which branches will not be. A true Jew is not one who is one outwardly. A true Christian is not one who is one outwardly. A true *church* member is not one who is one outwardly. I would apologize for not having made this clear before, but there are at least five chapters on it in *"Reformed" Is Not Enough*.

THE VISIBLE PART OF THE INVISIBLE VISIBLE CHURCH APRIL 7, 2007

On an earlier post, Green Baggins posted a link to his blog, marking a place where Andy Gilman had responded to something I had written on Scott Clark's blog. Andy had responded to it on yet another blog, and then sent a copy of it over to Green Baggins, and so GB came over here and asked me what I thought of it. Isn't the Internet great?

So here's Andy*:

> Doug Wilson posted something on Scott Clark's blog back in early January regarding the visible/invisible church distinction. Here's something I wrote to another forum after that exchange:
>
> Doug Wilson:
> [begin quote]. . . if you want to have the invisible church existing "in history," in a way that is distinct from the visible church, then you are out of accord with the Confession. That is because the invisible church "consists of the whole number of the elect." A partial number of the elect is not the invisible church because it is not the whole number of them. It would make sense to speak of the whole number of the truly regenerate at this moment of 2007, but this is just a partial congregation within the invisible church. It is a subset of the invisible church, not the invisible church itself—just as Christ Church here in Moscow is a congregation within the visible church; we are a subset.
>
> If the invisible church includes the whole number of the elect, then it exists right now in the mind of God. I affirm this, as does Wilkins. If

* Comment number 61 here: greenbaggins.wordpress.com/2007/01/05/the-church-its-definition-in-terms-of-visible-and-invisible-valid.

you want it to exist right now in history, then you have to do something about the "whole number of the elect," which includes current atheists who will be converted tomorrow and saints yet unborn. In short, you cannot have the invisible church, as the WCF defines it, in history. You can have a invisible congregation of the invisible church, but how helpful is that? January 4, 2007 [end quote]

Back to Andy:

According to the WCF definition, says Doug Wilson, the invisible church is an abstraction which exists only in the mind of God. "A partial number of the elect is not the invisible church because it is not the whole number of them." To speak of anything less than "the whole number of the elect" as the invisible church is contrary to the WCF definition of the invisible church. Yet when the WCF defines the visible church as consisting of "all those throughout the world that profess the true religion," or when the LC says the visible church is "made up of all such as IN ALL AGES and places of the world do profess the true religion," Doug seems to have no problem allowing the visible church to exist in history, and to be subdivided. He seems to have no qualms about referring to Christ Church in Moscow (which I'm sure he will allow is not "all those throughout the world that profess the true religion"), as a partial expression of the visible church, without doing injury to Westminster's definition of "visible church."

My point is that the "visible church" according to the WCF definition is no less an abstraction than is the "invisible church." If Doug is going to be consistent he will have to limit himself to talking only about "particular churches," like Christ Church in Moscow.

But if he takes that logical step, then he should be careful not to talk about the members of his "particular church" enjoying "union

> and communion" with Christ, because, according to LC 65, "union and communion" with Christ is reserved to those who are members of the invisible church, an entity which doesn't exist in history according to Doug's reading of Westminster. It would follow then that "union and communion" with Christ is occurring only in the mind of God, where also the invisible church actually exists. LC 82 and 83 speak of the "communion in glory which members of the invisible church have with Christ," IN THIS LIFE. So by Doug's reading of Westminster, we would have members of the invisible church, a thing which doesn't exist in history, somehow enjoying communion with Christ "in this life."

And now, back to me:

To review some of the essential issues here, let me just assert a couple things at the outset. I could cite numerous places where I have said these things in my published writing on this subject, but I have done this enough now that I think the average reader will just let me say them again.

1. I agree with the *substance* of visible/invisible distinction. That is, I agree that there is a "whole number of the elect" and that the word Church is an appropriate way to speak of these people. I agree that there are professors of the true religion, together with their children, not necessarily elect, scattered throughout all ages, who also should be called by the name Church.

2. In agreeing with the *doctrine* set forth in the Westminster Confession, I have said that the terms visible/invisible are susceptible to misunderstanding at the popular level, and that I believe the terms historical/eschatological captures the same substantive meaning and are not susceptible to the same misunderstandings. That is my point. Okay so far?

Now, having said this, I agree with Andy's point about the definition of the visible church in the Westminster Confession. It is an abstraction. But this does not hurt my point at all—it *reinforces* it. If my point is that the language of visible church and invisible church is clunky, how does it undermine my point to show another area where it clunks?

Andy said this, "My point is that the 'visible church' according to the WCF definition is no less an abstraction than is the 'invisible church.'" But Andy, Lane . . . *anybody*! Doesn't this reveal that according to this definition the visible church is just as invisible as the invisible church is? When we use a descriptive adjective like *visible*, it naturally raises the questions, "Visible to whom? From what vantage? When is it visible? Who can see it?" If the answer is that only God can see the visible church, and this is what we have set up by definition, wouldn't it be good to find a phrase that points *to the same group of people*, but does not mislead in this way? To define it in a way that combines the limited perspective of human eyes, but then extend it way past the point where human eyes can take it in, is, it seems to me, clunky. I say this while agreeing that the elect deserve the name of the true Church, the ultimate Church, the real Church . . . dare I say it? the eschatological Church. I say this while agreeing that there are people who do not have a connection to this ultimate Church, but who have professed the true religion and are attached to the Church in time and in history. Let's call them the historical church.

It seems to me the problem should be obvious. We could illustrate this problem, if we wanted, by speaking of the audible church and the inaudible church. Only God hears the inaudible and genuine cry of the heart, and hypocrites can join themselves to the church, and offer up their lengthy (and very audible) prayers. We are not accustomed to this kind of language, and we have to think about it. Isn't it obvious that it creates the problem of vantage point? Audible to whom? When?

Now if someone wants to work with the terms visible/invisible church distinction, and bring it down into history by means of stipulated definitions, *that is absolutely fine with me.* On these issues, I am not trying to grab anybody where the pants hang loose and frog-march them out of the Reformed faith. What I am saying is that these stipulated applications of the Westminster definitions have to be carefully applied because the application is not nearly as easy as it looks. If the confessional definition of invisible church is "the whole number of the elect" and you bring it down to April 7, 2007, are you staying with the *elect*, or are you shifting to the *regenerate*? This is not a simple move, and missteps are common.

That said, I agree with Andy that the visible church in 2007 is a subset of the visible church as Westminster defines it. But I would prefer to use words to describe this that won't collapse when we put pressure on them. If I say the historical church in 2007 is a subset of the historical church generally, I don't have to change definitions of *historical* in mid-discussion. It means the same thing throughout. But the visible church in 2007 is a subset of the visible church throughout all ages, *which is invisible to everyone except God.* The visible church now is the visible part of the invisible visible church, because most of the visible church doesn't exist to be visible yet. But when I say *historical church*, it does not create these questions and situations, and, brethren, *please believe me*, I am referring to the same people. I just believe it is a more effective way to make the same distinction, and it is not subject to the same objections.

ADVANCED STAGES OF ENDUSTMENT
APRIL 10, 2007

I don't have a lot to say about the next chapter of *By Faith Alone*, other than that I enjoyed it. It was written by C. Fitzsimmons Allison, who also wrote a very good book that I also enjoyed entitled *The Cruelty of Heresy*. Allison is the retired Episcopal bishop of South Carolina, and so he knows a good deal about heresy—having studied it up close and in its native habitat. Kind of like those guys who live with wolves in National Geographic specials.

Part of the reason I enjoyed it is that it didn't really have anything to do with the current dust-up through which we are all in advanced stages of endustment. Allison proves that the historic standards of the Anglican church are entirely unambiguous on the question of justification, despite a great deal of learned and ecumenical mumbling to the contrary these days. And he also does a good job showing that "ancient pastoral wisdom and contemporary depth psychology testify to the reality that many intractable patterns and compulsions are symptoms of unconscious roots" (p. 105).

This in turn creates a real problem with Romanist definitions of mortal sin—because bringing the root issues out into the open where a pastor can help a parishioner is to jeopardize that parishioner's immortal soul by making that sin realized and conscious. Anyway, I refer you to that discussion, which was interesting.

But the only way this chapter contributes anything to the Federal Vision controversy is by means of a hidden premise. That hidden premise (hitherto unproven, unestablished, but *not* unasserted) is that FV guys deny justification by faith alone. If *that* is assumed, then historical discussions of *other* bad guys who did the same thing become relevant. But of course, if we affirm *sola fide*, as we *do*, then the hidden premise has disappeared, leaving us with less of an enthymeme and more of a gap in the argument. But you can't have everything.

One thing that Allison commented on made me think of a separate principle that needs to be mentioned, and so I might as well do it here. This is not really an interaction with Allison's point, but he provides me with a good excuse to talk about it.

> Bishop N.T. Wright, another who wishes to give up on imputation, was interviewed in *The Christian Century* and stated that his studies had undermined his earlier views, and that 'the big question about justification for Paul was not, 'How do I find a gracious God?' but 'How do Jews and Gentiles who believe in Christ share table fellowship?.' (p. 109)

One of the things that I have found exasperating in this whole debate is the practice of setting up dichotomies that are not really dichotomies. One of the points I made in *Angels in the Architecture* is that the medieval mind had a harmonizing tendency. This can obviously be overdone, and they overdid it, but there are times when you wish for that harmonizing spirit. For example, when I look at the statement above from Wright, the first thing I want to do is see them together. Why on earth would we have to choose?

Consider the two questions: How do I find a gracious God? How do Jews and Gentiles who believe in Christ share table fellowship? The answer to the second is the answer to the first. The way Jews and Gentiles share table fellowship *is by finding a gracious God*. In fact, the first is included in the second. We can rephrase the second question this way: How do Jews and Gentiles who have found a gracious God share table fellowship? The answer is contained in the statement, and the two are intertwined. Unless we hear the gospel message of how to find a gracious God, we will have no interest whatever in finding gracious table fellowship with anybody else. In short, they are not detached questions, any more than the two great commandments——love God and love your neighbor——are detached commandments.

AND THE WINNER IS . . .
APRIL 10, 2007

You should recall that some time ago, I invited contributions to a Federal Vision haiku contest. Rather than apologize for my tardiness in announcing the winners, let me just say that we all know that *time* is one of the tests of a classic.

First prize is 15 clams off any purchase at Canon Press, which goes to Chris Witmer for the following two submissions. Second prize is ten dollars off at the same establishment and goes to Joost Nixon. Honorable mention isn't worth anything substantive, which is good, because that one goes to Nate Wilson's entry.

Chris Witmer

You don't resemble
My caricature of you
Because you're lying.

SJC judgment
The sound of two hands clapping
Unanimously

Joost Nixon

RC is aging
who will assume his mantle?
Bombasticity

Nate Wilson

Cherry blossom spins
dropping charges, elusive,
brave debate partner

GERONIMO!
APRIL 11, 2007

The next chapter, "Reflections on Auburn Theology," is by T. David Gordon, and I would like to return a compliment in the same words he uses. My father used to quote this poem when I was a kid, and Gordon applies it to us. I, not surprisingly, think that it is more apropos when swiveled around and pointed the other way. "It is like the girl who had a curl right in the middle of her forehead: When it was good she was very very good, and when she was bad she was horrid" (p. 114). But in the version I learned, it was the little girl, not the curl, who was good or otherwise.

Anyhow, Gordon has more polemical voltage directed at the FV than many of the others, but he contextualizes it in a way that I really appreciated. This is one of the places where he was very good. He attacks the FV through the theologian he considers to be the grandfather of the movement, John Murray. And he has some strong things to say about Murray, about which there will be more shortly. But when it comes to "actions that must be performed," Gordon is positively judicious.

> Rather, I would like to indicate that I think his view ought to be given due and serious consideration because of Murray's stature within the Reformed tradition, and because of his otherwise orthodox views on most matters . . . I think we should discuss his views for a few generations. (pp. 120–121)

> I also think we should always be open-minded about our tradition, and when an individual of Murray's ability and stature suggests a recasting of our tradition, we should consider that challenge seriously for at least a generation or two. (p. 121)

And then, a few pages later, talking about the FV, he says this, and I think it is probably the most significant contribution coming from this book.

> Again, I do not wish us to remove advocates of Murray's view from Reformed church courts; in this I deliberately distinguish myself from those who views are identical to mine, but who feel the Murrayans must go. But I do wish us to be candid about his own candid disagreement with the historic covenant theology, and I wish us to stop regarding Professor Murray's recasting of covenant theology as we do the drunk uncle, as something we cannot discuss openly. And further, I'd like to retain the right, after a generation or two of discussion, to remove Murrayism if we discover that his views are genuinely fatal to consistent federalism. (p. 123)

We need a lot more of this demeanor. I believe that Gordon gets some things really wrong, but he is not doing it in a lynch mob. And it is because of this that his polemical voltage is appreciated, at least by me. I can answer it, perhaps in kind, but neither of us is getting ready to slap the horse's rear.

Consistent with this judicious temperament, Gordon objects to the role of the Internet in advancing these discussions at breakneck speed (p. 124, 125). We can take his point without necessarily seeing the history of the dispute the way he does. He says "the Auburn men must accept responsibility for the controversy that has ensued" (p. 125). This overlooks the little matter of a "may God have mercy on their souls" judicial statement by the RPCUS, unimpeded by any discussion with the men concerned, which was then heaved by John Robbins, via the Internet, into the middle of the Reformed world, in much the same manner that a couple twelve-year-old boys might heave a dead cat over the fence into the middle of a ladies afternoon luncheon. Nevertheless, however he applies it, he is right that *abuse* of the Internet has played a role in this.

I want to spend a little bit of time on a short list of claims that Gordon makes, and then lay me down and rest a while.

> Generally, those who think they are working within a new paradigm have a tendency to dismiss counterarguments without engaging them or refuting them. (pp. 114–115)

Okay, where do I go to start engaging? I am resolved to do better on this. Maybe we could set up a debate or something.

Gordon says that we insist on using biblical language only (p. 115), and then points out that our widespread use of the phrase *the covenant* violates this rule. The Bible speaks of covenants in the plural (p. 116). The problem is that we do not object to historic terminology, or systematic terminology. We do not insist on using biblical language *only*. We are fine with theological language. We object, however, to the language of systematics when it disallows the use of biblical language at *any* time. We are not strict biblicists; we don't believe that we have to talk in biblical language all the time. But, and here is the rub, can we speak in biblical language *some* of the time?

Gordon quotes Cal Beisner's observation of our "anachronism of perceiving the fifteenth or sixteenth centuries as influenced by the Enlightenment" (p. 116). That would be anachronism aplenty, were it true. But there is a stark difference between maintaining, as we do not, that the Enlightenment influenced the writing of the Westminster Confession, and maintaining, as we do, that Cal Beisner's reading of the Westminster Confession is influenced by the Enlightenment. The former is silly. The latter is self-evident.

> Calvin Beisner has additionally (if pointedly) criticized the Auburn objection to logic or careful definitions. (p. 116)

Right. This is why I am the co-author of a logic textbook? This is why I sit on the board of Logos School, which teaches a year of formal logic to our eighth graders? This is why I am working with the Association of Classical and Christian Schools, which requires all member schools to follow the curriculum of the Trivium—grammar, dialectic (*logic*), and rhetoric? And, to seal the point, I wish that Cal would *carefully define* what it means to object to logic.

Gordon believes that Murray jettisoned the wrong things from covenant theology, and one of the innovations that he accused Murray of is the idea that all covenantal relations are gracious (p. 119). This is just breathtaking. The idea that all God's covenantal relations are fundamentally gracious is, in the Reformed landscape, as old as the Reformed hills.

In an interaction with an unobjectionable comment by Rich Lusk, Gordon says something remarkable. Rich said, "the Mosaic law was simply the Gospel in pre-Christian form" (p. 119). To this Gordon responds by saying it is analogous to saying "early 1944 Hiroshima was simply a Japanese city in pre-nuclear form." This is funny, but those who live by the analogy die by the analogy. For the bombardier apostle Paul, when he was about to drop the big one, was asked by a comrade, "Do we then destroy the pre-nuclear Japanese city?" replied, "Nay, but we uphold the pre-nuclear Japanese city. Geronimo!"

Just one more. He attacks John Murray's monocovenantalism with an appeal to Galatians 3 and 4. But please note. In responding to Gordon here, I do *not* share Murray's view that there was no covenant with Adam in the garden.

> Paul contrasts the Abrahamic and Sinai covenants and illustrates them at the end with the figure of Sarah and Hagar, saying, "These are two covenants." (p. 120)

They are two covenants all right, but which two? There is the Abrahamic and the Sinaitic, clearly, but what was the form of the covenant from Sinai here? Was it the covenant at Sinai as God actually made it, or was it the covenant of Sinai as construed by those *who desired to be under the law* (Gal. 4:21)? The Judaizers, by their self-righteousness, transformed an historic manifestation of the covenant of grace into a contemporary covenant of works. This is why they were condemned. Elswhere, Gordon tells us his rule of thumb for identifying Auburnites——anyone who speaks generally of "the covenant" (p. 116). The problem is that this would include the Westminster Confession, which plainly identifies the Sinaitic covenant as a manifestation of the covenant of grace. So, my questions at this point for Gordon would be these: did the Westminster theologians misread Galatians 3 and 4? Do you take an exception to the Westminster Confession when they identify the Sinaitic covenant as an outworking of the covenant of grace?

Be all that as it may, in conclusion, let me say that this chapter was a good one in the context of this controversy. Gordon displayed a real judiciousness, mentioned earlier, and even where he got a bunch of things wrong, he was actually seeking to interact with FV stuff, and was not content with the kind of oblique critiques employed in the other chapters. If we have a couple generations, this kind of interaction could make real headway.

PICKING UP FEATHERS
APRIL 14, 2007

Gene Veith comments on Worldmagblog here*. A friend drew my attention to this post of a few days ago. I have included below a comment which I posted at his site, but I also need to say something here. Given the climate in the Reformed world today, and given how many people go to Worldmagblog, it is not possible to set the record straight completely. But something is better than nothing, and maybe the people who are feeding Gene bogus information will eventually regain some sense of shame. I wish that everyone who is so hot for Westminster would carefully review what the Larger Catechism says about the ninth commandment.

Here is my comment from his blog:

> Well, it appears that the damage is already done, but I might as well say something for the record. I hold to the idea of penal substitution as being at the heart of the gospel, I subscribe to the Westminster

* cranach.worldmagblog.com/cranach/archives/2007/04/the_gospel_with.html, no longer available.

Confession and its views on the atonement, I drafted the NSA statement of faith which includes a statement which I will include below, and I helped to name the building where our church offices are housed—Anselm House.

"Because all sons of Adam are spiritually dead, they are consequently incapable of saving themselves. But out of His sovereign mercy, God the Father elected a countless number to eternal salvation, leaving the remainder to their sinful desires. When the time was right, the Lord Jesus Christ died on the cross and was raised to life as an efficacious redemption for the elect. Thus He secured the salvation of His church, for which He laid down His life. And at the point of each individual's conversion, the Holy Spirit brings resurrecting grace, effectually calling him by His power, with the result of repentance and faith."

It is a grief to me that Christians can be so careless about the reputations of others. It is not appropriate to walk up to the top of a hill and empty a feather pillow into a brisk wind. With the feathers all over everywhere, it is not adequate to anticipate problems with, "Someone correct me if I am wrong." Okay, now I am doing that a few days later, when I first heard of it. Who are we going to ask to pick up the feathers?

CELL BLOCK E
APRIL 14, 2007

I do have a couple of things to say about David VanDrunen's contribution to *By Faith Alone.* First, he is guilty of continued misrepresentation of those he is debating with.

> Although recent criticism of the traditional Reformed doctrine of justification has taken many forms, nearly all critics seem to concur in dismissing the idea of active obedience. This is true of figures associated with the New Perspective on Paul and the Federal Vision. (p. 127)

Second, when he gets into particulars, he interacts with Rich Lusk and Jim Jordan in such a way as to reveal that he does not really understand the ground of their objections. For example, when he quotes Jim Jordan, he selects a quote that affirms double imputation and rejects the idea of merit (p. 132). The issue is not imputation; *the issue is merit.* And you cannot prove that the merits of Christ's obedience are imputed to us by proving that all of Christ's life and death and life again are reckoned to His people. I affirm the latter, and deny the former. Those who want to argue that those who deny the former must of necessity deny the latter need to do something more than assume it to be true. Something like that needs to be *shown.* I maintain that it is possible to hold to the doctrine of imputed obedience (both active and passive) while rejecting the idea of accumulating merit.

Third, I would like to raise the question of the relationship between imputation and union with Christ. This is not a particular point in VanDrunen's chapter; what he was writing just made me think of it. Does God impute the righteousness of Jesus Christ to us as a consequence of uniting us to Christ, or does He unite us to Christ as a consequence of imputing the righteousness of Jesus Christ to us? Or a third option like *neither*—both happening together?

And last, I would like to comment on a typical misunderstanding of the relationship of the new covenant to the law of Moses. Speaking of Galatians, VanDrunen says this:

> In context, the yoke of bondage clearly in mind here is life under the Mosaic law. Remarkably, Paul has just associated life under the Mosaic Law with life under paganism, referring to them by similar terms (4:3 and 4:8–9). (p. 138)

At best, this is confusing. It makes sense to say that Israel corporately in the time of the first century was in this condition, and it makes sense to say that Caiphas was. But Zecharias and Elizabeth? Mary and Joseph? David and Jonathan? Isaiah and Jeremiah? Indistinguishible from pagans?

And it makes sense to say that if any of the Galatians *returned* to this old Judaism, they would find it impossible to be an Isaiah, or David, or Mary. That time had passed, and to return to it was indistinguishable from paganism——that was what was behind Paul's equation of circumcision to pagan self-mutilation. This is what the Galatian temptation was, and this is what Paul was writing about. But we also have to take into account (*full* account) the fact that Hebrews 11 is filled with a list of names who lived by faith, and who therefore lived in the liberty of faith. God did not deliver Israel out of the bondage of Egypt into a different kind of bondage. The Exodus was not a transfer from Cell Block D to Cell Block E.

WHY NOT NOW?
APRIL 15, 2007

The next chapter in *By Faith Alone* is entitled "Covenant, Inheritance, and Typology," and is co-authored by R. Fowler White and Cal Beisner. Their argument is ingenious, intricate, and, I believe, entirely unsatisfactory. What they are seeking to do is understand the covenant of redemption, the covenant of works, and the covenant of grace in their archetypal, typical, and antitypical relations. The end result is very complicated, but some of their basic assumptions are easy to identify and answer. And because this is an architectonic project, when those foundational assumptions are addressed, the larger argument is addressed also.

The first is that they insist that grace must be defined as *de*merited favor. This, in contrast to the preferred understanding in FV circles, where grace is understood as *un*merited favor. White and Beisner say this:

> The term grace presupposes the state of sin and demerit brought about by the fall . . . Grace is favor in the presence of demerit of negative desert, that is, in the presence of the transgression of righteous requirements. Thus, to teach that the Adamic covenant did not differ in substance or principle from the covenant of grace is to compromise the Scriptural doctrine of grace. (p. 164)

There are a couple responses to this that are necessary. The first is that the scriptural doctrine of grace would have to include scriptural uses of the word grace (*charis*), would it not? "And the child [Jesus] grew, and waxed strong in spirit, filled with wisdom, *and the grace of God was upon him*" (Luke 2:40). This does not eliminate the legitimate possibility of using the word *grace* in certain theological circles to refer to demerited favor only. Fine. But surely it should be recognized by those doing this that *other* theological circles might have reasonable scriptural grounds for seeing it as unearned or unmerited favor? Without being told that they are compromising the scriptural doctrine of grace because they give it the same lexical range that Luke did?

The second is that White and Beisner need to acknowledge here (which they do not) that the idea that God's graciousness was foundational to the covenant with Adam in the garden is a common, historic view among the Reformed. Since they are writing to defend the Reformed faith against "redefinition" (p. 147), it would seem particularly important for them to note that their insistence on raw merit as a settled consensus among the Reformed is itself a fine example of redefinition. *Numerous* Reformed theologians, from the Reformation down to the present, have seen God's covenantal dealings with Adam as essentially gracious. It would be tedious to list them all, but I can if I need to.

Next, White and Beisner argue this:

> The Mosaic covenant was a republication of the covenant of works modified to be compatible with the covenant of grace. Specifically, the covenant of works was modified in the Mosaic covenant by limiting the application of the principle of personal merit to the retention (vis-a-vis reception) of earthly and temporal (i.e., typological) blessings by Israel and their king. (p. 167)

This is actually a strange amalgam of covenant theology and dispensationalism. In dispensationalism, the Jews are God's earthly people, and the Church is made up of God's heavenly people. White and Beisner have a more layered and nuanced view, and to do this they argue that the Mosaic covenant (as type) is part of the covenant of grace, but also that it was a recapitulation (as antitype) of the broken covenant with Adam in the garden.

But to see the move from old covenant to new as a move from earth to heaven is problematic on a number of levels. At the same time, there are many issues and as many texts to work through. Whatever it is, the relationship between Israel and the Church is not a *simple* one. The pull of dispensationalism is powerful for a reason. In my view, the Lutheran take on this is similar to the dispensational one, and again, this is not intended as a slam. There are reasons for it. White and Beisner want to see limited earthly blessings in the Old Testament, apportioned on a principle of works. But they want all matters of *salvation*, however, in both Old and New Testaments, to be by faith alone. This desire to maintain the perimeter around our enclave of all salvific grace motivates Lutherans and dispensationalists as well. Whether it is seen as special pleading, or as what happens when you are painted into a theological corner, it is still understandable. Given that the subject is difficult enough, it is unfortunate that White and Beisner ramp up the stakes in their conclusion, by saying that their opponents hold to "no gospel at all" (p. 170). Now, how can that be helpful?

I do not see works as the principle whereby Jews maintained their earthly privileges. I see salvation (in the heavenly sense) as being appropriated by evangelical faith alone, plus nothing. At the same time, I also see a faithful Jew appropriating earthly blessings by that same kind of evangelical faith alone, plus nothing. Without living and real faith, God hates everything we do. The first commandment with a promise was given to the Jews at Sinai, that it might go well with them in the land the Lord their God was giving them. Earthly blessing, right? But Paul takes that same promise and applies it to a bunch of Gentile kids in Ephesus. How were they to appropriate the promise, that it might go well with them in the earth? In chapter six of Ephesians they were called upon to remember chapter two of Ephesians. They were to appropriate this blessing the same way the Jews in the Older Testament were to appropriate all their blessings—by grace through faith, lest anyone should boast.

How am I put right with God? By grace through faith. How do I earn money to feed my family? By grace through faith. How do I keep the weeds down on my three acres? By grace through faith. How do I see answered prayers? By grace through faith. There is nothing whatever that any obedient creature can ever do, in this world or in any other, in this generation or any other, in this covenant or any other, that is not done by efficacious grace appropriated by living faith. Ever. Period. For this doctrine of mine, I am sometimes accused of trying to undermine the doctrine of *sola fide*, which I don't quite understand either.

And last, to see the covenant with Adam as essentially gracious does not require us to then say that the Adamic covenant does "not differ in substance or principle from the covenant of grace." This is a *non sequitur*. The latter does not follow from the former. Let me pick on my colleague Doug Jones, who is a swell guy. If, in his swell-guyness, he offers a book contract to someone who sends in a manuscript to Canon Press, and also, equally in his swell-guyness, he resolves a dispute with a neighbor over that neighbor's dog barking endlessly at midnight, it does not follow from this that the manuscipt was written by the guy with the barking dog. God's graciousness to His creatures is a given. This does not drive or predetermine the stipulated requirements of any covenant He might make with those creatures. It does not require that all His covenants must amount to the same covenant. It just means that any of the covenants He makes must be consistent with that gracious character.

In this chapter, White and Beisner argue that the covenant of redemption (as they explain it, between Father, Son, and Spirit) is archetypal of the covenant of works between God and Adam.

> This covenant of redemption, being pre-creational, preceded and was archetypal of the covenant of works between God and Adam. (p. 150)

This (broken) covenant of works was then a type of the coming (unbroken) covenant of grace. This is the pattern they are following: archetype, type, antitype. The way they are arguing here is almost a mirror image of the way Ralph Smith argues in his book *The Eternal Covenant*. The ultimate reality (for both sides) is the intra-Trinitarian covenant before all worlds. But Smith sees that relation as being one of covenantal *love*. White and Beisner see it in terms of strict covenantal *merit*.

> The Father and the Son being equally God, it is proper to posit strict merit between them, and that is the case in the covenant of redemption . . . The similarity between the two is that God (in the covenant of redemption, the Father toward the Son; in the covenant of works, the Trinity toward Adam) binds himself by his justice to reward a certain performance. (p. 150)

There is no way to argue this point without making it personal, but I do not intend it to be personal here in any kind of *ad hom* sense. I take it as a fixed biblical reality that you become more and more like the God you worship. Idolaters become like the idols they worship (Ps. 115), and Christians who behold the glory of God in the face of Christ become more and more like Him. We are being transformed from one degree of glory to another. When we finally see Him, we will become like Him because we are going to see Him as He is. Now the good news is that *all* of us—White, Beisner, Clark, Waters, Lusk, Leithart, and even me—are worshipping the same God. When we've been there ten thousand years, bright shining as the sun, we've no less days to laugh about this particular tangle we've gotten ourselves into. We will also laugh about how much better Heaven is than Ft. Lauderdale.

At the same time, our conceptions of God still matter now. For example, many Arminians know and love the Lord, but their doctrinal formulations of what He is like still affects what they do here and now. If a doctrine is false, then true Christians can find themselves pursuing false ideals of sanctification in the name of the true God. All this to say, the idea of strict book-keeping transactions of merit at the ultimate level between the persons of the Trinity is an idea that is sure to affect how we deal with one another down here, and not positively. Ironically, the template of raw justice being applied by some to fellow ministers in the Reformed faith has led to a great deal of raw injustice.

And lest this point be seen as a self-serving observation, let me apply it this way. Let me urge all my brothers on the FV side of things to layer grace upon grace in our dealings with those who allege we are denying, undermining and attacking the gospel that we would actually die for. Well, if that is the case, here's the opportunity. Let's die for it now.

I KNOW MY BAPTISTS
APRIL 16, 2007

Well, I am done with *By Faith Alone*—done with the book, that is, not the doctrine. I want to deal with the last three entries in one post all together because I don't really have a great deal to say about each one.

John Bolt, a professor of systematic theology at Calvin Theological Seminary, defends the covenant of works as a necessary doctrine. The vast majority of the article was just fine, a perfectly orthodox piece of academic writing. In the chapter, he interacts with Anthony Hoekema and John Stek, two men for whom he has a great deal of respect. He also deals with some of John Murray's views, and he does this with a great deal of respect also. All of these men reject the phrase *covenant of works* in various ways, and Bolt is unpersuaded by them—and in this chapter he indicates his "own reasons for rejecting the challenge" (p. 172).

I really only have two objections here, and they are closely related. The first is that in a footnote he says this:

> While considerations of space and potential accessibility to their works by readers, along with my personal relationship with and respect for my teachers, led me to focus on Hoekema and Stek, their challenges, thankfully, are also free from the various tendentious theological agendas characterizing much of the contemporary discussion about covenant of works. (p. 172)

Tendentious means partisan or controversial. Since those who are guilty of such an attitude are left unnamed, we can only guess at their nefarious identity. But, given the theme of this book, I think we could *probably* guess right. But this is the oddity. In the previous chapter (also on the covenant of works), the concluding words warned us that to misstep on this subject lands us in another gospel entirely (p. 170). This is clearly bad in chapter seven, but here in chapter eight, it is okay to mess around with these ancient landmarks, so long as you do it in an academic manner and are not tendentious. So, if you are going to deny the gospel, be sure to be sweet about it.

The second question is this: Bolt teaches at Calvin Theological Seminary and he doesn't have other fish to fry? Now I don't have any problem with sound conservative men going into questionable places and fighting the good fight there. *Go, fight, win* is my take on all such valor. But I do wonder about men who go off to live in the Louisiana swamps to fight alligators and whose published articles are directed against Montana mosquitos.

The last chapter in this book was by Gary Johnson, one of the editors of this volume. And it may surprise you to learn that I thought this chapter was *fantastic*. My only complaint would be that the editors included it in the wrong book. The chapter title was "The Reformation, Today's Evangelicals, and Mormons." The chapter was directed at the current gooey definitions of *evangelical* in today's theological climate, and how it has led (in the fevered imaginations of some) to the inclusion of Mormons among the ranks of evangelicals. My sentiments in response are summed up by *ptooey*, which pretty much encompasses Johnson's conclusions also. Johnson's problem here was the reverse of Bolt's. By its placement in this book I was expecting a fight with the Montana mosquitos, but he wound up killing and skinning several gators. Well, okay. I am all for that. But what is it doing in *this* book? This is the mosquito book, not the gator book.

The only substantive criticism I would offer is that on the last page of the chapter, Johnson included Wesley in a list of "our evangelical forefathers" (p. 204). But you can't have everything. Even though he was probably referring to the historical development of evangelicalism, and not to the semi-Pelagianism as such, *still*. But maybe I am just a little jumpy. At the same time, if I were the editor of a volume on the deterioration of confessional evangelicalism, and if Johnson were to submit this chapter for consideration, I would be happy to include it. Good stuff.

The Afterword was written by Albert Mohler, and I am just sorry about it. He takes the contributions of the writers of this book at face value, and says that FV represents "a repudiation of the tradition received from the Reformers" (p. 205).

> The Federal Vision is gaining influence among Reformed evangelicals who should be *least* likely to move in the direction of Trent rather than Geneva and Wittenberg. (p. 207)

There is not really any pleasant way to respond to this, so let me just preface it this way. I think Al Mohler is a great man, and I believe he has done wonderful things for the church today. I really like him, and I like the way he goes about his business. I thank God for him.

That said, let me present my credentials for what I am about to say. I was brought up in a Southern Baptist church. I was baptized in a Christmas Eve service as a ten-year-old at my home church, College Avenue Baptist in Annapolis, Maryland. I was surrounded throughout my childhood and most of my adult life by conscientious and *godly* Baptists. I was steeped in the baptistic worldview, and it wasn't a dopey or hypocritical version of it either. Some of the people I still respect most in this world are Baptists. And despite great initial reluctance on my part, I became a paedobaptist around the age of forty. I am fifty-four now. All this to say, I know my Baptists.

The dominant form of Christian faith in North America is baptistic. The thought-forms are baptistic. The cultural expectations are baptistic. And the influence on paedobaptist denominations *has been baptistic.* A large number of Presbyterians do not have infant baptisms anymore so much as they have wet dedications. So when someone like Mohler encounters a paedobaptist who has *not* been domesticated by the prevailing set of expectations for all evangelicals, his natural reaction is to think of someone who is Trent-ward bound. As I once said in another setting, I set out for Geneva (and have been settling in here for almost twenty years now), but a bunch of my American friends think that I moved to Rome. They can't tell the difference between Rome and Geneva because both of them are across a lot of water and are *way* east of Kentucky.

Mohler is further excused because a lot of the people telling him that FV is bad whiskey are confessional Presbyterians. Why should we expect him to sort out this paedobaptist squabble, and why would we expect him to side with the group farther away from his own baptistic convictions? I sure don't. But we do need to notice how odd this is. Now I don't want to say that these Presbyterians attacking us have apostatized—not a bit of it. But they *have* baptisticized. This can be easily shown—for the contributors to this volume, the differences they have with a Baptist like Mohler are *minor*. Who did they ask to write the Afterword? I can think of a multitude of subjects that I would ask Al Mohler to contribute a summary statement for . . . but this subject is not one of them.

REFORMED OR "REFORMED"?
APRIL 21, 2007

Green Baggins[*] is a website critical of the FV. While some of the standard issue misunderstandings are on display there, and the language of *heresy* is unfortunately employed too quickly for my taste, nevertheless there is an obvious personal and theological integrity, displayed in a willingness to correct things once they have been worked through.

Lane (the man behind Green Baggins) has begun a series of posts on *"Reformed" Is Not Enough*[†], and I will try to keep a discussion going as he does so. I would like to keep this more like a discussion than a debate, and maybe we can all learn something.

He doesn't like the title of my book, even when the scare quotes around "Reformed" are noted. And he caught a typo in the book—an instance where the scare quotes were omitted, which they certainly should not have been. Let me

* greenbaggins.wordpress.com

† Currently available at canonpress.com/products/reformed-is-not-enough.

first make a comment on what the title was *intended* to mean, and then a statement on the context of its use. The title means that it is not enough to *call* yourself Reformed; for those in our confessional tradition, it is necessary to actually *be* Reformed. Now a central part of the FV critique of the broader Reformed world is that we have accommodated ourselves too much with the American baptistic tradition, and this has affected how we read our confessional standards (which do not represent such an accommodation). For example, a number of our critics think they have put distance between themselves and the baptists (as they have, some) by saying that the sacraments are means of grace. But they hasten to add that this is always *sanctifying* grace. The language of salvation is inappropriate here. The problem with this is that the Westminster Catechisms both ask how is it that the two sacraments are effectual means of salvation. And so, I say in this title that you are not necessarily in the confessional tradition just because you call yourself "Reformed." That is what it meant.

Was it a provocative title? Well, I don't think you could call it provocative, but it *was* combative. I reject the charge of provocation because it was not an attempt on our part to start anything—the controversy was already in full swing. *And remember how all this started.* We had a pastors conference, of the ordinary kind, and we had absolutely no idea of starting anything. It was just the theme of that conference that year. About six months later, we were blindsided by the pronouncement of the RPCUS, and it was a jumbled theological hash of a pronouncement too. But one thing was clear—the bottom line was a "may God have mercy on their souls" kind of dismissal. John Robbins then assiduously made sure that the news was spread all over Reformed tarnation. We were in the middle of a firestorm created by some ignorant and envious men, and so, yeah, the title of my book was a challenge. I had just been consigned to hell for affirming a bunch of things I actually don't affirm, by men who had never talked to me about it, and I knew for a fact that John Calvin's twin brother would be run out of Joe Morecraft's church for sacerdotalism. This was all being done in the name of being *Reformed*, and so I answered the "Reformed."

At the same time, the issue was not their doctrine. It was their narrow sectarianism. I know that the "TR" *position* has been an honorable part of the

Reformed faith from the beginning, and I have no difficulty in fellowshipping with such men, up to and including baptists. From our side, these are not heresy issues at all. But men who think that their little blinkered corner of Toad Flatts, Alabama represents the variegated richness of the Reformed faith need to drive to the nearest big city and check a book out of the library.

So then, the strict TR position is not "Reformed." The position of the sacramental Calvinists is not "Reformed." The Kuyperian position is not "Reformed." But any subset of of the historic Reformed world, *taking itself for the whole*, is "Reformed." The problem is not holding to certain convictions within the Reformed context. The problem is Reformed sectarianism, and when that happens, I call it "Reformed."

It looks as though, from the initial comments that Lane made, a good portion of this discussion will revolve around the question of sacramentalism, touched on above, so I will hold on that for the time being. The one thing I will say here is that my views on sacramental union in the Lord's Supper are basically the same as Calvin's (and as rejected by Dabney), and as articulated by Keith Mathison in *Given for You*[*].

JUDAS THE CHRISTIAN
APRIL 25, 2007

In his treatment of my chapter on whether or not Judas was a Christian, Green Baggins does a good job[†] catching the distinctions I was seeking to make. He hears my qualifications, and is willing to believe them.

He says that he has no real problem with the chapter and had just a few quibbles/questions. One of them had to do with the passage in Acts 26 where Agrippa says something obscure to Paul (as represented by all the different translations). Was he saying that Paul had almost made him a Christian, or that he was astonished at Paul's impudence in even thinking about it? I don't really have a dog in that translation fight (which is a fancy way of saying I don't know). What matters for my argument is that the word *Christian* is used by Agrippa, not by Paul.

* amazon.com/Given-You-Reclaiming-Calvins-Doctrine/dp/087552186X

† greenbaggins.wordpress.com/2007/04/22/judas-was-a-christian

This issue came up in the comments section of Lane's post, and it illustrates well the nature of this discussion. Even if my argument in this chapter fails (with regard to the use of the word *Christian*), we still do not have any distinctive New Testament use of the word *Christian* with regard to regeneration. For many modern evangelicals, the phrase *becoming a Christian* (in the effectual call sense) has sacramental status. You cannot mess with that phrase without getting in trouble—and that phrase is not required by any usage in the New Testament. I argued that all the uses in the New Testament were from a pagan perspective, or at least from the vantage of an outsider looking in. Even if that is not the case, there is nothing there that warrants a scriptural insistence that this is is what "becoming a Christian" means. In other words, I think our modern use of it is lawful and reasonable—but it is not exegetically self-evident.

The other question Lane raises is about the distinction of benefits. I have two definitions of *Christian* in this chapter—someone who is born again by the Spirit of God, and someone who is baptized in the triune name. Suppose we have someone who is a Christian in both senses, and the guy right next to him is a Christian in the latter sense only. Do I believe in a distinction of benefits between the two? Yes, I hold to a radical distinction of benefits. As Lane pointed out, I use the analogy of marriage often. Suppose two married men, one faithful and the other adulterous. Given the fact that marriage (generally) is a blessed estate, is there a distinction of benefits in what the two men receive from their marriages? Yes, there is a radical distinction of benefits. And any "benefit" that the adulterer believes himself to have with this arrangement will be a benefit that comes back later to haunt him in the judgment.

SOME STANDARD MISUNDERSTANDINGS
APRIL 29, 2007

I have been on the road, and have only now had the opportunity to read the recently released PCA report‡ on the Federal Vision. This is just an initial response; more will *probably* be forthcoming.

‡ Currently available here: pcahistory.org/pca/studies/FVreport_2007.pdf.

First, I appreciated the response of the Bayly brothers, which can be found here.* And, like Mark Horne, I greatly appreciated the fact that we were identified as brothers in Christ. In line with this, the timbre of the report was judicious, and it looked to me as though the committee members *did* labor to understand us. But I also agree with the observation that the committee was stacked with critics, and I believe that this resulted in some of the standard misunderstandings.

Here is a sample of a standard misunderstanding

> Moreover, to affirm the Standards, and then redefine the terms used in the Standards, is not to affirm the Standards. For example, to affirm the decretal view of election, and then to say that the Bible teaches that the elect may fall from their election, is to set the Bible over against the Standards.

Well, sure. But this is not the case if you do not redefine the terms, but rather suggest an additional stipulated use of the same term, while not denying the first stipulated. If I say that I believe in the Westminster Confession's red use of the world *election*, but that I also believe that the Bible in various places uses *election* in the blue sense, I am not maintaining that blue is red. This is not redefinition; it is an additional definition.

> The Committee would suggest that the FV proponents have in effect provided an alternative hermeneutic for interpreting Scripture. They have done so 1) by concentrating their efforts on the "objectivity" of the covenant, 2) by stressing the "covenantal" efficacy of baptism, 3) by focusing on the undifferentiated membership of the visible church, 4) by holding the view that the "elect" are covenant members who may one day fall from their elect status, and 5) by highlighting the need for persevering faithfulness in order to secure final election.

This reveals, again, some of the standard misunderstandings (and yes, I know, *another* misunderstanding is that FV advocates constantly complain

* baylyblog.com/2007/04/now_that_the_pc.html

about imaginary misunderstandings. Nothing imaginary about it.) First, these five things are not a hermeneutic we bring to Scripture. They are, to the extent that we hold them, doctrines we believe are derived from Scripture. My views on the efficacy of baptism, for example, are *not* a hermeneutic. But notice that I also said, "to the extent that we hold them." 1. We do emphasize the objectivity of the covenant, but not as a hermeneutic. 2. We do stress the covenantal efficacy of baptism, but again, not as a hermeneutic. 3. We do not believe in an undifferentiated membership of the visible church. For example, I believe the visible church can be differentiated into two categories, converted to God and unconverted to God—i.e., those headed for heaven and those headed for hell. 4. We believe that the covenantally elect (blue) can fall from their elect status; we deny that the decretally elect (red) can do so. 5. We deny that there is anything we can do to "secure" decretal election. This means that 3 out of the 5 representations here are just flat wrong, and the other two are fuzzed over with that hermeneutic business.

Here is a more striking example. The report says:

> Doug Wilson has implied that all baptized covenant members are participants in Christ in the same "strong sense," writing that "the person who did not persevere was not given less of Christ."

I read that and thought something like, "Huh, that doesn't sound like me." So I went to the footnote and found a thread on this blog cited, a thread called "Life in the Regeneration." Here is the section they footnoted.

> In order to take all baptized covenant members as participants in Christ in the "strong sense," we would have to distinguish what is objectively given in Christ, and not what is subjectively done with those objective benefits. Perseverance would, on this reading, be what was subjectively done with what God has objectively given. In this view, the person who did not persevere was not given less of Christ. But this necessarily means that persevering grace is not an objective gift or grace. God's

> willingness to continue "the wrestling" would depend upon what kind of fight we put up, or cooperation we provide, and because no one's fundamental nature has been changed, those natures remain at "enmity with God." In this view, whatever total depravity means, it is not ontologically changed, just knocked down and sat upon. The Spirit pins one snarling dog, but not another. But this in turn leads to another thought—eventually at some time in the process we stop snarling and start cooperating (if we are bound to heaven), and what do we call this change or transformation. The historic name for this change has been regeneration, and I see no reason to change it.

In this section, I am arguing *for* the traditional use of the word regeneration, I am arguing *against* a particular view ("on this reading," "in this view"), and the PCA report here represented me as arguing 180 degrees from what I was in fact arguing. This is upside down and backwards. If they read that entire thread of posts, they would know that I believe it is incoherent to say that anyone receives "all of Christ" in the strong sense without receiving perseverance. This was simply sloppy.

There will be more later, particularly on the nine declarations at the end of the report.

MAY 2007

A CLARIFICATION

MAY 1, 2007

Green Baggins has come* to the chapter of *RINE* where I seek to establish my Calvinistic bona fides. Some have interpreted the FV as though it were some form of Arminianism or semi-Pelagianism. So early in the book, I set aside a chapter to demonstrate that I wish that the Synod of Dort had promulgated a couple extra points so I could believe them too.

The review of this chapter is fair, with Green Baggins mostly wanting to have a few questions clarified. So here I go.

The first is whether I am a compatibilist when it comes to questions of free will. The answer is yes, if we are talking about creaturely choices, like whether to go left or right, or whether to pick this flavor or that one at the ice cream store. But when it comes to *moral* choices, I believe that unregenerate men are not free unless and until God creates that freedom in them by granting them a new heart.

Second, when I said that God ordained us making free choices, one of the commenters at Lane's blog was correct in assuming that I was referring to the teaching of the Westminster Confession at that point—that God's ordination is the foundation and establishment of our creaturely freedom, not the annihilation of it. But I want to keep categories distinct. Lane appealed to the "coercive" nature of Saul's conversion. And okay, I would agree that the new birth is "coercive" in the same way my first birth was. Nobody consulted me in 1951 about whether I wanted to be born in 1953. But we don't normally describe that kind of thing as coercive, but it *is* clearly monergistic. And I affirm that as well.

* greenbaggins.wordpress.com/2007/04/30/calvinistic-bona-fides

And last, Lane points to a place where I say that I am not denying the Reformed faith—the objectivity of the covenant is the Reformed faith. He is right to catch me here; this was an unfortunate overstatement. I have said in other places that there are those in the Reformed stream who do not emphasize the objectivity of the covenant, and yet should be recognized as Reformed (Reformed Baptists). I should have said that here. I do believe that this understanding is the best understanding of the Reformed faith (which is why I hold it), and that this part of the stream in which I am floating goes all the way back. But I did not mean to say that there were not disagreements over these issues all the way back.

ED VEITH AND ME
MAY 4, 2007

A week or two ago, you may recall we had some discussion here about a question Ed Veith had raised on his blog about my views on the penal nature of the substitutionary atonement. Well, he was doing some traveling, as was I, but we finally connected a couple days ago. We had a good chat on the phone, and Ed posted this* on his blog as a result. And since I had commented on the affair in this space, I wanted to publicly note that everything is square between us, and that I consider Ed to be a fine example of a godly Christian scholar and gentleman.

NO REAL DISAGREEMENT YET
MAY 4, 2007

Green Baggins is continuing his review of my book *"Reformed" Is Not Enough*, and he continues to do a fine job†. In his review of the next chapter where I seek to establish my evangelical *bona fides*, he basically has one question that he wants clarified, and it has to do with my views on the "detectability" of regeneration.

* cranach.worldmagblog.com/cranach/archives/2007/05/doug_wilson_and.html, no longer available.

† greenbaggins.wordpress.com/2007/05/01/evangelical-bona-fides

If you believe, as I do, that baptized covenant members can be either converted or unconverted, this sets up a very practical problem for pastors. If our task is, as St. Paul put it, "warning every man, and teaching every man in all wisdom, that we may present every man perfect in Christ Jesus" (Col. 1:28), then this means that pastors have to know how to watch for warning signs that a baptized someone is headed in the opposite direction. That's what shepherds *do*.

I don't believe that any of us can *prove* the internal spiritual condition of other people with any kind of absolute certainty, and I have seen some pretty arrogant attempts. But at the same time, over the course of people's lives, we can have evidences of their spirtual condition. Jesus says that the nature of the tree determines the nature of the fruit, and so long as we are not running our spiritual evaluations of other people's hearts out to the tenth decimal point, I have no problem with prudent judgments in terms of those evidences. Paul says that the works of the flesh are *manifest*, and those who live that way won't inherit the kingdom of God. In a similar way, godly fruit is manifest over time as well.

My central problem with how many contemporary evangelicals handle this problem is not that they look for fruit to determine the nature of the tree. That is biblical enough. My problem is that the "fruit" that they look for is often radically unbiblical. "*He's* a Christian because he threw a pine cone in the fire on the last night of youth camp." "He's *not* a Christian because I saw him order a beer in a restaurant last week."

Lane wonders if he has come to our first substantive disagreement in this chapter. I do not believe that he has.

MORE FV CLARIFICATIONS
MAY 9, 2007

My apologies to Green Baggins‡ for taking so long to answer his questions. I have been up to my neck in discussions with atheists. For the same reason, my answers here will be brief, and may come across like a laundry list, but I hope they will still be able to do the work of clarification.

‡ greenbaggins.wordpress.com/2007/05/04/reformation-bona-fides

I affirm the traditional three uses of the law. One of those uses, that of convicting sinners and making them aware of their need for a savior is the use of the word *law* in the law/gospel distinction. The only quirk I bring to this is that I believe that the law is not found in one part of the Bible and the gospel in another. The whole thing is law and the whole thing is gospel. So I reject a law/gospel *hermeneutic*, but I do not reject a law/gospel *application* in the lives of men by the Holy Spirit. For a man in rebellion, everything about the Bible convicts, including the gospel. The message of the cross is the stench of death to those who are perishing. For a man forgiven, the whole thing is good news—even the preamble of the Ten Commandments is a promise of gospel. God is the one who brought us up out of the land of bondage.

My beef with merit is grounded in its medieval use, as though it were a fungible currency. But if someone poetically says (or one of our hymns say) that we are saved by the merit of Christ plus nothing, I have no problem with it. I prefer to say that the (entirely praiseworthy) obedience of Christ is imputed to us, rather than that the merit of the obedience of Christ is imputed to us. This is not because I want to take anything away from Christ, for I do not. And I prefer to stay away (if I can) from distinctions like condign, congruent, and pactum merit. I don't think it is a biblical way of speaking. At the same time, if you persisted, you could probably get something out of me on it, just as you could get me to come down on the infralapsarian/supralapsarian debate if you held a gun to my head. "Okey," as a character in Chandler would say. "Infra. I'm an infra."

The next question is this:

> Would Wilson be willing to affirm that Christ's perfect obedience and full satisfaction gives us pardon of sins and the acceptance of our persons as righteous?

This is a simple one. Absolutely.

The last question concerns of the "aliveness" of justifying faith. Lane and I agree that the sole instrument of justification is faith, and we both agree that this faith is alive, and not dead. But we do have a disagreement after this, although I do not believe it is insurmountable.

Lane says:

> My position is that it is *not its aliveness* which makes it fit for justification, although justifying faith is *always alive*. . . . However, it is not because it is alive that it is the instrument of justification, but because it receives and rests on Christ that it justifies. . . . By saying "because of aliveness" one has introduced a ground that is different from Christ's righteousness. This is not sound.

Here's the difficulty. I have no problem granting that the aliveness of the faith is not the ground of our justification, just as the faith itself is not. God does not look at the aliveness of the faith and say, "Good job there, Wilson!" He does not accept me on the *ground* of anything in me, including my faith or the aliveness thereof. But He does justify me through the *instrumentality* of my faith and the aliveness thereof. Lane appears to worry that people might get the wrong idea from this aliveness and set themselves up to boast. This is a mistake, I grant, but our ability to screw the theology up does not even slow God down. Far more people have made this same mistake with regard to faith than they have with faith and aliveness. But God established faith as the instrument anyway. When Lane says, "This is not sound," I would urge him to defer judgment until after he has asked a few more questions. "Do you believe that the faith which is the instrument of justification is always alive?" Yes. "Do you believe that God looks on this aliveness as part of His ground in justifying?" Not at all. "Do you believe that a living faith is a ground of justification or an instrument of justification?" An instrument only. And I cannot for the life of me see how such answers even begin to threaten the doctrine of *sola fide*.

FVS, TRS AT PCA GA, ASAP, SHOULD READ . . . MAY 10, 2007

I have a suggestion. FVs and TRs headed for the PCA GA, should read, as soon as possible, the subject of this post. They should do this so that we don't wind up with any new denominations with too many Cs, Rs, and Ps in the name.

There is an old blues song that starts out "Twenty-nine ways to make it to my baby's door . . ." Well, my friend Jeff Meyers has gone one better in writing a response to the PCA study committee's report on the Federal Vision. It is entitled, in good, sturdy Puritan fashion, "30 Reasons Why It Would be Unwise for the PCA General Assembly to Adopt the Federal Vision Study Report and Its Recommendations."* In my view, you could summarily throw any fifteen of his reasons out the window before you start reading, and his response is still devastating. Anyone who is going to General Assembly this year should have a copy of this report, and I would urge any such individuals to make a few extra copies so that they could have some to give away.

One the "two birds with one stone" front, I recently became aware of a new Reformed news site. My link to Jeff's response goes through that site, so take a look as you pass through.

ALL PASSAGES WORK TOGETHER FOR GOOD
MAY 12, 2007

Before Green Baggins goes on to my next chapter, he had some follow-up questions† to my last response.

First, law and gospel. As I said, I affirm the three uses of the law. My position is this: when the law reveals to me my need for a savior, and prepares me for the gospel proper, that is part of the story of how God undertook to save me. The law that condemns, indeed, the very passage that pierced me to the heart, is now understood by me in a framework of grace.

I don't deny that Scripture contains many imperatives, and I acknowledge that such imperatives condemn those who are in rebellion and remain obligatory for those who have been forgiven. But if I am elect, regenerate, and forgiven, all things work together for good. If all things work together for good, then this means that all passages work together for good for those who love God and are the called according to his purpose.

* Currently available here: auburnavenue.org/documents/30ReasonsFinal.pdf

† greenbaggins.wordpress.com/2007/05/09/reply-to-wilson-2

Flip it around. What could be more gracious than John 3:16? And yet, for those who are perishing, this grace is to them the stench of death. I therefore conclude that the law and gospel application is not a matter of different kinds of texts as it is a matter of different kinds of human hearts—law hearts and grace hearts. In order to be transformed into a grace heart, a law heart must be convicted. But that conviction can come from "law texts" or "grace texts." And once the person is converted, the "law texts" that terrified take on a completely different appearance.

In the comments, Chris Hutchinson asked when I was going to call Steve Schlissel and Rich Lusk on the carpet for their explicit rejection of the law/gospel distinction. First, the fact that they have been accused of doing this in this controversy is not even slightly compelling to me. As I pointed out recently, in their report the PCA study committee quoted me as arguing *for* something that I was actually arguing *against*. I have corrected this mother of citation errors, and I will be very interested to see if that egregious error still shows up in the copy that will be distributed to all the delegates attending the PCA's General Assembly. In this controversy, multiple accusations have been entirely unreliable. I know this to be the case with regard to many aspects of my own teaching. Why should I drop everything and condemn my friends simply because they have been accused *by the same unreliable people*? And secondly, my formulation of the law/gospel distinction seems to be a little strange to you, but it is *kind* of okay, you guess. And I guess I don't believe that Steve or Rich would have any problem with what I have argued for here.

With regard to the Larger Catechism 55, I have no problem affirming it if the language is taken in a straightforward, ordinary way. I am justified by Christ's good work, and not in any way by my good works. But if someone said that this question requires that merit be understood in its technical, theological, covenant of works sense, then I would want to take an exception there.

Lane says, "One must also deny the errors that attack such truth. This is an equally binding and equally important aspect of orthodoxy." I do believe this is true. But is it possible to deny Nestorianism (which I do) while doubting if Nestorius was one? And it sometimes seems to me that Barth is not the best representative of Barthianism, not that I agree with either. If you want me to deny as a soul-destroying error the doctrine that sinful men can in any way contribute to their own salvation, I am happy to do so. If you want me to condemn Wilkins or Lusk for teaching that, you will have to first convince me of two things—that you got your *facts* right, and that you are above petty *politics*. I am currently settled in the conviction that with certain notable exceptions (you, Lane, being one of them) the response to both of these criteria of mine is negative. Your GA delegates are going to be rolling into a vote on this *inaccurate* report of your study committee without having been given time even to *read*, let alone digest, the report. This is why we have clichés like "the smell test."

For Lane's last question, I believe that there is a practical distinction between faith and virtue, not only an abstract distinction. I am saying we can distinguish, but never separate. What is easier to distinguish than height and breadth? But if I remove the height of an object, I am simultaneously removing the breadth. I cannot separate them. To use the example offered by St. James, it is like the body and spirit, which are two entirely different things. But if we separate them, that is the condition that we call death.

A STACKED COMMITTEE?
MAY 15, 2007

Sean Lucas has apologized to me for the tone of something he wrote about me a few years ago. He did this publicly on his blog (here*), and given the widespread attention this whole thing has received, I thought it would be good to extend forgiveness in a public way as well, which I am happy to do. I am happy to accept his apology and am grateful for the way in which he extended it.

I understand that he is not retracting the substance of his criticisms, but rather for the tone of them. Nevertheless, I honestly appreciate him coming this far, and am happy to respond as far as I am able.

In the same spirit, I continue to express concern about the stacked nature of the FV study committee that Sean Lucas served on. If every member of

* seanmichaellucas.blogspot.com/2007/05/reprocessing-bad-process.html

that committee had publicly rejected the FV in a *gentlemanly* way, it would still be a procedural problem of the first order to assign nothing but gentlemanly critics to the committee. A committee can be stacked without being snarky, and at the end of the day, injustice is still done. And so that remains a central concern of mine.

MANGLE TANGLE
MAY 17, 2007

I recently accepted an apology from Sean Lucas over a review he had written of *"Reformed" Is Not Enough* a few years ago. He did not apologize for *what* he had written, but rather for the *way* in which he had written—he apologized for the tone. I am not taking any of my response back, but I hunted down the review in question, and just now finished reading it. My problem now is that, considered in isolation, I didn't see anything wrong with his tone. I thought that in terms of manner he was well within bounds. The content, for which he did not apologize, was a typical mangle-tangle of misunderstandings, and that created a tone of its own, one dependent on content. It was perfectly fine if he was right, and it was patronizing if he was wrong. Those misunderstandings were a good representation of the kind of prejudiced thinking that you don't want to put on a study committee. Or, if you do, you certainly don't want to put "nothing but" that perspective on a study committee. Be that as it may, I am still grateful for the apology and I still accept it. I did need to state for the record, though, that I don't think an apology for tone detached from content was necessary. At the same time, anything that helps ramp down the level of indignation—on both sides—going into the PCA's General Assembly is a good thing in my book.

THEOLOGIANS ARE FROM MARS
MAY 18, 2007

I just now finished looking over a statement from Mid-America Reformed Seminary—"Doctrinal Testimony Regarding Recent Errors." What a dog's breakfast.

The testimony is suitably coy and nebulous about exactly who the particular error-mongers might be, but they do refer darkly to "the present controversies," "contemporary discussion," "current climate," "theological errors," and whatnot. The most specific statement is this:

> With no animosity toward persons, and recognizing that we all see as "through a glass darkly" (1 Cor. 13:12), we humbly but resolutely stand against the theological errors now current, propagated by certain teachings of what has become known as the Federal Vision, by certain teachings of what has become known as the New Perspective on Paul, and by certain teachings of other individuals and theological movements. (p. 6)

We all see through a glass darkly, but some more darkly than others. Here is the problem, and it is a glaring and grotesque one. Their testimony includes a "Digest of Errors" (pp. 17–20). This is a list of 45 errors taught by "the various proponents of the current set of errors." I am an FV guy, right? I should be able to find myself in there, right? But out of their list of 45 errors, I find that I could be able to join them in rejecting 43, and maybe 44 of them. The "error" I recognize as a reasonable expression of my own position is #36, that of paedocommunion. The others on the list participate in overt misrepresentation, with varying degrees of high-handedness. The degrees of misrepresentation range from mild to jaw-dropping. This was an unbelievably shoddy bit of scholarship. This was atrocious. This was violation of the ninth commandment with a chainsaw.

I would offer to debate someone from MARS over this, but what's the use? Does anyone really believe that any member of the faculty there would allow himself to be put in a position where he would have to answer specific questions about this "testimony"? I think I'll save my breath for cooling my porridge.

John Frame wrote a famous essay on *Machen's Warrior Children*, and his central point about the travesty of Reformed fractiousness and bloodletting was certainly well taken. But I am having doubts about whether the word *warrior* is the word we are looking for. We aren't dealing with warriors anymore; we have lever-pullers, agenda-setters, drive-by report-makers, schmoozers, politicians, non-argument-followers, and hide-behind-deskers.

TESTIMONY ON THE MARS TESTIMONY
MAY 21, 2007

The official testimony of the Mid-America Reformed Seminary has a digest of errors. I stated in an earlier post that I could join with them in rejecting about 43 of their list of 45. But the reasons for this vary. In some cases, it was because I agreed with them in rejecting the errors of actual people. But in many other instances, I can only agree with them in rejecting the views of someone who would be in error if he ever were actually born. But I don't just want to state this generally, and so I decided to offer a brief comment on each of their 45 points. My comments are in bold.

Here is the MARS Digest of Errors:

> By way of summary, the various proponents of the current set of errors, which find their focus in an erroneous and moralistic doctrine of justification, teach some or all of the following errors:
>
> 1. that a doctrine of a covenant of works is unbiblical;

I hold that God made a covenant with Adam in the garden, and Adam by his rebellion broke the terms of that covenant.

> 2. that gospel precedes law in the divine/human relationship before the fall;

I hold that the gospel presupposes disobedience. Gospel is good news in response to the bad news of our condemnation. But graciousness is not the same thing as gospel. I do believe that the standards of law are a manifestation of God's gracious character. Adam enjoyed that graciousness before the fall, and the standard that God's graciousness required of him had been made very clear to him.

> 3. that, before the fall, grace circumvents God's law in this relationship; or that, prior to the fall, for God to demand obedience and righteousness from humans in order to enjoy fellowship with him is works righteousness;

I hold that grace cannot circumvent God's law under any circumstance. I do believe that grace is the context of God's law, but that is hardly a circumvention. Obedience was required of Adam, but it was required in the context of grace. For a groom to turn to his bride right after the "you may kiss the bride" part, jab his palm with his forefinger and *demand* fidelity from her now would be grotesque. But to say this, as I do, doesn't mean that I believe that her fidelity is somehow optional.

> 4. that God required only faith, not works of obedience, from Adam in paradise;

I hold that faith was required, and it has always been the characteristic of true faith that it obeys. The only route to the work of obedience required in the garden (staying away from the tree) was to trust God, believing Him. True faith and works of obedience are never in opposition.

> 5. that there was no probationary period or test of man's obedience in paradise;

I hold that God permitted the serpent to test Adam's faith and faithfulness in the garden. This would not have continued indefinitely, so it was a probationary period.

> 6. that the pre-fall covenant in paradise contained or implied no eschatological promise;

I hold that the covenant in paradise did imply an eschatological promise—what Jim Jordan has described as an eschatological maturity.

> 7. that the stipulations and restipulations in the pre-fall covenant are identical to the stipulations and restipulations in the covenant of grace—namely, man lives under God's grace, must trust or have faith in him, and enjoys blessing so long as he keeps covenant;

I hold that the means of keeping covenant (faith in God who supplies the grace to obey) are not to be confused with the stipulations of the covenant (e.g., stay away from that tree). The grace of covenant-keeping is not to be confounded with the terms or stipulations of the covenant. A man whose wife dies is free to marry another, and he is to exhibit *the same fidelity* to each wife. That doesn't make the two women into one woman.

> 8. that the covenant of grace is not primarily about God's provision of Christ as the Savior of his people but about each party of the covenant meeting their obligations, so that God's grace and human responsibility are correlated: God must give Christ for salvation, and the human party of the covenant must meet his or her covenant obligations in order for the covenant to come to fruition;

I hold that God has provided an efficacious Savior for His people, and that salvation will come to encompass the world. This salvation is in no way contingent on our making it work. We will in fact meet our obligations, but this flows from God's monergistic work, and does not contribute to a synergistic work.

> 9. that the covenant of grace is as breakable and precarious as the covenant in paradise, since its promises and threatenings are objective realities that await the human party of the covenant to determine which reality is subjectively appropriated;

I hold that the covenant of grace can only be broken by those members of it who were not determined by God before the foundation of the world to inherit eternal life. For those who *were* so determined to that eternal salvation, the covenant of grace is a slab of titanium fifty feet thick.

> 10. that the covenant of grace is basically a divine proposal in which God offers salvation on the condition that the human party of the covenant repent, believe, and continue in obedience to the demands of the covenant;

I hold that this only true if we remember that God then gives to the "human party," provided he is elect, the needed repentance, faith, and perseverance to the end.

> 11. that the covenant of grace is not a testamentary covenant or a covenant by testament;

I hold that there is no such thing as a non-testamentary covenant.

> 12. that the covenant of grace may not be defined as being made with those ordained to eternal life or with the elect in Christ, or with Christ, the second Adam, and the elect in him;

I hold that the covenant of grace may be defined as being made with those ordained to eternal life. I deny that we can say that it is made *only* with those. The Westminster Confession (7.5–6) requires us to believe that the covenant of grace is not an ethereal covenant, but rather a covenant made on the ground with sinners, including reprobate sinners. The administration of the covenant of grace includes activities that made certain reprobate individuals like Caiphas ministers of that covenant. But these individuals missed the point of the covenant, which is always Christ.

> 13. that it is wrong to speak of a dual aspect of this covenant;

I hold that this doesn't mean anything to me. Dual in what respect? Is this talking about the Mosaic covenant being a recapitulation of the covenant of works? Then it would be accurate. But if it is talking about the covenant of grace having two aspects in the sense that some members of the covenant were decretally elect and others were not, then this dual aspect is something that I insist on.

> 14. that the distinction between law and gospel is erroneous;

I hold that the distinction between law and gospel is healthy and good. But we have to locate it in the right place so that we do not divide the Word of God.

> 15. that the law is gospel and the gospel is law;

I do hold that law is gospel for those who are forgiven. The law of the Lord is perfect, converting the soul. And I hold that the gospel of the cross is law for those who are perishing. But this just refers to the attitudes of love or hatred that the converted and the unconverted have respectively. It does not turn indicatives into imperatives, or vice versa.

> 16. that the use of the idea of merit involves a paradigm of works righteousness contrary to God's covenant relationship of love for or friendship with man both before the fall and after the fall;

I hold that this *could* be true, depending on how the word *merit* was being used. But it is not necessarily true.

> 17. that justification entails only the forgiveness of sins, not the righteousness of Christ imputed to the believer as the complete fulfillment of the law of God;

I hold that in justification God imputes to the sinner all the good things that Jesus ever said or did, and that this is an important part of justification.

And then I hold that God does the same thing over again, just to make sure. I would subscribe to the imputation of the active obedience of Christ three times if I thought it would convince somebody.

> 18. that the Reformation doctrine of justification by faith alone is false;

I hold that . . . jeepers, *what*?

> 19. that justification primarily means to belong to the people of God, rather than to be forgiven and accepted by God through Christ's imputed righteousness to believing sinners;

I hold that this is a false dichotomy. I would drop the word *primarily*, and say *as well as* instead of *rather than*.

> 20. that justification is not to be defined by the idea of imputation;

I hold that justification is applied by means of imputation, which is the result of God's legal and forensic declaration.

> 21. that not all so-called good works of believers are excluded from their justification before God, and so some of the believer's good works are included in their justification before God;

I hold that if any of my good works attempted to contribute to my justification before God, then they should be slathered with bacon grease and thrown into hell.

> 22. that justification is by faith through its works of love or faith in its working or doing good works;

I hold that justification is by faith alone, but not by a faith that is alone.

> 23. that the (non-meritorious) good works of believers are the basis for or determinative of one's final destination;

I hold that this is just the snout of Pelagius, peeping out from under the wooly white sheepskin that he bought somewhere.

> 24. that justification is not by faith alone but by faithfulness, that is, by works of human obedience which qualify faith as the instrument for receiving Christ;

I hold that this sounds a lot like #23.

> 25. that Jesus Christ's active obedience serves to qualify him to be Savior and Mediator, but this fulfillment of righteousness is not imputed to believers as part of the ground of their righteousness before God;

I hold that Jesus Christ is a federal head, and consequently, it is not possible for anything He said or did to be withheld from His people. All that He did, whether positive obedience or obedient suffering, is imputed to us.

> 26. that good works, or what are termed non-meritorious good works, are not simply the fruit of faith and justification but (partly) constitute the ground or the means or the instrument of justification;

I hold that good works do not constitute the ground or means or the instrument of justification.

> 27. that the good works believers perform are necessary for being accepted by God;

I hold that there is a difference between necessity and causation. Good works are necessary, but they are *not* necessary as part of the ground of justification. It is necessary for them to be necessary somewhere else.

> 28. that justification is incomplete, and that there will be a final or second justification on judgment day;

I hold that the justification that occurs in the life of a person truly converted never has to be repeated or improved upon. But I do believe that there will be a final vindication of all God's people. This second justification is not to be thought of as an improvement upon the first. But there will be an eschatological vindication, when the sons of God are revealed and the creation rejoices.

> 29. that the distinction between 'the sign' (such as the water of baptism or the bread and wine in the Lord's Supper) and 'the thing signified' (Christ's redemptive work) is false, since they are one and the same;

I hold that the sign and the thing signified are not one and the same thing.

> 30. that the sign of the sacraments is in itself the reality;

I hold that through a faithful use of the sacramental signs we are privileged to meet with the reality.

> 31. that the sacraments offer a different grace than the Word of God, such that unless infants and small children receive the Lord's Supper they are being starved of grace;

I hold that all God's grace is the same grace, routed through different means. And this means I only believe that infants and small children are being starved from grace when they are held back—as they frequently are—from *all* offers of God's grace to His people.

> 32. that the efficacy of baptism is tied to the moment of baptism—that is, baptismal regeneration is true and right doctrine;

I hold that the *covenantal* efficacy of baptism is tied to that moment. But the regenerative efficacy of baptism is *not* tied to the moment of baptism, as the Westminster Confession plainly teaches (28.6). Baptism, together with the Lord's Supper, are effectual means of salvation to worthy receivers *only* (WSC #91).

> 33. that God's grace is conveyed through the sacraments *ex opere operato* (by the act performed);

I hold that God's covenantal authority is conveyed through the sacraments *ex opere operato*, saving some and condemning others. But God's grace is *never* conveyed by any instrument *ex opere operato*.

> 34. that all the baptized, head for head, are united to Christ and saved;

I hold that this, taken as an isolated statement, should be considered a false one.

> 35. that some of those who are baptized *and saved* can (and do) lose their salvation;

I hold that, if by *saved* here they mean decretally saved, then this is incoherent. But if "saved" means united to Christ in a John 15 sense, then it makes good sense of at least that text. The only thing that is sure here is that you cannot have one kind of salvation, and then go and lose the other kind that you don't have. That kind of impossibility cannot be accomplished, even if it would make the donors happy.

> 36. that small children and infants should be admitted to the Lord's Table prior to a responsible profession of faith;

I hold that this is the only one on this list that reasonably represents my position.

> 37. that, unless covenant children partake of the sacrament of the Lord's Supper, they are being spiritually starved;

I hold that children are being starved when they are cut off from all means of grace, or, when the one contact with grace they have been allowed (e.g., infant baptism), is in effect negated or insulted by other devices intended to supplant the Word of God for the sake of some tradition.

> 38. that the sacrament of the Lord's Supper imparts to its recipients a grace or blessing distinct and different from the grace of the Word of God and the sacrament of baptism;

I hold that grace is grace is grace.

> 39. that divine grace is resistible unto eternal damnation on the part of those who are elect, saved, forgiven, and united to Christ;

I hold that this is just crazy talk.

> 40. that the blood of Christ is not sufficient and efficacious in all for whom it was shed and applied, inasmuch as among those who enjoy forgiveness, justification, and reconciliation through Christ's blood, some lose these blessings since they break the covenant and subsequently perish eternally;

I hold that the blood of Christ is absolutely efficacious, accomplishing everything that God intended for it to accomplish, including the securing of the salvation of those who are the decretally elect.

> 41. that there are two kinds of election—one unto temporary salvation, another unto eternal salvation;

I hold that this should have been #39. And I would have agreed with this one, just like Calvin did, except that the surrounding statements showed that this one was completely skewed.

> 42. that eternal election is conditional—namely only those are elect unto eternal salvation who continue in the way of covenant obedience and faithfulness, whereas those who are counted under the covenant and do not meet this condition enjoy genuinely saving but not eternally saving election;

I hold that the MARS faculty are representing us exactly backwards. The decretally elect are beneficiaries of an unconditional decree on the part of God, which is the only reason why they are saved.

> 43. that being saved and united to Christ does not necessarily or inevitably mean that one will persevere in that salvation by God's grace, for his grace can be resisted unto the loss of salvation and a permanent falling away;

I hold that God's grace can only be resisted by those who are not decretally elect. And *they* can do nothing but resist it.

> 44. that the distinction between the visible and invisible church is invalid, since each and every member of the visible church is said to be elect and saved;

I hold that the distinction between the visible and invisible church is just fine, just so long as it is not made to be the only distinction within the church. Every member of the visible church is said to be united to Christ *in some sense*, but this is not the same thing as saying that every member of the visible church is "in."

> 45. that the invisible church refers to the church in eschatological glory.

I hold that the invisible church refers to the same group of people as are referred to under the heading of the eschatological church. But this does not mean that they mean the same thing. The church in eschatological glory will be anything but invisible.

MORE ON MARS
MAY 22, 2007

Just so that you all know, I had a phone conversation this morning with Alan Strange, Nelson Kloosterman and Mark Vander Hart, all faculty members at MARS. While we did not come to any agreement, we began and closed with prayer, had a cordial and frank exchange of views, and intend to do it again. The only disruption occurred when my youngest daughter and son-in-law came into my office during the phone conference and handed me an ultrasound photo that revealed she is carrying twins. *That* threw me off my game for a minute, but the other guys were understanding and didn't take any unfair advantage.

Paul tells us that we are to be "endeavoring to keep the unity of the Spirit in the bond of peace" (Eph. 4:3). This means that hard work is frequently involved, and I believe that we should be eager to undertake that work with anyone who is willing for it. I have no intention of just slapping a happy face sticker on all this—the MARS testimony and my response to it reveal that we have an awful lot of work to do. But still, my thanks to these three gentlemen for a God-honoring conversation.

CHASING MONKEYS
MAY 22, 2007

The fact that I am talking with our brothers from Mid-America does not mean that we should not continue to pursue the issues before us. And because this thing continues to erupt in public, we have to deal with it in public. As God gives opportunity we can have some "behind-closed-doors" discussions with the zookeeper. But the fact remains that the monkeys are all out of the cage, and so we have to spend at least some of our time chasing monkeys. So let me chase a particularly lively one for just a moment.

Let me illustrate the ninth commandment problem another way. This remains the center of my concern about the MARS testimony, and why I think it is such a problem.

> We affirm that the covenant of works and the covenant of grace are distinct covenants, and should not be confused or amalgamated, for the first covenant deals with man in a state of integrity, whereas the second covenant finds man corrupted, wholly depraved, and under the penalty of death . . . . (*MARS Doctrinal Testimony*, p. 22)

Here is the difficulty. This is clearly applicable to Westminster West, and their tolerance of the recapitulation view. But MARS has not only said that the covenant of works and the covenant of grace are distinct, they have said they are *necessarily* distinct because of the spiritual condition of those with whom they were made. This makes it impossible for the covenant of works to be re-given at Sinai in any sense—how could the covenant of works be made with man "corrupted, wholly depraved, and under the penalty of death"? But this is what the recapitulationists do.

So then, the doctrinal testimony of MARS is general enough to apply to NPP, FV, WW, and nameless others (NO). If the bugle blows indistinctly, then how is this a help in preparing for battle—if battle indeed is called for? When your adversary is not named, then there are only two things that the average pew sitter can do. He can conclude that it must not be important for him to know (but then why do it?), or he can *guess*. When he guesses, as many will do, he will frequently guess wrong because the MARS testimony names the FV, and then describes the FV position in ways that all FV men that I know would repudiate (to varying degrees). And that is a ninth commandment issue.

IS NORMAN SHEPHERD FROM MARS?
MAY 23, 2007

Let us assume for a moment, for the sake of discussion, that the criticisms contained in the MARS testimony are right on target. This will help us set up something that will reveal (with a great deal of clarity) why the testimony is a plain violation of the ninth commandment. Let us also take the naming of names on page six in the most broad and charitable sense, which is that NPP and FV are not coterminous with these errors, but rather that they are "carriers" of these errors.

Here is the problem, and it boils down to the relationship of Mid-America to Norman Shepherd. Norman Shepherd has visited there to lecture, his works have been assigned in class (and not in the way New St. Andrews assigns Darwin), and he (most significantly) served for a number of years on their board. John Barach is one of the original Auburn four, and a graduate of

MARS. He has Norman Shepherd's signature on his diploma, and he graduated in 1997.

It seems to have been recognized by all previous lumpers-together that this stew needs to have Norman Shepherd in it, and not just N.T. Wright and Steve Wilkins. It is remarkable therefore that MARS did *not* identify Norman Shepherd by name. Neither did they identify their own seminary as carriers of these errors as well.

Shepherd's previous connection to Westminster is not comparable, because he was forced out of Westminster as a result of a previous incarnation of this same controversy. But one of the places that "gave refuge" to Shepherd after that controversy was MARS. This was after his views became known, and became known in controversy. This is just another way of saying that MARS is in the process of changing sides and is trying to do so in such a way that no one notices.

This kind of inconsistency has been seen before, and it is one of the central reasons for seeing this whole imbroglio as ecclesiastical politics instead of ecclesiastical reformation. Norman Shepherd *has* been used as a scarecrow in all this, but those who were previously associated with him in ministry have been pressured to simply back away. If they just drop their support *quietly*, then nothing so messy as public repentance will be required of them. Presbyterian & Reformed is now publishing attacks on the FV, but they previously published Norman Shepherd's *Call of Grace*. And Richard Gaffin blurbed it.

Clearly, MARS is no longer willing to stand with Shepherd, as they were once willing to do. But in this testimony of theirs, they did not even mention Shepherd. If this were a matter of biblical principle, and not politics, MARS would have started with themselves. This is Biblical Ethics 101. Instead they lumped a bunch of disparate groups together, excluding *only* the one citation that would have involved them in it. In their defense, if it can be called that, at least they did not cast the *first* stone.

In that famous story of the woman caught in adultery, Jesus famously tells the accusers that the one without sin should cast the first stone. I take this as the Lord saying that whoever is without the sin of adultery, the sin in question, should cast the first stone. And they all, beginning with the oldest, slowly went away.

So I have a very simple question for Alan Strange—and let me say again that I do appreciate his willingness to interact with me on these things. Here it is: consider this set of errors that you are attacking, and of which the NPP and FV are carriers. Was MARS in the 1990's a carrier of these same errors also? If not, why not? In what ways are other critics of NPP/FV/NS mistaken? If so, then why was an expression of institutional repentance not included in the testimony? Why attack others publicly for doing something that your own institution did privately for many years?

The accusation made against us is that we are messing around with justification by faith alone. This is not true, but suppose for a moment that it were true. If the anti-FV critics were right and correct in lumping all the carriers together as well, then this would include Norman Shepherd along with the rest of us. But MARS cannot afford to name him, because that would be too glaring. Too many people would say, "Hey!" all at once, and go off to look at their diplomas, and there would be Norman Shepherd's signature, staring back at them in silent rebuke. They would then haul out their old class notes and say, "Huh. He didn't used to be a bad guy."

We have no textual basis for asserting that this happened, but let me expand the story of the woman caught in adultery. I am not making a historical claim here, but rather trying to illustrate something about human nature. I do believe that Jesus was referring to the sin of adultery when He says that the one without sin should cast the first stone. I believe that *is* implicit in the text. But here is the expansion. Human nature being what it is, I do not find it incredible to believe it possible that one of the men with a rock in his hand had himself slept with that condemned woman before. And I also believe that he could feel terrible about it, feeling the pangs of conscience terribly. But that doesn't mean that he would have the backbone to drop the rock and stand up to the vigilante mob around him.

If the testimony of MARS is to be believed as a statement of principle, then I think that they must publicly repent of their own connivance with these errors, as well as repent of trying to sidle away from those errors instead of repudiating with them openly. If they are not willing to do this, then at a bare minimum, they need to withdraw their testimony as it now stands. The way they have grouped the offenders together is not just too confusing, it is too convenient.

SOME REASONABLE QUESTIONS

MAY 30, 2007

A group of ten PCA pastors have written an open letter about the PCA Study Committee on the "Federal Vision, New Perspective and Auburn Avenue Theology." In the second paragraph of this letter, these men say, "We are not FV men." Nevertheless, they have a number of very reasonable questions about the report, and good reasons for saying "it would be premature for us to ratify their report." You can find out more about these men here*, along with a link to their letter.

CHILDREN OF ABRAHAM

MAY 29, 2007

In a battle, foot solders focus rightly on the conflict right in front of them. Generals don't have the luxury of that simplicity, and so they also have to think constantly about the larger strategic issues. Great generals do not just think of tactics on the field, but also of the larger strategic issues, up to and including the geo-political ones.

When doctrinal controversy erupts in the Church, the same realities are present. There are local church members and local pastors who find themselves swept up into a particular conflict that is a small part of a larger battle. They are required to be faithful in that conflict, and part of that faithfulness includes recognizing that the conflict includes their issues but is not "about" their issues. An infantryman in WWII France is trying to take a particular farmhouse, but he does not believe that the war is over that farmhouse.

We have been praying for reformation in the Church for many years now, and I believe there are reasons to believe it is beginning to arrive. One of the

* reformednews.com/2007/05/news-pastors-draft-pastoral-letter-on.html, no longer available.

reasons for believing this is the explosion of chaos and confusion. In *The Last Lion*, William Manchester described Winston Churchill's participation in one of the last cavalry charges of the modern world. Before the forces collided, everything was distinct and in its place. The flags were snapping briskly. The sides were clear, and everything was magnificent. Once the armies met, there was complete pandemonium. Only a wise general could keep his head in that situation and remember what was actually supposed to be occurring.

As I said, we have been praying for reformation in the Church for many years now. But what on earth made us think that *any* reformation *ever* came without making a glorious mess? When did new wine in old wineskins not result in wine all over the floor?

The problem is this: when men build the tombs of the prophets there is a large measure of self-deception going on. They tell themselves that they are the true heirs of the prophets when their actions betray them (to the wise) as heirs of those who opposed the prophets. Christ took just one glance and told them what they were doing. The curators of the Reformation Museum want everyone to stay behind the velvet ropes, to leave the old books on their shelves, and coo over the wax reproduction of John Knox confronting Mary Queen of Scots. Then everyone is given a brochure reminding everyone to not try this at home.

People just do this, and they don't know that they do. This is a deep sociological reality, and all the wishing in the world can't make it unfold differently. In this reformation, just like the last one, there will be the old guard, refusing to budge. There will be the defenders of the old, those who are willing to retrench somewhat, introducing some reforms under pressure. There will be the magisterial reformers, with significant differences between them, outlining a vision for the future. There will be the sane anabaptists, trying to stay out of trouble. There will be the opportunistic lunatics, who set up some kind of Federal Vision wife-swapping deal.

One of the earmarks of shrewd insight is the ability to see what corresponds to what. Who is like this person? Who is like that one? Who are the reformers, speaking the language of Scripture afresh? Who are the heretics, flaming with the *rhetoric* of reformation, but denying the substance? Who are the curators and librarians, custodians of treasures they cannot understand anymore?

When the massive confusion of real reformation breaks out, how do you decide what to do? Simple. The children of Abraham will do the works of Abraham.

JUNE 2007

GOOD STUFF

JUNE 7, 2007

For those who are following the Auburn Avenue fracas, and especially those who are going to be attending the General Assembly for the PCA, I heartily commend to you Joel Garver's interaction with the PCA study committee report. You can find that here.*

GETTING THE RIGHT LID FOR THE JIGSAW PUZZLE BOX

JUNE 4, 2007

Now that my schedule has recovered some of its equilibrium, perhaps I can catch up on answering some of Green Baggins's questions.

On the law/gospel distinction, Lane says of me that "if there is any distinction, it is in the person, and not in the text, whereas I hold that there is a distinction in the text." He doesn't really want to argue this point, but I think there is still room for clarification. I am not rejecting a distinction between law and gospel, or between demand and promise. What I am rejecting is the use of these two categories *as a hermeneutic*. In short, the abstract categories of law and gospel are not to be used as an aid in exegesis. But I do not reject the application of Scripture in these categories, with due notice of what the text says and the spiritual condition of the one to whom it is applied.

In the discussions about this I have not seen any attempt to answer the examples I have given, examples that show that the function or use of "law"

* sacradoctrina.blogspot.com, no longer publicly available.

can be performed by any passage and that the function or use of "gospel" can be performed by any passage. The law of the Lord is perfect, converting the soul. The message of the cross is a stench to those who are perishing. If we have a law/gospel *hermeneutic* then we must categorize these passages as one or the other, but then we find God applying them in the other category. The way I am handling the categories allows us to see Christ's words *follow me* as being either law or gospel, depending (Matt. 4:19; 19:21). So I affirm the three *uses* of the law, but I deny that the law should be used as a hermeneutical principle, whether conjoined with the gospel or not. What the text is saying *can* be determined apart from a law/gospel hermeneutic. What the text means for me *cannot* be determined apart from law/gospel considerations.

I completely agree with Lane that the Church can enter into periods of declension (we are in a big one now), and that progress is not automatic. So just because something is "new" doesn't make it good. I also concur with him that openness theism is just warmed-over Socinianism.

Lane raises the question of what my point was in talking about nebulous tradition—was it directed at those who encounter sacramental Calvinism and assume (because of the sacramental efficacy) that it has to be the teaching of Trent. I don't have my copy of *RINE* with me, and so I can only say I *think* that was my point on that page. I certainly believe this to be the case. It happens a lot.

He also raises the question of the relationship between systematic theology and the exegesis of a particular passage. Lane says that it is dangerous to "engage in exegesis with no reference to ST at all." I couldn't agree with this more. For any Christian who believes the Bible to be inspired by God, and therefore coherent throughout, systematic theology is nothing more or less than remembering what the Bible says everywhere else when you come to study what it is saying here. Various forms of systematic theology are found in the Apostles' Creed, Nicea, Chalcedon, Westminster, Hodge, Turretin, and N.T. Wright. No one systematic theology covers everything, and many of them get key features positively wrong—like a guy putting a jigsaw puzzle of a sailboat together, when he is working from the wrong box top, a picture of a lighthouse. By the end, he will be putting pieces in with a mallet.

I would even go so far as to deny any antithesis between systematic theology and biblical theology. What is called biblical theology is simply a more refined systematics—a system with many more features, subtleties and workarounds. And I agree with Lane that all exegesis must be conducted with faithfulness to the teaching of the entire Scriptures in the forefront of the mind.

When I say that a man is not defined by his internal essence, I do not mean to *exclude* the state of his heart from a summary of who he is. I simply do not want it limited to that. His family matters, his story matters, his baptism matters, his relationships matter, and so on. But of course, whether his heart belongs to God in truth also matters.

My last comment concerns Lane's question about my egg and omelet analogy. In this illustration, what do we do with the rotten eggs, the reprobate eggs in the omelet of the historical church? Doesn't this give us a "scrambled mash"? Yes, it would, and this is where I would appeal to the scriptural pattern of multiple analogies, because, as we know, at some point, any given analogy will break down. Mine does at this point. The egg/emelet illustration is simply meant to show that there is an individual component to this, as well as a corporate component. The question arises as to whether there is any differentiation between elect eggs and reprobate eggs. Yes, there is, and my illustration (not being about that) tends to blur that distinction. At the eschatological breakfast, the best cook in the world can't take the rotten eggs out of the omelet before serving. The best gardener *can* prune the fruitless branches.

I would apologize for this deficiency in my illustration, but I think that it is how illustrations are supposed to work, so long as we use a lot of them. The scriptural illustrations sometimes really accent this differentiation (wheat and tares), sometimes get the two kinds of believers too close for comfort (fruitful and fruitless branches in Christ), and sometimes pay no regard to that differentiation (because a different point of the illustration is in view). For an example of this latter, in the parable of the sower, there is no difference at all in what kind of plant is trying to grow. Going back to my point about systematic theology, we have to remember all of our illustrations whenever we are using one of them.

LIVE IN THE HOUSE, NOT ON THE MANTEL
JUNE 7, 2007

I am continuing to interact with Green Baggins's review* of my book, *"Reformed" Is Not Enough.*

When I draw a distinction between a law/gospel *hermeneutic* (which I reject) and a law/gospel *application* (which I accept), this is what I mean. With a law/gospel hermeneutic, each text is either demand or promise, and it is the job of the interpreter to find out which one it is, and then apply it according to its nature. Certain verses are the carrot and the other verses are the stick. Misapplication would be to use the carrot as a stick, or the stick as a carrot.

Law/gospel application depends upon the hearer. To a "law-hearer," the Bible is all demand. Do this, do that, do the other thing. Believe in Jesus. Get baptized. Tithe. Go to church. Be faithful to your wife. All that. The law-hearer receives all this as *law*. The legalist thinks he can do it. The rebel doesn't care to do it, and rejects it all. But they both hear it as demand. Do this and live.

The gospel-hearer listens to Christ say, "Follow me," and it strikes him as a glorious privilege and invitation. It is good news. The ten commandments are heard as further grace from the one who brought us out of Egypt, out of the house of bondage. And when someone is converted, they are being converted from a law-hearer to a grace-hearer. There is a transition from the one condition to the other.

Now, to the point of Lane's disagreement, now that a person is converted, can we make distinctions in the text? Certainly we can distinguish imperatives from indicatives, laws from promises, and so on. But now that I am saved, everything is contextualized within that grace. That grace surrounds everything, making it lovely. It is in that grace that we now stand. I can tell grammatically when God issues a requirement for His people. This is the vase of demand, on the mantlepiece of law, situated in the middle of the house of grace. And I live in the house, not on the mantle.

And when we are doing evangelism, we will encounter people who don't have the context of that "house of grace." For them, everything is a stench.

* greenbaggins.wordpress.com/2007/06/06/reply-to-wilson-the-sequel

Law condemns. He would not have known what sin was if the law had not said, "Do not covet." But equally, the glories of grace strike him the same way. The name *Jesus* gives him the creeps just as much as *no drunkenness* or *no fornication* do.

The next thing is my egg/omelet analogy. Lane says this:

> If Doug is willing to say that *in terms of the invisible church*, reprobate eggs are *not part of the omelette*, then I am just fine with the illustration. The corporate omelette, considered in terms of the visible church, has good eggs and bad eggs. The corporate omelette, considered in terms of the invisible church, has only good eggs in it.

Now this is where analogies get really helpful, as well as silly. First, I agree with Lane here, and I know what he is getting at, but would point out that this analogy doesn't work as well as we might like. There is no such *thing* as an invisible omelette. But suppose we tried historical omelette and eschatological omelette? The cook is a master cook. In the historical omelette, we have some reprobate, stinky eggs in there. But this cook is so good that by the time of the eschatological breakfast, He will have snaked all of those eggs out of there. I trust this makes the point, but it is not a good analogy because ordinary cooks never get rotten eggs out of the omelette after the cooking starts.

But that is not true of the scriptural analogy for this. Gardeners do prune fruitless branches. And the historical vine really has fruitless branches which the eschatological vine will not have. And the gardener knew the entire time which branches were going to go, and which were going to stay.

On the point about Post-Reformation scholasticism, I went back and looked at my quotations from Joel Garver in chapter five. I am not sure where he has changed his views since then, but those quotations still represent my views. I do believe that the Reformed scholastics had to fight off a lot of bad stuff, and that they used a certain rationalistic approach to do so. This was necessary, but cautions are always in order. As I put it there, "Such *lawful* interpretations can require technical and high flown language. This is *not necessarily bad, so long as we remember* what we are doing" (*RINE*, p. 55, emphasis added). My concern is not so much with them, as with some of their curators.

A DOUBLE ORDER OF GOLDEN-BROWN BUTTERMILKS JUNE 9, 2007

A reply to some of the (very deserved) criticisms of the PCA study committee on the Federal Vision can be found here.* The PCA will be addressing this issue at their GA in the coming days, and so I would urge everyone to pray that God would protect that denomination from an act of theological folly and high-handedness.

I am not going to interact with the "humble answers" *seriatim*, but I do want to say one thing about how they answered the most glaring problem with the study committee—that being the stacked nature of the committee. To put it in terms that the average layman can follow, that committee was as stacked as a double order of golden-brown buttermilks.

Read the answer to this charge and try to read it out loud without laughing. Here you go.

> First, it has been suggested that the composition of the Committee was unfairly weighted. On the contrary, the Committee represents a broad range of thought within the PCA, bringing together many who have in the past disagreed on less essential (though important) issues. These seven elders are from seven different presbyteries and have between them served faithfully in at least 20 different churches across the PCA. One is a former moderator of the PCA, another is the Vice President for Academics of our denominational seminary, and a third, the chairman, was an active member of the Presbyterian Pastoral Leadership Network (PPLN) that spearheaded the passing of the "Good Faith Subscription" amendment. Three others are faithful and active ruling elders that have served the PCA in a variety of capacities. This broad composition

* This blog (humbleanswers.wordpress.com) was closed after the GA.

> highlights the tremendous opportunity for different "camps" across the PCA to join together at the 35th General Assembly to reaffirm what unites us most as a church: the centrality of God's grace in all of salvation. Further, such accusations reveal a mistrust of the motives of the Committee and the denomination's moderator, who has faithfully served our church, beginning in the RPCES, for over 35 years, including service as the editor of the PCA's news website. This is a form of ad hominem and does not address the substance of the report itself, nor the report's nine clear declarations which represent straightforward readings of the Westminster Standards with which few could disagree.

Here, allow me to translate. *Charge:* the committee assigned to investigate the issue of the Federal Vision was stacked so that there would be no one representing FV concerns on committee, and hence there would be no minority report. *Reply:* on the contrary, the seven men on that committee are a walking embodiment of diversity. They live in different *towns*, they order different entrees at *restaurants*, and, after checking, we discovered that none of them have the same make of automobile. Thus, the *ad hominem* charge that this committee was stacked against the Federal Vision is a charge that stands both confounded and abashed. We hope, dear reader, that we can get past this nonsense.

Well, it is kind of hard to get past it so long as you continue to roll around in it.

THAT HE'D BEEN IN HIS BUNK BELOW
JUNE 11, 2007

I read on Reformed News that Sam Duncan, former moderator of the PCA, has provided a summary of the FV in preparation for the big doings at the General Assembly of the PCA this week. But before I start in on my war dance, let me just say that you ought to check out Reformed News† far more often than you do.

† reformednews.com, no longer available

Anyhow, Sam Duncan's summary can be found here*. Let me just record and interact with a handful sample quotations. But before I do, let me just say, as a *general* point, that this is just freaking unbelievable.

> The business that comes before the Assembly will be highlighted by discussions of the Federal Vision, New Perspectives (on Paul), and Auburn Avenue theologies (the "Federal Vision").

Three problematic positions are listed here, the FV, the NPP, and the AA theologies, or, lumping them all together, "Federal Vision" for short. Never mind that FV and AA can't be anything *but* lumped together, being synonymous and all. And then another set of issues entirely, the NPP, is thrown in to add a little stickiness to this doctrinal taffy pull that we have going on here.

> For the layman, who is not familiar with this topic, the Federal Vision basically teaches that membership in a local church makes one elect; once one is elect, his salvation may be lost; baptism results in regeneration; and justification is achieved through both faith and good works.

Let me just say that there is a difference between holding to the five points of historic Calvinism, which I do, and holding to the five talking points of Calvinism. For a representative sample of latter, just check out the quotation we just retrieved our left rubber boot from. There are four substantive claims being made here about the FV, and *all* of them, one hundred percent of them, are, as the French say, le wrong. According to us'ns, decretal election is dependent in no way on membership in a local church. We *are* talking about decretal election, right? Decretal election cannot be lost, period. Baptism does not result *ex opere quasimodo* in personal regeneration. And our justification is not in any way "achieved" by any personal characteristics, ethical decisions, moral contributions, or boyish smiles we might try to come up with.

* fpcpca.net/News/NewsStory.aspx?guid=2a56dad4-0d7d-46ec-a3db-24e0cec60ea9, no longer viable.

We have gotten to the point in this controversy where this kind of summary leaves us with only two options for understanding what is being said. Either we are dealing with (as the papists would put it) invincible ignorance, or we are dealing with a willful determination to shatter the ninth commandment. If *this* is the kind of reasoning that is going to be the guide for the men at the PCA helm, it will soon become apparent to the world that they are steering by the mast in front of them, and not by the North Star at all.

> The Federal Vision, many believe, takes election out of the hands of the Lord and places it on man's shoulders.

"Many believe" this, do they? I have what might appear to be an impertinent question, but it seems to *me* to be relevant. The "many" who believe this, and I hesitate to make such a gauche appeal to an old-fashioned concept like this, but, are they *right*?

> This is to be contrasted with the Federal Vision's teachings that an individual's good works and his faith are required for one to be justified.

I scarcely know how to start. I am not going to refute this. I will describe it. Breath-taking. High-handed. Pole-axing. Serpentine. Devious. Wrong.

"Who is at the helm of the PCA?" This was a question tellingly raised on a listserv I am on, and the good folks who raised it set a train of thought in motion that made me remember a song I learned as a child.

> A capital ship for an ocean trip was the *Walloping Window Blind.*
> No wind that blew dismayed her crew or troubled the captain's mind.
> The man at the wheel was made to feel contempt for the wildest blow,
> Though it oft appeared when the gale had cleared
> That he'd been in his bunk below.

There was one other item that I thought needed a comment.

> Other business that will come before the Assembly will be in the form of Overtures to change our Book of Church Order or requests to take other actions. This year, the Assembly will consider requests to . . . recognize the 500th anniversary of John Calvin's birth in 2009.

I suggest that on this last item there needs to be a rider that says something like, "honoring a worthy man of God, while eschewing his sacramentalism, his views on regeneration, the Church, and temporary election, all of which have helped create the FV mess that we have just now cleaned up. Calvin, however worthy he might be of receiving a shiny prophet's tomb, is, at least according to *some*, at the heart of all this trouble."

A CAREER MOVE?
JUNE 11, 2007

I just got an email from my son-in-law Ben, to whom the credit for this insight belongs. He was responding to the current PCA embarrassment and, here . . . let him talk:

> I was thinking about how for the last generation the thing that has always been presbyterianism's real strength has been its intellectualism. Liberals could be intellectuals but unorthodox, and evangelicals could be orthodox but were always goofy. The Reformed always managed to be orthodox and intellectually engaging. But with the death of Falwell and the retirement of that generation of evangelicalism, it seems like our presbyterians, with their willful ignorance on the FV issue, are shifting over to take the place of orthodox shallow thinkers. If that happens it is going to leave a real vacuum for orthodox believers looking for challenging thinkers . . .

This is a new angle for me. Perhaps these men are doing all this because they are applying for another job opening entirely. What Jim Jordan refers to as the closing of the Calvinistic mind may not be theological Alzheimer's. It might be a career move.

PCA AT THE CROSSROADS
JUNE 13, 2007

Please be praying for the PCA. This afternoon they will be considering the Federal Vision issue. Or, more accurately, they will be considering what some people *deem* to be the Federal Vision issue. Unfortunately, depending on the outcome, there are accurate names connected to inaccurate summaries of doctrine, and so this really is a crossroads for the PCA.

There are enough genuine doctrinal issues involved in this controversy that it *could* have been a doctrinal choice. But because the choice has come to this point in the way it has, the choice is actually between nativism and catholicity.

There are (at least) two ways to get rid of heretics from a denomination. One is to study the issues, grasp them, determine if your opponents are actually teaching them, and then make the decision. The other is generate some slogans, doggedly persevere with those slogans ("that's my story, and I'm stickin' to it"), pull some levers, stack some committees, and then ban anyone who has read a book by N.T. Wright without glowering the entire time.

There may not be fireworks this afternoon, but this is a really big deal. Pray that God would protect the PCA from nativism.

GOLD IS HEAVY AND HARD TO CARRY
JUNE 13, 2007

By now all those who have been following the Federal Vision situation in the PCA will have heard that the General Assembly of the PCA approved the report by the study committee. That was *not* what we were praying for, and so I thought I needed to make just a couple of brief comments here.

First, I would encourage everyone associated with the FV to take care that they not speak publicly about this out of frustration, exasperation, fear or anger. The situation will still be here in a couple days, and calm heads will be better at figuring out what to do then than hot heads will be now. As I sometimes tell people in counseling situations, there is no situation so bad but that you can't make it worse.

Second, I think it would be spiritually healthy for us on our side of the line to ask for God's particular blessing to fall on some of the men who were instrumental in getting this report accepted—R.C. Sproul, Lig Duncan, et al. As my father has taught me, God requires us to love our neighbors, our wives, all men, and our enemies. The chances are excellent that *anyone* we can think of is covered by at least one of those categories. If Christ can tell us to bless those who despitefully use us, then how much more should we be able to see our way to bless brothers in Christ who thought they were doing nothing more than affirming *sola fide*?

And last, Jesus the Lord is not only sovereign over the details of each of our individual lives, He is also sovereign over the course of all history. He is the Head of the Church, and so this includes church history, which in its turn includes denominational histories. If we are His servants, and we are, then we can trust Him with what He is doing here. Someone once said that the advancement of the kingdom of God is a long series of spectacular victories cleverly disguised as disasters. In our local church, here at Christ Church, when I became a paedobaptist in the early nineties, some of the things that happened in that mess were among the most difficult events of my life. But looking back at them, I can see now that I did not have the eyes to see exactly how *much* God was blessing our congregation. In other words, the greatest trials were the greatest blessings. Gold is heavy and hard to carry. This is God's way, and He loves to do it this way. We do not know what the future holds, as the hymn says, but we know who holds the future.

CONTRA MUNDUM?
JUNE 18, 2007

Contra mundum is a nice slogan if you can get it. I have been watching some of the internet discussion in the aftermath of the PCA decision at GA, and I decided I needed to say a little something about the following argument: "*All* these venerable alphabet combinations have condemned the Federal Vision—URC, OPC, RPCNA, PCA, GM, NATO, and countless others—and still you guys whine and complain. What makes you think that *the entire world* has failed to comprehend what you guys are saying? Hey?"

The use of this argument, with virtually no self-awareness at all, is actually an argument in favor of *another* observation I have made about all this. Those who go by the nickname TR are actually curators of the Reformed mausoleum, and not scholars in the Reformed tradition. The way we can tell this is that—in defense of keeping the marble floors of their mausoleum polished and shiny—they deploy Eck's argument against Luther. Their blood stirs when they hear the story about Athanasius saying that he was *contra mundum* because they really like that kind of thing when is it behind glass in the museum of church history. But when someone actually stands up against the living and breathing ecclesiastical Mitred Ones, they haul this argument out as shamelessly as a theologian who thinks he is *supposed* to have an infallible *magisterium*. And they do this against people who they say are trying to "lead them to down the road Rome." But how can you lead people to Rome when they are already there?

NO APPEAL TO SCRIPTURE
JUNE 19, 2007

My (hopefully helpful) interactions with Green Baggins* continue apace. This segment includes his response to a recent post of mine (on Eck's argument against Luther), as well as our continued interaction as he works his way through my book, *"Reformed" Is Not Enough*. This should not have to be too long a post because I think I can answer the questions he has posed without a lot of explanation.

The question raised by my Eck argument was this: am I seriously saying that tight-shoed Calvinists are on a doctrinal par with Roman Catholics? Was I talking about the *content* of the Establishment's doctrine, that which always motivates them to clamp-down down on the courageous dissidents?

Now, there is always the possibility of rhetorical overstatement with Wilson, and I hope he will clarify this point. Maybe he is only claiming that the method of argumentation tends towards ossification, and not the actual doctrinal content.

Whaddaya mean, "rhetorical overstatement?" Most of the time I am holding *back*. And, all kidding aside, Lane is starting to read me pretty well. I was

* greenbaggins.wordpress.com/2007/06/19/ossification-and-defining-the-covenant

talking about the method of argumentation, and not the actual content. This does not mean that this is unrelated to content, but that was not my point there. But the relationship to content is this: when a church begins defending itself by means other than the assigned scriptural means, then in my book the content is not really being defended. The Roman Catholic church still teaches a great deal of truth (Trinity, Incarnation, etc.), but the methods they allow in arriving at some of their errors are a standing threat in principle to the truths that remain. The same thing is true about ossified Reformed denominations. The apostasy from the central content may still be centuries off—but when an ecclesiastical culture defends its traditions by raw authority, minimal debate, one-sided investigations, no appeal to Scripture, and so on, all the godly content that remains in their confessions is certainly *vulnerable and exposed.* I say this as someone who subscribes, in good faith, to the *Westminster* Confession, holding to it with rowdy enthusiasm.

But Lane is correct. I was not saying that those Reformed folk who did this thing deny the truth of the Confessions, or that they have embraced heretical doctrines. I *am* saying that they have adopted a means of defending their Confession that is at odds with the content of the Confession itself, and hence they will not be able sustain a defense of the Confession over any extended period of time. If there are any leading lights in the PCA who are *able* to defend the truths of the Reformation against those who contradict it (as it is claimed we in the FV do) by means of open debate, relevant interaction, and appeal to Scripture, this controversy has not revealed their names to us. A stacked committee, followed by time for debate on the floor of GA that could be measured in minutes. What a *joke.*

I am on the road, and don't have my copy of *RINE* with me, so I don't think I can answer as specifically as Lane might like (with page numbers and everything), but I think I can answer his questions about this section of the book.

First, I do believe in a continued "first use" of the law for Christians. We are constantly in need of re-learning why we need a Savior. Lane goes on to anticipate a disagreement here, because he is right that I do believe that, for believers, everything is contextualized in ultimate grace. I don't buy the "equal ultimacy" of grace and law. But I do believe that law is grounded in the character of God, and am not trying to denigrate it in any way. Grace has a backbone, and that backbone is law. I agree (partly) with Lane that grace and law "are both equally ultimate . . .in Christ, the Law-Keeper and Grace-Giver." Of course, Christ is the Law-Keeper, and of course, He is the Grace-Giver. That is where we agree. We differ because I think they are obviously *not* equally ultimate. Christ giving grace is grace. And Christ keeping the law is also grace—He didn't have to do that, and He gave it to us anyway. His grace is grace, and His obedience is grace. There is nothing in the life of a believer that cannot be reduced to grace, within two or three steps.

We then come to Lane raising the question about my views of Reformed scholasticism. I went back and looked, and this is what I previously said.

On the point about Post-Reformation scholasticism, I went back and looked at my quotations from Joel Garver in chapter five. I am not sure where he has changed his views since then, but those quotations still represent my views. I do believe that the Reformed scholastics had to fight off a lot of bad stuff, and that they used a certain rationalistic approach to do so. This was necessary, but cautions are always in order. As I put it there, "Such *lawful* interpretations can require technical and high-flown language. This is *not necessarily bad, so long as we remember* what we are doing" (*RINE*, p. 55, emphasis added). My concern is not so much with them, as with some of their curators.

Lane responds to this by asking (quite respectfully) if I have read and interacted with Muller on this. The answer there is (with equal respect) that I have not. I have Muller's big monga-set but haven't read it yet. I have read and appreciated his work elsewhere, and I guess I am not quite sure how the sentiments I expressed above would differ with how Lane is representing him here. I don't believe that the Reformed scholastics were rationalists, but I also believe that the apostle Paul would have been quite amused with any *detailed* displays of Ramian logic. But I don't even believe that it is bad to use that kind of logic, just so long (as I noted above) as you remember where you are and what you are doing. And that Ephesians and Second Kings weren't written that way.

Lane stated the principle this way: "No one can state a position with authority on this question unless he has read Muller and interacted with his arguments." I think this would be reasonable to apply to someone who was setting up *challenge* someone of Muller's stature. But I don't see myself as doing that. And so my question to Lane would be—does this same high threshold apply to critics of the FV? Should those hundreds of men who were simply voting on something that many of them had barely heard of, and were doing so because RC Sproul said that *sola fide* shouldn't be up for grabs, did they meet this threshold of yours?

The last issue is where it would be nice to be able to point to page numbers in *RINE*, but oh, well. From the quotations that Lane supplied, it looks as though I may have unwittingly caused some confusion. I am *not* a monocovenantalist. I believe that God made a covenant with Adam in the garden, which Adam then broke. God then made a second covenant, distinct from the first, but not unrelated to it. It was not unrelated because one of the blessings of the second covenant was to reverse the curses that had fallen on our race because of our disobedience to the first covenant. In a very limited way, they are like the Articles of Confederation and the Constitution—not the same at all, but not unrelated. When I said that there was only one covenant throughout covenantal history, I was assuming the Fall as having already happened. In *all* history, two covenants. Since the fall, only one, contra the dispensationalists.

As I use the word *bond* in my definition of a covenant, I mean a relationship and everything that goes with a true and godly relationship (which would include love, agreements, standards, and parties of the first part).

And last, when I reject morbid introspection, I am rejecting the *morbidity*, and not godly self-examination. My problem with morbid introspectionists is not that they examine their hearts, but rather that they absolutely *refuse* to examine their hearts. I wish that they would learn how to examine their hearts.

LIKE SOME BLONDE IN A TIGHT DRESS
JUNE 21, 2007

Three quick responses to the latest at Green Baggins*.

The first is that when I denied the equal ultimacy of gospel and law, Lane responded with this:

> One important point here is the relationship of law and grace in the mind of God. Wilson says that he doesn't buy the equal ultimacy of law and grace. I would answer: is God more gracious than He is holy? Is the righteousness of God more or less important than the love of God?

The problem here is that law and holiness are not synonyms. I have no problem at all in declaring the ultimacy of God's holiness. He was thrice holy before any creature was made, and I see the holiness of God as the sum total of all His perfections. But holiness is not the same as law. Law derives from His holiness, and is dependent on it, but it is not the same thing. For example, God gives law to His creatures, and He forgives sinful creatures. This is what His mercy, and justice, and grace, and law do when He is interacting with fallen creatures. But these unmanifested attributes (a readiness to forgive, say) were not operative at all in the timeless aeons before the first creature was spoken into existence.

Second, Lane asks (with regard to my affirmation of two covenants), "Was eternal life for Adam conditioned upon perfect and personal obedience?" I wouldn't put it that way. I would rather say that avoidance of eternal death was conditioned upon not disobeying. The gift that Adam was receiving could be forfeited by disobedience but did not need to be earned by continued obedience. Disobedience would wreck it, and did, but obedience wouldn't earn it.

And last, the treatment of the FV position was a political move, and really slick, but transparently obvious. Part of the elegance of the thing lies in how obvious it is, and how the people running the play don't care. It reminds of a baseball player who, when my dad was a boy, and there was only one umpire on

* greenbaggins.wordpress.com/2007/06/20/the-covenant-of-works-2

the field, would do the following whenever he got on first. If a ball was hit to the outfield, the ump had to run out to see how it was handled because he was the only guy there. Our man on first would take the opportunity to run behind the ump, skipping second base, and running straight to third. Everybody in the stands saw it, of course, but the ump didn't. And what mattered (at least to him) was the fact that he got what he wanted. He was on third after all.

Large assemblies in part must rely on their committees to do the spade work, and I am not faulting the GA for that. You can't have high level of theological discourse within the limits that a big assembly necessarily has. That is why it is so important to get the fairness thing right before the GA—in the committee. So I am faulting those who stacked that committee like it some blonde in a tight dress, and who then try to brazen it out after the fact. "What's this? What do you mean? Perfectly modest attire."

THE REV. RICK JAMES
JUNE 22, 2007

Just so you know . . .

In any controversy, it is always easy to move on to the next thing. And the next thing can be the next argument, the next bone of contention, the next chapter, the next dust up, the next round, and so on. When this happens, all the participants move on and the controversy continues. It is often the case that key moments in the early stage of the controversy are almost completely forgotten by the participants. But until that happens, as long as Asahel is dead in the road, people stop and look, and it slows the battle down.

This principle is why people do things that they are willing to brazen out. People brazen it out because *brazening it out works*. And this is why I intend to bring up the stacked nature of the PCA committee every chance I get, for as long as I can remember to do so. Not only will I do this, but I intend to memorialize it with as many metaphors as I can manage to come up with. That committee was as stacked as a double order of buttermilks, as stacked as some blonde in a tight dress, and as stacked as a brick house. The PCA, she's mighty, mighty.

GREASING THE SKIDS WITH A HOLY UNCTION
JUNE 22, 2007

Green Baggins* has raised the spilt milk issue and is wondering whether my repeated raising of the stacked committee issue is worthwhile, now that the vote has gone down. But before I answer this, now that we are on the subject again, let me just say that the committee was as stacked as a Campbell soup display in the front aisle of Safeway. But my metaphors aren't getting through to Lane, and he now argues that for me to keep *returning* to this issue betrays a lack of confidence in God's sovereignty.

> And yet, look at Wilson's last post. What good will it do to continue to state that the deck was stacked? Is he going to convince anyone of it? Question to Wilson: was the composition of the study committee somehow outside the providence of God?

There are two issues here. First, I do not believe that the fact that God has decreed something is in any way inconsistent with the free agency and responsibility of man. This is because He decrees everything, and we remain responsible for our little portion of that everything. If I sinned yesterday, I know as a good Calvinist that this was part of the decretal will of God, settled before all worlds. But I also know that His decrees do not annihilate my responsibility to confess my sin heartily and honestly. So of course God decreed that the PCA General Assembly would do exactly what they did. And that does not in any way remove the moral responsibility of the men who greased the parliamentary skids with an holy unction.

The second part of Lane's question is this. "Is he going to convince anyone of it?" Well, yes, actually. I intend to convince quite a few people of it, and I don't have to do a lot of talking. This is not a hard sell. It is, to use a theological phrase, stinking obvious. All I have to do is continue to point out that the committee had no minority report, and the fact that it was not *going* to have a minority report was assured and settled from the very beginning, from the moment the committee assignments were first given.

* greenbaggins.wordpress.com/2007/06/22/the-visibleinvisible-church-distinction-again

I have said for a number of years that this is a battle over the second-year seminarians. There are any number of young men who do not yet have a dog in the fight. They are in the "reading up on it" stage. They do not have a job yet (meaning that they don't have a job that can be *threatened*), and these young bucks are just sitting there watching this whole thing. Their heads are going back and forth, like the crowd at Wimbledon watching a really hot tennis match. Huh, they think. Look at that. Whoa, they think. Look at *that*. Does Lane really think that the rigged nature of this charade is not obvious to any disinterested observer? Does he really think I would have any trouble persuading people that a stacked committee was a stacked committee?

There are some who are suspicious of the Federal Vision who are men of integrity, and they don't like the *way* this thing is being done. Lane should join them. I have a good friend, deeply skeptical of FV, who is consistently embarrassed by the behavior of the anti-FV national leaders.

And David Bayly, no friend of the FV, said this:

> Tim and I believe the Ad Interim Report would have been stronger if the committee had contained representatives of Federal Vision views. Our experience both in authoring and in taking part in such committees leads us to believe that the inclusion of foes uniformly sharpens the thinking—and ultimately the reporting—of such committees.*

This is exactly correct, and the fact that this was *not* done is the standing legacy of that hand-*picked* committee. You know, the committee that was as stacked as all the Miles Davis LPs in an FM radio station basement. Lane would be well-advised to give up the vain task of defending men who ought to be able to defend themselves, but who, in the political world they live in, won't need to at all. They don't need Lane to carry water for them because they are going to just brazen it out. This was a parliamentary power move—"because we *can*"—and we on the receiving end are all grown-ups.

* David's bog post, "Why I voted against the Novenson procedural motion..." is here: baylyblog.com/blog/2007/06/why-i-voted-against-novenson-procedural-motion

We understand what is being done to us. And we trust the sovereignty of God in the midst of it. But the sovereignty of God over sin *sanctifies no sin*. Only the blood of Jesus Christ does that.

AS STACKED AS . . .
JUNE 23, 2007

Since a volunteer competition is breaking out already, let's put them all in one place. I may have missed some in the gathering, and so if I did just add them again in the comments section. And if any new ones occur to you, please add them as well. I think we could have at least as much fun as the haiku contest.

As stacked as:

1. A double order of buttermilks;
2. Some blonde in a tight dress;
3. A brick house;
4. As Rick James on his way to detox;
5. As a deck of cards at a Magician's Convention;
6. As the Library of Congress;
7. As a new-mown hayfield;
8. As a deck of cards at a casino;
9. As a lottery ticket;
10. As cordwood in November;
11. As a Harry Potter display, July 20, 11:59 p.m;
12. As Bay Bridge traffic on Memorial Day weekend;
13. As the odds against me winning the lottery;
14. As little brown pellets under a neglected rabbit cage;
15. As the assumptions required to support a claim for atheistic moral objectivity;
16. As a polygamist's honey-do list;
17. As a dozen rocks in the middle of the Jordan;
18. As the odds against a productive study actually being accomplished by a stacked committee;

19. As the ballot box in a Mexican election (but I repeat myself);
20. As a double-decker bus with Japanese tourists;
21. As a Nigel Tufnel Marshall rig at the amusement park gig;
22. As the national debt;
23. As the strata in the Grand Canyon;
24. As plywood at Home Depot;
25. As a Campbell soup display in the front aisle of Safeway;
26. As all the Miles Davis LPs in an FM radio station basement;

A couple different verbs:

1. As stuffed as Derek Small's spandex at the airport checkpoint;
2. As choreographed as a WWF match.

IN SEARCH OF A REAL EXAM
JUNE 23, 2007

Bob Mattes, one of the members of the PCA committee, has written his only Wilson post*. He is limiting himself to just one because I am not in the PCA. In his post he makes four basic points. One is that I created the CREC in my own theonomic image rather than join a denomination that would hold me accountable for my teaching. The second is that I have a lot of nerve, accusing the PCA of stacking their committee—when *I* my own self was examined at a CREC presbytery meeting concerning my views on the Federal Vision. I was examined by a committee that I "handpicked." Third, if I want a real exam I should go out to Westminster West and Scott Clark and Michael Horton would show me what a *real* examination was supposed to be like. And last, it appears that within the last few weeks he has discovered that I believe a number of icky things about slavery.

Okay, this won't take long. The first accusation would at least have had some surface plausibility when we established the CREC a little over a decade ago with just three churches. The church I pastor being one of the three,

* reformedmusings.wordpress.com/2007/06/22/my-only-wilson-post

someone at that time could have made the big frog/small pond accusation. I think some did. But with the way God has blessed us, it is not plausible at all any more. With the varying circumstances of the churches kept in mind (mission, candidate, member), there are around sixty congregations now. We are extremely grateful to God for His continued kindness to us. If you want to know more about the CREC, you can check it out here†.

Second, of course my examination did not involve any real risk. It wasn't supposed to. I wasn't on trial. I requested a detailed examination so that others outside our circles could see clearly what I taught on these subjects, and so that this teaching would be "on the record" and available. I didn't request to be brought up on charges. I requested that my friends and colleagues within the CREC ask me the questions that my adversaries outside the CREC *should* have been asking me, but were refusing to. The exam was recorded and both it and a written portion of it are available. And that exam has been, um, *underutilized* by those who pretend in public and in their judicial settings to know what I think.

Third, I would be happy to go out to Westminster West to be examined by Scott Clark and Michael Horton. But I will have to ask Bob to set it up for me, because I have requested face to face interaction/debates/discussion multiple times. Scott Clark turned off the comments section of his blog because his assertions always have a way of squirting sideways on him. His examinations always go much better when there is no one there to answer the questions. So, here it is again. I would be delighted to be examined by Clark and Horton. Bob, please, set this one up.

And last, the slavery thing. He quotes me saying, "Our humanistic and democratic culture regards slavery in itself as a monstrous evil, and it acts as though this were self-evidently true. The Bible permits Christians to own slaves, provided they are treated well. You are a Christian. Whom do you believe?" He doesn't engage with this, but just offers it up as ludicrous on the face of it. Nothing necessary here but a horse laugh, right? His plausibility structure clearly comes from our surrounding secularism, and not from the Bible.

† crechurches.org

What I would like to do is provide Bob with a couple of quotations, one from the Bible and the other from the Westminster Confession, and then ask a small cluster of questions.

> Let as many servants as are *under the yoke* count their own masters worthy of *all honour*, that the name of God and his doctrine be not blasphemed. And they that have *believing masters*, let them not despise them, because *they are brethren*; but rather do them service, because *they are faithful and beloved*, partakers of the benefit. These things *teach* and *exhort*. (1 Tim. 6:1–2, emphasis added).

And from Westminster:

> By this faith [saving faith], a Christian believes to be true *whatsoever is revealed in the Word*, for the authority of God Himself speaking therein" (WCF 14.2, emphasis added).

And here's my small set of questions: In the first century, where slavery existed, would you have taught and exhorted these things? And do you have saving faith?

For those who are interested in what the Bible actually teaches about slavery, and want to read more about my views on the subject, with those views presented *in context*, they can get this book.*

FAR WORSE THAN A STACKED STUDY COMMITTEE JUNE 24, 2007

I did not see the video feed on the floor debate at the PCA General Assembly, but I understand that R.C. Sproul Sr. argued there that putting FV guys on the study commission would be akin to putting the defendant on the jury. Okay, so let's take that as our model of what the proceedings were supposed to be like.

* *Black & Tan: Essays and Excursions on Slavery, Culture War, and Scripture in America,* currently available here: canonpress.com/products/black-tan..

If it were simply a study committee, then you would expect to get the various perspectives, a majority report and minority report and so on. If it were a judicial proceeding, then you would not expect that—in that context, R.C.'s comment makes sense. But of course, in order for a judicial proceeding to make to the floor of GA, other things would have had to have happened first—little things like charges, proof, trials at presbytery, that kind of thing. But let's leave that aside for the nonce.

Now I believe that it was the former, a study committee, and so I advance the argument that the committee was as stacked as . . . as . . . as, I don't know, stacked things. But what happens if it is the latter? A jury, not a study committee? *That* presents me with another argument, and this one is actually far more potent than the argument I ought to have. Study committees sit around in the library. Juries handle the lives and reputations of others. And so of course, you exclude the accused from the jury. *You also exclude men who are hostile to the accused,* and who are out to get them. You exclude the personal friends of the accused, and—because Almighty God inhabits the highest heaven and considers the ways of men—you *also* exclude the professional adversaries of the accused. The point of a jury is to find disinterested parties, who will listen to both sides, and make a determination. Instead, what do we have? So the committee was a jury. Did it meet the biblical standards of justice for the composition of juries? Ha.

As a study committee, the PCA Ad Interim committee was stacked and risible. But if you want it to be a *jury*, it was far worse than that.

REFORMED CATHOLICITY
JUNE 24, 2007

In the thread of a recent post, the question of sectarianism and the CREC was raised, and I thought I needed to make just a few comments about it. This is one of those issues where context matters a great deal.

I became a paedobaptist in 1993, and this happened in a church with some staunch baptists in it. Without going into the details, some of the baptists left unhappy, but the vast majority of the church, and the vast majority of the baptists in the church, did not want to divide over such an issue. So we didn't. We worked out a baptismal cooperation agreement, one that we still honor and use. As a friend and a pastor to some of these godly and charitable baptists, I was not about to conduct a purge of them from the church. These were people who had stood by me in a very difficult time. Now, with this mutt of a credobaptist/paedobaptist congregation, what Reformed denomination would you have us go join? We had absolutely nowhere to go.

At the same time, we had become convinced of presbyterian polity—the difficulty of sorting out the baptism question had revealed some pretty sorry gaps in our polity as well. And so we joined together with two other congregations here in the Northwest, congregations that had had a historic connection with us—lots of friendship and common ministry together. That is how the CREC formed—not as a schismatic attempt to increase fissures in the Reformed world, but rather as an attempt to reduce the disunity in our small corner of it. Since that time the Lord has blessed us greatly, and we have seen many congregations come into our confederation. We are very grateful for all of this.

But in the discussion of the catholicity (or lack thereof) in the CREC, this comment was made.

> Unfortunately, for Wilson, arguably the CREC founder, and others, that is not enough. Additionally, they insist all Presbyterians must tolerate equally these practices equally and there is zero respect for the decision of the presbyters of other (than CREC) denominations, that do not happen to allow for these convictions that landed you in the CREC. By becoming yoked with the CREC, you are yoked with men and woman who enjoy mocking their enemies (in this case presbyters), and have elevated it to an artform. At some point, this recklessness must become indefensible to the real leadership of the CREC, if such a thing exists outside of Moscow.

Just a few things need to be said here. The first is a factual one, and concerns what we demand from others. Take paedocommunion, for example. I believe that paedocommunionists in the PCA have a moral obligation to honor the decision of their denomination *against* that practice. I would believe them to be in sin if they unilaterally rejected the authority of their broader church in this. But take it a step further. Could a nonpaedocommunionist church join the CREC? Absolutely. We have room for credobaptists, and so why on earth would we reject credocommunionists? On what principle would we reject them?

There is one restriction in this regard, but it applies to everyone—and it is in my mind the "catholicity" requirement. An individual congregation in the CREC can be a credobaptist congregation and allow only credo-baptists on the session. This could be what is taught from the pulpit and settled in their statement of faith. But if a family from a paedobaptist CREC congregation moved to their area, and joined their church, they could not require that the children who had been already baptized be baptized again. They would have to *receive* those infant baptisms. They would not have to *administer* them, but they would have to receive them in all charity.

A similar kind of thing could happen the other way. If someone baptized in infancy came to credo-baptist convictions, I could not in good conscience conduct such a baptism myself. But I could help the person find a minister who could do this, and when the deed was done, I should have no problem receiving such a person into fellowship with us.

All CREC congregations have to adopt the Apostles Creed, the Nicene Creed, and the Definition of Chalcedon. After that, they have to choose between one of six reformational creeds—the London Baptist, the American Westminster, the original English Westminster, the Three Forms of Unity, the Savoy Declaration, and a modern Reformed Evangelical Confession. There has even been talk about adding the original Augsburg Confession and/or the 39 Articles, but we haven't gotten very far on that. Christ Church here in Moscow has adopted a Book of Confessions, with the central confession being the original Westminster, but the larger book includes the 39 Articles. All of this represents a very practical attempt at Reformed catholicity. We are very serious about this.

So what about the point that we (meaning me) mock our enemies? It should be extremely obvious by this point that we do not treat fellow believers this way simply because they hold different doctrinal convictions than we do. We are building a confederation that has fellowship and cooperation between such groups built into it *as a design feature*. And the credocommunionists in the PCA, were they to visit us here in Moscow, would be welcome at the Table with us any and every Sunday. The same goes for all CREC churches. Their children would be welcome too, but let us not get distracted from the point we are discussing. The credocommunionists who hold their convictions sincerely and honestly have nothing but respect from me. I do feel sad for them, but no mockery. *None.*

What I mock is Pharisaism. What I mock is stacked study committees, and the long, solemn, indignant faces whenever somebody mentions this screamingly *obvious* fact. What I mock is the bum's rush for ministers in good standing with no charges filed, no evidence submitted, no proof offered, just raw power from on high—but plenty of *that*. What I mock is a study committee that gets an important quote from me bass-ackwards, drops it sheepishly when caught, promising to explain it on the floor of GA. By the way, did that happen? What I mock is exactly the same thing that we find mocked in the pages of the New Testament—ecclesiastical stuffed-shirt *pretentiousness*, and an inability to maintain a sense of godly *proportion*. You know, camels and gnats, gold and altars, and justice and mercy and tithing from the spice rack. You know, *justice and mercy* and parsing the covenant of works under a meritscope. What I mock are those who are *so* concerned for merit in the pages of their systematics, but when it comes to any merit their judicial proceedings might be lacking, they don't give a rip. What I mock are the traditions of the elders—even though I love, honor, and keep those traditions. But the ones who have those traditions draped over their heads like so many Westminster tablecloths have only obscured their vision and have started bumping into things, knocking them over. When I say something about *that* peculiar custom, I am upbraided for not honoring the tablecloth. Not at all. Put it on the Table, and sit down, you and your children. You are supposed to eat the *food*, people, not argue over the silverware.

In short, if you want to know, I am a *Puritan*. The trouble some are having with understanding this just reveals that they are dutiful curators at the Puritan Waxworks (day pass $9.95) and need a night in the museum. You know, where some Elizabethan pamphleteers come to life and show us all that Reformation is more like chopping down the redwood of Self-Righteousness with the ax of the Gospel than it is like threading the needle of Condign Merit with the gossamer thread of Supralapsarianism. Whatever that might mean.

OTHODOX JOE
JUNE 27, 2007

Green Baggins* is continuing our discussion, and this exchange revolves around two basic questions. The first has to do with my examination by the CREC presbytery (in 2004, before we divided into two presbyteries). Lane asks if the CREC has any TRs in it, and if they were invited to participate in the exam. And pressing his point home, he asks if there were no TRs on the examination committee, then how would this do anything to allay the charge that the CREC is nothing more than a "rubber stamp denomination," the better to enable me to say things like *bwah hah hah*. Lane goes out of his way to say that *he* is not saying this but wonders what good the exam did in a world where people *are* saying that.

Several things. First, I actually think the CREC does have some TRs in it, but I don't know that they would be owned as such by those who are currently wearing the mantle. At least one of the gentlemen I have in mind in this category was on the examination committee. But in addition, I have to point out that I did not form the committee. I requested the examination, and the committee was formed by our moderator. I do know that the goal of the committee was to ask questions that TRs would acknowledge as the questions that needed to be asked, and I believe they did a very good job of this.

The committee did decide that I was orthodox, but that was not the real point. I acknowledge it was not exactly a Perry Mason courtroom moment. So Lane's point is correct as far as it goes—if someone wanted to dismiss the

* greenbaggins.wordpress.com/2007/06/25/notae-ecclesiae

verdict, that would be easy enough for them to do. The verdict was that I was okay, but of course I was judicially okay *before* I requested the exam. I didn't need to go through an exam to establish that. The point of the exam was to establish a public record, *on* the record, of how I answer certain controverted questions. And since the time of that exam, we have not trumpeted the results of the verdict—as though the CREC took me behind closed doors, pretended to examine me, and then came out to announce that I was Orthodox Joe. No, what we have circulated is *the exam itself*—the questions and the answers. We have circulated written questions and answers, and we have circulated recordings of the oral exam.

This means that if someone says that the verdict was rigged, all we have to do is refer them to the contents of the exam and ask where the problem lies. And, given the content of that exam, there are only three responses that an honest to goodness TR can have. The first is to ignore everything. This has been the path not less traveled. The second is to acknowledge that the questions and answers were really good, and that I might actually be descended from A.A. Hodge. The third is to say I am lying. But whatever happened, we did not think that a verdict by itself would persuade anybody. Honest answers to obviously good questions *should* be able to do that though.

Lane worries a bit that I might go off on a little bit of rhetorical terryhooting in response to his blog post, but I have no intention of doing that. I do that sometimes but never when someone is honestly trying to communicate with me—as Lane obviously is trying to do. I have been known to make light-hearted comments about grand exalted potentates and wizards running freethinkers out of their moose lodge of a church, but this is all in good fun, and not directed at guys who are honestly trying like Lane.

The second point resumes his interaction with my book *"Reformed" Is Not Enough*, and his basic question here concerns my "minimizing" discipline as one of the marks of the Church. The traditional marks of the Church in Reformed theology have been Word, sacrament, and discipline. I tweak this slightly, making discipline the fence that protects the two marks of the Church, Word and sacrament. Lane gets my illustration exactly. A church without discipline has no immune system; it is a church with AIDS. But people with AIDS are very sick people, not dead people. Churches without Word and sacrament are not sick churches, but rather dead churches. One of the commenters at Lane's blog suggested that I was "minimizing" discipline like this because of my supposed baptismal nominalism. But those who know what the church culture in Moscow is like know that this is really wide of the mark. We *do* practice church discipline. My reduction of discipline to a "semi-mark" of the Church was simply an attempt to answer a theological puzzle, not an attempt to shy away from discipline. A church with no discipline is a church with AIDS.

I see Word and sacrament as essential to life, right now—like breathing or the circulation of the blood. I see discipline as essential to the protection of those things which are essential to life, but as not necessarily essential to life right this minute. A man with AIDS can live for years. A man whose heart stops, or whose lungs collapse, dies immediately. I was simply trying to account for this analogous difference.

Lane asks if I allow exceptions to the rule that no salvation is to be found outside the Church. Absolutely. I much prefer Westminster's formulation of this to Cyprian's—outside the church there is no *ordinary* possibility of salvation. I grant that the last day will reveal the salvation of many who never had any connection to the visible church. But this is not the way it ordinarily goes, and this is not the way the New Testament usually speaks.

JULY 2007

CHESTERTON DOWN THE HIGHWAY

JULY 3, 2007

Green Baggins has reviewed some commentaries here*, among them Peter Leithart's new commentary on Kings.

Apart from demonstrating that he is a young man in a hurry—he expresses his disappointment with the commentary without having read it, on the basis of the bibliography alone—he also misses an important aspect of theological development in the Church. This is understandable because Lane is a product of seminary, and modern seminaries are very much in the tradition of measuring theological development in one way, a way that certainly has its place. But when it forgets the other way (which it almost always does), trouble is brewing. Scholars are soon replaced by fussers and there we are.

There are two ways to measure a man by his footnotes and bibliography. One is to measure his footnotes and bibliography. The other is to measure how many footnotes and bibliographies he is likely to wind up *in*.

The two usually don't go together, but occasionally they do—as they do in Leithart. For another rare example, C.S. Lewis was capable of writing scholarly books that showed a mastery of the literature in his field, and these books (like *The Allegory of Love*, or *English Literature in the Sixteenth Century*) are still valuable today. But he wrote another way as well, with virtually no footnotes or scholarly apparatus. These are the books by which he is chiefly remembered, and they will show up in footnotes and bibliographies for the next five hundred years or so.

* greenbaggins.wordpress.com/2006/10/27/some-recent-new-books

Chesterton was quotable above virtually all men, and one looks in vain for him to handle the requirements of the footnote-mongers with sufficient gentleness and respect. Chesterton roisters merrily down the highway of thought, with the more precise-minded following after, picking up after him, correcting a citation here or a date there. And yet the footnoters highly respect him (now that he's dead), and will quote him until the cows find two in the bush, as they say.

My point, and there is one around here somewhere, is that Peter Leithart has made, is making, and will make an enormous contribution to theological development in the twentieth and twenty-first centuries. Disagreeing with him is fine, and he is the kind of gracious Christian gentleman who welcomes that kind of thing. But patronizing him is just embarrassing.

PLUG AND CHUG LEGALISM?
JULY 8, 2007

Kevin Johnson quotes* from an article in the most recent *Credenda*, and admonishes me for something I didn't say in it.

> Correspondingly, the Reformation was first about our repentance and embracing of Christ something which Wilson never mentions in this article.

This was curious on two counts. First, it should be possible to write an article about liturgy and not incur someone's displeasure because I didn't mention something else that I believe equally strongly. You can't say everything everytime—it's a time management thing.

But the curious nature of the second count was even more odd. That is because, as it happens, I *did* mention a "genuine love for Christ" in the article, along with how certain kinds of people need "learn something fundamental about God." I also mentioned, twice as it turns out, the fact that Holy Spirit can be grieved by our behavior in worship. What Johnson dismisses as mere moralism and legalism, checking things off a spiritual to-do list, was actually

* reformedcatholicism.com/?p=1214, no longer available.

an exhortation to function within the context of triune *personalism*, never forgetting that God is always present with us in worship and will not be fooled by our mummeries, high or low.

Actually, there was a third oddity in Johnson's response. That was the fact that one of the main thrusts of the article was the point that a simple "liturgical to-do list" won't cut it. Here is another snippet from that article and, you tell me, is this the kind of "plug and chug" approach that legalists like to take?

> To say up front that liturgy is extremely important—that having a defined, biblical structure to the worship service is crucial, and that formality does not necessarily drive our genuine love for Christ—does not require us to then embrace any particular practice that some Anglicans might be doing. To follow the covenant renewal pattern of worship [the pattern we follow at Christ Church] not only does not require us to adopt any proposal (provided it is 'higher' than what we were all doing ten years ago), it actually requires us to be suspicious of all such tendencies to overshoot the goal.

In other words, there are any number of ways to honor Christ in worship. The next paragraph describes two pastors *doing the same thing*, one out of obedience to Christ and the other not. The legalist wants everything cut and dried. The wise response to such questions and situations is usually something like "it's not that simple." Two men can do the same thing and one be received by God and the other not. Two other men can do very different things and both be received by the same God.

Johnson's critique is comparable to challenging my writing or preaching because I don't use the King James Version of the Bible. To which I could respond, "But I do use the King James." Now what do we do? It is apparent that Johnson wants very much to find a crucial area where he and I differ, and I am sure there are plenty of them. But whether or not the Reformation was first brought about by "our repentance and embracing of Christ" is not one of them.

APROPOS OF NOTHING
JULY 20, 2007

In the tension-filled room full of systematic theologians and biblical theologians, it is perilously easy to juxtapose "timeless truths" to "story." But this is not necessary, and this is another plea to all get along. It should go without saying that I affirm what the Reformed systematicians have distilled out behind their magisterial barn. And when they are serving up *Old Turretin* (200 proof) I drink it down gladly. Nevertheless, I have great sympathies with the biblical theologians also.

But in the current debates, since I am more or less aligned with the latter group, let me just say this as an admonition to our guys. A lot of what goes out as biblical theology, marketed as "Story Theology" is actually "Literary Criticism Theology." And those are not the same thing at all.

WALK LIKE A NINJA
JULY 24, 2007

Green Baggins continues to review my book *"Reformed" Is Not Enough*, and he does so here*. He begins this post by asking where I have been hiding.

> I sent an email to Douglas Wilson asking if he is desirous of continuing the debate. I believe that since June 28th, which was the first post on the sacerdotalism chapter, and July 2nd, which was the second post on that chapter, and July 12th, which was my first post on the baptism chapter, Wilson has had adequate time to respond. I think that if those who are benefitting from this exchange between a critic and a proponent of FV are desirous of keeping this a two-way street, some pressure will need to be exerted on Wilson to continue on his side. I plan on finishing the book review. I am not sure why Wilson has not continued the debate. But lack of time can hardly be the reason, especially since he has posted on the Federal Vision here. I do not mean to bully Wilson in any way. If he is not desirous of continuing the debate, then

* greenbaggins.wordpress.com/2007/07/23/baptism-now-saves-part-2

> that is certainly his prerogative. At the same time, I think it odd that he has been clamoring for debate, and yet now does not seem to want it. Was it because I came down hard on his (mis)take on Warfield? I make no attempt to read his motives. I am somewhat puzzled, I confess. Maybe Wilson will be so good as to clear it up for us.

So let me address that first. What with a book project I was finishing, some pastoral time-munchers, catching up in the office after time on the road, shoveling away at small mountains of email, and having five extra grandchildren back from the UK, I have been up to my neck in plenty of good things to do. During such seasons, priorities shift, some of them downward. But interacting with Green Baggins is still something I intend to finish, and because I have just gotten through this most recent bottleneck, here we are. No pressure necessary. All I need are some extra hours.

At the same time, in the spirit of full disclosure, it should be said that my enthusiasm for answering Lane had been dampened by his treatment of Leithart on Kings. That was just the royal limit, but still I soldier on. What I intend to do here is respond briefly to this most recent post, and, as I have opportunity, go back and respond to the ones I missed. I hear rumors that I got my rear end kicked over a Warfield quote and so I really need to go back to that one and check for bruises.

One of the reasons I have been willing to interact with Lane is that he has been willing to acknowledge a number of my qualifications and explanations. This is not the case with some of the other FV guys, but, for whatever reason, he does do it with me. This could cut both ways, of course. At the end of this process I might find that I am reluctantly included among the orthodox. The other possibility is that Lane might have to start defending himself against charges that *he* is denying *sola fide*. There are some people out there on a hair trigger, and whenever one goes to presbytery one must walk like a ninja.

For example, in this last response, he is sailing pretty close to the wind—at least as far as some critics of the FV are concerned.

> In this [on the question of deferred grace from baptism], I would certainly side with Wilson. Indeed, as carefully read and qualified (I don't at all like the language of baptismal regeneration, as it carries an enormous weight of baggage), Wilson's position seems to be in accord with the Standards on baptism.

Yikes. Criminy. An implication of this is that Lane is arguing here that FV critics who have accused me of sacerbadthingsism have misunderstood and misrepresented me. This is quite true, and so I'll take it with grateful thanks.

So let me explain my use of the phrase *baptismal regeneration.* I actually agree with Lane that the phrase carries a lot of baggage that I don't want to carry. This is why you won't hear me preaching any sermon series on *Why We Hold to Baptismal Regeneration.* What happened was this.

I got accused of holding to baptismal regeneration, and a bunch of other unflattering things, by a number of hostile Injuns who had the warpaint on, and who were wearing the Westminster Confession of Faith as a ceremonial headdress, feathers and all. Without me having used this kind of language provocatively (for obvious reasons of prudence), I was accused of holding to the substance of baptismal regeneration by men who did not know the history of their own confession. Because of their compromises with the American baptistic ethos, they had institutionalized a number of "workarounds" to the language of their own confession and baptismal formulae. This they did, serenely unaware of how much they owed to the Southern Baptist Convention.

The point of that section in *RINE* was to point this glaring problem out. Now I cheerfully admit, acknowledge and say that the Westminster doctrine on this is clearly *not* the doctrine of the Lutherans, Anglicans, or Roman Catholics. But if you are going to get whipped up into a lather over language, or logical inferences from such language, then why don't you guys start with your own confessional totem? It is just as clear that Westminster's is not the doctrine of the bapterian critics of the FV.

Lane says that he differs with me over my lack of qualification over *sign* and *thing signified.* But I do make this qualification and have made it repeatedly. My central point here is that if heresy charges can be leveled on the basis of "ambiguous" language, then the bapterians have only succeeded in indicting the Westminster Confession. It is the Westminster Standards that say both sacraments are effectual means of salvation to worthy receivers. It is the Westminster Confession that says one of the things signified by baptism is regeneration. It is the Westminster Confession that says the things signified by baptism (among which we include regeneration) are really exhibited and conferred by baptism at the time of the effectual call. So fine. Don't use the language of baptismal regeneration if you don't want to. I don't want to either. That is not a problem. But it is a problem when your reluctance to use that language yourself prevents you from reading a seventeenth century document in its historical setting. It is a problem if you cannot discern the undeniable presence of massive Presbyterian compromises with American revivalism in the evangelical world today. Such confusion is not biblical, it is not historical, and it is not confessional.

WESTMINSTER SACERDOTALISM
JULY 26, 2007

I said that I was going to try to get caught up with Green Baggins's review of *RINE*, and here is the next payment on that particular debt.

In his review of my tenth chapter, Lane says that my criticism of Warfield is based on a confusion of *sacerdotalism* and *sacramentalism*. "Sacerdotalism," he says, "has to do with a priesthood caste in the church." This is different from the idea that the sacraments work *ex opere operato*, which he calls *sacramentalism*. He also says that if something works *ex opere operato* it is tantamount to magic.

He then cites Warfield at various places to show that Warfield was objecting to the idea of a "human intruder in the pathway of God's grace." Now I take Warfield to be objecting to the idea of a *created* intruder, not just a human intruder. For Warfield, God's immediate grace does not need a priest to funnel it, certainly. But neither does it need bread or wine, or water.

But let's work with Lane's distinction and see what happens—even though, in one sense, the whole discussion is beside the point because Lane acknowledges that Warfield would reject sacramentalism also.

First, how can there be sacraments without someone to administer them? And if there must be someone to administer them, and they are means of grace, then presto, we have our human intruder getting in between the worshipper and the grace of God. The Westminster Standards are very strong on sacraments not showing up by themselves, or in the hands of agents not lawfully ordained to the task.

> The Lord Jesus has, in this ordinance, appointed His ministers to declare His word of institution to the people, to pray, and bless the elements of bread and wine, and thereby to set them apart from a common to an holy use; and to take and break the bread, to take the cup, and (they communicating also themselves) to give both to the communicants. (WCF 29.3)

> To these officers the keys of the kingdom of heaven are committed; by virtue whereof, they have power, respectively, to retain, and remit sins; to shut that kingdom against the impenitent, both by the Word, and censures; and to open it unto penitent sinners, by the ministry of the Gospel; and by absolution from censures, as occasion shall require. (WCF 30.2)

Lane's take on Warfield means that Westminster Presbyterians are sacerdotalists. The fact that we don't call the "human intruder" a priest is just a matter of terminology. The grace of God is available in the sacraments, and the sacraments are only available through those who are lawfully ordained. This means that the grace of God for God's people is dependent on human agents. This means that Lane must either change his definition of sacerdotalism or take an exception to Westminster.

My second point here has to do with Lane's take on *ex opere operato* being necessarily magic. Certainly, when a Roman Catholic priest utters the words of consecration, the results come about *ex opere operato*. In other words, with the sacraments, a "magic" utterance would be an *ex opere operato* utterance. But it doesn't need to go the other way. All cows have four legs, but not all four-legged beasts are cows.

Peter Leithart does a wonderful job in his most recent book *The Baptized Body* in showing the potency of ritual. And in his discussion, it is very clear that there is no "magic" at all. A man can lawfully make love to a woman on Monday when it would have been unlawful for him to do so the previous Friday. The difference was the wedding ritual on Saturday. A man takes the oath of office as president, and can send troops into battle where before he was powerless to do so. There is an *ex opere operato* efficacy in this kind of thing *which is not magic*, but which is no less potent for all that.

SANCTIONS AND THE SACRAMENTS
JULY 27, 2007

I believe that this next interaction with Green Baggins promises to be pretty helpful. He is still critiquing the tenth chapter of *RINE*.*

> In other words, for Wilson, the objective nature of baptism means that all people who are baptized come into the same relationship to the covenant, in this sense: that they are all under the same sanctions of the covenant, either for cursing, or for blessing. In fact, he identifies the sacrament with the blessings and curses of the covenant (p. 90). What I would ask is this: what kind of union does he mean? Saving union? Unsaving union? The union of a branch, or the union of a parasite?

The short answer first. The kind of union I mean is *covenantal union*. And when the tree in the scriptural metaphor is the covenant, then I mean the union of a branch. When wheat and tares in the scriptural metaphor are distinguishing true faith from false, then I mean the union of proximity, as with a parasite. Scripture speaks to this issue both ways, and so should we. Wheat and tares are always ontologically different. When you wash a pig you have a clean pig. When a dog vomits, you have a hungry dog. At the same time, when Jesus cuts the fruitless branches out of the Vine, He is removing them from a position which they share entirely with the fruitful branches

* greenbaggins.wordpress.com/2007/07/02/sacerdotalism-part-2

(John 15). Same thing in Romans 11, when Paul talks about the olive tree. We need to layer our illustrations, and not treat them as discrete billiard balls that cannot occupy the same space at the same time.

And I looked at page 90 of my book, and the closest thing I could find to Lane's summary was this. "There is no power in the sacrament itself; there *is* power in that which the sacrament is identified with—the blessings and curses of the covenant itself." I can see that my phrasing here could have been more, um, as the present writer would say, were the present writer a Victorian, felicitious. I did not mean that the sacrament should be identified with sanctions, as though I was talking about the essence of the sacrament, or as triangles are to be identified with three-sided figures. I meant that the sacrament was closely identified with sanctions, as I (the present writer) am identifed with Moscow. I was not saying that there is a definitional identity between the sacrament and sanctions.

I think that this helps address the next question as well.

> But if that is the case, then I have this question: how can the thing signified in the sacrament (which I do not believe is the sanctions, but rather the promise of benefit) be said to be given to the non-elect?

I don't believe that the sacrament signifies sanctions, but rather than it signifies Christ. When this Christ is seen in faith, the necessary result is blessing. When Christ is rejected through unbelief, the result is a curse.

> And I realize the danger of inappropriate partaking of the Lord's Supper (see 1 Corinthians 11:27). But does this constitute part of the essence of the Sacrament? Or is it a distortion of the Sacrament?

> The thing signified is a positive thing, not a negative one

So we are not talking "things," or "essences," but rather Christ. In the personal encounter between Christ and the covenant member, there is either love or enmity. Love is the characteristic of the regenerate heart, and this love sees Christ (accurately) as Savior. Enmity is characteristic of the unregenerate heart, and this enmity sees Christ (*accurately*) as Judge. Christ viewed rightly is of course a blessed Savior. But when the sinful heart rejects Him, and that sinful heart belongs to a covenant member, the result is covenantal sanctions.

So I agree with Lane that the sacrament is given to us in a positive way, expecting the best. The cup is described as the cup of blessing, not the cup of blessings and curses. But, because certain Corinthians despised that blessing, many were sick and some had died. Uzzah died because he got too close to the *mercy* seat.

GREEN BAGGINS TAKES AN EXCEPTION
JULY 27, 2007

And in his latest response* to my response, Lane says this in the course of his continued discussion of Warfield.

"Regeneration can happen before baptism, during baptism, or after baptism. Therefore, it is not dependent on baptism."

This really gets at the crux of the matter between us, and it illustrates why I believe that Lane (and Warfield) *don't really believe* that sacraments are means of grace. They say they do (because as confessional Presbyterians they have to use that phrase), but they take away with the left hand what they gave with the right. Let me quote Lane again, and juxtapose his words with a pertinent section of the Westminster Confession.

> Regeneration can happen before baptism, during baptism, or after baptism. Therefore, it is not dependent on baptism.
>
> The efficacy of Baptism is not tied to that moment of time wherein it is administered; yet, notwithstanding, by the right use of this ordinance, the grace promised is not only offered, but really exhibited, and conferred, by the Holy Ghost, to such (whether of age or infants) as that grace belongs unto, according to the counsel of God's own will, in His appointed time. (WCF 28.6)

* greenbaggins.wordpress.com/2007/07/27/warfield-vindicated

Lane has said that regeneration is "not dependent on baptism," and he says this because of the varying temporal relations that are possible between the moment of baptism and the moment of regeneration. That latter part is true enough. On that point, Lane, I, and the Westminster divines all agree. Regeneration can occur before, during or after baptism. But Lane concludes from this that regeneration is not dependent upon baptism. This is almost a photo negative of the Westminster doctrine.

In stark contrast, Westminster says that the efficacy of baptism *is not tied* to any temporal considerations like this. So why does Lane make an argument out of temporal considerations? And what is the efficacy of baptism? What is included in this efficacy? *Regeneration*, among other things (WCF 28.1). Now Westminster says that, at the appointed time, for those to whom the grace belongs, regeneration is not only offered, but *exhibited* and *conferred*, and this is done by means of *an efficacious baptism*, regardless of when the water was applied. All this is accomplished in the power of the Holy Ghost "by the right use of this ordinance." They do *not* say that regeneration is not dependent upon a "right use of this ordinance."

So let me ask Lane a question here. Do you believe that the Holy Spirit uses the instrumentality of a "right use of this ordinance" as His way of really exhibiting and conferring the grace of regeneration on one of God's elect at the appointed time? If so, would you like to retract or modify your statement above? If not, would you be willing to take an exception to the Westminster Confession at this point?

WHAT IT MUST HAVE MEANT
JULY 28, 2007

One more and I am caught up in my exchanges with Green Baggins. But before answering the questions he raises about my chapter on baptism, I think it is important to address a question raised in the comments of my previous post.

> You make it sound like you're boys playing king of the dirt pile. Say uncle! A lot of theologizing is like that, isn't it?

Yes, it does sound like that if all we were doing is *talking*. But we are in a situation where the ministries of friends of mine are under assault, and not just verbal assault. The FV guys are bringing charges against no one, challenging the ordinations of no one, and we are not trying to get anybody removed from their pulpit. The same cannot be said in the other direction. In other words, this is not a *neener-neener* debate. Ministries and livelihoods are on the line. Yes, the reply might come, but this is what confessional faithfulness to the truth requires. But that is where we encounter the kick in the teeth. As I showed in the previous post, the people who are bringing accusations that we are out of accord with the Westminster Confession are in fact themselves out of accord with the Confession. And they are accusing us of being out of accord with the Confession at just the place where we hold to the Confession and they do not. In such a situation, that anomaly should be pointed out.

This reveals that in conservative American Presbyterianism, the governing doctrine is not the Westminster Confession, *but is rather the agreed-upon-consensus of what the Westminster Confession must have meant*. And whatever it must have meant, it cannot stray too far from the baptistic ethos of American evangelicalism. But when you go back to the words of the Confession, you find out that at the appointed time, for anyone to whom the grace of regeneration belongs, the Holy Spirit exhibits and confers that grace through a right use of the baptismal water. Folks have every right to disagree with this, but they don't have the right to disagree with it on the basis of their "consensus" in the name of Westminster. It *is* Westminster. Sometimes I feel like a speaker at a Fourth of July picnic who gets himself accused of being un-American because I mentioned that "we hold these truths to be self-evident, that all men are created equal, that they are endowed by their Creator with certain unalienable Rights."

The basic question Lane asks here is "with whom is the covenant of grace made?" I have no trouble with some of the distinctions he makes, particularly if you take them all together. I do have trouble with internal/external if no other metaphors are used, and none at all if it is used in conjunction with a cluster of other metaphors. I think that the distinction of narrow/broad is particularly helpful. In the broad sense, the covenant of grace is made with believers and their children. In the narrow sense, the covenant of grace is made with the decretally elect.

One other quick thing. Lane also asks why I identify the unregenerate within the covenant as covenant breakers. "Aren't unbelievers *already* covenant-breakers *in Adam*? . . . Are we going to say that they become covenant breakers of both the covenant of works and the covenant of grace?" Well, yes, that is exactly what I want to say. If Adam is their covenant head, they share in his rebellion. That's covenant breaking. And if they are in the covenant of grace in the broad sense required by the Westminster Confession (remember that even the Mosaic economy is described there as an administration of the covenant of grace), and they fail to keep the covenant because of their unbelief, then why would we not consider them covenant breakers there as well?

> Of how much sorer punishment, suppose ye, shall he be thought worthy, who hath trodden under foot the Son of God, and hath counted the blood of the covenant, wherewith he was sanctified, an unholy thing, and hath done despite unto the Spirit of grace? (Heb. 10:29)

How is such a person not a covenant breaker? How is he not a covenant breaker *beyond* the covenant made with Adam in the garden? He tramples underfoot the blood of the covenant by which he was sanctified. How could this be anything other than covenant breaking?

GREEN BAGGINS DOES TOO TAKE AN EXCEPTION
JULY 28, 2007

Under the heading of "No Exceptions,"* Lane has responded to my last post this way:

> I do not take any exceptions to the Westminster Confession of Faith. Wilson conveniently forgot to mention WCF 28.5, when he argues that I need to take an exception to the Standards: 'Although it be a

* greenbaggins.wordpress.com/2007/07/28/no-exceptions

> great sin to contemn or neglect this ordinance, yet grace and salvation are *not* so inseparably annexed unto it, as that no person can be regenerated or saved without it; or, that all that are baptized are undoubtedly regenerated' (emphasis added). This clearly states that regeneration is not dependent on baptism.

Actually, I haven't forgotten this section of the confession, and I agree with it whole-heartedly. But Lane doesn't—notice how he modifies the straight reading of this portion also. The premises stated don't yield the conclusion that "regeneration is not dependent on baptism." Rather, they yield the conclusion that regeneration is not *necessarily* or *absolutely* dependent upon baptism.

A man can be baptized and still be lost. Amen. A man can be unbaptized and still be saved. Amen again. This does not prove that there is no link between baptism and regeneration, but rather that there is not a "no exceptions link."

> If regeneration can happen without baptism ever happening (such as the thief on the cross), then regeneration is simply not dependent on baptism. One does not have to have baptism in order for regeneration to happen. And, as the Confession equally clearly states, just because one has baptism does not mean that one is regenerated, either. So, I am in perfect conformity with the Confession in saying that regeneration is not dependent on baptism.

The Westminster divines say that saving grace is not "inseparably annexed" to baptism, and they give two obvious examples. A man can be saved without it, and a man with it can be lost. But in the section of the Confession that Lane differs with, we were not talking about an unbaptized regenerate soul or a baptized unregenerate soul. We are talking about a baptized regenerate soul. Now, in *that* circumstance, does Lane agree or disagree that in the right use of the sacrament of water baptism that saving grace is really exhibited and conferred by the Holy Spirit at the appointed time?

> Lack of baptism does not mean lack of regeneration, and baptism does not automatically confer regeneration.

Sure, but if someone is baptized *and* regenerate, what is the teaching of the Confession about the relationship between the two? Does the Confession teach—only for those to whom the grace belongs—that regeneration is exhibited and *conferred* by baptism?

> If regeneration happens at the time-point of baptism, I am willing to say that the Holy Spirit uses baptism as a means through which a sinner is regenerated, although the baptism without the Word can do nothing. And before the TR's jump all over me for being FV, hear the rest of this out carefully. It is crystal clear it is really the Word that the Holy Spirit uses to regenerate someone. Even in baptism, I would argue that it is the Word which regenerates if regeneration happens at that time.

This does not whisper an exception to the Confession; it shouts it. The Confession says that the efficacy of baptism is not dependent on the "time-point" of its administration at all. Lane says that potential efficacy of baptism is limited to the time of administration and, even then, baptism isn't really doing anything. This is called *disagreeing* with the Westminster Assembly.

> But that will only be because the thing signified is also given, not because of the sign only being given. FV guys are fond of pointing out that the norm appears to be that the sign and thing signified are normally annexed one to the other. But the grace promised in 28.6 is the efficacy of baptism as a sign and seal. This must be distinguished (however closely one wants to tie the sacramental union) from the thing signified.

I would answer this, but I don't know what Lane means by it. I think there is something important in there, but I don't know what it is. For the elect, the sign seals the thing signified. That's why we can say that the thing signified is really exhibited and conferred.

> That being said, Wilson seems not to want to answer my query about Warfield. I would still appreciate it if Wilson would engage the Warfield quotations from the Shorter Writings, those books out of which Wilson forgot to read when formulating what Warfield supposedly believed about the Sacraments. In other words, I refuse to allow any kind of derailing of the discussion from Warfield's beliefs to my beliefs. We are really talking about Warfield's beliefs, not whether I should take an exception to the Confession. My own beliefs are tangential to this discussion.

Lane's answers here illustrate the point I was making about Warfield in *RINE.* I interacted with Warfield's doctrine on this as stated in *The Plan of Salvation.* At the same time, I acknowledged that Warfield would elsewhere confess that the sacraments are means of grace. Lane produced quotations that show this and challenges me on that basis. But I am going to stick to my guns here. Lane and Warfield have the same kind of "workaround" for the confessional language. Notice how Lane says that that baptism does something—but before his trigger-happy brethren empty their clips into him, he hastens to add this this is okay because *he doesn't really believe it.* The *Word* does it, not baptism. I understand something very similar to this being what Warfield means by the immediacy of God's grace in salvation, which goes back to my original point in my book.

Last thing. Lane says that whether he is in accord with the Confession if "tangential to this discussion." This is a nice little set up. Wilkins and Leithart—our presbyterial heavens will tumble to the ground if we find that *they* are out of accord with the Confession at any point. But is Lane out of accord with the Confession? An irrelevant detail. A trifle. Let us not get distracted. We have work to do. What is that work? Nailing *other* people for being out of accord with the Confession.

RC SR. DENIES THE GOSPEL
JULY 30, 2007

I am listening to the August message of the month from Ligonier, where RC Sr. is talking about the Noahic covenant. Imagine how I felt when I heard him say that the distinction between the "covenant of works" and the "covenant of grace" was somewhat "artificial" and even "superficial." Imagine further how I felt when he made of point of insisting that the covenant of works should be understood as fundamentally *gracious*. Whoa. Scott Clark, call your office. The rot of grace is spreading.

It seems clear now that RC's comments at the PCA General Assembly may have been necessary to throw certain heresy hunters off the scent. The bloodhounds of Westminster West are clearly restless, and are pawing at the locks of their kennels.

CONTINUED REJECTION OF WESTMINSTER
JULY 31, 2007

The next issue of *Credenda* is going to be addressing the whole issue of the Federal Vision, and in that issue you will find a statement of convictions signed by some of the leading participants in this conversation—we have released that document early so you can take a look at it here*. For hard copy, get a hold of the next *Credenda*.

Green Baggins is continuing his conversation with me here†, and I respond below.

There are places where I don't differ with the substance of what Lane is saying, but I wouldn't put it the way he does.

> The elect participate in the *ordo salutis* and the non-elect don't, even if they are all participants in the administration of the covenant of grace. I'm not sure that Wilson would disagree with this. And least, I hope he doesn't.

* Currently available here: federal-vision.com/ecclesiology/joint-federal-vision-statement

† greenbaggins.wordpress.com/2007/07/30/sign-and-seal

No, I don't disagree. But let me make this qualification. The *ordo* is not a car you ride to heaven. Rather, presupposing election, it is a description of what happens to a person throughout the process of his salvation. I do agree that it accurately describes what happens to the elect, and does not at all describe what happens to the non-elect. But at the same time, I do believe that the reification of certain theological abstractions sometimes gets in the way.

Lane asks what covenantal union is, and how that covenantal union relates to the ordo salutis. But he sets the stakes in a truly odd way.

> In order to be Reformed, the FV would have to prove that "covenantal union" confers **zero** *ordo salutis* benefits.

But what is this? There are at least a couple ways to take the word "prove" here. One is to establish to somebody's satisfaction that there is no inherent logical contradiction between our view of covenantal union and decretal theology. But this is not a requirement we apply elsewhere. In order to avoid hyper-Calvinism, you need to affirm that man is responsible along with an affirmation that God is exhaustively sovereign. But do you need to *prove* it? Yes, in the sense that you have to prove each of these tenets from Scripture. No, if you mean that you have to prove there is no logical contradiction between them. I can't do that—I can't show the math. But I can easily affirm both as being taught in the Bible. But this leads to the next sense of the word prove.

It could mean that we need to prove that we really do hold to both covenantal union *and* decretal theology—in short, the demand might be that we have to prove that we're not lying. But when distrust has escalated to the level it has, something like this is almost impossible to prove as well. How do I prove that I am not a lying skunk? But, for what it's worth, I do affirm that all God's people, elect and non-elect, share in a covenantal union with Christ. I also affirm that the fullness of this heritage belongs in truth only to the decretally elect. And so, Bob's your uncle.

> Would Wilson agree that the Covenant of Grace is made with Christ and with the elect seed in Him (LC 31)?

Yes, I would—in the narrow sense. In the broad sense, the covenant of grace is made with all believers and their children. I do this for the sake of making basic doctrinal distinctions, and the difference beween the elect and non-elect is one of those distinctions. Just let it be noted that the "broad sense" should not be read as the "not really sense." What is lacking is efficacy, sealing, assurance, and security. Connection to Christ is *not* lacking.

The next issue is an important one. Speaking of the place where I said he was out of accord with the Westminster Confession, Lane says this.

> The second point that needs to be addressed is the refreshing honesty of Wilson on the Confession here. He is right in this: the FV interpretation and the critics' interpretation of the Confession CANNOT both be right and allowable. Wilson is of course specifically applying this idea to the issue of baptismal efficacy, which is the topic under discussion. However, Wilson's statement seems to have a broader application. In other words the FV should drop the facade that the Reformed world is just one big umbrella that can house many different views, and that the Confession allows both FV views and TR's to exist simultaneously. No, it cannot. The FV interpretation and the TR interpretation contradict one another. That is what the TR's have been saying all along. It is refreshing to see an FV guy say so.

I want to respond to this with a series of short responses so we can get on to the question of baptismal efficacy. First, Lane is right that I believe our interpretations of the section on baptismal efficacy contradict one another. But it was not my point to extend that point to the entire Confession. Second, this can only be done if it is assumed that the Confession is infallible and inspired. A uninspired consensus document (as Westminster was) most certainly *can* make room for different views in a way that, say, the book of Romans doesn't. Now I believe that what we call the TR view of things has had an honored place in the Reformed mainstream since the Reformation. But so has the position that we are now calling FV. Simple question: did any of the delegates to the Assembly affirm baptismal regeneration (in the traditional sense) and did any deny it? And did they all vote?

Now, leaving aside baptismal regeneration in the classic sense, let us rather talk about the nuanced Westminsterian take on baptismal efficacy. Here Lane is simply wrong about the Confession and needs to take an exception. He says:

> But the grace promised in 28.6 is the efficacy of baptism as a sign and seal. This must be distinguished . . . from the thing signified.

What Lane is saying here is that the grace that is exhibited and conferred is not the grace itself, but rather the grace of a promise of grace. But his point is tautological. Baptism exhibits and confers baptism.

> I would say that in the case of the baptized regenerate soul, the sacrament of water baptism really exhibits and confers the grace of baptism as sign and seal at the appointed time.

Compare this to the statements of Westminster itself.

> The efficacy of Baptism is not tied to that moment of time wherein it is administered; yet, notwithstanding, by the right use of this ordinance, the grace promised is not only offered, but really exhibited, and conferred, by the Holy Ghost, to such (whether of age or infants) as that grace belongs unto, according to the counsel of God's own will, in His appointed time. (WCF 28.6)

But if the efficacy of baptism refers to the impartation of the sign and seal of baptism, then the "efficacy" of it *is* tied to the moment of administration. That is when the sign and seal is applied, right? The *grace promised* is not the same thing as the grace inherent in the act of *promising*. God shows His gracious nature in making this promise, true enough. But the grace *promised* is clearly the grace *signified.* Now grace signified only belongs to worthy receivers, it only belongs to those to whom it properly belongs (the elect). But for those elect, the Westminster divines taught, explicitly, that the grace promised in baptism is really exhibited and conferred on the elect at the moment of their regeneration. Lane doesn't have to like it, but this is what the words say. It cannot be what Lane is arguing for here. If it were, then the efficacy of baptism *is* anchored to the moment of administration. The only reason for detaching the sign and thing signified in time is because the thing signified often comes at a different time in a person's life than the moment of their baptism.

And just a quick comment on Lane's reasoning about this.

> If baptism confers regeneration upon the elect only, and not on the non-elect, then it does not confer regeneration for the elect either, since such a position requires that regeneration be located within baptism itself. And if it is located within baptism itself, then regeneration would also be conferred on the non-elect, as indeed some say.

Here's the problem with Lane's reasoning. Just substitute the word *Word* for *baptism*, and his reasoning applies just as well (or as poorly). The Word cannot regenerate because two men sat under the same sermon, and one was converted and the other not. If the Word regenerated *in itself,* then all who heard it would have to be born again. If the reasoning doesn't apply to the Word as a means of grace, then it doesn't apply to baptism either.